GRADES 2–3

The IDEA MAGAZINE FOR TEACHERS®

The MAILBOX®

2010–2011 YEARBOOK

The Education Center, Inc.
Greensboro, North Carolina

The Mailbox® *2010–2011 Grades 2–3 Yearbook*

ISBN13 978-1-61276-140-4
ISSN 1088-5544

Printed in the United States of America.

The Mailbox® Yearbook
PO Box 6189
Harlan, IA 51593-1689

HPS 232522

Contents

Learning Centers

Seasonal

Teacher Resources

Language Arts

READING Tips & Tools

Family Photos
Modeling, motivation

Emphasize the importance of reading with this family-themed activity and display. Ask parents to send a photo to school showing their child reading with someone at home. As each student brings his photo to school, have him share it with the class, explaining what he's reading and why. Then post the photos in your reading area. Not only will students get to share information about their families, but they'll also see the benefits of reading outside of school.

Amy Tyner, Falls Elementary, Zanesville, OH

Dad and I are reading a recipe so we can make breakfast for Mom.
I am reading a bedtime story to my brother so he can learn.

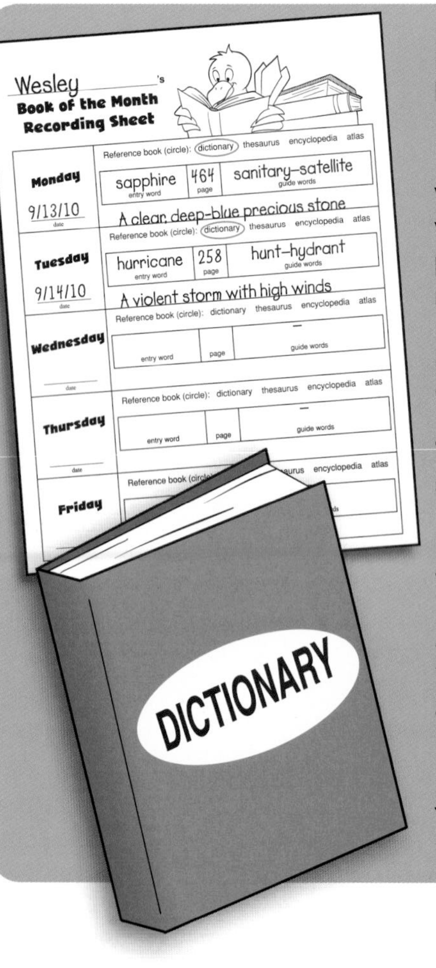
Wesley's
Book of the Month Recording Sheet
Monday
9/13/10
Reference book (circle): dictionary thesaurus encyclopedia atlas
sapphire
464
sanitary–satellite
A clear, deep-blue precious stone
Tuesday
9/14/10
Reference book (circle): dictionary thesaurus encyclopedia atlas
hurricane
258
hunt–hydrant
A violent storm with high winds
Wednesday
Thursday
Friday
DICTIONARY

Book of the Month
Introducing and using reference materials

Use this quick activity as morning work, center work, or a whole-class warm-up to familiarize students with different reference materials and new words. At the beginning of each month, introduce a different resource. Then post a different entry word each day. Have students use the featured reference material to complete a section of a copy of page 18 as detailed below.

Dictionary: Write the entry word, page number, and guide words. Then write the first definition.

Thesaurus: Write the entry word, page number, and guide words. Then write three synonyms.

Encyclopedia: Write the entry word, page number, and guide words. Then write one fact about the person, place, thing, or event.

Atlas: Write the location (in place of the entry word) and its page number. Mark through the guide word section. Write one or more facts about the location's geography. (If desired, instead of having students write just any fact, include the location in a question and have students use the atlas to determine the answer.)

Jean Erickson, Milwaukee, WI

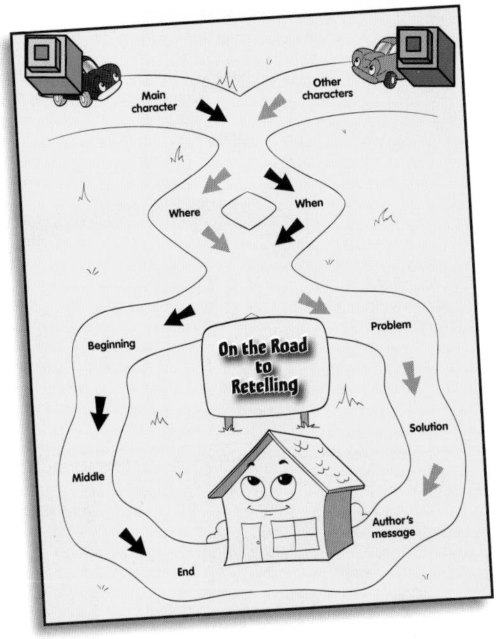
Main character
Other characters
Where
When
Problem
Beginning
On the Road to Retelling
Solution
Middle
Author's message
End

Two-Way Street

Retelling story elements

With this partner activity, students take two trips to the same destination—a better understanding of a common story. Give each duo a copy of the map on page 19 and two different-color Unifix cubes. Have each child place his cube on a different car. The student with Car 1 moves his cube along his retelling road, pausing at each prompt to provide that information from the story. Then the student moving Car 2 takes a turn along her road in the same manner.

Barclay Marcell
Roosevelt School
Park Ridge, IL

Editor's Tip:
Instead of a cube, have each student move a toy car along his road.

Great, Fantastic, Excellent...

Synonyms

In advance, gather a variety of stickers that feature words that are synonymous with *great*. To begin, give each child a sticker and instruct her to place it at the top of a sheet of paper. Next, have each student decide whether her sticker has a word that means about the same as *great;* if so, she shares her word aloud. Make a list of the words on the board and remind students that synonyms are words with the same or nearly the same meaning. Have each student copy the list onto her paper; then direct students to write two or more words on their papers as synonym headers. (If desired, have students decorate the words to look like stickers.) Instruct students to keep the papers in a handy place so they can list synonyms they find in their readings below appropriate words.

Mary Lou Michael, Conrad Weiser West Elementary, Womelsdorf, PA

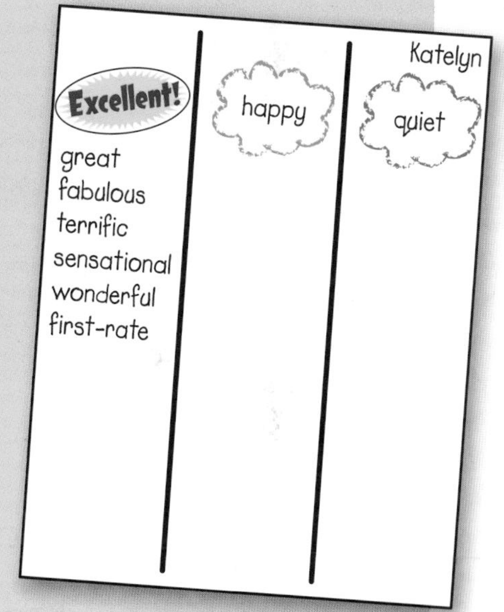
Katelyn
Excellent!
happy
quiet
great
fabulous
terrific
sensational
wonderful
first-rate

Read and complete each sentence.
Before I Read
I already know ______.
As I Read
I just learned ______.
After I Read
I used to think ______,
but now I know ______.

Thinking Along

Activating prior knowledge, making predictions

Strengthen students' reading habits with these reproducible desktop prompts. Provide each child with a copy of a prompt card from page 20. Review the sentences on the card and explain to students that, as they read independently, they should complete each sentence in their heads. Direct each child to tape her card to her desktop and encourage her to use it each time she reads.

Lisa Russo, Flushing, NY

READING Tips & Tools

Wise Owls
Comparing and contrasting

Showing how two topics are alike and different is a hoot when students use this variation of a Venn diagram! First, direct each child to label the wings on a copy of page 21 with two recently read topics. Then instruct the students to write below the headings how the topics are different from each other and write on the chest how they are alike. If desired, have students personalize their completed diagrams. Post the papers on a display titled "Reading Is a Hoot!"

Nancy Ramsey, Allgood Elementary, Dallas, GA

Name Andy
Date Oct. 25, 2010
Comparing and contrasting
owls
bird
Both
wings
bats
mammal

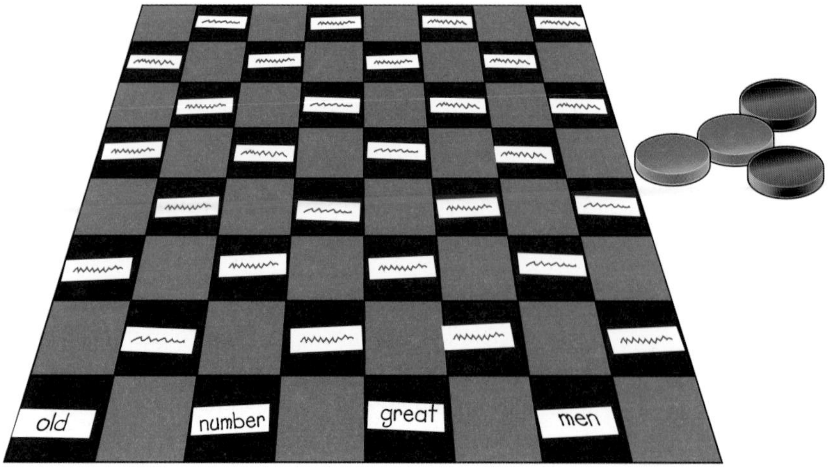
old
number
great
men

Read and Play
Reading sight words

Give the game of checkers a literacy twist! Print different words on small labels and attach one label to each black square on a checkerboard. Set out the checkerboard with a supply of checkers. Direct students to play according to traditional rules with one exception: before moving a checker, the student reads the word on the checker's current square.

Nikki Gillitzer
Bluff Creek Elementary
Chanhassen, MN

Editor's Tip:
Need an activity for an adult volunteer to do with a student? Use this game!

To the Point

Understanding cause and effect

To begin, invite students to reacquaint the class with the nursery rhymes shown. Next, instruct each child to fold a 12" x 18" paper in half vertically and then fold it in half two times horizontally. Direct the student to unfold the paper. Next, have the child cut out the cause patterns from a copy of page 22 and glue each one on a separate row, being sure that each arrowhead is touching the middle fold. Then have the child write each effect on the right side of the row. Review students' effect statements and then lead students to understand that the event written on each arrow led to, or caused, the event they wrote about (the effect).

Carolyn Burant
St. John Vianney School
Brookfield, WI

"Jack and Jill"
"The Itsy-Bitsy Spider"
"Little Miss Muffet"
"Georgie Porgie"

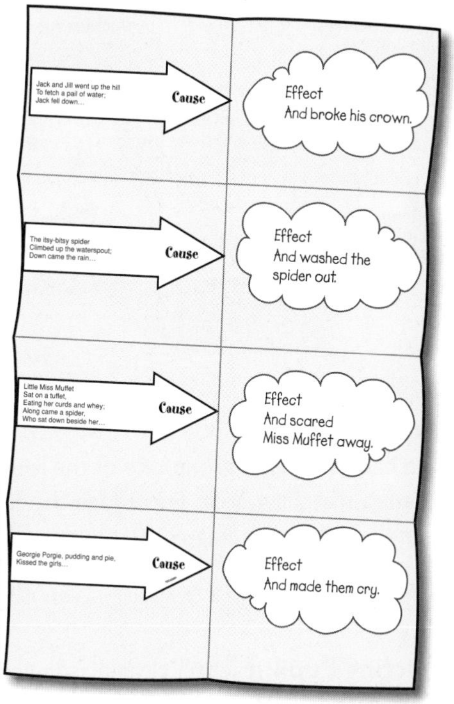
Jack and Jill went up the hill
To fetch a pail of water;
Jack fell down...
Cause
Effect
And broke his crown.
The itsy-bitsy spider
Climbed up the waterspout;
Down came the rain...
Cause
Effect
And washed the spider out.
Little Miss Muffet
Sat on a tuffet,
Eating her curds and whey;
Along came a spider,
Who sat down beside her...
Cause
Effect
And scared Miss Muffet away.
Georgie Porgie, pudding and pie,
Kissed the girls...
Cause
Effect
And made them cry.

A **thesaurus** lists words that are related. For each entry word, you will find **synonyms** (words with the same meaning). You might also find **antonyms** (words with the opposite meaning).

Name Aisha, Jayden Date Nov. 16, 2010
Using a thesaurus

A "Dino-mite" Discovery

Use a thesaurus to complete the chart.

Word bent	Page 32
Synonyms	Antonyms
curved twisted warped bowed crooked contorted	straight

A "Dino-mite" Reference

Using a thesaurus

Make an enlarged copy of the dinosaur pattern at the top of page 23 and post it near your reference materials. Tell your students that this area is home to many helpful books that they can use to improve their reading and writing skills. Then introduce students to Thesaurus, a modern-day dinosaur that lives in your classroom and wants students to use the reference material with its name. Show students a thesaurus; then explain how and when to use it. Give each student pair a copy of the bottom of page 23, assign the students a recent vocabulary word, and have them use a thesaurus to complete the page.

Steph McHugh, Bristol Bay Elementary, Yorkville, IL

Help Is on the Way!

Fictional-reading terms

Prepare students for post-reading retellings and discussions with this easy-to-use reading helper. Simply direct each student to color a copy of page 24 and glue it to his reading folder. Encourage the child to use the questions and directions to help him when he works on reading tasks.

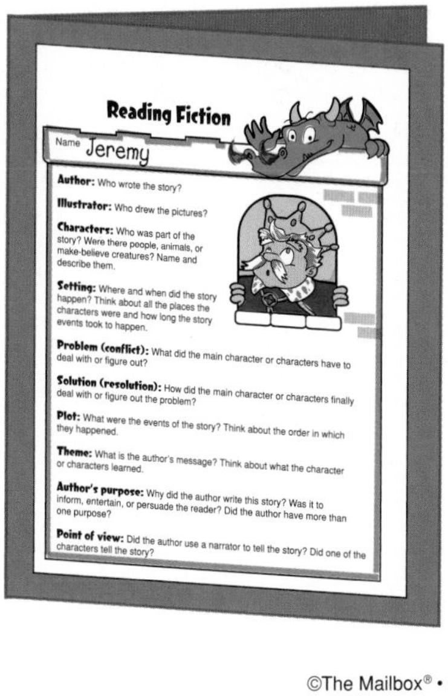
Reading Fiction

Name Jeremy

Author: Who wrote the story?

Illustrator: Who drew the pictures?

Characters: Who was part of the story? Were there people, animals, or make-believe creatures? Name and describe them.

Setting: Where and when did the story happen? Think about all the places the characters were and how long the story events took to happen.

Problem (conflict): What did the main character or characters have to deal with or figure out?

Solution (resolution): How did the main character or characters finally deal with or figure out the problem?

Plot: What were the events of the story? Think about the order in which they happened.

Theme: What is the author's message? Think about what the character or characters learned.

Author's purpose: Why did the author write this story? Was it to inform, entertain, or persuade the reader? Did the author have more than one purpose?

Point of view: Did the author use a narrator to tell the story? Did one of the characters tell the story?

READING Tips & Tools

Role-Playing

Literature circles

Assign each child in a group one of the jobs listed. Then, for each job, give the student a matching prop. Encourage the child to wear or hold the prop while completing his reading-related duties.

Rebecca Boudin, Fiddlers Canyon Elementary, Cedar City, UT

Predicting Pupil: places a clear plastic bowl (crystal ball) upside down on his workspace while sharing predictions about the reading

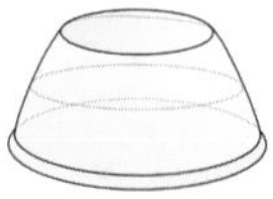

Discussion Director: holds a rolled-paper megaphone while sharing questions he prepared about the reading

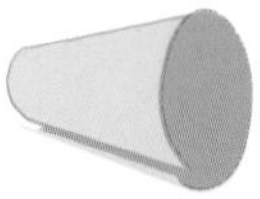

Word Wizard: holds a dowel or drinking straw (wand) while identifying tricky vocabulary words or finding their meanings in the dictionary

Artful Artist: holds a paintbrush while sharing a picture of his favorite part of the reading

Cool Connector: wears sunglasses while sharing a text-to-text, text-to-self, or text-to-world connection

Super Summarizer: wears an apron loosely tied around his neck (cape) while providing a summary of the reading

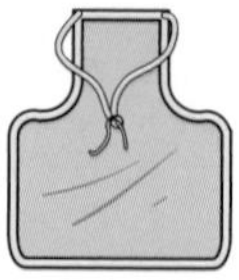

Biography
Dr. King

All Kinds of Books

Genres

With this ongoing activity, students identify different types of literature while creating a visual reminder of the books the class has read. To prepare, cut out an enlarged copy of the header patterns on page 25 and display them on a wall. Each time the class reads a story, take a picture of a child holding the book. Print the photo and invite the student to post the picture under the matching header. If desired, write the title of the book on a sentence strip and tape the photo to the strip.

Renee Plant, Verdigris Elementary, Claremore, OK

Award Winners
Fiction book reports

Use this oversize award as a simple postreading project. First, have each child cut out the summary form and ribbon patterns from a copy of page 26. Then have him complete the summary. Next, direct the student to make two tracings of the ribbon pattern and cut them out. On one ribbon, instruct the child to tell what he liked about the book. On the other ribbon, have the student tell about a connection he made to the book. Guide the child to glue the ribbons to the back of a paper plate and then glue the organizer onto the plate. If desired, have the child use art supplies to personalize his award.

Sharon Vandike, Visitation Inter-Parish School, Vienna, MO

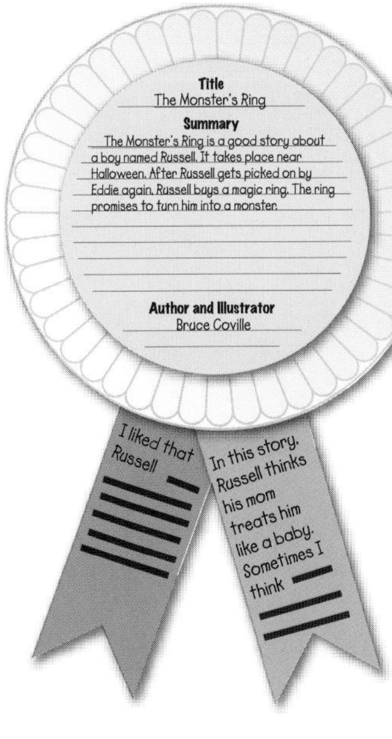
Title
The Monster's Ring
Summary
The Monster's Ring is a good story about a boy named Russell. It takes place near Halloween. After Russell gets picked on by Eddie again, Russell buys a magic ring. The ring promises to turn him into a monster.
Author and Illustrator
Bruce Coville
I liked that Russell
In this story, Russell thinks his mom treats him like a baby. Sometimes I think

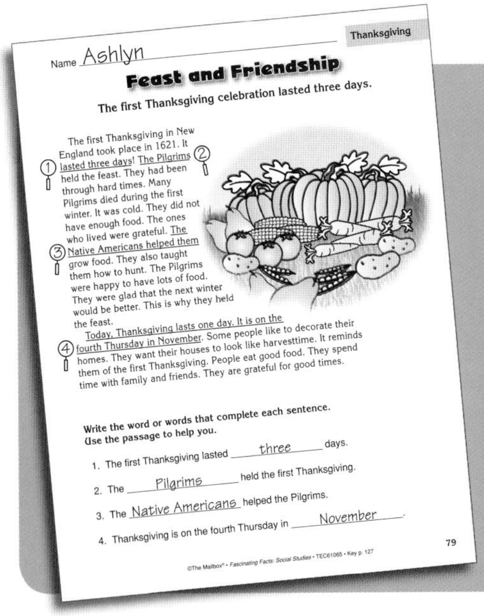

Thanksgiving

Name Ashlyn

Feast and Friendship

The first Thanksgiving celebration lasted three days.

The first Thanksgiving in New England took place in 1621. It lasted three days! The Pilgrims held the feast. They had been through hard times. Many Pilgrims died during the first winter. It was cold. They did not have enough food. The ones who lived were grateful. The Native Americans helped them grow food. They also taught them how to hunt. The Pilgrims were happy to have lots of food. They were glad that the next winter would be better. This is why they held the feast.

Today, Thanksgiving lasts one day. It is on the fourth Thursday in November. Some people like to decorate their homes. They want their houses to look like harvesttime. It reminds them of the first Thanksgiving. People eat good food. They spend time with family and friends. They are grateful for good times.

Write the word or words that complete each sentence. Use the passage to help you.

1. The first Thanksgiving lasted three days.
2. The Pilgrims held the first Thanksgiving.
3. The Native Americans helped the Pilgrims.
4. Thanksgiving is on the fourth Thursday in November.

79

©The Mailbox® • Fascinating Facts: Social Studies • TEC61065 • Key p. 127

Detective Work
Reading for details

Who's on the case? Your students are when they become reading detectives! Before starting a selection, have each student read the follow-up comprehension questions. As she reads the selection, encourage the child to look for clues to crack the case (find answers to the questions). When a student finds a clue, have her draw a simple magnifying glass on her paper near the matching text. Then have her write the number of the case file, or question, inside the magnifying glass and underline the clue. To close the case, direct the student to reread the questions and choose the best answers based on the clues she found.

Brooke Beverly, Dudley Elementary, Dudley, MA

Ready for Reading
Choral reading, vocabulary development

Pump up students for their reading block with this fun chant. Post the chant shown on the overhead, writing on each line a different student descriptor. Before starting your reading instruction for the day, review the underlined terms. Then invite students who match those descriptions to read their parts aloud as you lead the chant. Update the underlined terms daily or weekly, introducing new descriptors as students' vocabularies and reading skills improve.

Kim Minafo, Apex, NC

Boys: Cheer, cheer. Look who's here!

Girls: Ready to read and grow. *(Clap.)*

Students reading mysteries: Cheer, cheer. Look who's here!

Dog owners: Ready to start?

Everyone: Let's go!

READING Tips & Tools

Word Sandwich
Dictionary skills

This idea has all the fixings to be a class favorite! To begin, have each child cut apart a copy of the food cards on page 27. Next, direct him to locate a set of guide words in the dictionary and write a different one on each bread slice. Then have the student write a different word that falls between the guide words on each of the remaining cards. After the child has colored the cards, instruct him to make an answer key that shows the words in alphabetical order and put his cards and key in a resealable plastic bag. Instruct students to swap bags with partners to order each other's words or place the bags at a center for independent practice.

Cheryl Zellhoefer, Tecopa, CA

lunch
lung
lunge
lurch
lure
lurk

Mini Memoirs
Biography reports

Students summarize the main points of a person's life with this informative bookmark. After a child reads a biography, instruct her to complete a copy of the organizer on page 28. Provide time for proofreading and editing; then have her use the information from the organizer to complete a copy of a bookmark pattern on page 29. Then instruct the child to draw a picture or glue a photocopied image of the person she studied on the bookmark. Put the completed bookmarks near the classroom library and encourage students to borrow a different bookmark each time they visit the library.

Susan Overton
Collegiate School
Richmond, VA

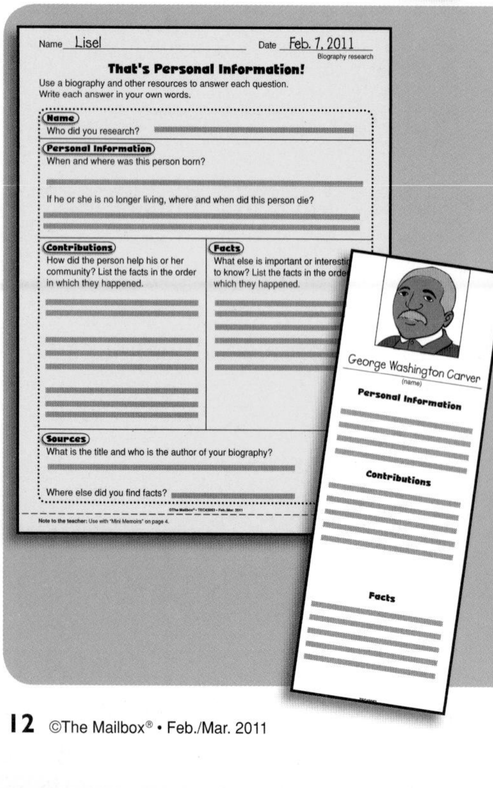
Name Lisel
Date Feb. 7, 2011
Biography research
That's Personal Information!
Use a biography and other resources to answer each question.
Write each answer in your own words.
Name
Who did you research?
Personal Information
When and where was this person born?
If he or she is no longer living, where and when did this person die?
Contributions
How did the person help his or her community? List the facts in the order in which they happened.
Facts
Sources
What is the title and who is the author of your biography?
Where else did you find facts?
George Washington Carver
(name)
Personal Information
Contributions
Facts

Hooray for Prefixes
Prefixes

Sing a few rounds of this song, and students are sure to remember some important prefix facts!

Prefixes
(sung to the tune of "When Johnny Comes Marching Home")

A prefix comes at the front of a word.
There's *pre-* and *mis-*.
A prefix comes at the front of a word.
There's *re-* and *un-*.
The base word stays the same, you know,
But the meaning changes, and there you go.
A prefix comes at the front of a base word.

Pre- means *before,* and *re-* means *again.*
Prefix, prefix!
Un- means *not,* and *mis-* can mean *bad.*
Prefix, prefix!
The base word stays the same, you know,
But the meaning changes, and there you go.
A prefix comes at the front of a base word.

Denise Ketzel, Slippery Rock Elementary, Slippery Rock, PA

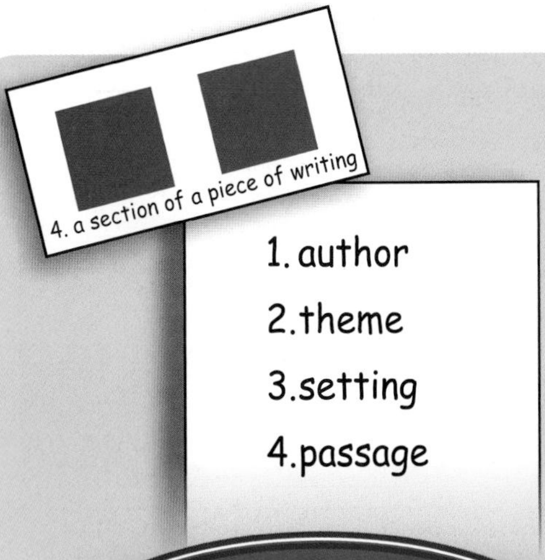
4. a section of a piece of writing
1. author
2. theme
3. setting
4. passage

An Extra Step
Vocabulary

What do you get when you combine a retired Candy Land game and important words to know? A sweet game your students will crave! To prepare, label each colored game card with a different number and definition. Then list on a key each number and its corresponding word. To play, students follow the traditional rules of the game, but a player can only move her game piece if she names the correct word for the definition on her card.

Catherine Kepler
Oak Park Special Emphasis School
Corpus Christi, TX

Editor's Tip:
Laminate the cards and use a fine-tip permanent marker to program the definitions. When you're ready to practice a new set of words, use rubbing alcohol to wipe the cards clean.

In Clear View
Homophones

Draw attention to sound-alike words with this supersize class reference. In advance, cut from butcher paper a three-foot-tall *H.* Assign each student pair a homophone and give them a supply of sticky notes. Direct the students to write one word on each sticky note and, if possible, to illustrate each word. Then have students post their notes on each leg of the *H.* For any homophones that have three words, guide students to post them along the horizontal bar of the *H.*

Heather Choffo, Marbrook Elementary, Wilmington, DE

we'd
we + would
toe
buy
road
be
read
bye
rode
weed
tow
by
rowed
bee
red

READING Tips & Tools

Reading Brings Riches
Retelling nonfiction

Students dig up important information with these fun-to-make treasure chests. To begin, direct each student to write the title of his book and its author on a copy of page 30. Then have him color it and cut it out. Next, instruct the child to cut from construction paper three jewel or coin shapes. Have him label each cutout with a different nonfiction element shown and list the corresponding information. The child glues the cutouts to the treasure chest and, if needed, fills any empty space with unlabeled coins and jewels. He refers to his project as he shares an oral report about his informational text. If desired, post the completed projects on a display titled "Reading Brings Riches." **As an alternative**, enlarge the pattern on page 30 for each child and have him cut six jewel or coin shapes. Instruct the child to label each cutout with a different nonfiction element shown and list the corresponding information on each.

Christa Burnette, Patrick Springs Primary, Patrick Springs, VA

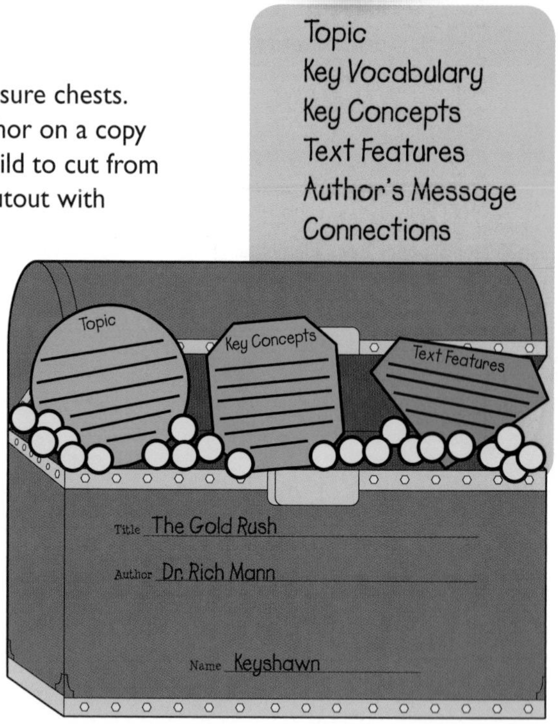
Topic
Key Vocabulary
Key Concepts
Text Features
Author's Message
Connections
Topic
Key Concepts
Text Features
Title The Gold Rush
Author Dr. Rich Mann
Name Keyshawn

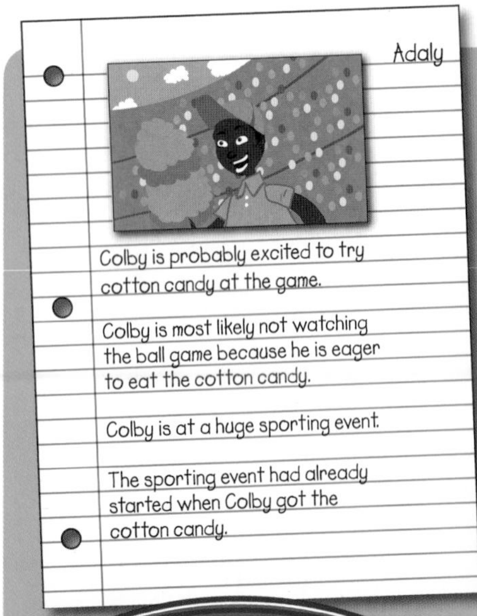
Adaly
Colby is probably excited to try cotton candy at the game.
Colby is most likely not watching the ball game because he is eager to eat the cotton candy.
Colby is at a huge sporting event.
The sporting event had already started when Colby got the cotton candy.

What's the Story?
Drawing conclusions

If a picture is worth a thousand words, why not use photos to reinforce this important reading skill? Invite each student to bring in an interesting photo of herself; then make a copy of each photo. Give each child a different copy, being sure not to give a student her own photo. Instruct each child to glue the photo to the top of a sheet of paper. Then have her use clues from the photo to determine what is happening and write as many sentences as possible about the event. After students have completed the task, have each child share with a partner how she determined what was happening in the photo. Then lead students to understand that sometimes all the ideas and details in a story aren't written out by the author. As a result, readers have to use story details and their own ideas to make a clear understanding of what is actually going on, similar to what students did when they described the photos.

Gina Zimmerman, Edgerton Elementary, Edgerton, KS

Editor's Tip:
Use interesting magazine and newspaper pictures instead of student photos.

Got the Hang of It?
Recognizing metaphors and similes

Draw attention to examples of figurative language with this easy-to-make chart. Cut apart the column headers from a copy of page 31 and glue them to a sheet of chart paper as shown. When you come across an example of figurative language in a read-aloud or a student reading, record it on the chart and discuss its meaning. After students understand what to look out for, hang the chart in an accessible location. Encourage them to add examples to the chart as they find them in their readings.

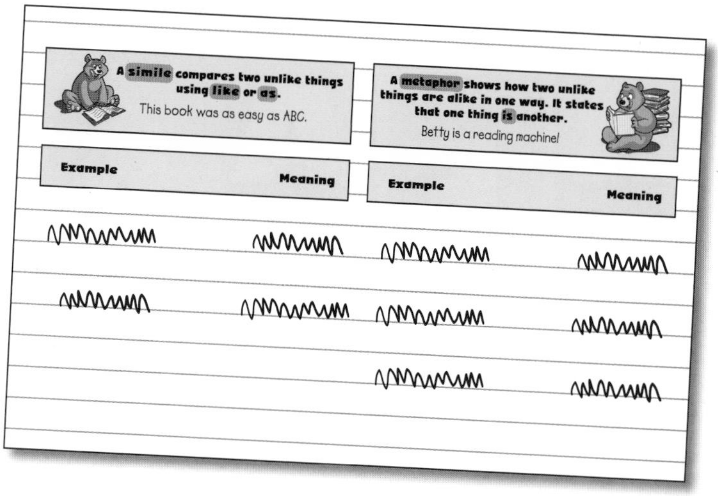
A simile compares two unlike things using like or as.
This book was as easy as ABC.
A metaphor shows how two unlike things are alike in one way. It states that one thing is another.
Betty is a reading machine!
Example
Meaning
Example
Meaning

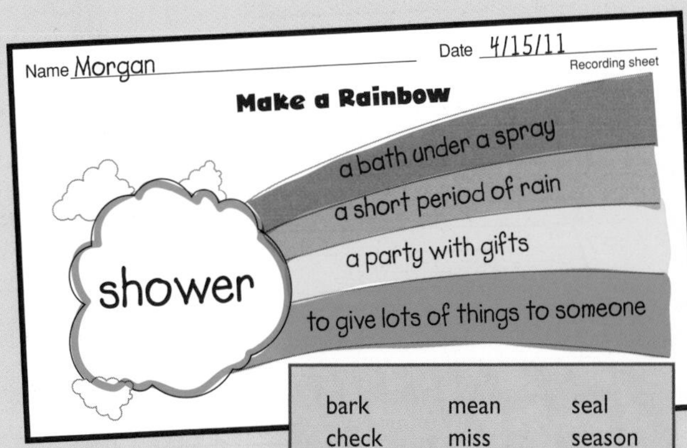
Name Morgan
Date 4/15/11
Recording sheet
Make a Rainbow
a bath under a spray
a short period of rain
a party with gifts
to give lots of things to someone
shower

bark	mean	seal
check	miss	season
date	pen	shower
fair	ring	squash
jam	rock	state
light	roll	well

Along the Arcs
Understanding multiple-meaning words

It may not be a pot of gold, but the reward at the end of this rainbow is just as valuable! To begin, give each child a copy of the recording sheet on page 32. Post the word list shown and have each child write one word in the cloud. Then have her write a different meaning in each arc. When she has written as many meanings as she can, have her lightly shade each arc a different color. **As an alternative**, have each child list synonyms or antonyms on each arc of the rainbow.

Colleen Reninger, Worth Elementary, Worth, IL

Top Secret Investigation
Reading for purpose, skill review

Small-group instruction makes the perfect setting for this partner activity. In advance, gather index cards in two different colors so each student will have a card. On each card of one color, write a skill related to the text; do the same with the other color using a different skill. Pair students and give each partner a different-color card and some highlighter tape. Tell students that they each have a top secret job: they must find examples of the skill listed on their cards in their readings. When students are finished, have partners swap books and determine what skill was highlighted. Provide time for students to share their ideas, encouraging them to support their responses with the highlighted text.

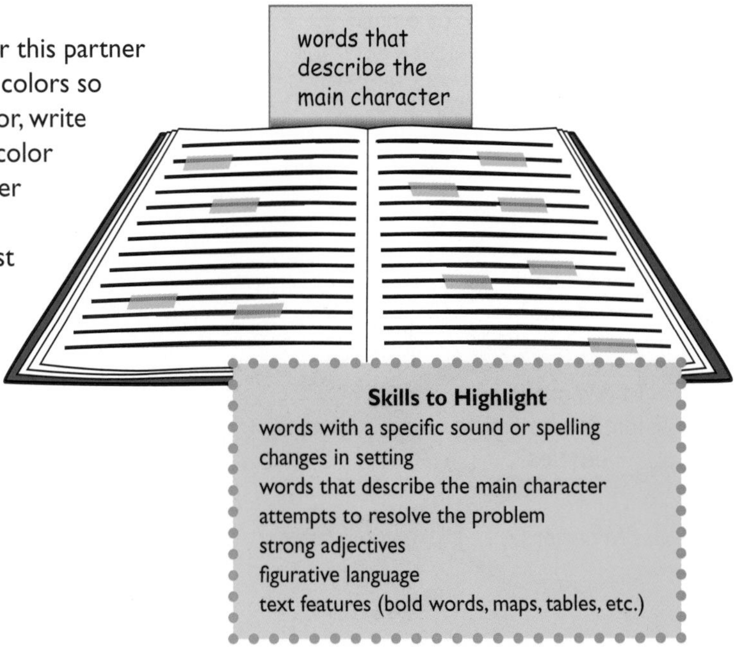
words that describe the main character

Skills to Highlight
- words with a specific sound or spelling
- changes in setting
- words that describe the main character
- attempts to resolve the problem
- strong adjectives
- figurative language
- text features (bold words, maps, tables, etc.)

READING Tips & Tools

Reading Relationship
Literature response

Get students personally involved in the current book study with this simple booklet. Guide each child to stack paper atop a sheet of construction paper, fold the papers in half, and staple them to make a booklet. Direct the student to write the title of the reading on the cover and then give him a copy of the prompts on page 34. Each day you work on the story, the child cuts out a prompt, glues it to the next page of his journal, and writes a response. At the end of the book study, he decorates the cover to represent the story.

Jennifer Cooper, Park Hills Elementary, Hanover, PA

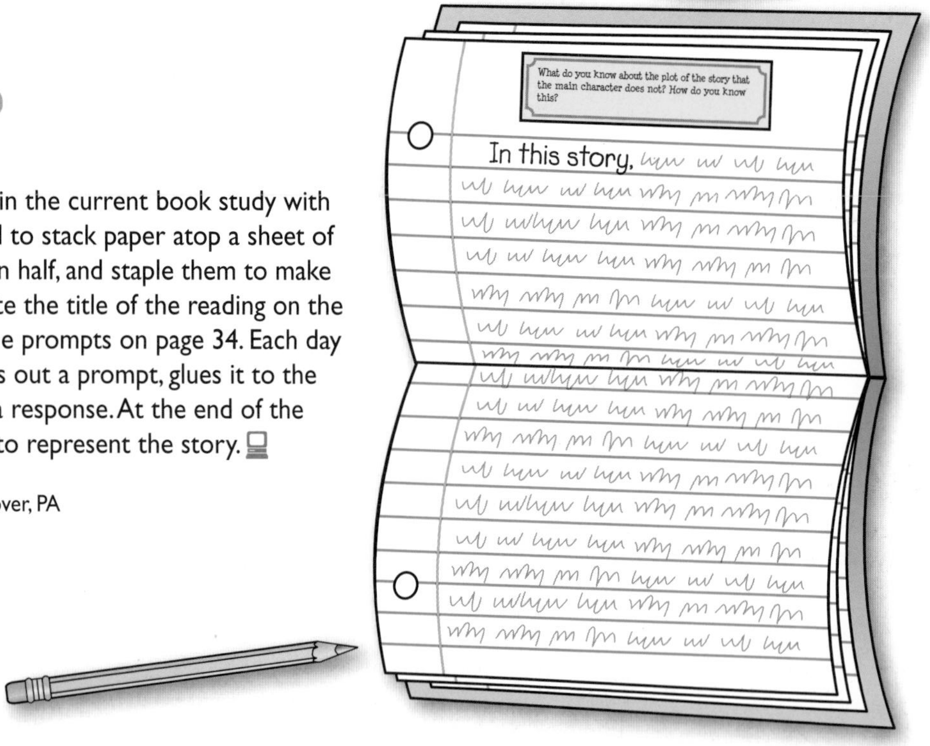
What do you know about the plot of the story that the main character does not? How do you know this?
In this story,

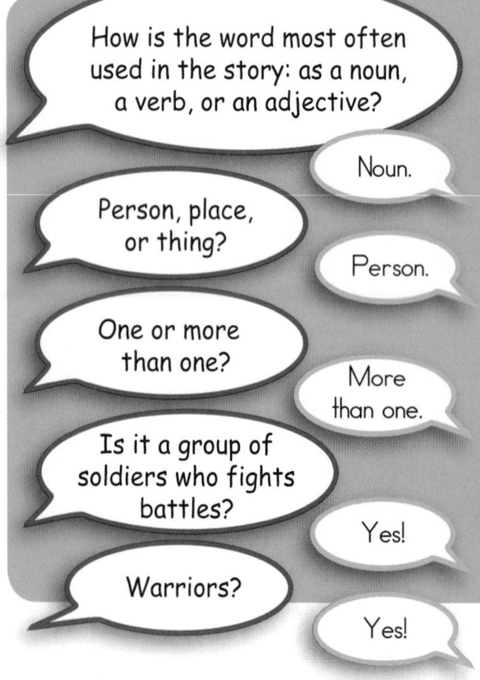
How is the word most often used in the story: as a noun, a verb, or an adjective?
Noun.
Person, place, or thing?
Person.
One or more than one?
More than one.
Is it a group of soldiers who fights battles?
Yes!
Warriors?
Yes!

Back to Review
Vocabulary

Build word knowledge with this fun question-and-answer game. In advance, program index cards each with a different vocabulary word. Instruct students to sit in a large circle and select one child to stand. Without letting the student see the word on the card, tape an index card to her back. Have her stand in the middle of the circle and slowly turn in place so others can see the word on the card. When everyone has seen the word, the child asks the group up to five questions that will help her determine the word. After she names the word, the child selects the next student to wear a card. If she's unable to name the word after five questions, provide a clue that will help her. **To make the game easier,** list the vocabulary words used in the game on the board.

Angela Farina, Washington Elementary, West Orange, NJ

Up There or in There?

Literal and inferential questions

This easy-to-make sign has two uses—one for you and one for your students! To make a sign, cut out a copy of the pattern at the bottom of page 34. Fold at the dotted lines and then unfold the paper. Turn the pattern facedown, glue a craft stick to the middle of one half, and then glue the backs of the paper halves together. **For teacher use**, lead struggling students to find the answer to a comprehension question by showing the matching side of the sign. **For student use**, direct each child to hold up his sign to indicate the kind of comprehension question you're reviewing.

Christine Kirley, Lincoln School, Hartford, WI

?
Find the answer in the reading.
?
Find the answer by thinking about the reading and what you already know.

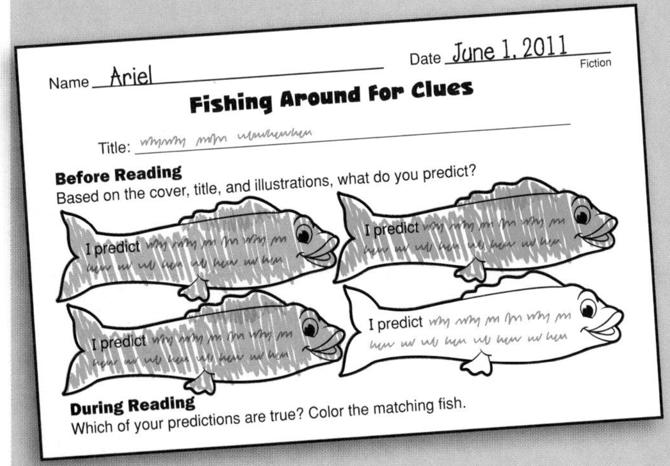
Name Ariel
Date June 1, 2011
Fiction
Fishing Around For Clues
Title:
Before Reading
Based on the cover, title, and illustrations, what do you predict?
I predict
I predict
I predict
I predict
During Reading
Which of your predictions are true? Color the matching fish.

Schooled on Previewing

Making and confirming predictions

Before reading, give each child a copy of the corresponding organizer (fiction or nonfiction) from page 35. Direct her to write the title of the reading on her paper and then preview the story or text. Guide the child to write a different prediction about the reading on each fish. Then, as she reads, have her lightly color each fish that lists an accurate prediction. **To extend the activity**, create an "After Reading" task. Have the student choose one inaccurate prediction and write on the back of the paper what really happens.

Renée Marie Plant, Verdigris Elementary, Claremore, OK

Pack Them In

Book reports

Save time approving book report books and create excitement for your next book report project! To start, label one side of a large, lidded box as shown. Put inside the box a class supply of books plus a few extras appropriate for the next book report. (Consider choosing books based on a topic, genre, or author.) If desired, place a few inflated balloons in the box as well. When you're ready to introduce the book report, set out the box so the labeled side faces you. Make a big fuss about discovering what's inside the box; then turn the box to reveal the label and remove the lid. Invite each child to select a book from the box. Refill the box at a later date with a different selection of books. Then, to increase interest and suspense, keep students from accessing the books until you're ready for the next project.

Kellie Henry, St. Joseph Grade School, St. Joseph, IL

Book Report Box

_______________________'s

Book of the Month Recording Sheet

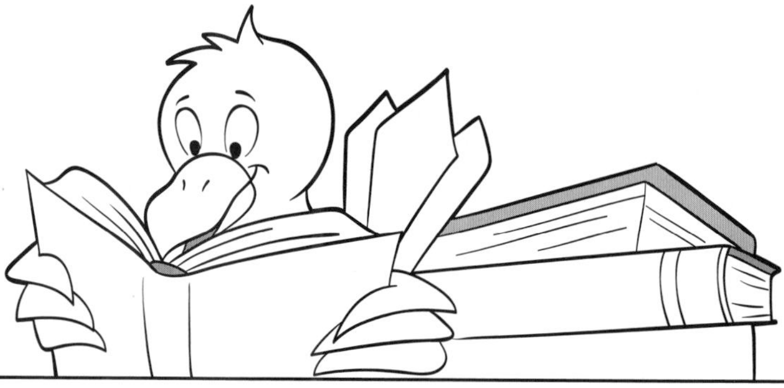

Monday _______________ date	Reference book (circle): dictionary thesaurus encyclopedia atlas entry word | page | — guide words
Tuesday _______________ date	Reference book (circle): dictionary thesaurus encyclopedia atlas entry word | page | — guide words
Wednesday _______________ date	Reference book (circle): dictionary thesaurus encyclopedia atlas entry word | page | — guide words
Thursday _______________ date	Reference book (circle): dictionary thesaurus encyclopedia atlas entry word | page | — guide words
Friday _______________ date	Reference book (circle): dictionary thesaurus encyclopedia atlas entry word | page | — guide words

 Note to the teacher: Use with "Book of the Month" on page 6.

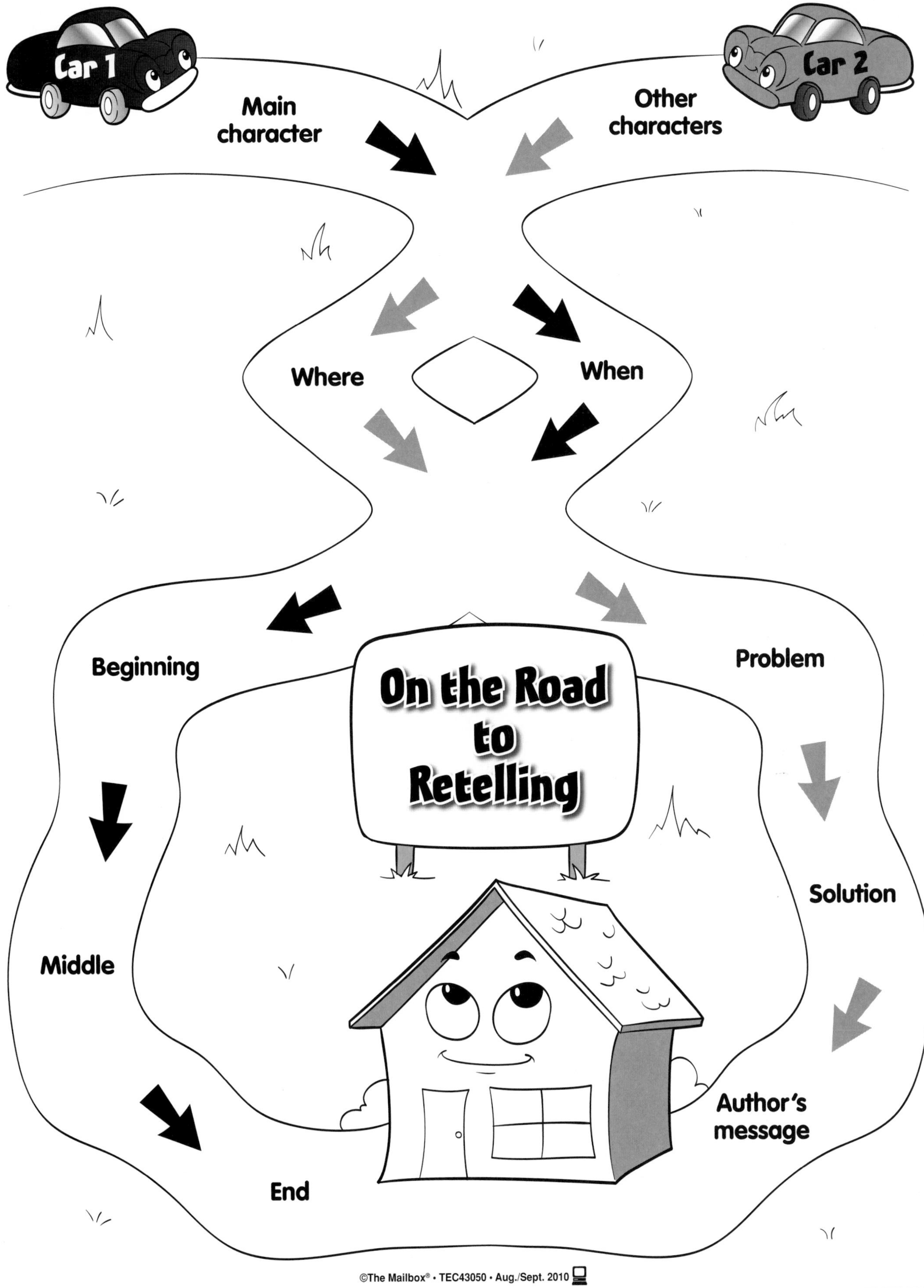
Car 1
Car 2
Main character
Other characters
Where
When
Beginning
Problem
On the Road to Retelling
Middle
Solution
Author's message
End

Note to the teacher: Use with "Two-Way Street" on page 7.

Prompt Cards

Use with "Thinking Along" on page 7.

Read and complete each sentence.

Before I Read

I already know ______________________________.

As I Read

I just learned ______________________________.

After I Read

I used to think ______________________________,

but now I know ______________________________.

TEC43050

Read and complete each sentence.

Before I Read

I already know ______________________________.

As I Read

I just learned ______________________________.

After I Read

I used to think ______________________________,

but now I know ______________________________.

TEC43050

Read and complete each sentence.

Before I Read

I already know ______________________________.

As I Read

I just learned ______________________________.

After I Read

I used to think ______________________________,

but now I know ______________________________.

TEC43050

Name________________________ Date ____________

Comparing and contrasting

Both

Note to the teacher: Use with “Wise Owls” on page 8.

Cause Patterns

Use with "To the Point" on page 9.

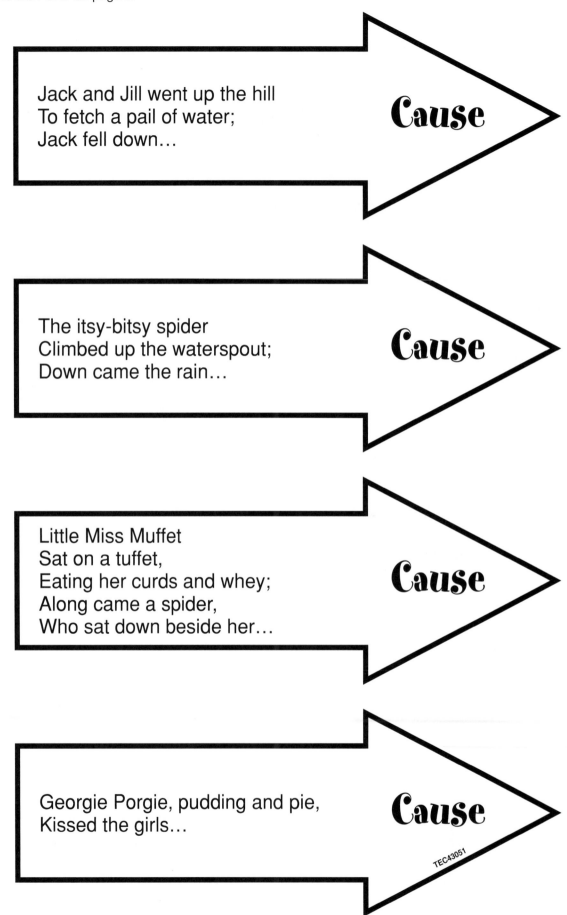

Jack and Jill went up the hill
To fetch a pail of water;
Jack fell down...

Cause

The itsy-bitsy spider
Climbed up the waterspout;
Down came the rain...

Cause

Little Miss Muffet
Sat on a tuffet,
Eating her curds and whey;
Along came a spider,
Who sat down beside her...

Cause

Georgie Porgie, pudding and pie,
Kissed the girls...

Cause

TEC43051

Use with "A 'Dino-mite' Reference" on page 9.

A **thesaurus** lists words that are related. For each entry word, you will find **synonyms** (words with the same meaning). You might also find **antonyms** (words with the opposite meaning).
HELLO!
My name is Thesaurus.
TEC43051

Name ______________________________ Date ________________

Using a thesaurus

A "Dino-mite" Discovery

Use a thesaurus to complete the chart.

Word	Page
Synonyms	Antonyms

Reading Fiction

Name

Author: Who wrote the story?

Illustrator: Who drew the pictures?

Characters: Who was part of the story? Were there people, animals, or make-believe creatures? Name and describe them.

Setting: Where and when did the story happen? Think about all the places the characters were and how long the story events took to happen.

Problem (conflict): What did the main character or characters have to deal with or figure out?

Solution (resolution): How did the main character or characters finally deal with or figure out the problem?

Plot: What were the events of the story? Think about the order in which they happened.

Theme: What is the author's message? Think about what the character or characters learned.

Author's purpose: Why did the author write this story? Was it to inform, entertain, or persuade the reader? Did the author have more than one purpose?

Point of view: Did the author use a narrator to tell the story? Did one of the characters tell the story?

 Note to the teacher: Use with "Help Is on the Way!" on page 9.

Use with "All Kinds of Books" on page 10.

Fantasy TEC43052	Mystery TEC43052
Realistic Fiction TEC43052	Historical Fiction TEC43052
Traditional Literature TEC43052	Science Fiction TEC43052
Informational TEC43052	Biography TEC43052
Autobiography TEC43052	Poetry TEC43052

Summary and Ribbon Patterns

Use with "Award Winners" on page 11.

Title

____

Summary

____

____

____

____

____

____

____

____

____

____

Author and Illustrator

____

____

TEC43052

Food Cards

Use with “Word Sandwich” on page 12.

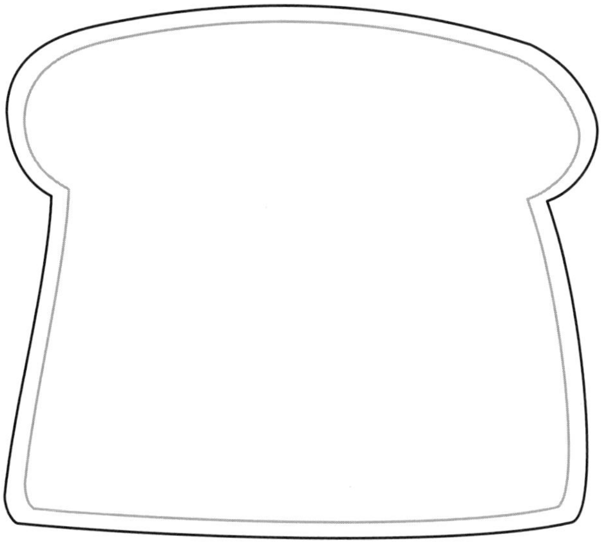

TEC43053

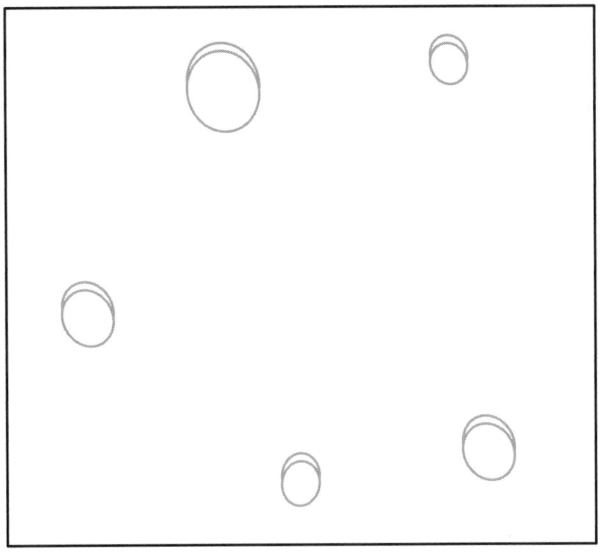

TEC43053

TEC43053

TEC43053

TEC43053

TEC43053

Name_______________________________________ Date ____________________

Biography research

That's Personal Information!

Use a biography and other resources to answer each question.
Write each answer in your own words.

Name

Who did you research?

Personal Information

When and where was this person born?

If he or she is no longer living, where and when did this person die?

Contributions

How did the person help his or her community? List the facts in the order in which they happened.

Facts

What else is important or interesting to know? List the facts in the order in which they happened.

Sources

What is the title and who is the author of your biography?

Where else did you find facts?

 Note to the teacher: Use with "Mini Memoirs" on page 12.

Bookmark Patterns

Use with "Mini Memoirs" on page 12.

(name)

Personal Information

Contributions

Facts

TEC43053

(name)

Personal Information

Contributions

Facts

TEC43053

Treasure Chest Pattern

Use with "Reading Brings Riches" on page 14.

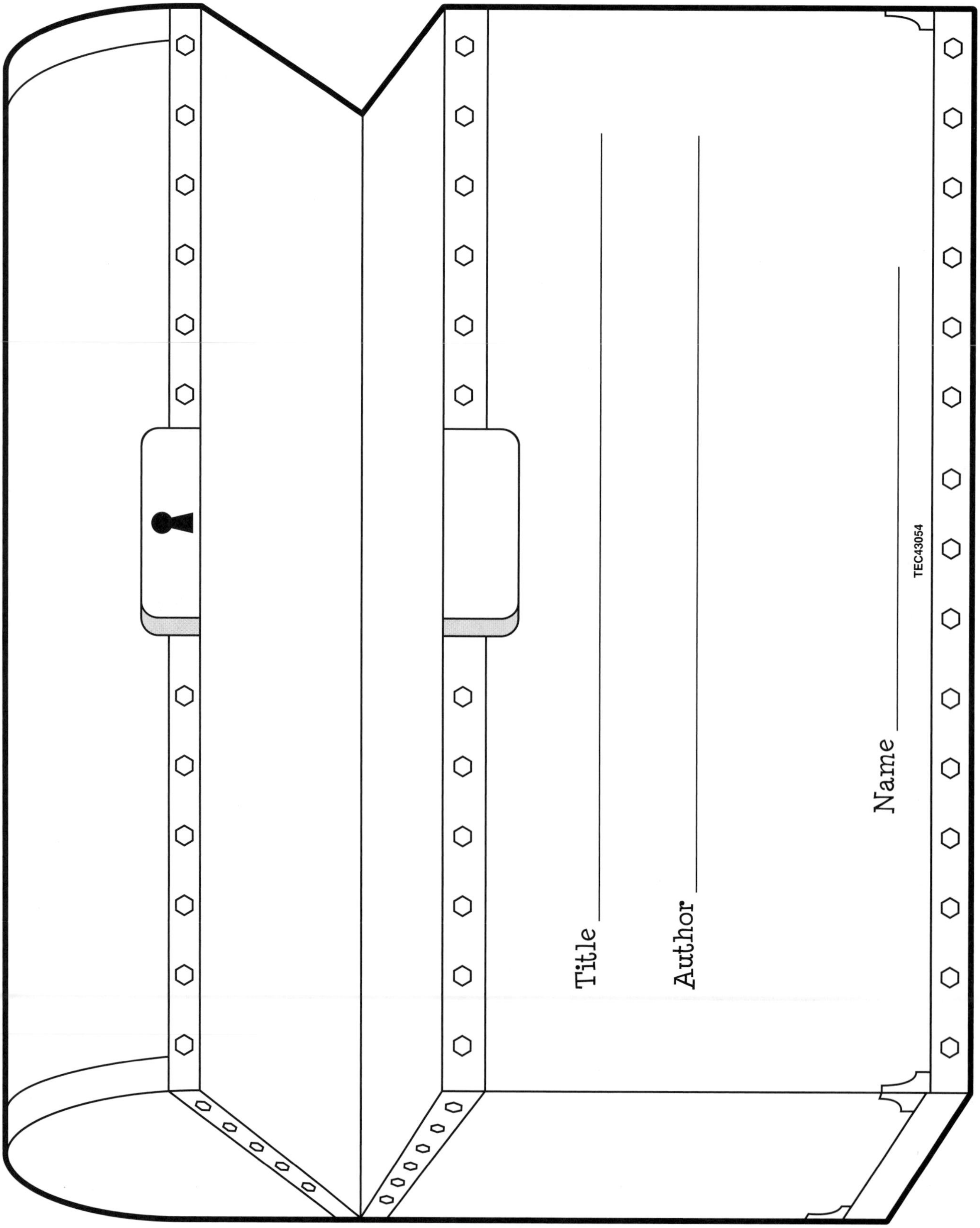

Title
Author
Name
TEC43054

A simile compares two unlike things using like or as.

This book was as easy as ABC.

TEC43054

A metaphor shows how two unlike things are alike in one way. It states that one thing is another.

Betty is a reading machine!

TEC43054

Example	**Meaning**

TEC43054

Example	**Meaning**

TEC43054

Name ______________________ Date ______________

Recording sheet

Make a Rainbow

Busy, Busy Ants!

Answer Key

1. exit	11. before
2. subtract	12. last
3. quiet	13. heavy
4. cold	14. useless
5. above	15. weak
6. inactive	16. destroy
7. never	17. pack
8. far	18. scatter
9. bumpy	19. defend
10. young	20. repair

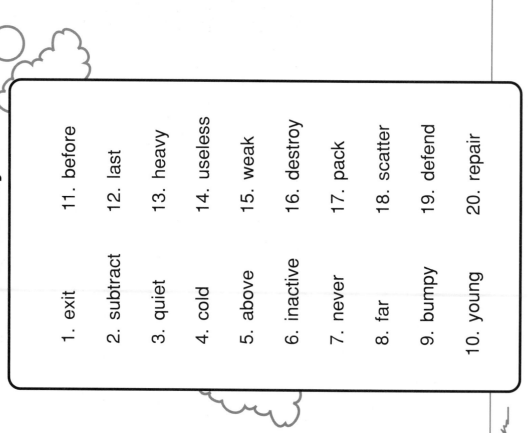

Note to the teacher: Use the recording sheet at the top with "Along the Arcs" on page 15 and the answer key at the bottom with "Busy, Busy Ants!" on page 33.

Busy, Busy Ants!
Antonyms

Word Bank

above	defend	heavy	pack	subtract
before	destroy	inactive	quiet	useless
bumpy	exit	last	repair	weak
cold	far	never	scatter	young

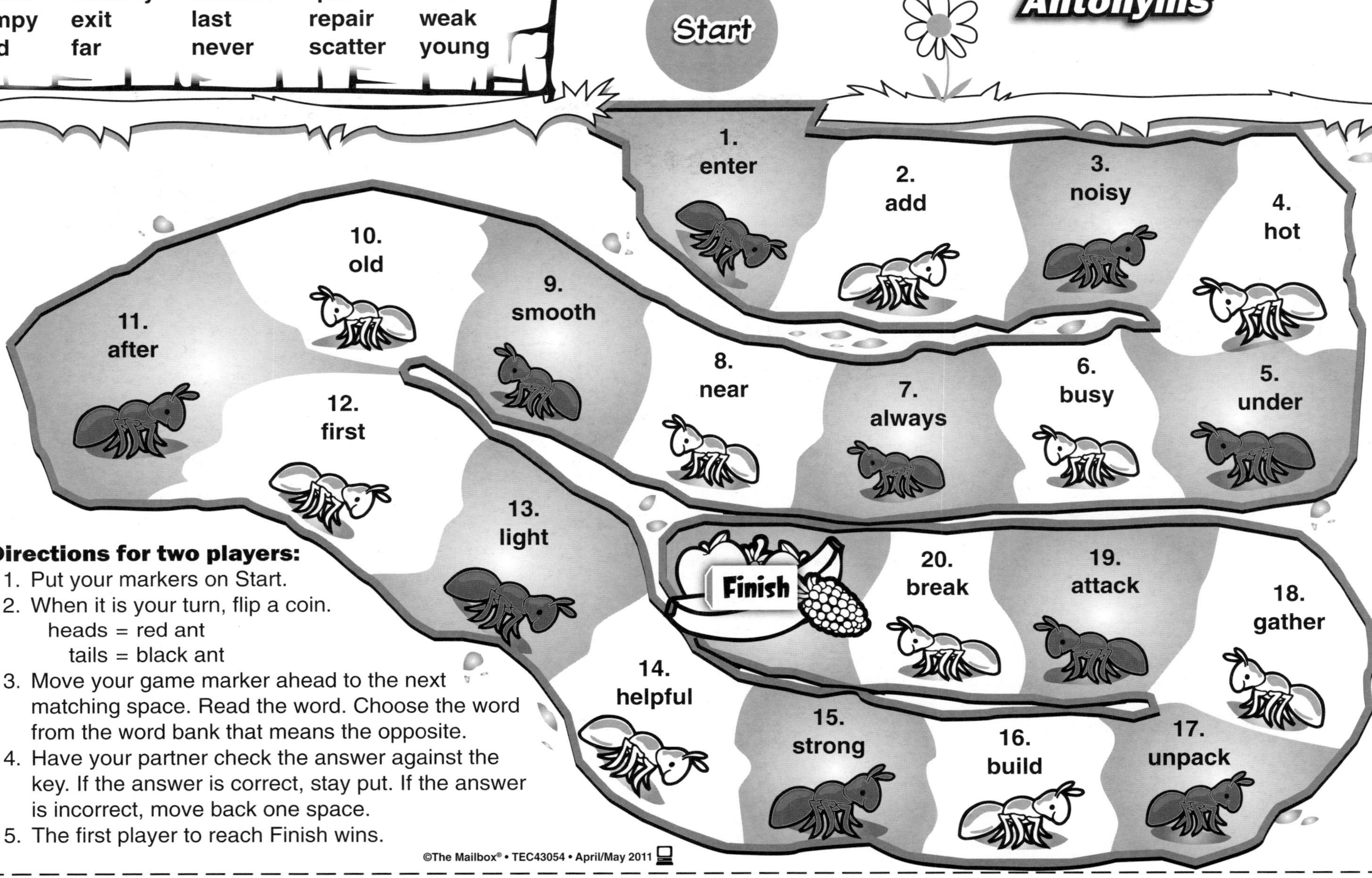

Start
1. enter
2. add
3. noisy
4. hot
5. under
6. busy
7. always
8. near
9. smooth
10. old
11. after
12. first
13. light
14. helpful
15. strong
16. build
17. unpack
18. gather
19. attack
20. break
Finish

Directions for two players:

1. Put your markers on Start.
2. When it is your turn, flip a coin.
   heads = red ant
   tails = black ant
3. Move your game marker ahead to the next matching space. Read the word. Choose the word from the word bank that means the opposite.
4. Have your partner check the answer against the key. If the answer is correct, stay put. If the answer is incorrect, move back one space.
5. The first player to reach Finish wins.

How to use Copy the gameboard on construction paper. Place at a center the gameboard, two game markers, a coin, and a copy of the key from the bottom of page 32.

Reading Prompts

Use with "Reading Relationship" on page 16.

Choose an event from today's reading. Describe how that event is like something that happened in your life. TEC43055	Choose a character from today's reading. Describe how that character's actions or feelings are like those of a character from a different reading. TEC43055	What do you know about the plot of the story that the main character does not? How do you know this? TEC43055	If you were the main character, what would you do next? TEC43055	What is the most exciting event from today's reading? Describe it and tell why it is exciting. TEC43055	What surprised you in today's reading? Why? TEC43055

Sign Pattern

Use with "Up There or in There?" on page 17.

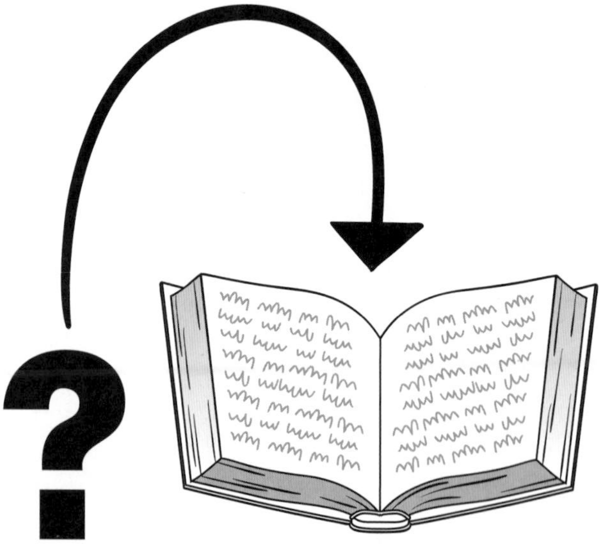

Find the answer in the reading.

TEC43055

Find the answer by thinking about the reading and what you already know.

TEC43055

Name ______________________ Date ______________

Fiction

Fishing Around For Clues

Title: ______________________

Before Reading

Based on the cover, title, and illustrations, what do you predict?

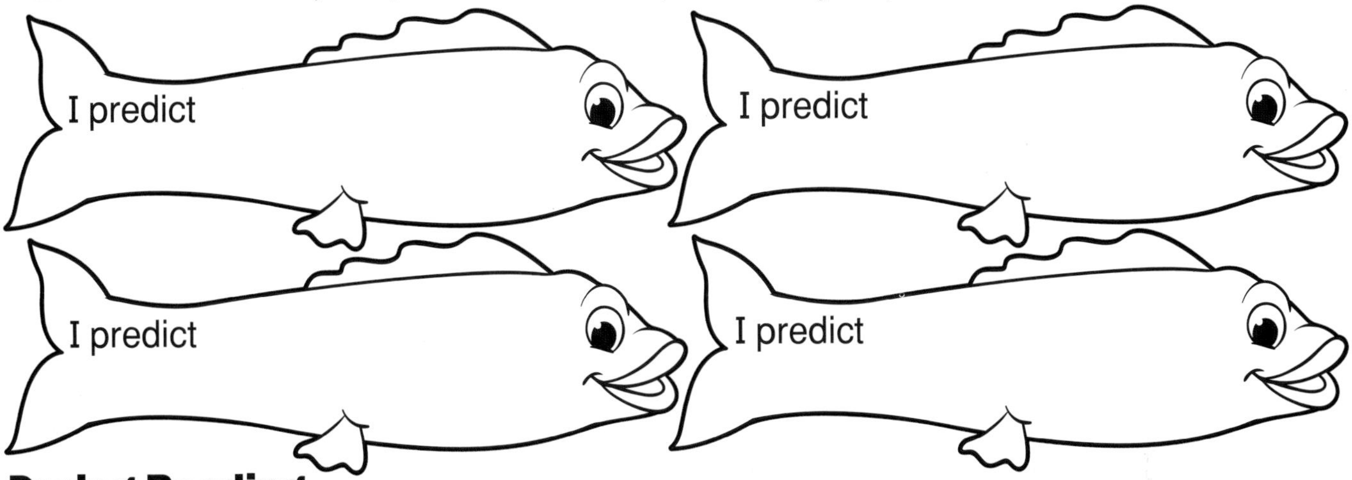
I predict
I predict
I predict
I predict

During Reading

Which of your predictions are true? Color the matching fish.

Name ______________________ Date ______________

Nonfiction

Fishing Around For Clues

Title: ______________________

Before Reading

Based on the charts, photographs, and other text features, what do you predict?

I predict
I predict
I predict
I predict

During Reading

Which of your predictions are true? Color the matching fish.

Note to the teacher: Use with "Schooled on Previewing" on page 17.

Name ________________________________ Date ______________

Beginning blends: *br, cr, fr, gr*

Sorting Mail

Add *br, cr, fr,* or *gr* to complete each word.
Write the word on the matching mail bin.

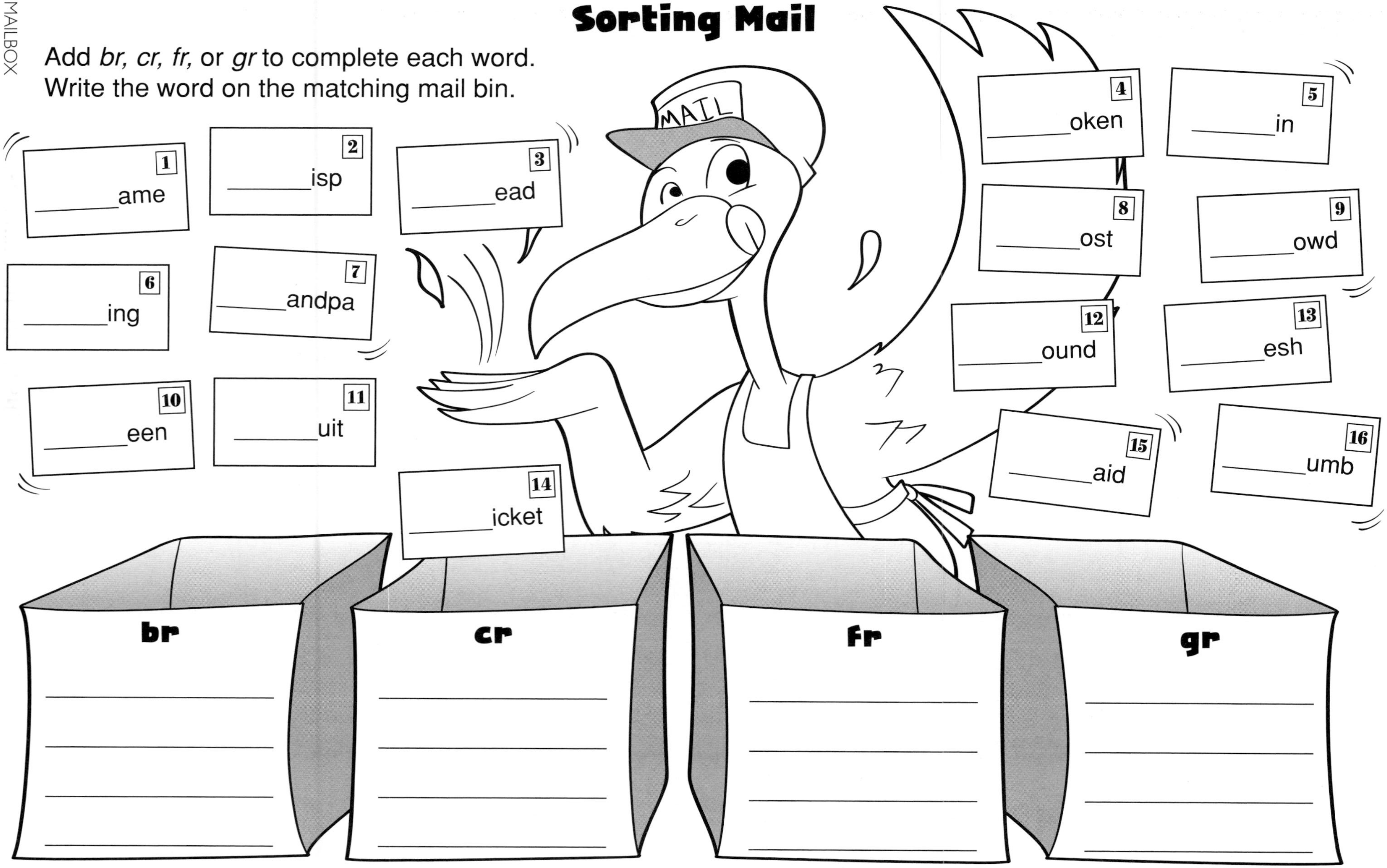
1 ______ame
2 ______isp
3 ______ead
4 ______oken
5 ______in
6 ______ing
7 ______andpa
8 ______ost
9 ______owd
10 ______een
11 ______uit
12 ______ound
13 ______esh
14 ______icket
15 ______aid
16 ______umb
MAIL
br
cr
fr
gr

Name ____________________ Date __________

Suffixes: *-er, -est, -ly*

Hitting Flies

Write the letter of the matching meaning next to each word.

____ 1. strongest	____ 7. smoothly
____ 2. trainer	____ 8. player
____ 3. loudly	____ 9. youngest
____ 4. longest	____ 10. quickly
____ 5. listener	____ 11. wildly
____ 6. pitcher	____ 12. deepest

Playoffs sponsored by
er = one who does
est = most
ly = in the manner of

A — in a quick manner

C — in a loud manner

D — one who listens

E — most young

O — one who pitches

F — most deep

H — in a smooth manner

N — most long

W — most strong

T — one who trains

L — one who plays

I — in a wild manner

Why did the frog like playing outfield?

To find out, write the letters from above on the matching numbered lines below.

__ __ (7 9) __ __ __ __ __ __ (1 10 4 2 9 5) __ __ (2 6) __ __ __ __ __ (3 10 2 3 7)

__ __ __ (10 8 8) __ __ __ (2 7 9) __ __ __ __S! (12 8 11 9)

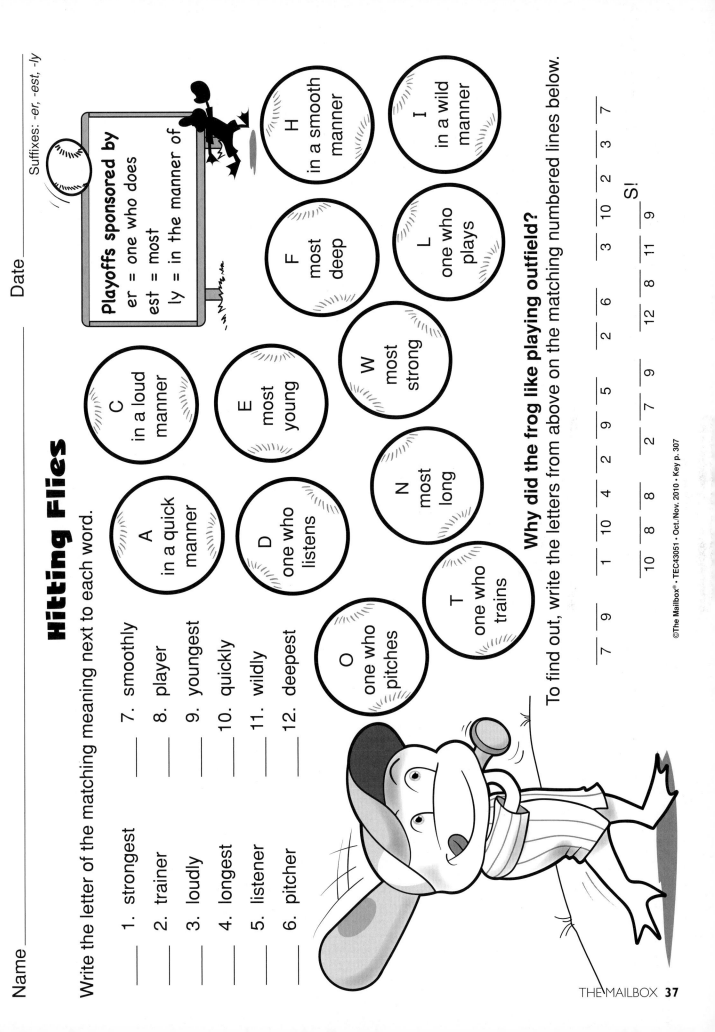

Name ______________________________ Date ________________

Squeaky Clean

Write a synonym (S) and an antonym (A) for each word.
Use the word bank.

1. fast
S ____________
A ____________

2. start
S ____________
A ____________

3. friend
S ____________
A ____________

4. little
S ____________
A ____________

5. neat
S ____________
A ____________

6. wealthy
S ____________
A ____________

7. strong
S ____________
A ____________

8. tight
S ____________
A ____________

9. correct
S ____________
A ____________

10. sick
S ____________
A ____________

11. follow
S ____________
A ____________

12. soft
S ____________
A ____________

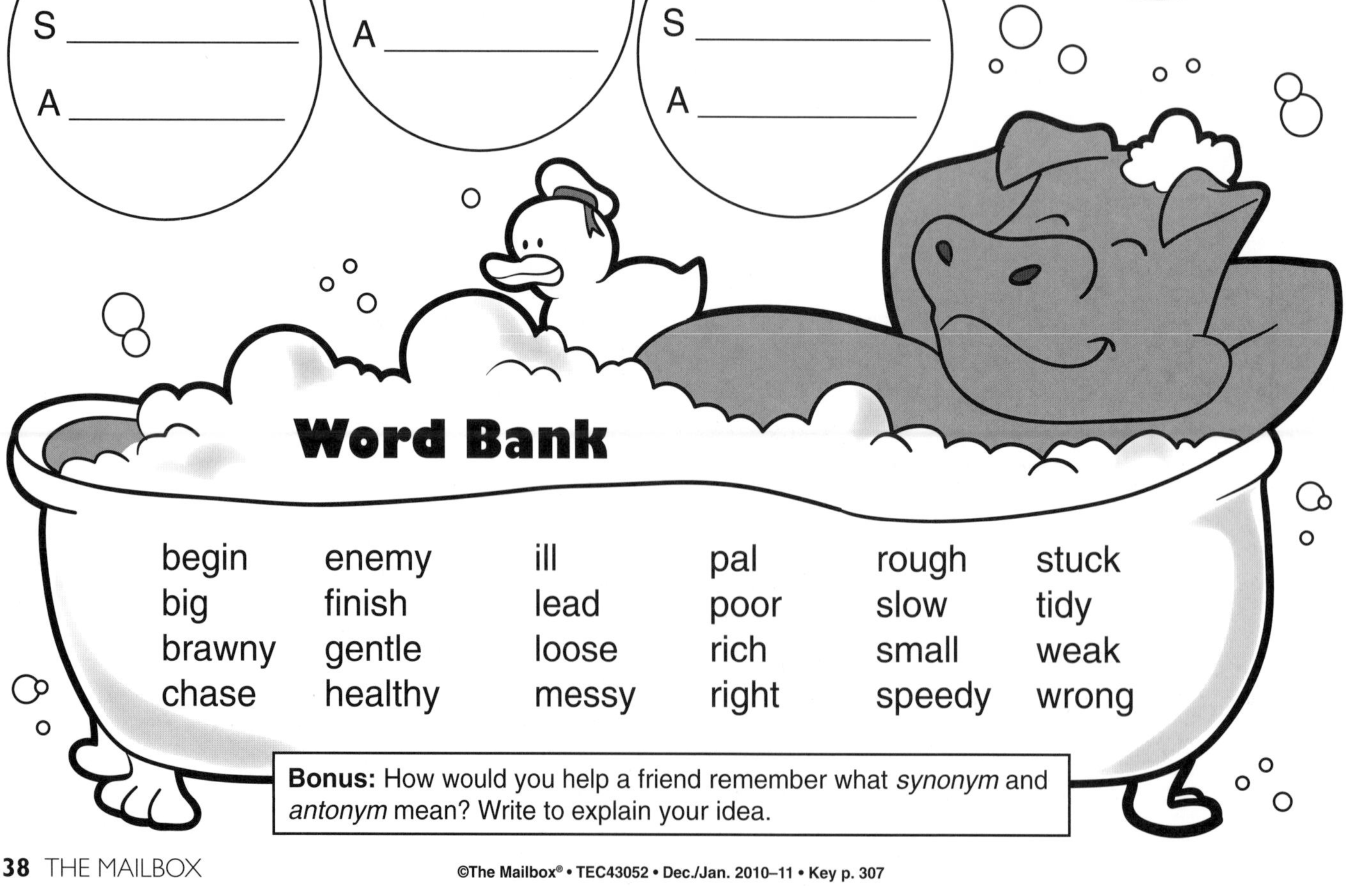

Word Bank

begin	enemy	ill	pal	rough	stuck
big	finish	lead	poor	slow	tidy
brawny	gentle	loose	rich	small	weak
chase	healthy	messy	right	speedy	wrong

Bonus: How would you help a friend remember what *synonym* and *antonym* mean? Write to explain your idea.

Name ______________________ Date ______________

Main idea and details

Shoe Shopping

For each set of sentences, draw a line through the detail that does not belong. Write the matching main idea on the box's lid.

1.

Many families have come to buy shoes.
It is a pretty, sunny day.
There is a long line to check out.
The salespeople are carrying stacks of shoes.

2.

The clerk must ring up lots of orders.
There are many boots in the corner.
There is also a big display of high heels.
Those sneakers come in every color.

3.

My brother gets sneakers with straps.
Mom picks out some brown flip-flops.
Dad gets a new pair of work boots.
My big toe hurts in those shoes.

4.

She picks out a shiny pair.
The salesperson measures her foot.
My brother wants cowboy boots.
Lucky for her, the shoes fit just right.

Main Ideas

- ☐ The shoe store sells all kinds of shoes.
- ☐ My sister needs new shoes.
- ☐ The shoe store is very busy today.
- ☐ My whole family is getting new shoes.

Name ____________________ Date ____________

Fact and opinion

Knitting Pretty

If the sentence is an opinion, color the yarn blue.
If the sentence is a fact, color the yarn red.

1. Spinning wool into yarn began about 6,000 years ago.
2. Wool often comes from sheep.
3. Everything made from wool is itchy.

4. Fleece is the wooly coat of a sheep.
5. Sheep are funny-looking animals.

6. Sheep make the best pets.
7. Fleece is taken off a sheep with clippers.
8. Sheep's fleece is clipped about once a year.
9. Shearing a sheep is not a fun job!
10. The fleece is used to make yarn for knitting.
11. People have been knitting for hundreds of years.
12. Knitting is a really hard skill to learn.

Bonus: Think about a favorite sweater or blanket. Write one fact and one opinion about it.

Name ______________________ Date ______________

Cause and effect

Hamster Happenings

Read about each event.
Highlight the *cause* in green.
Highlight the *effect* in yellow.

50¢ off!

1. Hazel saved money at the food store because she used coupons.

2. Harry saved his money for four months. As a result, Harry had enough money to buy the exercise wheel he always wanted.

3. Hildy lost her paycheck. She put the paycheck in her pocket, which had a hole in it. Poor Hildy!

4. Hal and Hallie pooled their money. Together they were able to buy a tunnel the entire family could use. Fun!

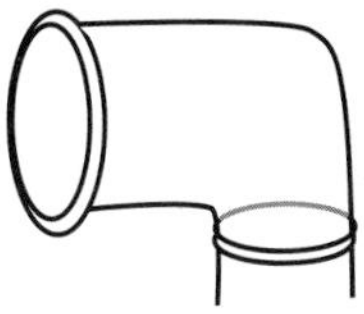

5. Hugh hid his money so no one could find it. He forgot where he put it.

6. Hannah put her babysitting money in the bank. Her money earned interest, which means her money amount grew.

Bank

7. Hank got a raise at work because he works hard, gets along with the other workers, and has a great attitude!

8. Henrietta spent her birthday money on candy. Not only did she buy something that didn't last very long, but she also got two cavities from the candy!

Bonus: Write to explain the difference between a *cause* and an *effect*.

How to use Have students work in pairs to complete a copy of this page. Instruct one child to highlight the causes and the other to highlight the effects. Or place student copies of this page, along with a yellow and a green highlighter, at a center.

Name ______________________ Date ______________

Using a glossary

Sensational Snakes

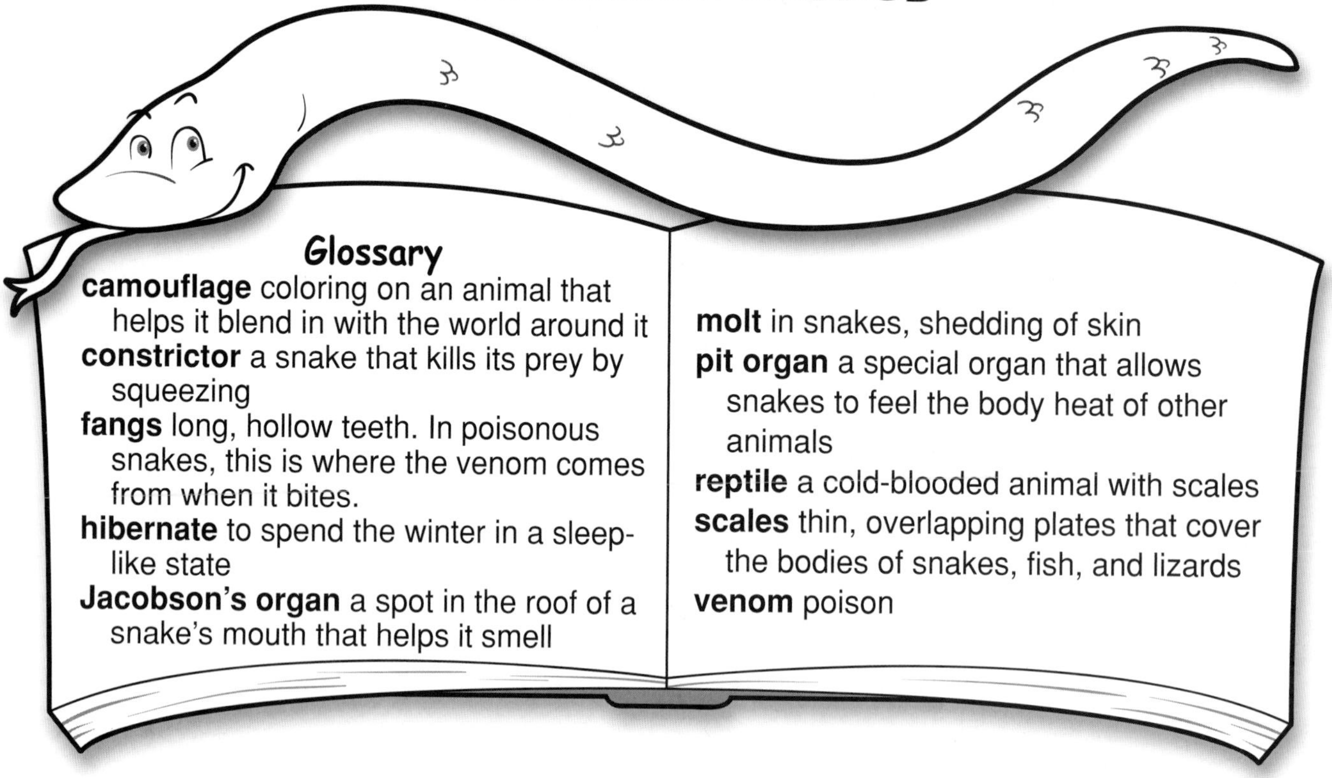

Glossary

camouflage coloring on an animal that helps it blend in with the world around it

constrictor a snake that kills its prey by squeezing

fangs long, hollow teeth. In poisonous snakes, this is where the venom comes from when it bites.

hibernate to spend the winter in a sleep-like state

Jacobson's organ a spot in the roof of a snake's mouth that helps it smell

molt in snakes, shedding of skin

pit organ a special organ that allows snakes to feel the body heat of other animals

reptile a cold-blooded animal with scales

scales thin, overlapping plates that cover the bodies of snakes, fish, and lizards

venom poison

Your fingernails and a snake's scales are made of the same stuff. What is it?

To find out, read the glossary.
Color the word that best completes each sentence.
Circle the answer at the end of the path.

1. A snake is a ____. It is cold-blooded.	reptile	venom
2. A snake's ____ may help it blend with the grass.	hibernate	camouflage
3. A snake will ____ in its den all winter.	molt	hibernate
4. The ____ on a snake cover its body.	fangs	scales
5. When a snake hunts, it uses its ____ to feel its prey's body heat.	camouflage	pit organ
6. As a snake grows, its skin will ____.	molt	camouflage
7. Sometimes a snake can smell its prey using its ____.	venom	Jacobson's organ
8. A python is a ____. It kills its prey by squeezing it.	pit organ	constrictor
9. Some snakes have ____ that release poison.	fangs	scales
10. The ____ from their fangs kills their prey.	venom	reptile
	keratin	**iron**

Bonus: How are a glossary and an index alike? How are they different?

Name ______________________________ Date ______________

Point of view, making inferences

Day at the Dog Park

Read each statement.
Write which fictional character would have made the statement.
Use the word bank.

Each statement is written from the **first person point of view.** That means the narrator uses pronouns such as *me*, *I*, and *we*.
Word Bank
big dog
little dog
dog owner
child
squirrel
dog trainer
stick

1. Ugh! Look at all the dogs. Can't a rodent get some peace and quiet? I guess I'll have to sit up in this tree until the park closes.

   ____

2. Goodness! Who brought all the big dogs today? A furry little princess like me can't prance around the park with them here. I guess I'll just have to sit and look pretty.

   ____

3. I wonder which dogs' owners need my help. That dog clearly needs a review of the *down* command, but that other one seems to have mastered *sit*.

   ____

4. Hooray for playtime! I'm so glad my owner brings me here. It's hard to find enough space to play in my house. Here I can stretch my long legs and run!

   ____

5. What a beautiful day. I am so lucky to have this park close to my house. My dog just loves it here. We could come every day.

   ____

6. Whee! That person threw me far. Here comes that big dog to take me for another ride!

   ____

Bonus: One character is left in the word bank. Write a statement as that character, using first person point of view.

Name ______________________________ Date ______________

Fiction comprehension

Fancy Nancy

N

The clock was ticking. Fancy Nancy had five minutes before she had to be dressed and ready to catch the bus for school. She had put on her sparkly shirt, her shiny shoes, and her brand-new jeans, but she could not find her lucky hat. Fancy Nancy couldn't start third grade without her lucky hat! So she looked all over her bedroom to find it. She checked her closet, she peeked under her bed, and she even looked in her desk drawers. Where was that hat? Fancy Nancy was getting upset. Her dad yelled that it was almost time to go. Fancy Nancy took one last look around her room. Then she grabbed her pink headband instead. "This will have to do," she said to herself. She put the headband in her hair and went downstairs. Just as she reached the bottom step, Fancy Nancy screamed. There, hanging on the coatrack, was her lucky hat! Before her dad knew it, Fancy Nancy had pulled off her pink headband and was wearing her lucky hat. She was ready to conquer third grade at last!

Use the story to answer each question.

1. Who is the story mostly about? ______________________________
2. When does the story happen? ______________________________

   ____
3. Where does the story start? ______________________________

   Where does it end? ______________________________
4. What is the problem? ______________________________

   ____

   How is it solved? ______________________________

   ____

Name ______________________ Date ____________

Comprehension: poetry

A Special Request

Read.

____

I've been waiting and waiting
But I've had no luck.
It seems that autumn
Is just stubborn and stuck.

Where is the snow?
No flakes have come down.
It's wintertime now
And the ground is still brown!

Let's go, winter!
You're making me sad.
Send me some snowflakes
And this kid will be glad!

Use the poem to answer each question.

1. What is the rhyme scheme (pattern) in this poem?
____
2. What is the poem's main idea? ______________________
____
____
3. What does the author mean by writing that autumn is just stubborn and stuck? ______________________
____
____
4. What is the poem's purpose? (Circle.)
   to entertain   to inform or teach   to persuade or convince
5. What would be a good title for this poem? Write it on the line over the poem.

Bonus: Circle the rhyming words in each stanza. Copy one pair. Write a list of five or more words that rhyme with the word pair.

Name ______________________________ Date ____________________

Generating questions about nonfiction

History of Hoops

Read.
Complete each question as you read.

Do you like to play or watch basketball? If so, you can thank a man named James Naismith. He invented basketball in 1891.

Why ______________________________ ?

Mr. Naismith was a PE teacher. His boss asked him to plan an indoor sport that could be played by teams during the winter.

What ______________________________ ?

Mr. Naismith came up with a game that used a soccer ball and two peach baskets. The baskets were attached to railings in the gym and were placed ten feet above the floor. The game had 13 rules.

Did ______________________________ ?

About two years later, the baskets were changed to metal hoops with net bags.

What ______________________________ ?

In 1894, the backboard was first used and the soccer balls were replaced with different balls.

What ______________________________

______________________________ ?

Bonus: Explain why asking questions as you read helps you better understand what you read.

Name ____________________ Date ____________________

Graphic organizer: comparing story elements

Packed With Details

Write two story titles.
Describe how the stories are the same and how they are different.
Use the word bank.

Book your trip today!

Word Bank

characters setting plot problem
solution theme author's message

Title

Both

Title

How to use Have each child complete a copy of this organizer after reading two different stories by the same author or two stories with some common story elements.

Name____________________ Date____________

Nonfiction text

Loads of Understanding

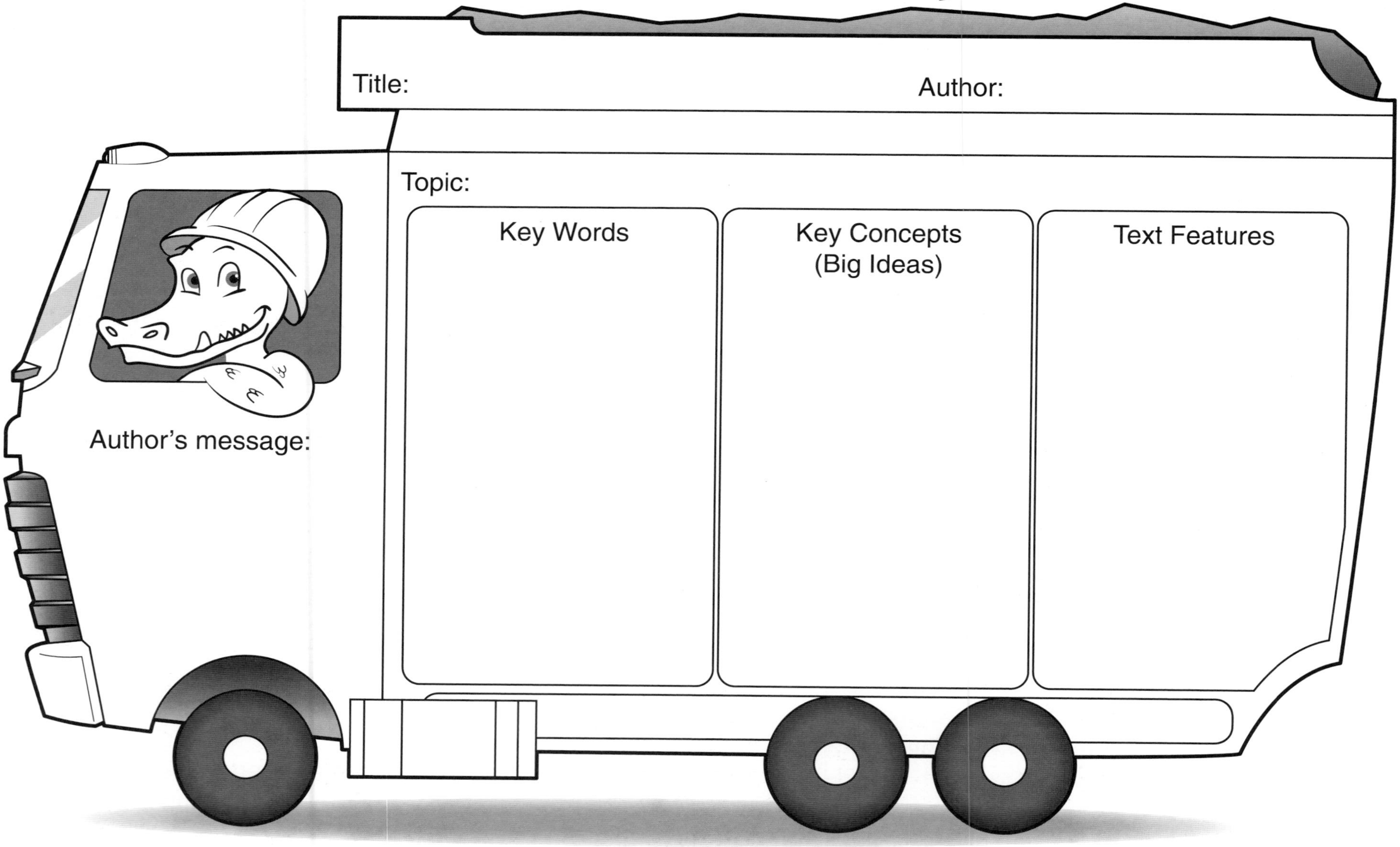
Title:
Author:
Topic:
Key Words
Key Concepts
(Big Ideas)
Text Features
Author's message:

How to use After reading a nonfiction selection, have each child complete a copy of this organizer.

Name ______________________ Date ____________

Book report

____

What is your opinion of the book? Use the code to write the title of this page.

liked it = This Book Will Take You Places
didn't like it = This Book Was No Vacation

Title:

The genre of this book is (circle)

autobiography	biography	fantasy	poetry
historical fiction	informational	traditional literature	
realistic fiction	science fiction	mystery	

Important things to know about this book are

•

•

•

Author:

The author's purpose is

☐ to inform
☐ to entertain
☐ to persuade

The author's message is

A+ Airlines

How to use Have each student complete a copy of this form as an organizer for a book report or have each child present the information from this form as an oral report.

Name ____________________ Date ____________

Graphic organizer: nonfiction text

Surfing for Information

Title: ____________________

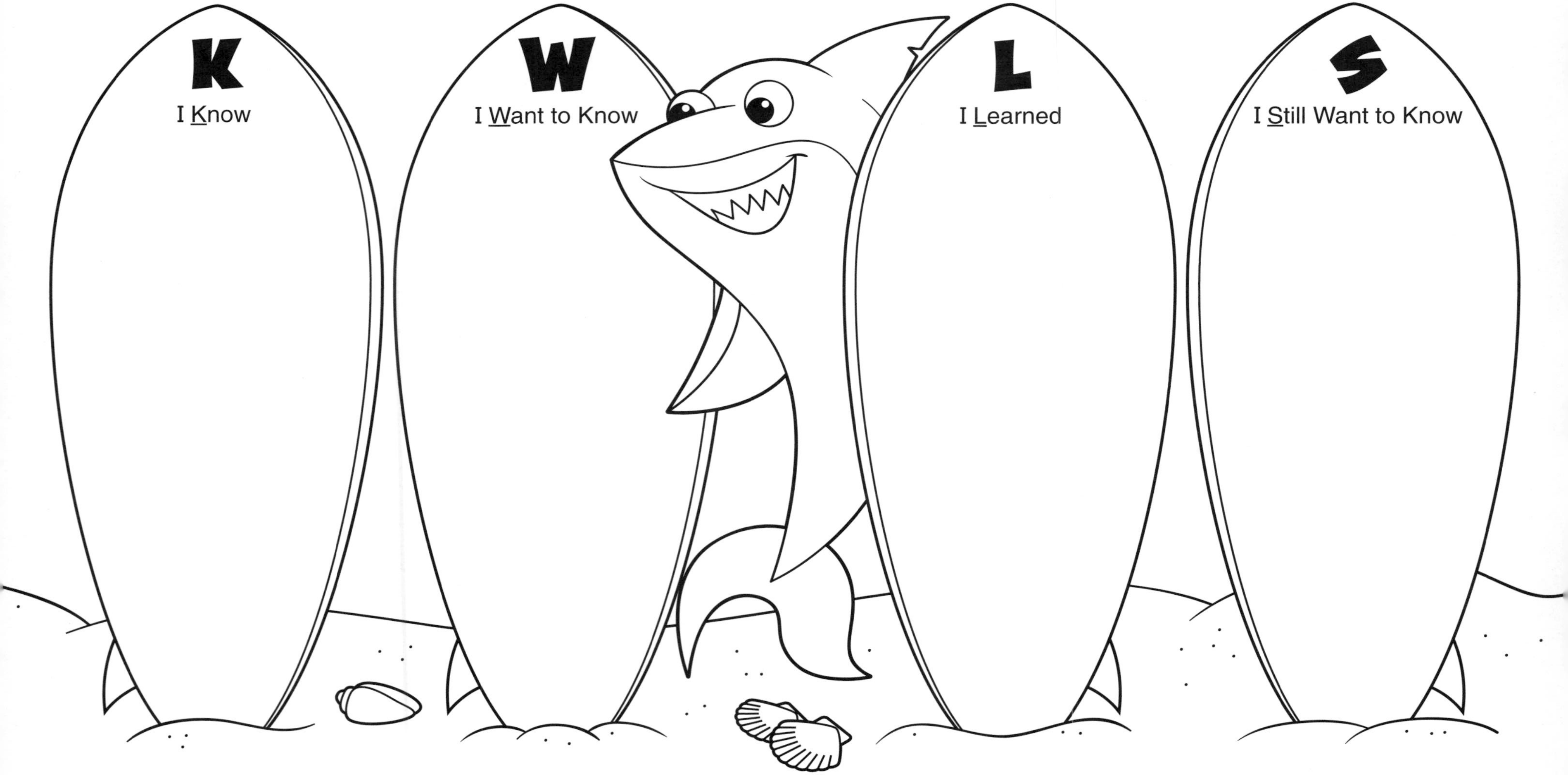
K
I Know
W
I Want to Know
L
I Learned
S
I Still Want to Know

Names ______________________________ Date ____________________

Partner game

Buzz Words

Making Words With Prefixes and Suffixes

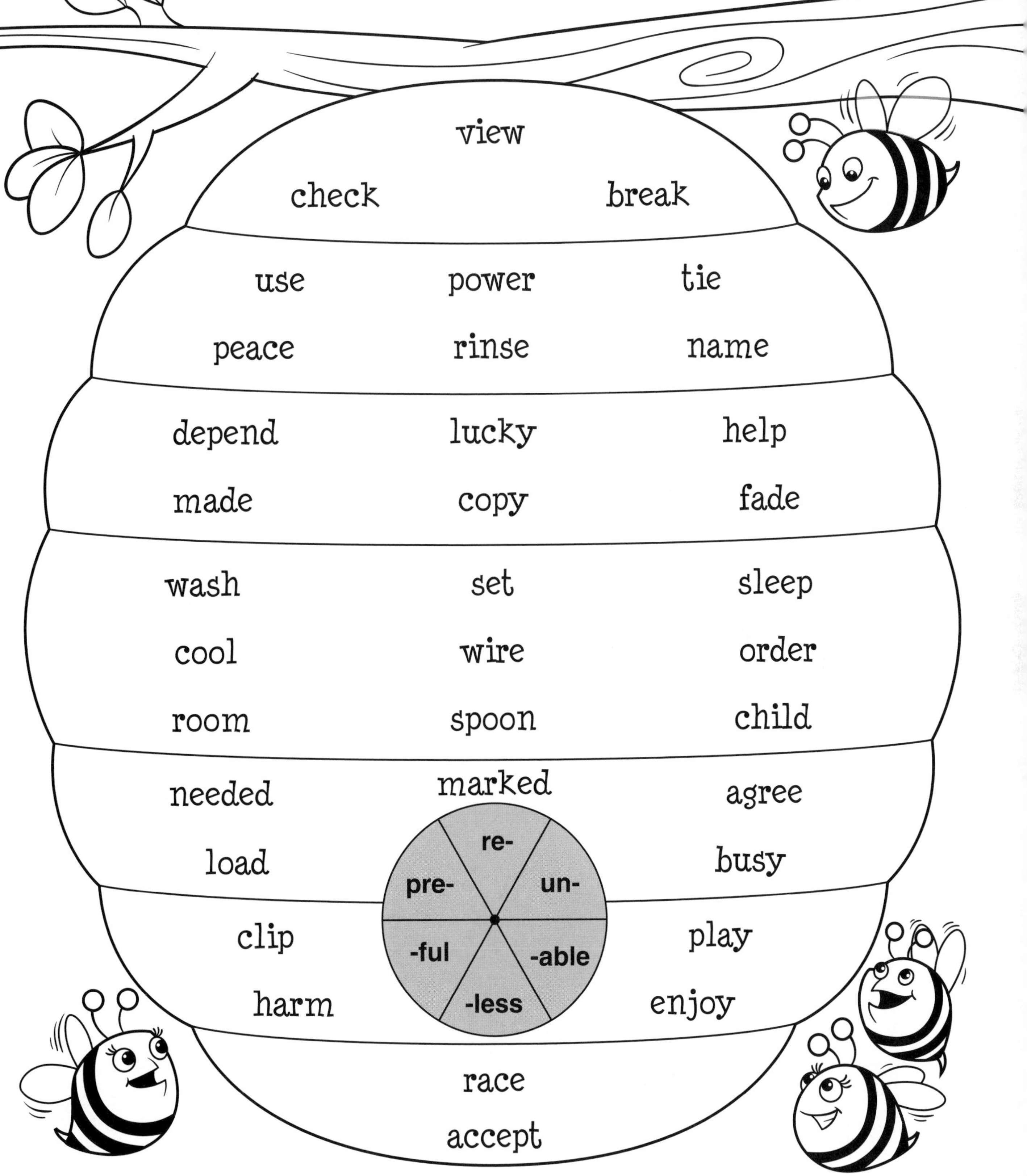

view
check
break
use
power
tie
peace
rinse
name
depend
lucky
help
made
copy
fade
wash
set
sleep
cool
wire
order
room
spoon
child
needed
marked
agree
load
busy
re-
pre-
un-
-ful
-able
-less
clip
play
harm
enjoy
race
accept

How to use Make one copy of this page for each student pair. Also make a copy of page 52 and fold the key under the directions. Set out the gameboard and directions with a paper clip and two different-color pens. Invite students to play the game as a center activity or during free time.

Buzz Words

Making Words With Prefixes and Suffixes

Directions for two players:

1. Make sure the key is folded under this page. Choose a pen.
2. When it is your turn, use the paper clip and a pencil to spin the spinner.
3. Use your pen to write the prefix or suffix spun next to a base word. If you are unable to make a real word, your turn is over.
4. Take turns until all the base words have a prefix or suffix added.
5. Turn this paper over to check the answers against the key. Award one point for each real word made. The player with more points wins!

Buzz Words
Key

view: preview, review, viewable, viewless
check: recheck, checkable, checkless
break: breakable
use: reuse, useable, useful, useless
power: repower, powerful, powerless
tie: retie, untie, tieless
peace: peaceable, peaceful
rinse: prerinse
name: prename, rename, nameable, nameless
depend: dependable
lucky: unlucky
help: helpful, helpless
made: premade, remade, unmade
copy: recopy
fade: prefade, fadeless
wash: prewash, rewash, washable
set: preset, reset, unset
sleep: presleep, sleepless
cool: uncool
wire: rewire, wireless
order: preorder, reorder, orderable, orderless
room: roomful
spoon: spoonful
child: childless
needed: unneeded
marked: remarked, unmarked
agree: agreeable
load: preload, reload, unload
busy: unbusy
clip: unclip
play: replay, playable, playful
harm: harmful, harmless
enjoy: enjoyable
race: prerace
accept: reaccept, acceptable

Note to the teacher: Use with page 51.

______________________________________'s
name

At-Home Reading Log

THE
FROG PRINCE

Please return this form to school by ______________.

Date	Title	Minutes Read	Parent or Guardian's Initials

Note to the teacher: Program the due date on a copy of this page before making student copies. For a monthly log sheet, make a front-and-back copy for each student.

Brain Booster 1

Write your title.

second grader
third grader

Write as many words as you can from the letters in your title.

TEC43050

Brain Booster 2

Copy each sentence.
Circle a hidden word.

best made sit these use wish

I am a dear friend. The seal is in the water.
Tom's it. I want to be Steve's friend.
How is he? What do you see?

TEC43050

Brain Booster 3

Write three ways the words are alike.
Write three ways they are different.

book
classroom
carpoolers

TEC43050

Brain Booster 4

Write two sentences.
Use an even number of syllables in the first sentence.
Use an odd number of syllables in the second sentence.

TEC43050

Brain Booster 5

Order each set of words to make a telling sentence, and then order them to make a question.

the an apple on table is
be will jack going us with

TEC43050

Brain Booster 6

Un- can mean *not,* and *un-* can mean *the opposite of.*
Write ten or more words that start with *un-*.
Write the meaning of each word.

unhealthy = not healthy

TEC43050

Brain Booster 7

Copy and complete the chart.
Only use words that start with the letter *m.*

States or State Capitals	Days or Months

TEC43050

Brain Booster 8

List all the words that can be nouns.
List all the words that can be verbs.
Rewrite each list in ABC order.

flea	flee	sea	see	tow	toe
stair	stare	tide	tied	meet	meat

TEC43050

Note to the teacher: Give each student a copy of this page (or one card at a time) to work on during free time.

Brain Booster 1

Write five or more words that start like *gum.*
Write five or more words that start like *gem.*

TEC43051

Brain Booster 2

Rewrite the sentences to show the correct use of capital letters.
Fill in each blank with a word of your choice.

FALL IS HERE. MY FAVORITE MONTH IN FALL IS ___. MY FAVORITE HOLIDAY IN FALL IS ___. I CAN ALWAYS FIND PLENTY OF ___ TO EAT IN FALL.

TEC43051

Brain Booster 3

Write the pattern or rule for each set of words.

A. cow, chicken, hummingbird, alligator
B. bird, dog, giraffe, elephant
C. game, flame, name, shame
D. sheep, moose, deer, swine

TEC43051

Brain Booster 4

Sort the words into two groups: singular *(*one) and plural (more than one).

turkeys	glass	dress
rivers	kiss	lens
boss	plates	holidays
meals	bus	houses

TEC43051

Brain Booster 5

Think of two or more vowel pairs that could take the place of each set of shapes.
Write the new words.

TEC43051

h _ _ t heat, hoot	b _ _
m _ _ n	br _ _ d
tr _ _ t	gr _ _ n

Brain Booster 6

List as many synonyms as you can for *scary.*

scary
alarming
frightful

TEC43051

Brain Booster 7

Copy and complete the chart.
Use the word bank.
Then add two more verbs of your own.

TEC43051

Past Tense	Present Tense	Future Tense
wrote	am writing	will write

Word Bank
write juggle eat travel rest

Brain Booster 8

What do a king and a tooth have in common?
They each have a **crown.**

Write a riddle like the one above for each of the answers below.

They each work in a **nursery.**
They each have a **bat.**
They each have many **stories.**

TEC43051

How to use Give each student a copy of this page (or one card at a time) to work on during free time.

Brain Boosters

Brain Booster 1

Rewrite each riddle.
Circle each punctuation mark you add.
Underline each compound word.

What do you get when you cross a tiger with a snowman Frostbite
Why dont mountains get cold in the winter They wear snowcaps

TEC43052

Brain Booster 2

How many words can you make?
Use only letters that touch on the grid.
List the words.

pair
colt

w	a	s	e
c	t	o	n
o	t	a	i
l	d	p	r

TEC43052

Brain Booster 3

Make a list of ten or more winter holiday words.
Rewrite the list in ABC order.

TEC43052

Brain Booster 4

For each word, write one synonym and one antonym.

cold **jolly**
bright **migrate**
hibernate **festive**

TEC43052

Brain Booster 5

For each clue, write a word that contains the letters *br*.

to look over br_ _ _ _
easily broken br_ _ _ _ _ _
never used before br_ _ _ _-_ _ _
to observe a holiday _ _ _ _ _br_ _ _
sweet houses are made of this _ _ _ _ _ _ _ _ _br_ _ _

TEC43052

Brain Booster 6

Write a list of steps telling how to put these words in ABC order.

peace **plump**
panda
pedal **pair**

TEC43052

Brain Booster 7

Write a proper noun for each common noun.

month	state	man
teacher	holiday	girl
river	company	building
pet	team	continent

TEC43052

Brain Booster 8

Copy the chart headings.
Add five or more words to each column.

Words Spelled With Prefix *pre-*	Words Spelled With *pre* (Not the Prefix)
pretest	present

TEC43052

How to use Give each student a copy of this page (or one card at a time) to work on during free time.

Language Arts

Brain Boosters

Brain Booster 1

How are these words alike?
How are they different?

snowfall **sunshine**

TEC43053

Brain Booster 2

Make a list of adjectives that describe yourself.

Make a list of adjectives that describe someone you love.

Draw a ♡ next to each adjective that is in both lists.

TEC43053

Brain Booster 3

Write a letter on each row to make a word in the bold column.

	u		e
r	o		e
c	a		s
	b		g
	o		
h	u		

TEC43053

Brain Booster 4

Copy each name.
Circle the hidden pronoun in each one.
Write each name and pronoun in a different sentence.

Shelly Henry Brittany Lexie
Gus James Wendy Courtney

TEC43053

Brain Booster 5

Read the clipped words.
Write the longer word.

A. bike = bicycle
B. champ
C. phone
D. teen
E. plane
F. exam
G. fridge
H. gas
I. auto

TEC43053

Brain Booster 6

What common expression does this nonsense sentence make if you fix the spacing and add an end mark?

Thee ar lyb ird cat chesth ew orm

TEC43053

Brain Booster 7

Explain what each underlined phrase means.

A. Farmer Fred has a green thumb.
B. My sister became a green-eyed monster when I got a new bike and she didn't.
C. My teacher gave us the green light to go to the playground.

TEC43053

Brain Booster 8

Wind (wĭnd) is moving air.

Wind (wīnd) means to curve or bend.

Make a list of ten or more words that are spelled the same but can be said differently and have different meanings.

TEC43053

How to use Give each student a copy of this page (or one card at a time) to work on during free time.

Language Arts

Brain Boosters

Brain Booster 1

Copy each word.
Circle the long *a* spellings.

afraid	daisy	grade
baseball	daylight	hallway
became	escape	May
bricklayer	explain	praise

TEC43054

Brain Booster 2

Write a short story about your day. (It can be fiction or nonfiction.)
Use at least four periods, three exclamation points, two question marks, and one comma.

TEC43054

Brain Booster 3

The topic is **butterflies**.
Write five or more questions about this topic.

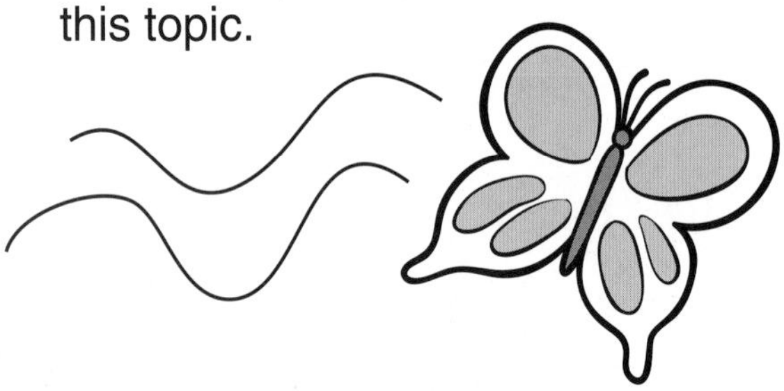

TEC43054

Brain Booster 4

Write three or more **facts** about eggs.

Write three or more **opinions** about eggs.

TEC43054

Brain Booster 5

Each of these words can be said more than one way and has more than one meaning.
Write two meanings for each word.
Tell how the words in each set are alike.

bass: a fish or a deep tone	close
does	lead
sow	tear

TEC43054

Brain Booster 6

What real compound words could take the place of the made-up words below?

A. femaleinsect
B. ranchdwelling
C. bedtimedress
D. oceaneats

TEC43054

Brain Booster 7

Name the word for each baby animal.

bear	cat	deer
goat	owl	sea lion
sheep	toad	whale

TEC43054

Brain Booster 8

Personification gives things the traits and actions of people.

The leaf danced across the playground.

Write a sentence about each topic.
Use personification.

pencil computer dismissal bell

TEC43054

How to use Give each student a copy of this page (or one card at a time) to work on during free time.

Brain Boosters

Brain Booster 1

Write as many different words as you can from these letters.

TEC43055

father

Brain Booster 2

Write these words in ABC order.

TEC43055

treasure	trip	toy
towel	treats	tugboat

How else could you order these words?

Brain Booster 3

What food, when written across the middle row, forms a three-letter word in each column?

TEC43055

s	g	a	o	n	e
y	t	e	d	w	g

Brain Booster 4

Write a pair of rhyming words for each set of clues.

TEC43055

A. **large branch** = big twig
B. **frog relative's signals**
C. **happy father**
D. **greatest bird home**
E. **best police officer**

Brain Booster 5

What do these words have in common? What words can you add to the set?

TEC43055

wow
Bob
radar
Hannah

Brain Booster 6

Write the meaning of each underlined phrase.
Then write your own sentences with each phrase.

TEC43055

This game is <u>as easy as pie</u>.
We'll be <u>roughing it</u> this weekend.
My sister <u>eats like a bird</u>.

Brain Booster 7

List each letter of the alphabet. For each letter, write something different you might do during summer.

TEC43055

A: act in a play
B: bounce a ball
C: catch fireflies

Brain Booster 8

Copy and complete each analogy.

TEC43055

Ice cream is to bowl as lemonade is to ____.

Scoop is to ice cream as ____ is to pie.

Flag Day is to June as ____ is to July.

How to use Give each student a copy of this page (or one card at a time) to work on during free time.

Writing Tips & Tools

Defeat the Monsters!
Descriptive writing

Tackle students' back-to-school fears head-on with this empowering activity. To begin, have each child identify something about school that scares or worries him. (Have students who claim nothing scares them identify something that might scare others.) Next, have the child copy and complete the sentence shown, using his fear to name his monster. Then have him imagine what his monster looks like and direct him to write a few sentences that describe the monster's physical features. Finally, instruct the student to write a few more sentences detailing real steps he could take to defeat his fear. **For added fun,** have each child create an illustration of his monster.

Sarah Nitsos, Juan de Anza Elementary, Hawthorne, CA

I am usually a very brave person, but sometimes I am afraid of the ___ monster.

The Test Monster
by Curtis

I am usually a very brave person, but sometimes I am afraid of the test monster. You have probably seen him. He's big and hairy. The test monster is always scowling, and when he's angry, he shoots bad grades out of his fingertips.

There are many ways I might defeat the test monster. One way is to keep up with my homework. That way I'm always practicing the skills I'll see on the tests. Another way to defeat the test monster is to find a study partner to help me get ready for tests. If I try these things, maybe the test monster won't be so scary!

Rylee
Writing
New Words to Use
Quick Writes
Story Ideas
Rough Drafts

Ready to Write
Preparing writers' notebooks

To involve your students *and* their parents in your writing program, give this idea a try. Have each child make a writer's notebook by cutting apart a set of four tabs from a tagboard copy of page 72 and gluing them to the pages of a notebook as shown. Also encourage her to personalize her notebook cover. Then, during open house, invite each parent to write an entry in the "Quick Writes" section of his child's notebook. By personally setting up their notebooks, students will have ownership of them, and with their parents' messages inside, students will have constant encouragement as well!

Nancy Fountain, John Greene School, Warwick, RI

Editor's Tip:
For those students whose parents are unable to attend open house, write an entry in their place or invite a student's former teacher to do so.

• Process • Descriptive • Expository • Narrative

Writing Tips & Tools

Searching High and Low
Identifying nouns

Capture students' attention while building their understanding of people, places, and things around your school. To prepare, divide a display into the categories "People," "Places," and "Things" and title it "We Went on a Noun Hunt." After reviewing the definition of a noun, lead students in reciting the chant on page 72. Then quietly guide the class around your school, encouraging students to take mental snapshots of the nouns they see. After returning to the classroom, invite each student to name a noun he saw and then write the word on an index card. Invite the child to tack his card in the matching section of the display. **For added fun and interest,** send students in small groups (with another staff member or parent volunteer) to take digital photos of their named nouns. When every child has been on a small-group noun hunt, print the pictures. Have each student post his picture near the matching index card.

People
Mr. Duckworth

Anndrea Dyer, Medina Elementary, Medina, TN

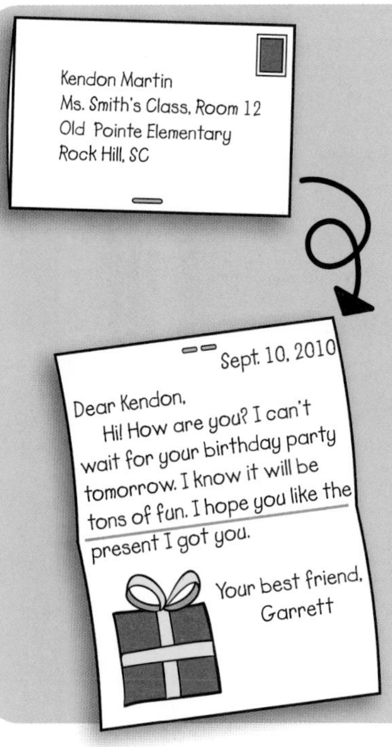
Kendon Martin
Ms. Smith's Class, Room 12
Old Pointe Elementary
Rock Hill, SC
Sept. 10, 2010
Dear Kendon,
Hi! How are you? I can't wait for your birthday party tomorrow. I know it will be tons of fun. I hope you like the present I got you.
Your best friend,
Garrett

Time for Mail
Writing friendly letters

These simple routines are sure to deliver plenty of letter-writing practice!

Weekly routine: Designate time each Friday as Friendly Letter Friday. During this period, have each student write a letter to someone at school, fold it in half, staple it, and address it. Collect the letters, have students sort them by recipient location, and designate a student mail carrier to deliver the letters.

Quarterly routine: In advance, request that each child provide four stamped envelopes, each addressed to a friend or family member outside of school. To celebrate the end of every grading period, have each child write to one of his designated recipients and place his letter into the corresponding envelope to be mailed. If desired, have students place their own letters in the school's outgoing mail bin.

Kimberly White, Old Pointe Elementary, Rock Hill, SC

A or *An*?
Using indefinite articles

In advance, label two sheets of paper with a different article as shown. Then label several more sheets of paper with different singular nouns, some beginning with a consonant and some beginning with a vowel. To start the activity, invite two students to hold the article papers. Pass out the other papers and direct those students to stand next to the sign with the matching article. Have the rest of the class use thumbs-up or thumbs-down signals to confirm their placement. To wrap up the activity, add an *s* to the end of each word and ask students holding those word papers to sit down. Ask the rest of the class why those students needed to sit, leading the class to understand that *a* and *an* are only used with singular words.

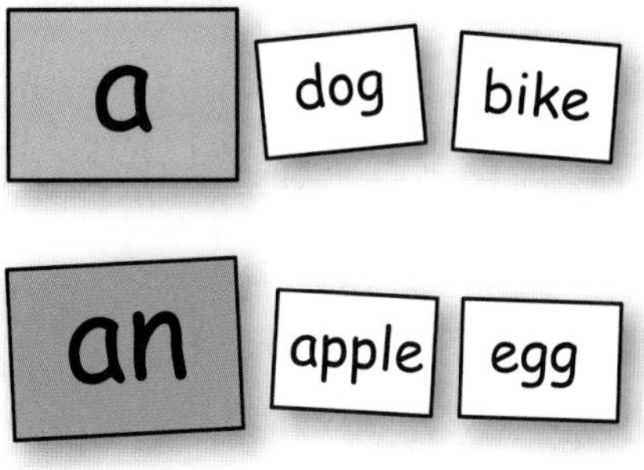
a
dog
bike
an
apple
egg

Katy Bastow, Provo, UT

Writing Tips & Tools

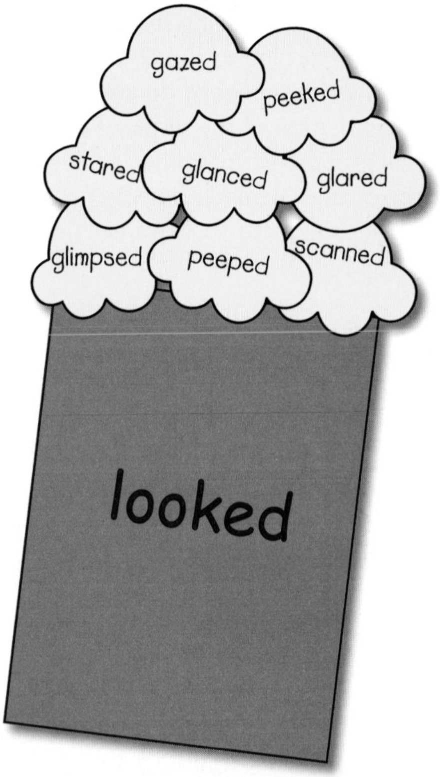
gazed
peeked
stared
glanced
glared
glimpsed
peeped
scanned
looked

Bursting With Fresh Words

Replacing overused words

In advance, label three large sheets of paper (popcorn bags) each with a different word students overuse in their writing. Show students the popcorn bags and discuss the words. Explain that overusing these words makes their writing seem stale and uninteresting to their readers. Then have each student independently generate one fresh word for each overused word. Direct each child to write his words on copies of the popcorn patterns from page 73. Then have him cut out the patterns and share his words with the class, telling which stale word each new word replaces. Display the popcorn pieces above the matching bags on a display titled "Give Your Writing Some Pop!"

Margaret Hines, Andersen Elementary, Yigo, Guam

Storyteller's Notebook
My Plan
Name Lauren

Clothing Chronicles

Imaginative narrative

Dress up your writing time with this inspired activity. In advance, gather a supply of interesting used clothing and accessories, such as hats, scarves, shoes, and costume jewelry. Give one item to each student to inspect. Also direct her to consider who might have worn the item, when, and why. Then lead the student to incorporate her answers into a creative story from the item's point of view. **To provide more assistance as students plan their stories,** give each child a copy of page 74.

Cindy Barber, Fredonia, WI, and Carolyn Burant, St. John Vianney School, Brookfield, WI

Jack-in-the-Box
Capitalization

To get students moving toward a better understanding of capital letters, write on the board or overhead sentences that are missing capitalization. Cover the sentences and then reveal one sentence at a time. Direct each child to push his chair away from his desk and sit on the edge of his seat. Read the sentence aloud twice, slowly the first time and a bit faster the second time. As you read the sentence a third time, instruct students to jump up like jack-in-the-boxes when you read a word that needs to be capitalized. Review the capitalization rules applied to the sentence. Then repeat the activity with the next sentence.

Brooke Beverly, Dudley Elementary, Dudley, MA

I am proud of my school!
Blue Lake Leopard says,
"I am proud of my school!"

Look Who's Talking!
Quotation marks

If your school mascot could speak, what would it say? That's the question students answer during this independent activity. To begin, show a picture of your school mascot. Then have each child fold a sheet of unlined paper in half two times, unfold it, and turn it to a vertical position. Direct the student to draw a picture of the mascot in the two middle sections and then write what the mascot might say in the top section. Instruct him to draw a speech bubble around the statement. Then have the child write the same sentence as dialogue in the bottom section, using the mascot's name and quotation marks. **To reinforce the quotation marks' placement,** have the student trace them using one of your school colors.

adapted from an idea by Bonnie Gaynor, Franklin, NJ

Collected Works
Published writing

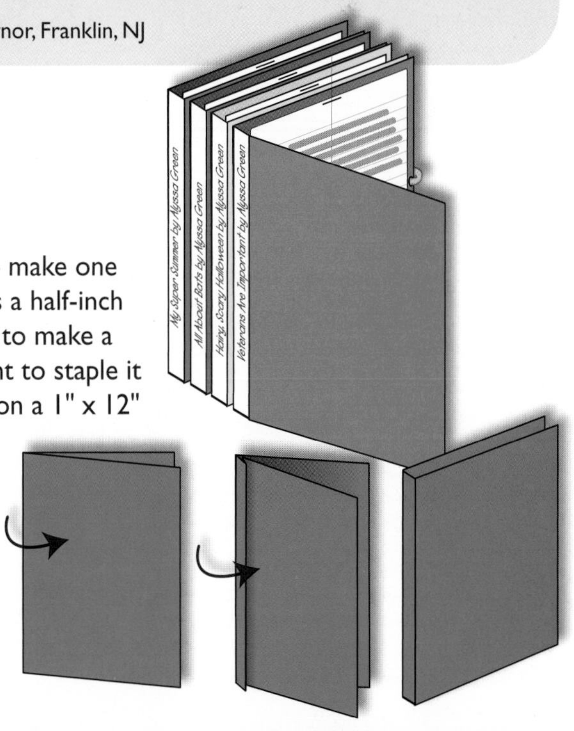
My Super Summer by Alyssa Green
All About Bats by Alyssa Green
Hairy, Scary Halloween by Alyssa Green
Veterans Are Important by Alyssa Green

Store students' published work in their very own bookshelves. To make one book, a child folds a sheet of 12" x 18" paper in half. Then she makes a half-inch fold from the crease and unfolds the newly made creases, as shown, to make a book spine. When she completes a writing project, direct the student to staple it inside her folded paper. Then have her write the title and her name on a 1" x 12" strip of paper and glue it to the spine of her folder. To add another book to the shelf, help the child punch a hole on the back cover of the first story's folder and the front cover of the next. Feed a length of yarn or ribbon through the hole, tie it off, and stand the project. Not only will students make a safe place to store their final drafts, but the resulting bookshelf also makes a cute keepsake at the end of the year.

Cori Mack, Chaparral Elementary, Gilbert, AZ

Writing Tips & Tools

Part by Part
Paragraph structure

Before students write a paragraph, guide them to recite the chant below and complete each action.

Christina Bainbridge, Central Elementary, White Pigeon, MI

A Good Paragraph

A good paragraph has four parts.	*Hold up four fingers.*
First part:	*Hold up one finger.*
Indent.	*Slide to the right.*
Second part:	*Hold up two fingers.*
Topic sentence.	*Hold hands overhead, as if making a roof.*
Third part:	*Hold up three fingers.*
Three sentences	*Hold up three fingers.*
That give details	*Hold hands out with palms up, signaling for more.*
And support	*Push hands up as if to raise the roof.*
The topic sentence.	*Hold hands overhead, as if making a roof.*
Fourth part:	*Hold up four fingers.*
An ending sentence	*Touch your toes.*
To wrap it up!	*Wrap arms around chest as if giving self a hug.*

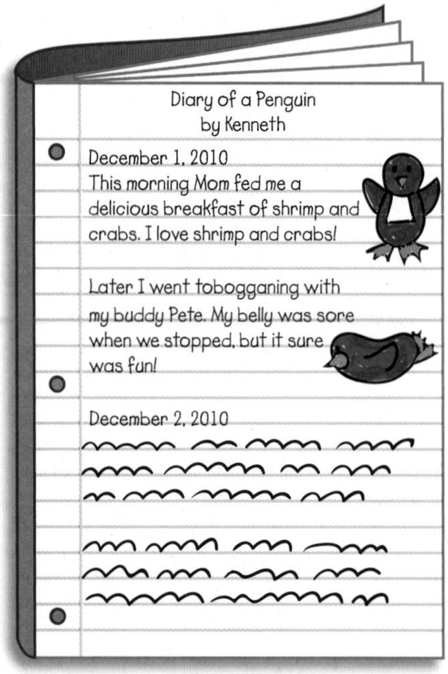
Diary of a Penguin
by Kenneth
December 1, 2010
This morning Mom fed me a delicious breakfast of shrimp and crabs. I love shrimp and crabs!
Later I went tobogganing with my buddy Pete. My belly was sore when we stopped, but it sure was fun!
December 2, 2010

Compare and Compose
Point of view

Read aloud two of the following stories by Doreen Cronin: *Diary of a Worm*, *Diary of a Spider*, or *Diary of a Fly*. Discuss with students how the details of the stories are specific to the main characters, who also narrate each story. Review the common format of the books, and then invite each child to consider an animal he knows well and write his own diary story. Remind each student to write as though he is the animal and to use details specific to that animal's life, while still writing a fictional story. Encourage students to add illustrations. Then bind the completed stories in a class book titled "Diaries of Our Favorite Animals."

Jennifer Cooper, Vestavia Hills Elementary East, Vestavia Hills, AL

Revealing Review
Spelling

Spell fuel.
5
4
3
2
1
0 1 2 3 4 5

In advance, make a coordinate grid on a large sheet of paper and laminate it. Next, use an overhead pen to draw a point on several coordinates, marking one point for each spelling word. Cover every coordinate with a small sticky note and then post the grid. To play, invite a child to name a coordinate. Remove the sticky note and, if a mark is revealed, direct the student to spell a word. If the child spells the word correctly, give the sticky note to his team; then invite a child from another team to play. If the student misspells the word or a mark is not revealed, return the sticky note to the coordinate. Continue play until all marks have been revealed or as time allows. The team with the most sticky notes, or points, wins!

adapted from an idea by Brooke Beverly, Dudley Elementary, Dudley, MA

Thinking Big
Sequencing

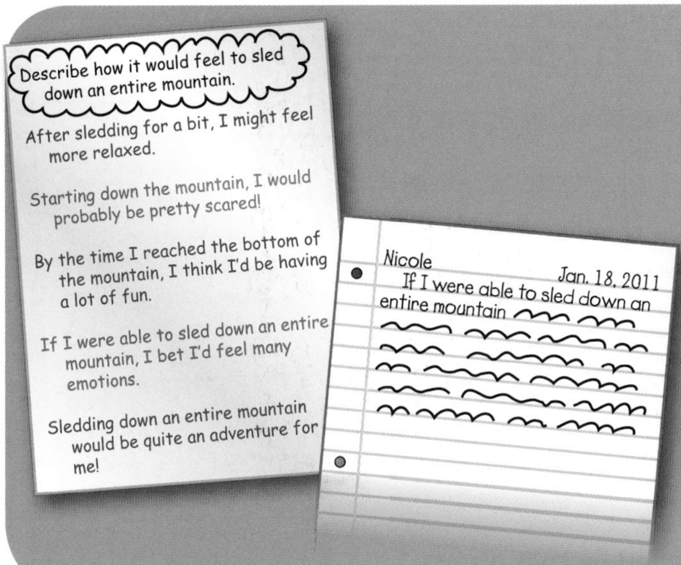
Describe how it would feel to sled down an entire mountain.
After sledding for a bit, I might feel more relaxed.
Starting down the mountain, I would probably be pretty scared!
By the time I reached the bottom of the mountain, I think I'd be having a lot of fun.
If I were able to sled down an entire mountain, I bet I'd feel many emotions.
Sledding down an entire mountain would be quite an adventure for me!
Nicole
Jan. 18, 2011
If I were able to sled down an entire mountain

This simple idea has benefits aplenty for your young writers. Before giving students a writing prompt, write your own response to it. Then copy the sentences in a scrambled order on an overhead transparency. Share the prompt with students; then display your scrambled response. Instruct students to copy the sentences on a sheet of paper in an order that makes sense. After reviewing the correct order, students will have had practice with sequencing, they'll have a solid example of your expectations, and they'll have one perspective on how to respond to the prompt!

Angie Ulrich, Millersport Elementary, Millersport, OH

Pint-Size Practice
Plurals

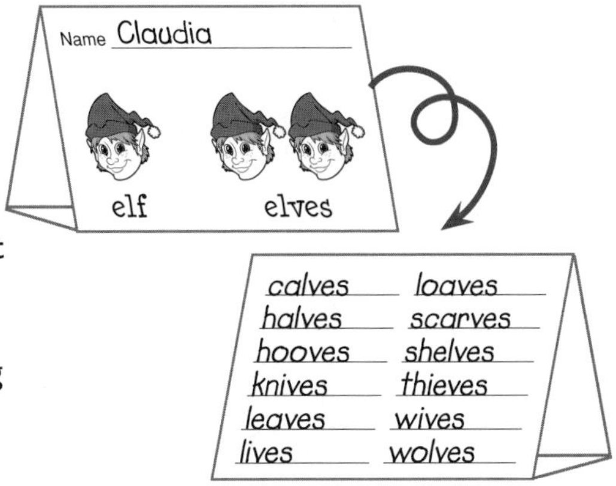
Name Claudia
elf
elves
calves
halves
hooves
knives
leaves
lives
loaves
scarves
shelves
thieves
wives
wolves

Images of fairies and elves will signal student understanding with this easy-to-prepare activity. Post the words shown and give each child a copy of page 75. Direct each student to write the plural form of each word on the strip with the matching rule. Then instruct each child to cut apart the strips, fold each one, and glue the ends together to make two tents. Guide each student to turn her tents so the words are facing her; then announce a word from the list. Have students hold up the matching tent so the fairies or elves face you.

ally	army	baby	berry	calf	city
country	duty	family	half	hoof	knife
lady	leaf	life	loaf	party	scarf
shelf	sky	spy	thief	wife	wolf

Writing Tips & Tools

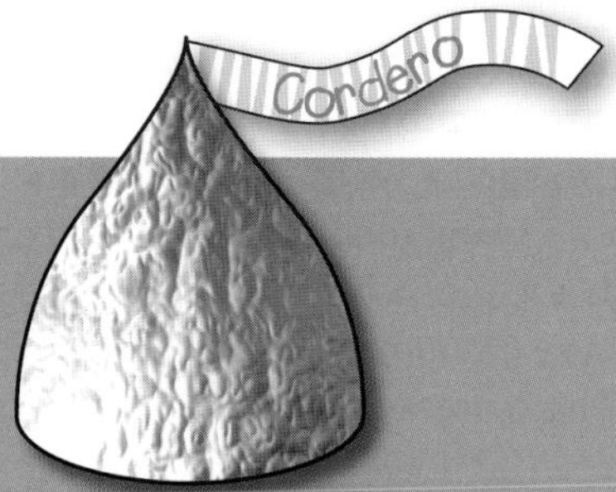

Cordero

Sweet and Simple
Writing poetry

Each child chooses a Valentine's Day–related topic and writes a synonym diamante poem using a copy of the poetry frame from page 76. To display the poem, the child traces a tagboard copy of the candy pattern from page 76 and cuts it out. Then the student covers the cutout with foil and writes his name along a strip of crepe paper. He tapes the crepe paper to the back of the cutout. Display each candy near the students' poem on a display titled "Kisses for Valentine's Day!"

Heather Meyer
Thornapple Elementary,
Grand Rapids, MI

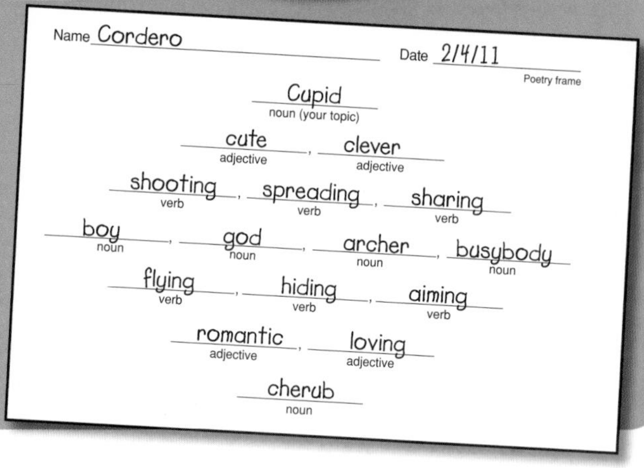

Name Cordero
Date 2/4/11
Poetry frame
Cupid
noun (your topic)
cute, clever
adjective adjective
shooting, spreading, sharing
verb verb verb
boy, god, archer, busybody
noun noun noun noun
flying, hiding, aiming
verb verb verb
romantic, loving
adjective adjective
cherub
noun

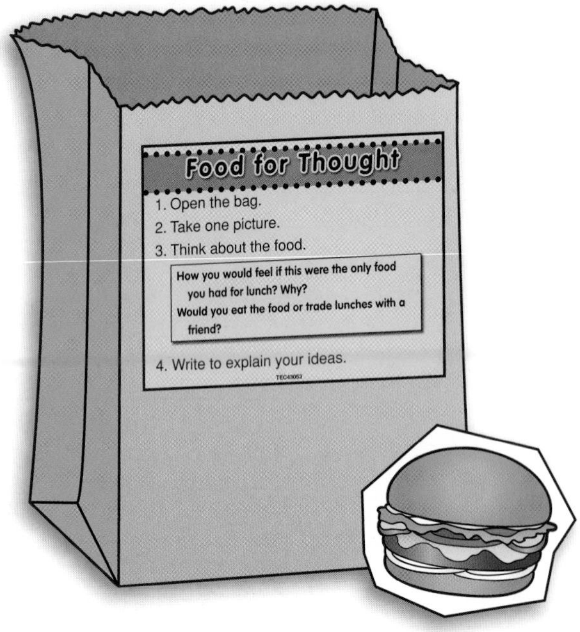

Food for Thought
1. Open the bag.
2. Take one picture.
3. Think about the food.
How you would feel if this were the only food you had for lunch? Why?
Would you eat the food or trade lunches with a friend?
4. Write to explain your ideas.

Food for Thought
Responding to prompts

Serve up some writing practice to go with this easy-to-prepare activity. Cut pictures of individual foods from magazines and store circulars. Place the pictures in a lunch bag. Tape a copy of one of the direction cards from page 77 to the bag and put it at a center. A child reads the card and responds to the prompt on a sheet of paper. **To prepare the activity for groups,** put a few pictures in each of a supply of bags. Tape one direction card to each bag and give one bag to every group.

Marie E. Cecchini, West Dundee, IL

St. Patrick's Day is March 17.

Punctuation Pointer

Spelling plural and possessive nouns

To begin, have each child cut a simple apostrophe shape from a half sheet of paper and tape the apostrophe to his pencil (pointer). Next, direct students to sit in a circle. Name a plural or possessive noun that ends in s and use it in a sentence. Direct a child to say the first letter of the word; then have each successive child to his left add another letter to spell the word. If the word uses an apostrophe, a student holds up his pointer to signal its place. When the word has been spelled, have the whole class repeat the spelling in unison, with every child holding up his pointer if the apostrophe is needed.

Case Closed!

Writing a mystery

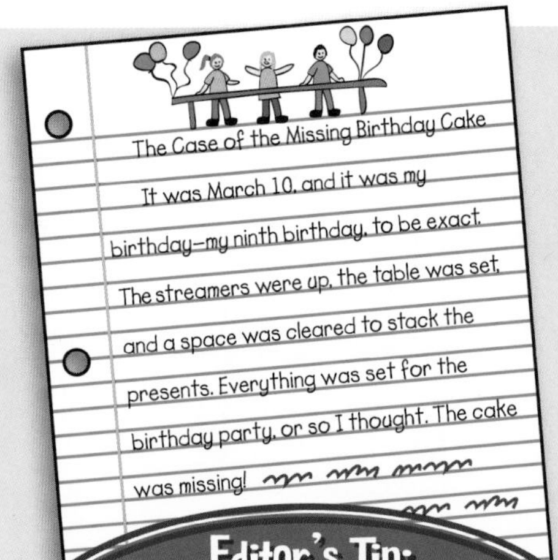
The Case of the Missing Birthday Cake
It was March 10, and it was my
birthday—my ninth birthday, to be exact.
The streamers were up, the table was set,
and a space was cleared to stack the
presents. Everything was set for the
birthday party, or so I thought. The cake
was missing!

Editor's Tip:
Make this a free-time activity instead. Set out a different bag of items every few weeks and display a new mystery title or prompt nearby.

Your student detectives will be clued into writing a well-detailed whodunit with this fun activity! To start, read aloud a favorite mystery story and then review the story elements found in it. Next, post on the board a mystery title, such as "The Case of the Missing Birthday Cake," or a prompt, such as "Everything was set for the birthday party, or so I thought. The cake was missing!" Give each group a bag filled with three unrelated objects, such as a glue stick, a plastic spoon, and a button. Challenge each group to determine how each object could be used to solve the mystery. Then have each student write and illustrate her own version of the mystery. Provide time for students to share their stories. Then compile the mysteries in a class book titled "Case Closed!"

VIP Paper Trays

Revising drafts

With this star-studded tip, your student authors will look forward to completing each draft of the writing process! Label each half of a white shirt box as shown to make two paper trays. Stock the "Rough Drafts" tray with white paper. Decorate the second tray with gold star stickers and stock it with yellow paper. Place the trays at your writing center. Direct students to use the white paper for first drafts and the yellow paper for revised drafts. If desired, label a third box half "Fancy Finals" and stock it with decorative paper for publishing students' writing.

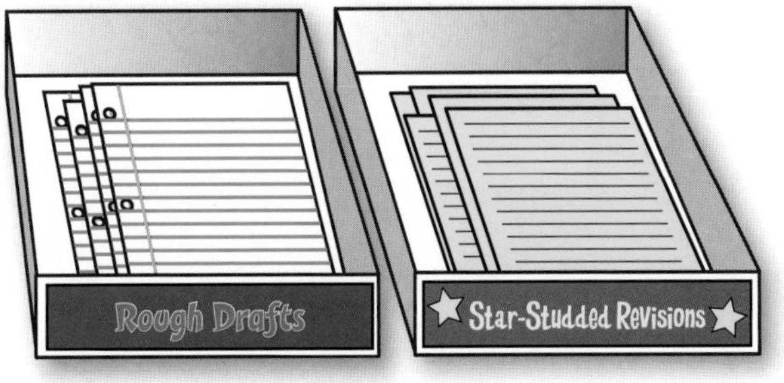
Rough Drafts
Star-Studded Revisions

Writing Tips & Tools

Building Understanding
Parts of speech

These student-made mini posters not only look great but also reinforce a number of language arts skills.

the tall tree
against
by
The squirrel ran up the tall tree.
around
Kylie
to run
How?
When?
Where?
What?
(degree)

To practice prepositions, a child writes a three-word phrase *(article, adjective, noun)* at the top of a sheet of colored paper. He folds four pieces of $2\frac{3}{4}$" x $4\frac{1}{4}$" paper in half; then he labels the top flap of each paper with a different preposition. Next, the student lifts each flap to write and illustrate a sentence using the preposition and the phrase. Then he glues the folded papers to the colored paper as shown.

To practice adverbs, a child writes a verb infinitive at the top of a sheet of colored paper. She folds four pieces of $2\frac{3}{4}$" x $4\frac{1}{4}$" paper in half; then she labels the top flap of each paper with a different question shown. Next, the student lifts each flap to write and illustrate a sentence that uses a form of the verb and an adverb to answer the question. Then she glues the folded papers to the colored paper as shown.

Caryn Fuiten, Garfield Montessori Magnet School, Decatur, IL

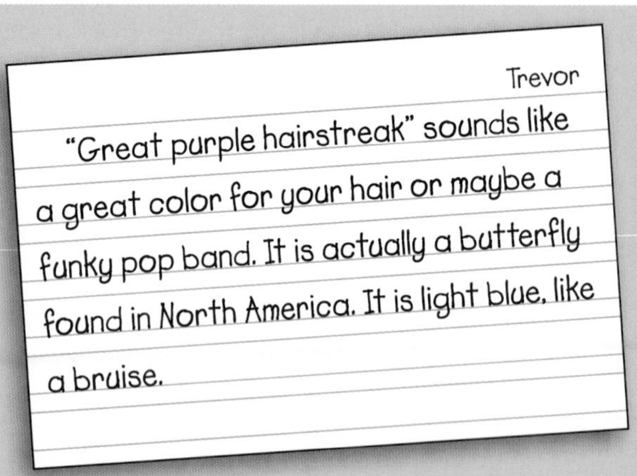
Trevor
"Great purple hairstreak" sounds like a great color for your hair or maybe a funky pop band. It is actually a butterfly found in North America. It is light blue, like a bruise.

Writers Take Flight
Descriptive writing

Combine one part imaginative writing with another part informational writing and the result is this sensational spring activity. To start, post the list of butterflies from page 79. Direct each student to choose a butterfly and complete a copy of the organizer on page 78. (Plan for students to use reference materials.) Next, guide him to write a descriptive paragraph that starts by telling what the butterfly name implies, or seems to be. Then have him tell what it actually is, where it can be found, and one interesting fact about it.

Lou Smeja, Emerson Elementary, Elmhurst, IL

Getting Noticed
Motivation

Before students begin a writing assignment, slip a pair of colorful socks over your shoes. Challenge students to do their best work in an effort to knock your socks off. When a child demonstrates excellent writing, pass him one of the socks to wear or keep at his desk for the remainder of the writing time. Then use a copy of one of the notes on page 79 to share the good news with the student's family.

Gina Zimmerman, Edgerton Elementary, Edgerton, KS

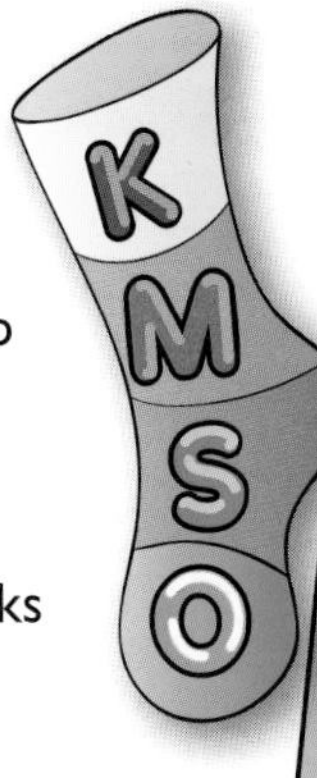
K
M
S
O

Wesley 's writing was so great it knocked my socks off!
April 4, 2011
Dear Family,
I was so impressed with Wesley's story-writing today. He did an amazing job describing his characters and explaining all the ways they tried to resolve the story's conflict. I look forward to more great writing from Wesley!
Ms. Zimmerman

Editor's Tip:
Embellish the socks with brightly colored foam letters and other craft supplies.

good
nice
stuff
awesome
happy

Ready to Recycle
Overused words

Write each word students commonly overuse in their writing on a separate sheet of chart paper. Explain to students that there is a time and a place to use each of these words but, since the words have been used so much in students' writing this year, they are worn out and it's time to recycle them. Have each child copy the words onto a piece of scrap paper. Then, with great fanfare, instruct students to crumple the papers and discard them in the recycling bin. Give each small group a sheet of chart paper and instruct the students to generate more specific words for the word listed. Post the completed charts as a class reference.

adapted from an idea by Mary Skelly, Salem, NY

Sweet and Simple
Story starters

Need to cook up a free-time activity for your early finishers? Try this! Place in a bag several different cookie cutters. Explain to students that the cookie cutters can be used to plan an interesting story. Direct an early finisher to trace two of the cookie cutters onto a sheet of paper and write within the outlines different words and ideas that could be used in a related story. If time allows, have her write the story.

April Lewis, Warsaw Elementary, Warsaw, NC

flowers
bloom
sweet-smelling
bee
bunny
hops
fields
sniffing

Writing Tips & Tools

Armed Against Repetition

Varied sentence lengths

With some help from this outrageous octopus, students will keep repetitive writing at arm's length. Give each child a copy of page 80. Have him program each arm with a different number or number range. Tell students that as they write they should try to vary the length of their sentences. After writing, have the child count the number of words in each sentence and draw a tally mark on the arm with the corresponding number or range. If tally marks are heavy on one particular arm, direct the child to revisit his writing and vary the length of his sentences.

Sue Fleischmann, Sussex, WI

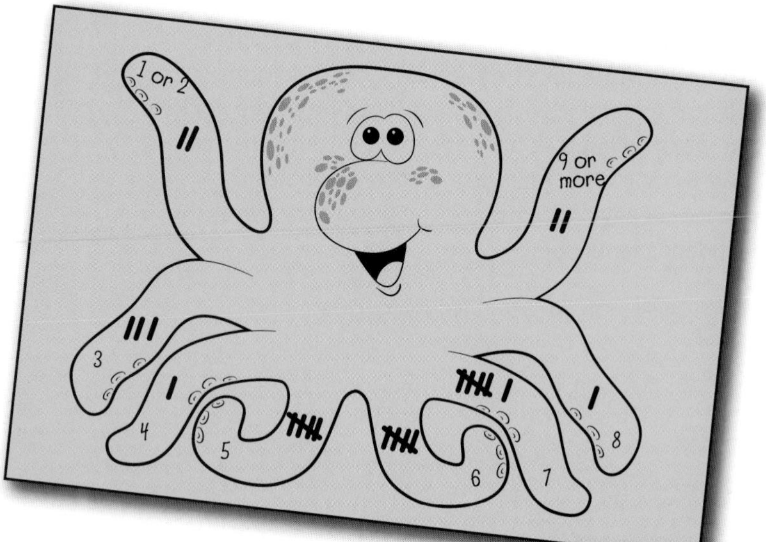

1 or 2
9 or more
3
4
5
6
7
8

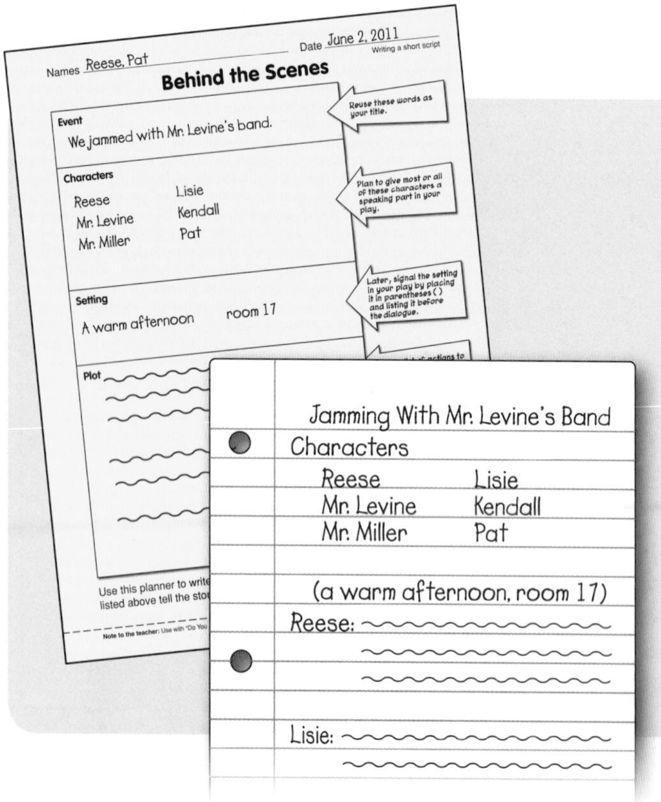

Names Reese, Pat
Date June 2, 2011
Writing a short script
Behind the Scenes
Event
We jammed with Mr. Levine's band.
Reuse these words as your title.
Characters
Reese
Mr. Levine
Mr. Miller
Lisie
Kendall
Pat
Plan to give most or all of these characters a speaking part in your play.
Setting
A warm afternoon
room 17
Later, signal the setting in your play by placing it in parentheses ( ) and listing it before the dialogue.
Plot
Jamming With Mr. Levine's Band
Characters
Reese
Lisie
Mr. Levine
Kendall
Mr. Miller
Pat
(a warm afternoon, room 17)
Reese:
Lisie:

Do You Remember?

Writing a short script

Reconstructing a memorable class event is the focus of this partner activity. To start, have each duo make a list of events from the school year and discuss which one would make an interesting short play. Next, guide the pair to complete a copy of page 81 as a plan for their play. Then provide time for partners to follow the format of the planning page to write the script. During the last week of school, invite students to present their plays to the rest of the class.

• Process • Descriptive • Expository • Narrative

Writing Tips & Tools

I Took My Skunk to the Library
by Jocelyn

Laughs in the Library

Imaginative narrative, cause and effect

Encourage a little year-end mischief with this fun writing project! To begin, read *I Took My Frog to the Library* by Eric A. Kimmel. Brainstorm with students other animals that might be taken to a library (causes) and the messes each animal would create (effects). Next, have each child write her own version of the story that features an animal other than a frog. Instruct the student to illustrate the most humorous event from the story; then provide time for each child to share her story and show her illustration.

Brenda Weston, Maple Elementary, Hoopeston, IL

Look Here

Proofreading

Draw students' attention to one area for improvement in their writing. When the class starts a writing project, tell students that they will later proofread a partner's paper with only one skill in mind. Announce the featured skill, such as a specific overused word or phrase, correct use of end marks, or correct capitalization. After writing rough drafts, let students swap papers and, as each child reads, have him circle any errors related to that skill on the paper. Then have the student draw a pair of silly eyes in the margin. When the paper is returned to its original author, the child revises the sentence beside each pair of silly eyes.

It was a beautiful summer day
at the beach, and I was having
a picnic with my friend Jordan.
We had a blanket spread out on
the sand, and we were enjoying a
yummy lunch of sub sandwiches,
fruit, and chips. Then, out of the
blue, a seagull swooped down and
took my sandwich, and before I

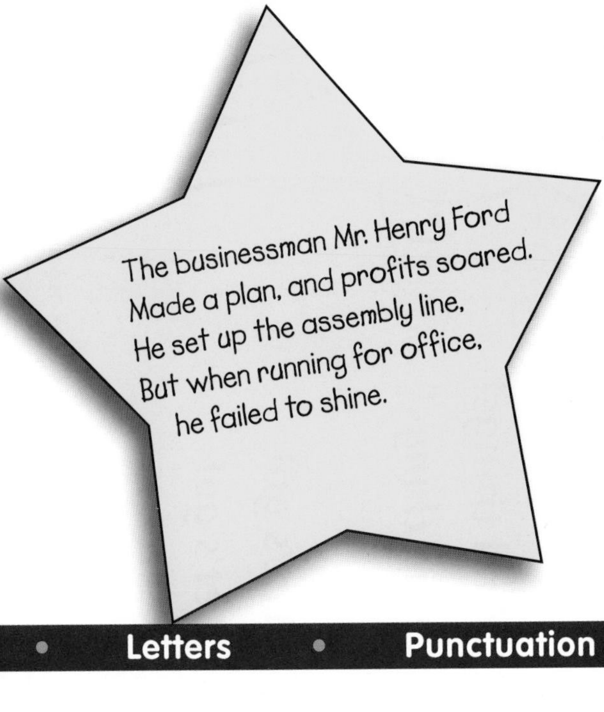
The businessman Mr. Henry Ford
Made a plan, and profits soared.
He set up the assembly line,
But when running for office,
he failed to shine.

Starring...

Writing poetry

Challenge student pairs to apply facts about a famous person in the form of a clerihew poem. Share with students the sample shown and discuss what they notice about its structure. Lead students to understand that this kind of poem incorporates humor and facts, has two rhyming couplets, and the first line ends with the person's name. Instruct each duo to select a famous person—such as a historical figure studied during the year or a favorite figure from pop culture—and list facts about him or her. Then have the students use the clerihew format to write a poem about the person. If desired, have each student pair write a final draft on a large star cutout; then bind the stars in a book titled "Superstars."

Natalie Tanner, Adam Elementary, Houston, TX

Notebook Tabs

Use with "Ready to Write" on page 60.

New Words to Use	New Words to Use	New Words to Use
TEC43050	TEC43050	TEC43050
Quick Writes	**Quick Writes**	**Quick Writes**
TEC43050	TEC43050	TEC43050
Story Ideas	**Story Ideas**	**Story Ideas**
TEC43050	TEC43050	TEC43050
Rough Drafts	**Rough Drafts**	**Rough Drafts**
TEC43050	TEC43050	TEC43050

We're Going on a Noun Hunt!

We're going on a noun hunt!
We're going on a noun hunt!

We're gonna catch some good ones!
We're gonna catch some good ones!

People, places,
People, places,

And things!
And things!

Let's go!
Let's go!

Note to the teacher: Use with "Searching High and Low" on page 61.

Popcorn Patterns

Use with "Bursting With Fresh Words" on page 62.

TEC43051

TEC43051

TEC43051

Storyteller's Notebook

My Plan

Name ____________________

Characters

____

____

____

Setting (time and place)

____

____

____

____

Plot (main story events)

Conclusion

____

____

____

____

____

____

The End

Note to the teacher: Direct students to fold a copy of this page in half horizontallly and then again vertically. Use with "Clothing Chronicles" on page 62 or anytime students plan a narrative.

To make most **nouns that end in a consonant and then *y*** plural, **drop the *y*** and **write *ies*.**

TEC43052

fairy fairies

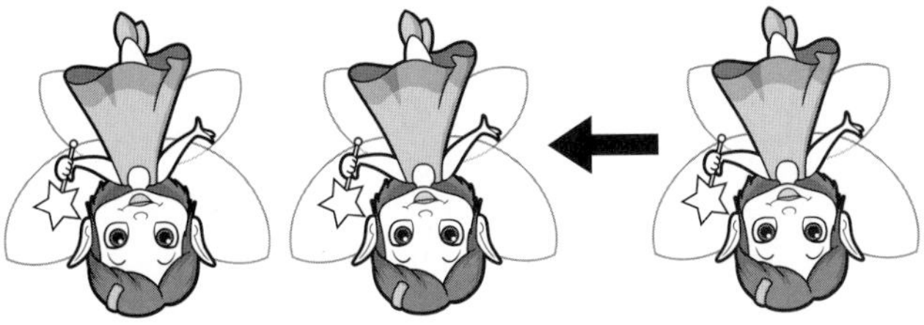

Name ____________________

To make most **nouns that end in *f*** or ***fe*** plural, **change the *f*** to ***v*** and **write *es*.**

TEC43052

elf elves

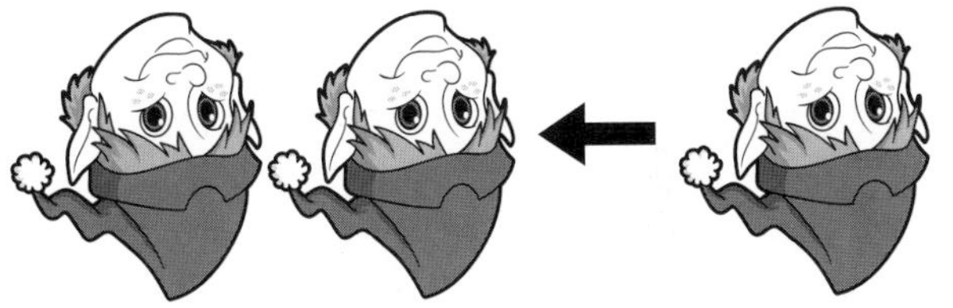

Name ____________________

Note to the teacher: Use with "Pint-Size Practice" on page 65.

Candy Pattern and Poetry Frame

Use with "Sweet and Simple" on page 66.

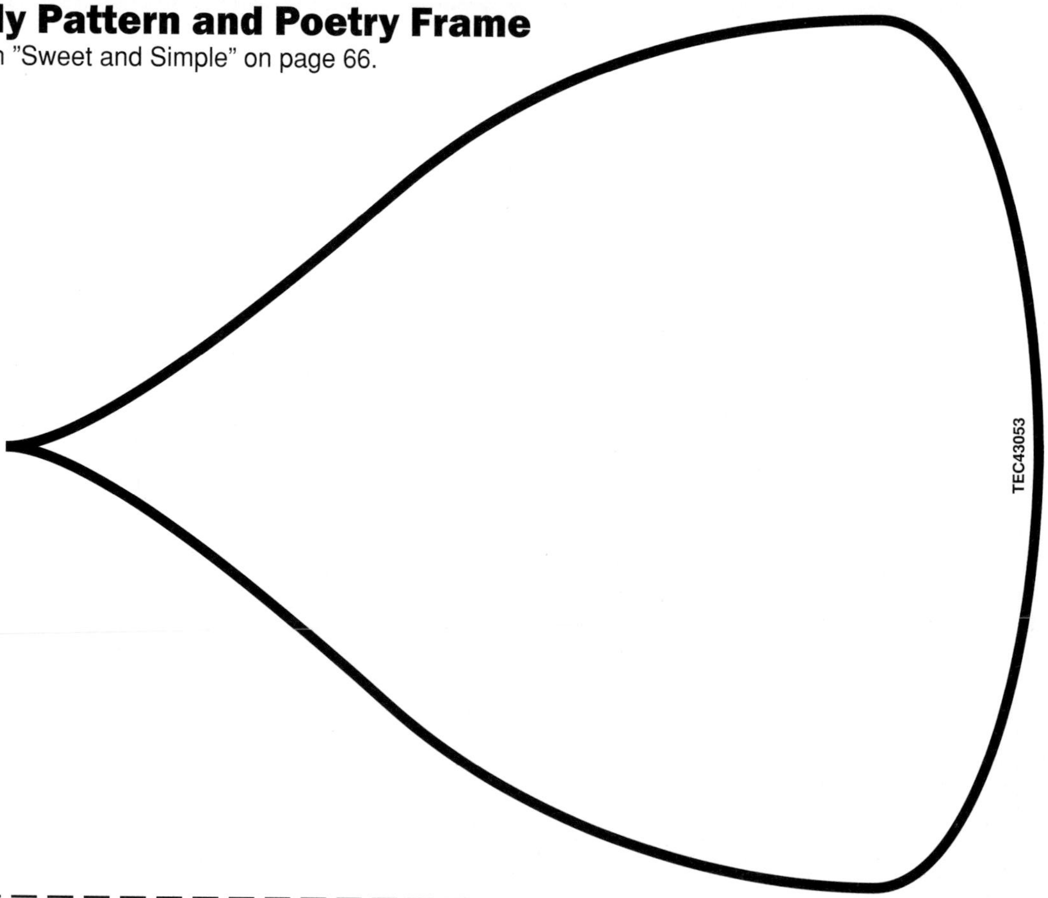
TEC43053

Name_______________________________ Date _______________

Poetry frame

____
noun (your topic)

_______________, _______________
adjective adjective

_______________, _______________, _______________
verb verb verb

_______________, _______________, _______________, _______________
noun noun noun noun

_______________, _______________, _______________
verb verb verb

_______________, _______________
adjective adjective

____
noun

Food for Thought

1. Open the bag.
2. Take one picture.
3. Think about the food.

Is this a healthy food? Why or why not?

4. Write to explain your ideas.

TEC43053

Food for Thought

1. Open the bag.
2. Take one picture.
3. Think about the food.

How you would feel if this were the only food you had for lunch? Why?
Would you eat the food or trade lunches with a friend?

4. Write to explain your ideas.

TEC43053

Food for Thought

1. Open the bag.
2. Take one picture.
3. Think about the food.

What other foods would you eat with this one to make a meal? Name and describe them.

4. Write to explain your ideas.

TEC43053

Food for Thought

1. Open the bag.
2. Take one picture.
3. Think about the food.

Pretend this food could talk. What would it say? Describe a conversation you might have with this food.

4. Write to explain your ideas.

TEC43053

Name______________________________ Date ______________

Descriptive writing organizer

It's a What?

butterfly

Based on the name, this sounds like it could be:

1. ______________________________
2. ______________________________
3. ______________________________

Facts about the butterfly:

Where does it live? ______________________________

____

What does it look like? ______________________________

____

____

____

The website or book where I found my facts:

____

____

 Note to the teacher: Use with "Writers Take Flight" on page 68.

Use with "Writers Take Flight" on page 68.

Western Tiger Swallowtail
Pearl Crescent
Great Purple Hairstreak
Mulberry Wing
Spring Azure
Mustard White
Purple Emperor
Grizzled Skipper
Dotted Checkerspot
Painted Lady
Gray Cracker
Southern Pearly Eye
Coyote Cloudywing
Dreamy Duskywing
Mourning Cloak
Baltimore Checkerspot
Southern Dogface
Question Mark

TEC43054

________________________________'s writing was so great it knocked my socks off!

TEC43054

Note to the teacher: Use with "Getting Noticed" on page 69.

Octopus Pattern

Use with "Armed Against Repetition" on page 70.

TEC43055

Names ____________________ Date ____________________

Writing a short script

Behind the Scenes

Event
Characters
Setting
Plot

Reuse these words as your title.

Plan to give most or all of these characters a speaking part in your play.

Later, signal the setting in your play by placing it in parentheses ( ) and listing it before the dialogue.

Use the list of actions to guide your dialogue.

Use this planner to write the story of your event. Have the characters listed above tell the story through their dialogue (conversation among characters).

Note to the teacher: Use with "Do You Remember?" on page 70.

August Prompts

Name ____________________

- [ ] What was the best part of your summer? What was the worst part of your summer?
- [ ] If you had one more day of summer vacation to do anything you wanted, what would you do?
- [ ] Orville Wright was born on August 19, 1871. He and his brother built the first successful airplane. How would life be different without airplanes?
- [ ] Do you like to eat outside? Why or why not?
- [ ] Write a story titled "My School at Night."

TEC43050

September Prompts

Name ____________________

- [ ] Would you rather have two 15-minute recesses each day or one 30-minute recess each day? Explain.
- [ ] What subject do you think should be taught in school but isn't? Explain your choice.
- [ ] How would school be different if there weren't any rules? Tell why you think so.
- [ ] Applesauce, apple pie, and apple juice are just a few ways to serve apples. What is your favorite apple-based food or drink? Convince others that your choice is the best one.
- [ ] If you wrote a book, in what part of the library would it be shelved? Explain.

TEC43050

Writing prompts: Have each child staple a copy of this page in his writing journal. Or cut copies in half and distribute only one month's prompts at a time to students. When a student uses a prompt, he checks it off in the box.

October Prompts

Name ______________________

- ☐ *Nocturnal* means active at night instead of during the day. Would you like to be nocturnal? Why or why not?
- ☐ Copy and complete the sentence. Then describe what happens next.

  I reached into the pumpkin to pull out the seeds, but instead I pulled out _____.
- ☐ Pretend your class has a new student. Explain to your new pal what to do and where to go during a fire drill.
- ☐ If you were invited to explore another planet, would you go? Why or why not?
- ☐ What is the coolest thing you learned this month? Describe it and tell why you think it is cool.

Whooooo

TEC43051

November Prompts

Name ______________________

- ☐ In honor of Veterans Day (November 11), write a thank-you note to a veteran.
- ☐ November is Family Stories Month. Write a story about a funny or important event that happened to your family.
- ☐ Is your Thanksgiving break too long, too short, or just right? Explain your choice.
- ☐ Copy the topic sentence. Then complete the paragraph.

  The best things in life are free.
- ☐ Write a fiction story titled "Why the Turkey Has a Wattle."

TEC43051

How to use Have each child staple a copy of this page in his writing journal. Or cut copies in half and distribute only one month's prompts at a time to students. When a student uses a prompt, he checks its box.

December Prompts

Name ______________________

- [ ] Write steps to tell how to unwrap a gift.
- [ ] Copy one of the topic sentences. Write three detail sentences.
  - I am always happy when winter begins.
  - I am not a fan of winter.

- [ ] If you could spend one day of your winter break doing anything you wanted, what would you do? Describe the day.
- [ ] Santa Claus wants to take a vacation after the holidays. Where should he go, and what should he do? Write a letter to tell him your ideas.
- [ ] Pretend you could redo any day from the last year. Which day would you redo and why?

TEC43052

January Prompts

Name ______________________

- [ ] Would you rather miss school because of snow but have to make up the day on a Saturday, or have no snow at all? Explain.
- [ ] What changes do you expect in the year ahead? Write a paragraph that tells about them.
- [ ] Think about the saying "Never judge a book by its cover." Why do you think this is important when dealing with other people?
- [ ] What is your favorite synonym for *cool?* Write a story that uses the synonym three or more times.
- [ ] Pretend a book character will join your class. Which character would you like to have as a classmate? Explain.

TEC43052

How to use Have each child staple a copy of this page in his writing journal. Or cut copies in half and distribute only one month's prompts at a time to students. When a student uses a prompt, he checks its box.

February Prompts

Name ____________________

☐ Copy the sentences shown. Fill in the blank. Then write the rest of the paragraph, explaining why you love what you love.

Don't you just love it when __? I do!

☐ You have a stack of pancakes on your plate. How do you get them ready to eat? Write the steps. Use details.

☐ You want to change seats with a classmate, but your teacher says you need his or her permission first. Write a paragraph to him or her. Give two or more reasons why you two should change seats.

☐ How would your life be different if peanut butter had never been invented?

☐ What's the best thing about February?

TEC43053

March Prompts

Name ____________________

☐ March is National Women's History Month. Describe an important woman in your life. Tell why she is important.

☐ Write a weather report for today. Then write a weather report for tomorrow based on what you hope it will be like.

☐ Write a story titled "My Lucky Day."

☐ What do you like to do for fun in the spring? Write a letter to a friend. Invite your pal to join you for this activity.

☐ Imagine that you ride the wind and it takes you to a faraway place. Describe your trip. Tell where you go and what happens when you get there.

TEC43053

How to use Have each child staple a copy of this page in his writing journal. Or cut copies in half and distribute only one month's prompts at a time to students. When a student uses a prompt, he checks its box.

April Prompts

Name ____________________

- [ ] April 1 to Mother's Day is National Card and Letter Writing Month. Write a letter or make a card for a different person each day.
- [ ] April 7 is No Housework Day. Describe what your home would be like if every day were No Housework Day.
- [ ] Imagine you have just discovered a new insect. Tell how you found it and what it is like. Use your senses!
- [ ] If you could grow anything you want in a garden, what would you grow? Why?
- [ ] Why is it important to care for the earth?

Thank you!

TEC43054

May Prompts

Name ____________________

- [ ] May is Get Caught Reading Month. Where would someone most likely find you reading? Describe the place.
- [ ] Suppose you are writing a story about your life (autobiography) and that each school year is a chapter. Write the chapter for this year.
- [ ] Write a story that has a pond as the main setting.
- [ ] What are the benefits of riding a bike to get from place to place? What are the drawbacks?
- [ ] Convince your teacher to change one classroom routine. Tell which routine should change, why it should change, and how it should change.

TEC43054

How to use Have each child staple a copy of this page in his writing journal. Or cut copies in half and distribute only one month's prompts at a time to students. When a student uses a prompt, he checks its box.

June Prompts

Name ______________________

- [ ] Which is the best place to stay cool during the summer: at the pool, at the beach, or at a water park? Explain.
- [ ] Each June, a holiday will be celebrated in your honor. Name the holiday and give its exact date. Then tell what you did to deserve this honor and how people will celebrate the holiday.
- [ ] You're having a picnic when an unwelcome guest arrives. Describe the guest and tell what happens next.
- [ ] Write a story titled "How the Ladybug Got Its Spots."
- [ ] Imagine you are at summer camp on another planet. Write a letter to a friend. Tell what you did today.

TEC43055

July Prompts

Name ______________________

- [ ] Think of a food you enjoy. Copy and complete the sentence. Then give reasons to support your opinion.

  __________ should be the official food of summer!

- [ ] If you could watch Fourth of July fireworks from any place in the United States, where would you be? Why?
- [ ] Pretend you are in charge of planning a family vacation. Tell where you would go, why you chose this place, and what your family would do there.
- [ ] On a typical summer day, where would you likely be found? Why? What would you be doing?
- [ ] Imagine you have invented a new game that can only be played in summer. Describe it.

TEC43055

How to use Have each child staple a copy of this page in his writing journal. Or cut copies in half and distribute only one month's prompts at a time to students. When a student uses a prompt, he checks its box.

Name________________________________ Date________________

Personal narrative: small moment

Starting the Big Day

Prompt: The first day of school can be exciting, scary, and fun. How was your first day of school this year? Tell the story of the first part of your day.

Plan:

Start

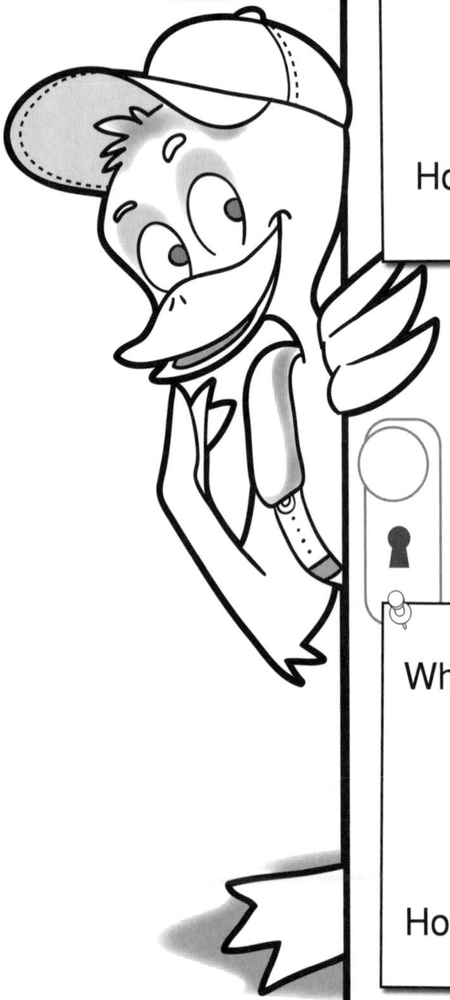

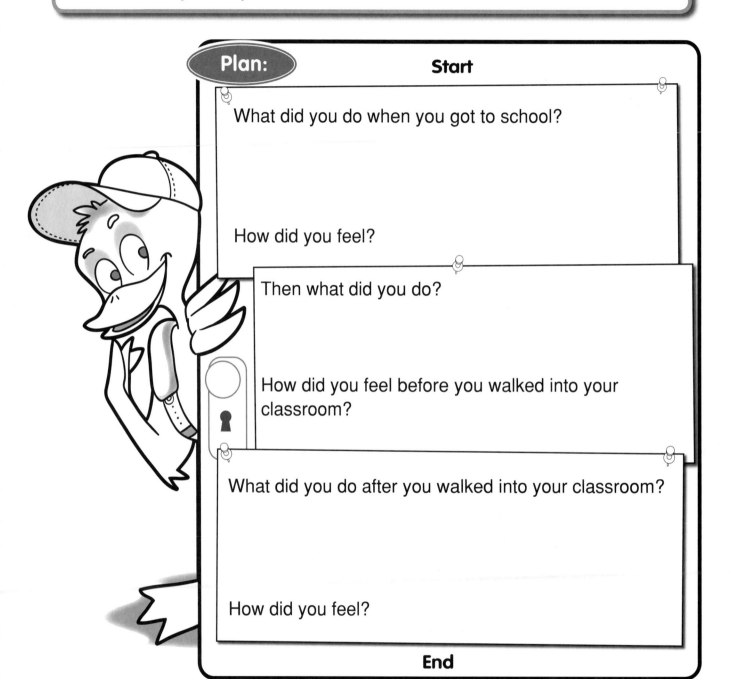

What did you do when you got to school?

How did you feel?

Then what did you do?

How did you feel before you walked into your classroom?

What did you do after you walked into your classroom?

How did you feel?

End

Write: Tell the story of how your first day of school this year began. Include what you did and how you felt each step of the way. Write so the reader feels as though he or she was there too.

Name ____________________ Date ____________

Logical sequence

Along Comes a Spider

Prompt: Imagine you are eating lunch. A large spider shimmies down its dragline and then crawls across your table. It is headed your way!

Plan: What is the problem?

What will you and the other characters do to solve the problem?

First

Next

Then

How will the story end?

Finally

Write: Write a story about your lunch with the spider. Use your plan to keep the events in order.

Name ______________________ Date ____________

Descriptive writing

Winter Wonderland

Prompt: It's winter. You've just opened your front door and gone outside. Describe your surroundings.

Plan:

What do you taste?

What do you touch?

What do you smell?

What do you hear?

What do you see?

Write: Write about winter where you live. Use details so that someone who lives far away will have a complete picture of what winter is like where you live.

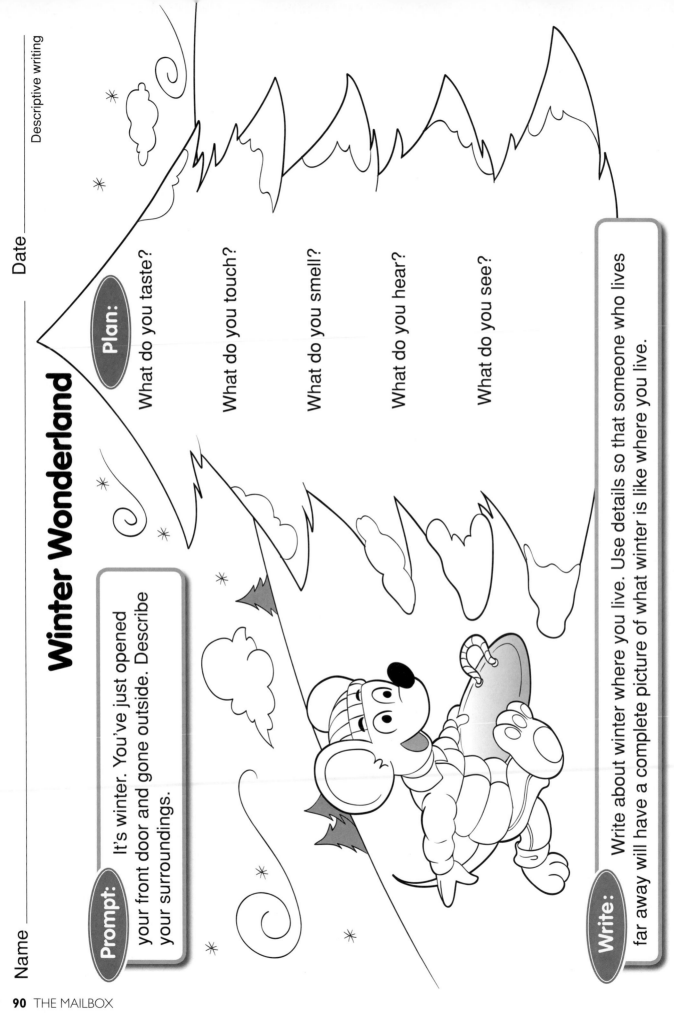

Name ______________________ Date ______________

Descriptive writing in a narrative

What Was That?

Prompt: You're playing outside when something strange catches your eye.

Plan:

Describe what you see.	Tell what happens next.

Write: Write a story. At the start of the story, you're playing outside. Give a good description of what you see. Then tell what you do and what happens.

Name ______________________ Date ______________

Writing to persuade

You Have to Try It!

Prompt: You have just been hired to sell a brand-new breakfast cereal in your local grocery store.

Plan: What is the cereal called?

How would you describe the cereal?

Which of these words would likely grab a shopper's attention? Circle them.

Why should a shopper buy the cereal?

1.

2.

3.

Piggy
Puffs

Write: Write a short speech that you might read to shoppers in the grocery store. Use words that will get the shoppers' attention and convince them to buy the cereal you are selling.

Name ________________________________ Date ____________________

Looking Ahead

Prompt: Your teacher needs your help writing a set of directions for next year's class.

Plan: Choose one classroom routine you know how to do really well.

- ☐ arriving in the morning
- ☐ lining up
- ☐ sharpening your pencil
- ☐ getting help during centers
- ☐ turning in your work
- ☐ choosing a book from the class library

List the steps.

Write: Explain to students in next year's class how to complete the chosen routine. Keep your audience in mind as you write. Since your readers will be new to the classroom, they may need lots of details.

Name ______________________ Date __________

Generating story ideas

Rustling Up Story Ideas

List ideas for each story element.
Check off each idea when you use it in a story.

Character (Who)

☐ ________ ☐ ________ ☐ ________
☐ ________ ☐ ________ ☐ ________

Setting (Where and When)

☐ ________ ☐ ________ ☐ ________
☐ ________ ☐ ________ ☐ ________

Problem (What)

☐ ________ ☐ ________
☐ ________ ☐ ________
☐ ________ ☐ ________

Note to the teacher: After each student lists his ideas on a copy of this page, have him keep the paper in his writing folder or notebook.

Name ______________________ Date ______________

Punctuation

At the Fair

For each sentence, write the missing end mark.
Color the ticket with the matching mark.

TICKETS
SOLD OUT!
!
!
!
!
?
?
?
?
.
.
.

1. We are at the fair today ☐
2. Do you like the fair ☐
3. Oh, there are so many things to see ☐
4. Let's buy some tickets for the rides ☐
5. I want to ride the Ferris wheel first ☐
6. What is your favorite ride ☐
7. Wow, that ride made me dizzy ☐
8. I love the food at the fair ☐
9. Do you want something to eat ☐
10. What a huge ice cream cone ☐
11. How many tickets do you have left ☐
12. We can watch the fireworks tonight ☐

Bonus Box: Write three sentences about the fair—one asking, one telling, and one exclamatory.

Name________________________ Date____________

Singular and plural nouns

Baking Biscuits

Write the plural form of each noun.
Color by the code.

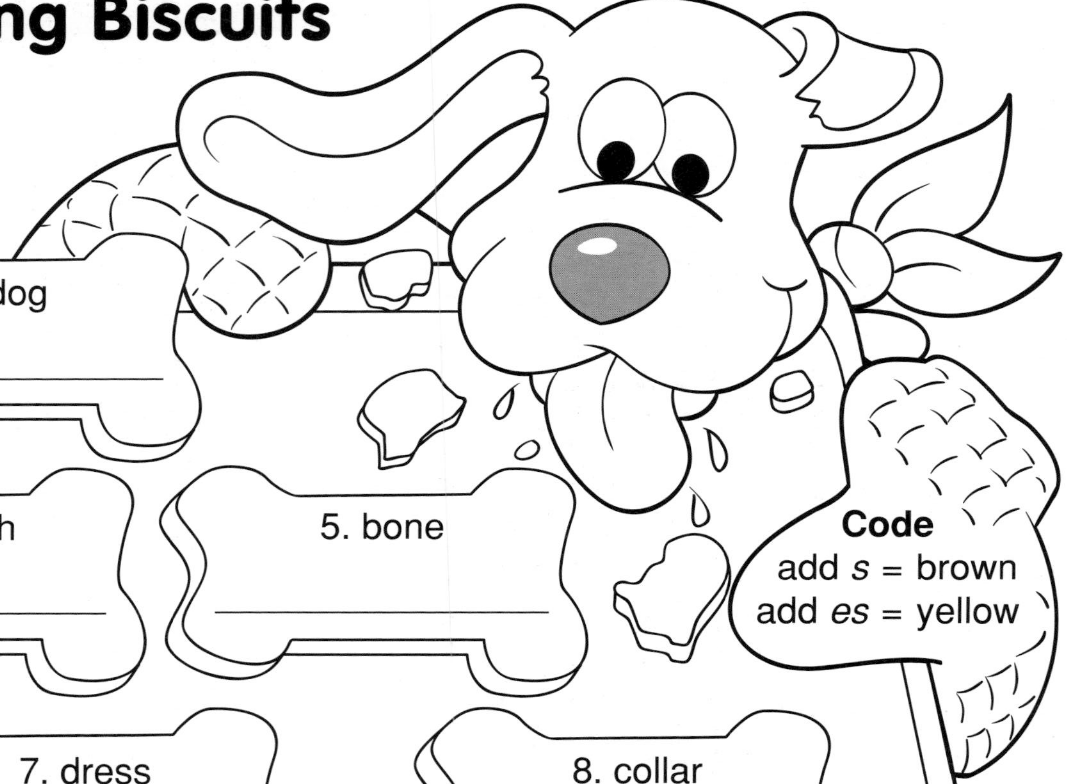

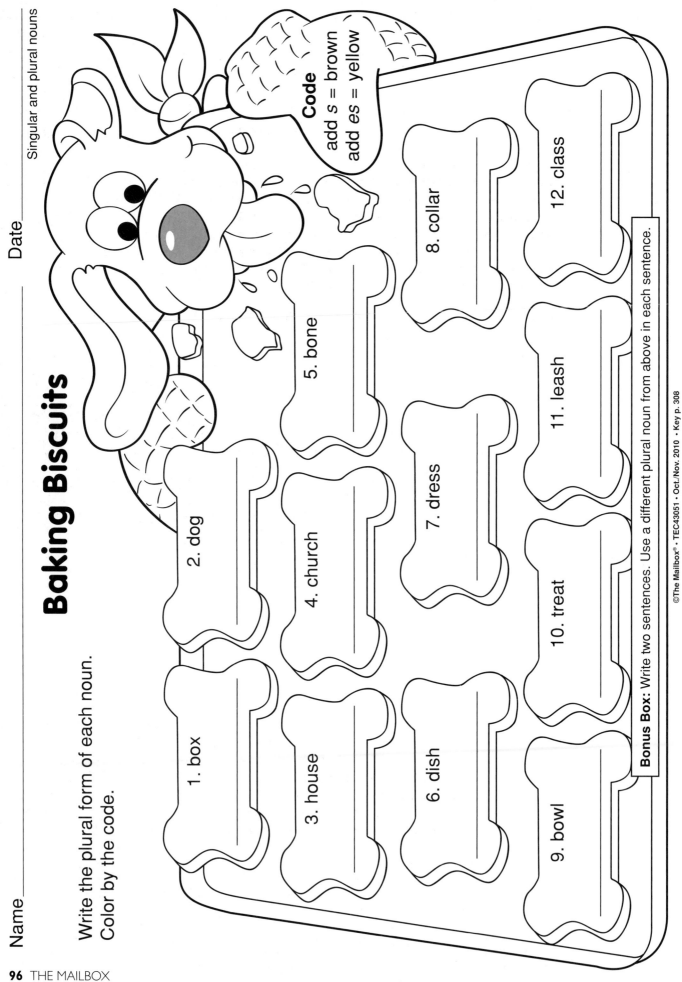

Code
add *s* = brown
add *es* = yellow

1. box ____________
2. dog ____________
3. house ____________
4. church ____________
5. bone ____________
6. dish ____________
7. dress ____________
8. collar ____________
9. bowl ____________
10. treat ____________
11. leash ____________
12. class ____________

Bonus Box: Write two sentences. Use a different plural noun from above in each sentence.

Name ______________________ Date ____________

Regular and irregular plurals

The Doctor Will See You Now

Lightly color the cookie that shows the plural spelling.

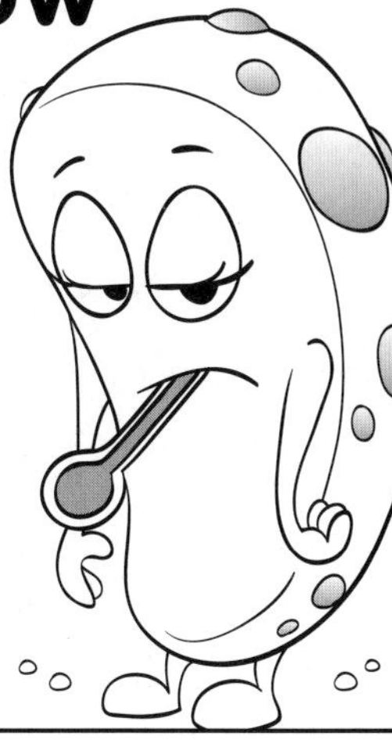

1. treat W treats Z treates	2. child X childs E children	3. sheep V sheeps G sheep	
4. tooth S tooths U teeth	5. farm I farms P farmes	6. ox K oxes S oxen	7. bus Q buss F buses
8. goose M geese T gooses	9. box Y boxes F boxs	10. doctor B doctores T doctors	11. mouse C mice H mouses
12. puppy N puppies J puppys	13. foot F footes R feet	14. man L men K mans	15. exam A exams D exames

Why did the cookie go to the doctor?

To find out, write each letter from above on the matching numbered line or lines below.

__ __   __ __ __   __ __ __ __ __ __ __   __ __ __ __ __ __!

5 10   1 15 6   7 2 2 14 5 12 3   11 13 4 8 8 9

Bonus: Explain how you know when to add *-es* to a word to make it plural. Then list three words that you must change the spelling of in order to make them plural, such as *man* to *men*.

Name ______________________________ Date ____________________

Action verbs

History in the Dirt

Use a crayon to outline each bone that names an action verb.
Then use the outlined bones to complete the sentences below.

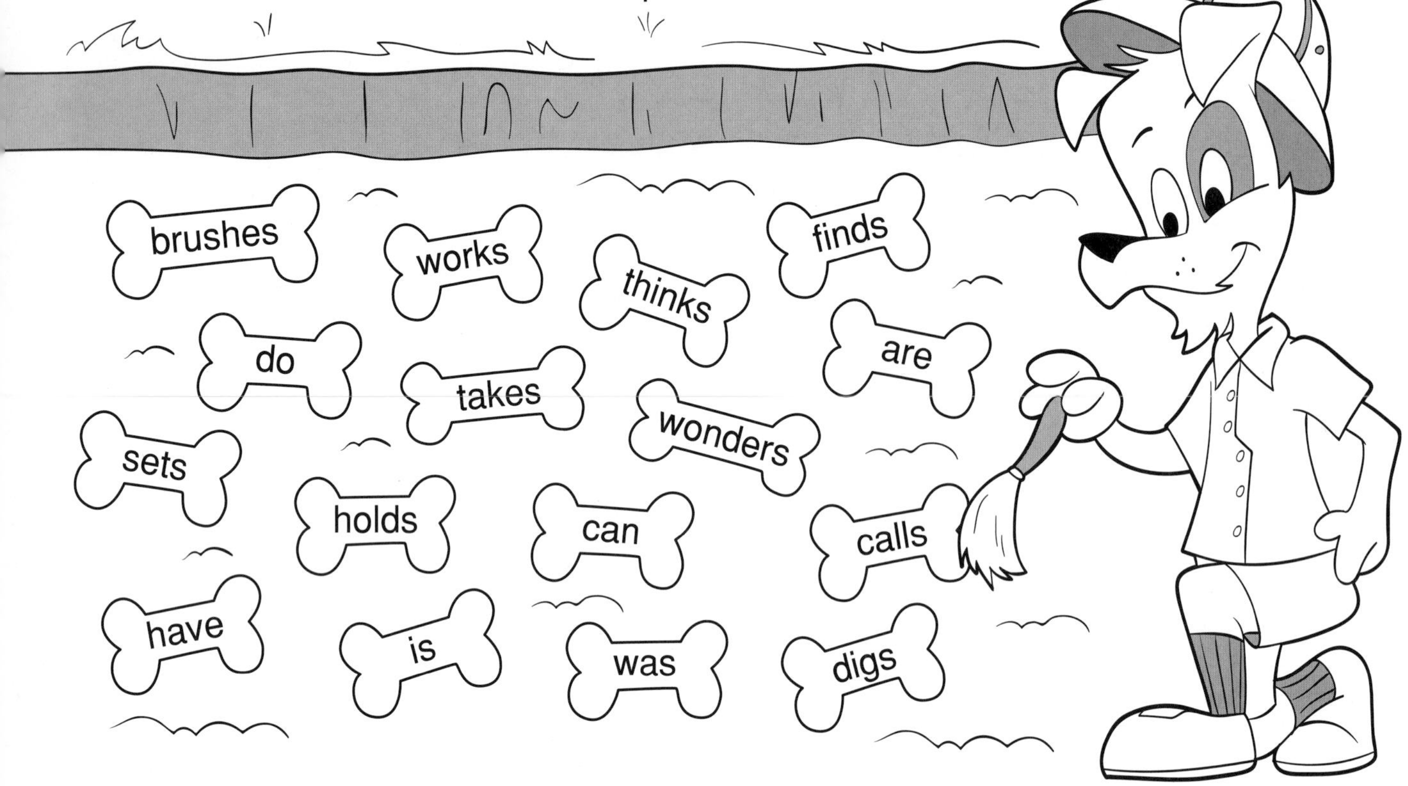

brushes
works
thinks
finds
do
takes
are
sets
wonders
holds
can
calls
have
is
was
digs

1. Professor Dino Saur ________________ he has found dinosaur bones.
2. He ________________ up his tent next to the site.
3. He ________________ into the soil.
4. The professor ________________ one huge bone.
5. He gently ________________ the dirt off the bone.
6. He ________________ a picture of the bone.
7. The professor ________________ his students over to see it.
8. One student ________________ the bone up in the air.
9. Everyone ________________ what dinosaur this could be.
10. The professor ________________ hard to uncover the rest of the bones.

Bonus: Write three sentences telling what you would do if you found a dinosaur bone. Circle the action verbs.

Names ______________________ Date ______________

Treasure Found!

Circle each letter that should be capitalized.
Color a coin with the matching letter.

C
I
J
D
H
H
G
H
M
O
P
T
S
T
P
V
W
Y
Bonus: Pretend you are Pirate Pete.
Write a letter back to Parrot Pegleg.
Circle each capital letter you use.

march 28, 2011

Ahoy, Pirate pete!

What a trip we had looking for treasure! we have made many stops. On sunday we anchored in Pirate's Cove. The map pointed to a hidden spot. We dug and dug. All we found was a forgotten box of valentine's day cards.

On tuesday we hiked to gold hill. The map took us to a hidden cave. There we found some halloween candy from last october. It wasn't gold, but it was yummy!

Yesterday we landed on treasure island. What luck! A big treasure chest was sitting right there by the shore. Captain john's keys were hanging on a palm tree. We peeked inside the treasure chest and took a sample of captain John's loot. To be fair, we left some cards and candy in its place.

how was your week? I hope it's been a "booty-ful" one!

your friend,
parrot Pegleg

Name ____________________ Date ____________

Writing dialogue

Character Conversations

Write the name of each dog by the statement it might say.

Puddles

Powder

Digger
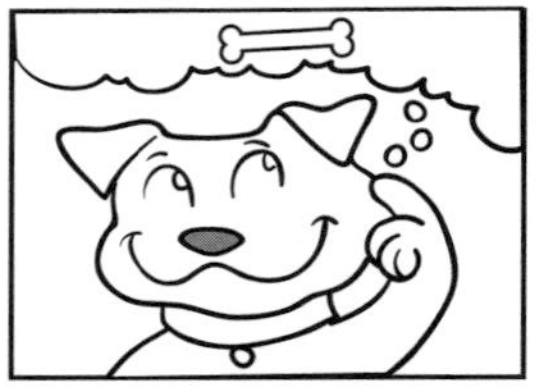

Snuggles

Cookie

Champ

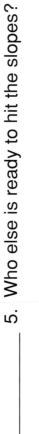

Digger 1. I don't know where I left my bone.

______ 2. Do you want to play catch?

______ 3. I just took a swim.

______ 4. Is it naptime yet?

______ 5. Who else is ready to hit the slopes?

______ 6. This is the best treat ever!

For each match above, write the sentence using dialogue.

7. "I don't know where I left my bone," Digger said.

8. ____________________

9. ____________________

10. ____________________

11. ____________________

12. ____________________

Bonus: Choose two classmates. For each classmate, write a sentence using dialogue. Include words they might actually say.

Name ______________________ Date ______________

What Do You Say?

Write eight different adjectives to describe each noun.
Start each word with the letter on its row.
Use a dictionary or thesaurus to help you.

	sandwich	friend	restaurant	necklace
D			darling	
E				
S	salty			
C				
R				
I		imaginary		
B				
E				elegant

Bonus: Make a list of adjectives to describe yourself.

Name ______________________ Date ______________

Irregular verbs

Night Game

Color the letter of the verb that best completes each sentence.

1. The game ___ right on time. (B) beginned (H) began	2. The first batter ___ the ball hard. (U) hitted (X) hit
3. A foul ball ___ over our heads. (Y) flew (T) flied	4. The batter ___ fast, but he was tagged out. (D) runned (M) ran
5. Another ball was ___ to right field. (W) sent (I) sended	6. The first baseman ___ to hold onto the ball. (C) fought (P) fighted
7. The outfielder ___ it by the fence. (A) catched (E) caught	8. Look, the runner ___ second base! (Z) stole (G) stealed
9. The home team ___ proud. (K) felt (H) feeled	10. By the fifth inning, it had ___ quite a lead. (S) builded (Q) built
11. That's when I ___ a hot dog. (R) eated (O) ate	12. The visiting team ___ the game. (F) lost (N) losed
13. Many people ___ the fireworks after the game. (E) seen (V) saw	14. We ___ home souvenirs. (Y) taked (J) took
15. I ___ all my friends about the game. (H) told (L) telled	**Why are baseball games often played at night?** To solve the riddle, write each uncolored letter on the matching line or lines below.

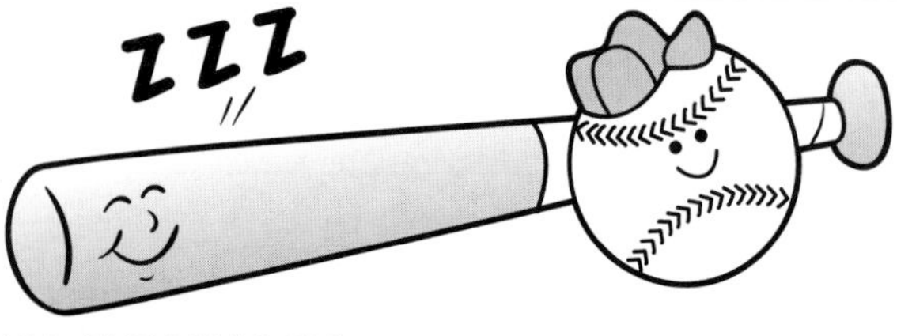
ZZZ

__ __ __ (3 9 13) __ __ __ __ (1 7 3 10) __ __ __ __ __ (10 15 13 13 6)

__ __ __ __ __ __ (4 2 11 5 12 8) __ __ __ (3 9 13) __ __ __. (4 7 14)

Name ____________________ Date ____________

Noun-pronoun agreement

Egg Race!

Circle the pronoun that best completes each sentence.

1. Ms. Hen's class was getting ready for ___ egg race. (their / its)

2. Nellie Nugget could not find ___ team's spoon. (her / their)

3. Rusty Rooster gave ___ extra spoon to Nellie. (our / his)

4. Soon, all the teams had ___ eggs and spoons. (its / their)

5. Each team took ___ place at the starting line. (its / their)

6. Ms. Hen blew ___ whistle. (her / his)

7. Rusty Rooster dropped ___ egg. (its / his)

8. His teammates cried, "___ egg!" as it bounced off the ground. (Our / My)

9. Soon after, Feathers and Peepster carried ___ eggs over the finish line. (our / their)

10. Ms. Hen stated, "I think it's time for a water break, ___ friends. You look 'eggs-hausted'!" (my / her)

Bonus: In each sentence, draw a box around the noun the circled pronoun replaces.

Start 1 TEC43050	2	3	4	5	6	7	8	9	Glue.
10	11	12	13	14	15	16	17	18	Glue.
19	20	21	22	23	24	25	26	27	Glue.
28	29	30	31	32	33	34	35	36 Finish	

Player 1

TEC43050

Player 2

TEC43050

Inching Across the Yard

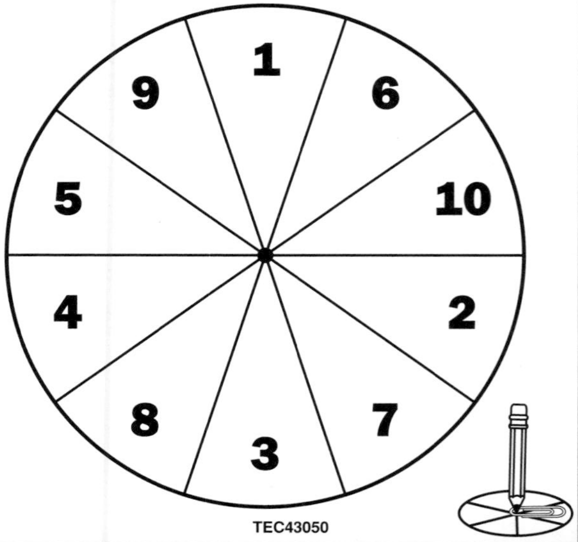
1
6
10
2
7
3
8
4
5
9

TEC43050

Spelling game

Inching Across the Yard

Directions:

1. When it's your turn, place your marker above or below Start. Use a paper clip and pencil to spin the spinner.
2. Have your partner read the numbered spelling word that matches your spin.
3. Spell the word aloud. Have your partner check your spelling against the list.
   If you are correct, roll the die. Move your marker the matching number of inches on the strip.
   If you are incorrect, do not move.
4. The first player to reach or pass Finish wins.

Partner Game To prepare, number a current spelling list from 1 to 10. (If you have more than ten words, choose ten to practice.) Copy this page; have the partners cut apart the four strips and glue them together to make one long strip. Also have them cut apart the spinner, directions, and marker cards.

MATH

Math Tips & Tools

Fun in the Sun

Collecting and graphing data

Thoughts of summer are put to good use with this collaborative activity. Divide students into small groups. After a brief discussion of summer memories, have each group brainstorm and list in a tally chart four vacations students wished they had taken over the summer. Give each group a copy of the class list and direct group members to divide the list among themselves; then instruct each student to survey those classmates to determine which vacation they'd choose. After gathering data, have each group compile its finding on a graph. Provide time for each group to share its results.

Laura Wagner, Austin, TX

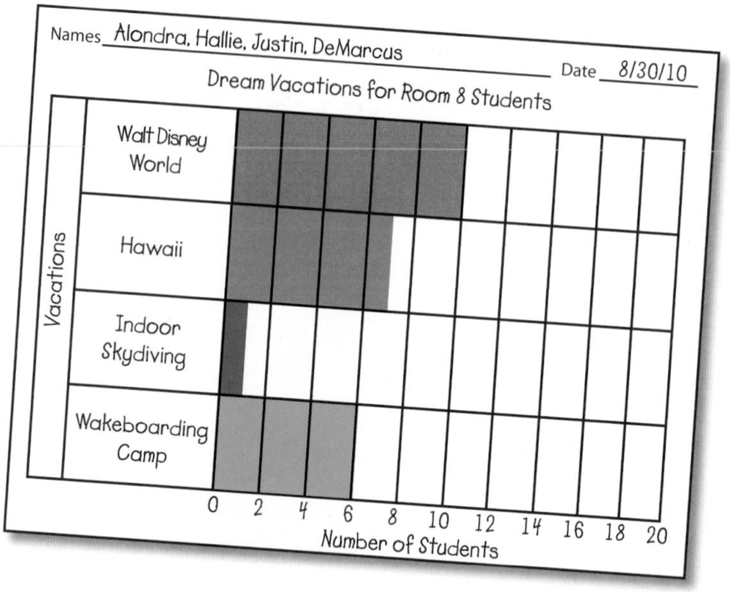
Names Alondra, Hallie, Justin, DeMarcus
Date 8/30/10
Dream Vacations for Room 8 Students
Vacations
Walt Disney World
Hawaii
Indoor Skydiving
Wakeboarding Camp
0 2 4 6 8 10 12 14 16 18 20
Number of Students

School-Home Link

Recording time, schedules

Help students learn their new schedule and build clock skills at the same time. To start, review the daily schedule with students. Have each child write on a copy of the strips on page 118 eight important subjects or activities from the schedule. Then direct her to draw the clock hands to show each starting time and also write the corresponding time. Next, have the student cut apart the strips and make a chain by taping the strips together in chronological order. Encourage the child to take the chain home and use it to explain to her family the important activities from her school day.

To make the activity less challenging, draw the hands on each clock before making a class supply of page 118. Simply have students write the times.

To make the activity more challenging, have students show the start and end times for each subject or activity and then determine the duration of each one.

Mary Burgess, Howell Valley Elementary, West Plains, MO

Math
9:00

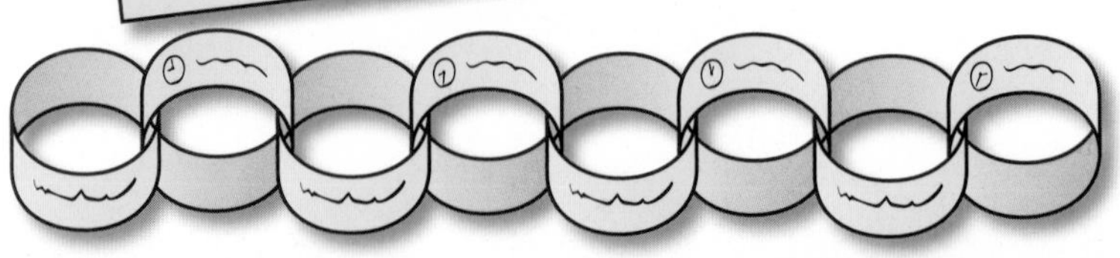

Math Tips & Tools

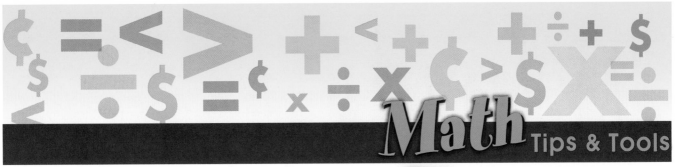

"Berry" Cool
Using ordinal numbers

Bree

Students put numbers in their places with this hands-on activity. To begin, have each child cut apart the cards and grid from a copy of page 119. Direct students to place the cards on their desks so they can easily read each name. As you provide clues like the ones shown, instruct students to place the named berry on the matching grid space. After all cards are placed, follow up with questions such as "In which position is Bailey?" To conclude the activity, have each child glue his cards in place or store the cards in a resealable plastic bag to use at another time.

Carolyn M. Burant, St. John Vianney School, Brookfield, WI

- ☐ Bree is first.
- ☐ Brooke is fifth.
- ☐ Blake is sixth.
- ☐ Bill is sixteenth.
- ☐ Bev is second.
- ☐ Brandt is twelfth.
- ☐ Beth is twentieth.
- ☐ Bailey is third.
- ☐ Bella is tenth.
- ☐ Bo is eighteenth.
- ☐ Ben is eighth.
- ☐ Bubba is eleventh.
- ☐ Bekka is seventeenth.
- ☐ Bob is fourth.
- ☐ Brian is fourteenth.
- ☐ Baxter is thirteenth.
- ☐ Betty is seventh.
- ☐ Bruce is fifteenth.
- ☐ Brady is ninth.
- ☐ Bart is nineteenth.

MILK

Many Shapes and Sizes
Understanding capacity

This variation of musical chairs will expose your students to different liquid measurements. In advance, ask each child to bring in an empty gallon, quart, pint, or cup container. Before beginning the activity, have each child name and show the container he brought to school; then direct each student to place his container on his desk. Play music and instruct students to move from desk to desk as the music plays. When the music stops, name one of the four container sizes. Have students who are standing at desks with those containers step out of the game. Restart the music and continue playing until one child is left standing.

Sima Silverstein, Bais Rivka Schools, Brooklyn, NY

Editor's Tip:
Have students who are out of the game serve as judges.

Bank on This
Making change, adding and subtracting money

To make working with money a daily transaction, set up a classroom bank. Designate a daily wage for students. Tell the class that for each day they complete their assigned classroom jobs, complete their work, and follow the rules, each child will earn the wage. If desired, also tell students that actions such as breaking a rule or failing to complete an assignment may result in a deduction of a child's wages. Assign students to serve as tellers and, at the end of each day, have the tellers distribute play money to each child equal to the value she earned for the day. Instruct each student to count her money and write her daily total on a page of her math journal. Then have her deposit her money in a resealable plastic bag. At the end of the week, have students calculate their weekly earnings and invite them to use their money to make purchases from a class store or goody box.

Sept. 13, 2010 $0.50
Sept. 14, 2010 $0.50
Sept. 15, 2010 $0.50
Sept. 16, 2010 $0.30
Sept. 17, 2010 $0.45
Weekly Total $2.25

Leonard Tarris, All Saints Catholic School, Pottsville, PA

Math Tips & Tools

A Mouthful of Math
Motivation, assessing prior knowledge

To make this math mascot, locate a box with a hinged lid. Line the inside of the box with red or pink paper and then decorate the box to look like a friendly monster's head. Introduce the math mascot to your students. Explain that it has just joined your class and has one weakness—it gobbles up math manipulatives when students are out of the classroom. To use the mascot, secretly place inside the box a sample of the materials to be used during the day's math instruction. When math begins, invite a brave student to reach into the mascot's mouth to retrieve what's inside. Then use the materials to introduce the upcoming lesson. **As an alternative,** use the math mascot each time you start a new unit. After inviting a student to reveal the manipulatives to the class, use the items to lead a discussion to determine students' knowledge of the upcoming skills.

Rachel Mueller, Millstone Township Elementary, Clarksburg, NJ

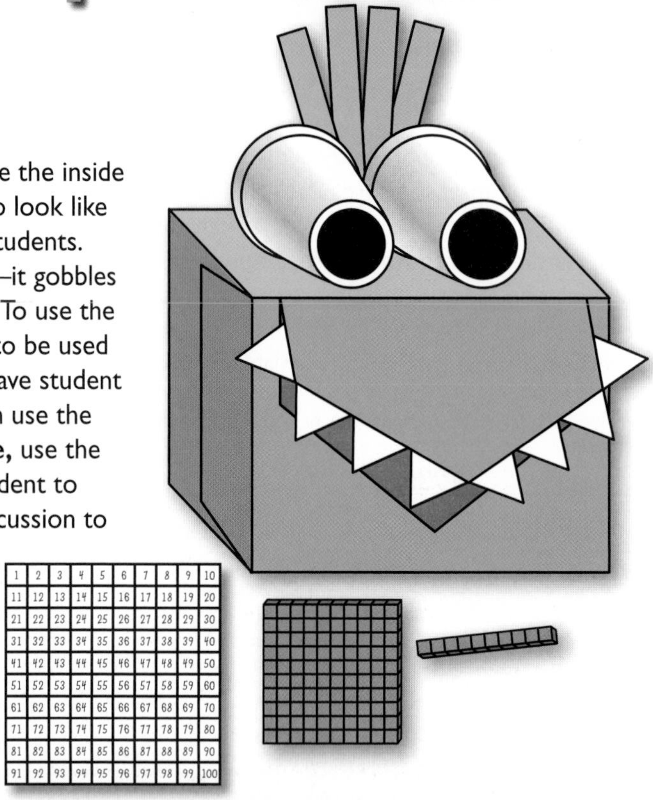

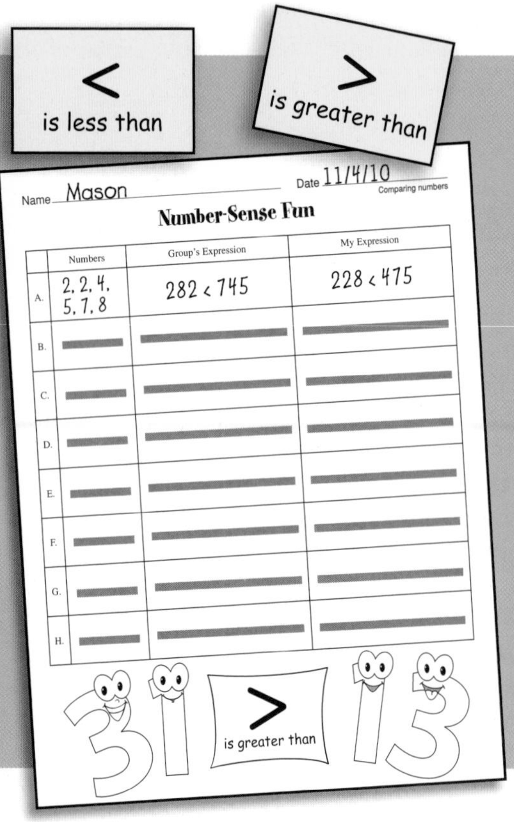
<
is less than
>
is greater than
Name Mason
Date 11/4/10
Comparing numbers
Number-Sense Fun
Numbers
Group's Expression
My Expression
A. 2, 2, 4, 5, 7, 8
282 < 745
228 < 475
B.
C.
D.
E.
F.
G.
H.
>
is greater than

In the Cards
Comparing numbers

Are you ready to deal out some number-sense fun? First, make a supply of inequality cards labeled as shown. Next, remove the face cards and tens from a deck of cards. Give each student a playing card and a copy of page 120. Then organize students into groups of four to make two two-digit numbers, groups of six to make two three-digit numbers, or groups of eight to make two four digit numbers. Deal one inequality card to each group. Instruct students in each group to organize their cards to make a true expression. Then, in turn, invite them to write their numbers and expression on the board. Confirm that the expression is accurate; then direct each student to copy the numbers and expression onto his paper. After each group has shared, challenge each student to write a second true expression for each set of numbers.

Carolyn Burant, St. John Vianney School, Brookfield, WI

Math Tips & Tools

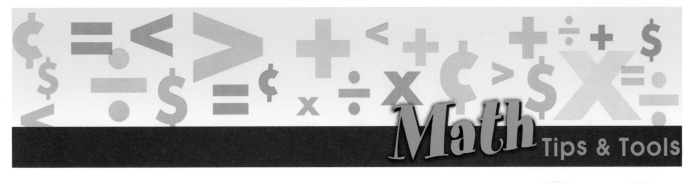

Show Me!
Estimating measurement

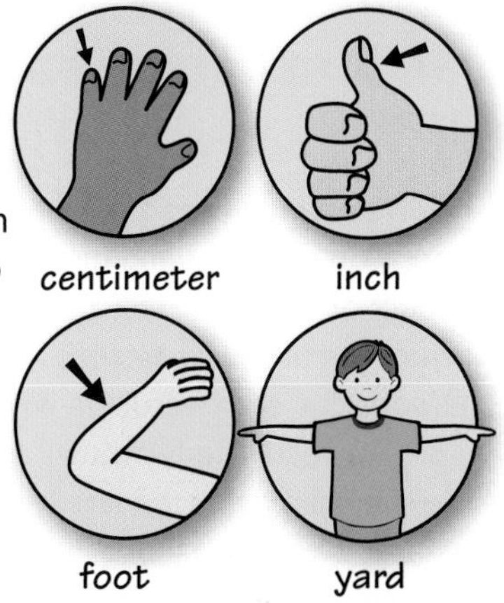
centimeter
inch
foot
yard

Build estimation skills and incorporate math vocabulary into your whole-class directions and transition time with this memorable tip. Explain to students that a centimeter is about the width of a pinkie nail while an inch is about the same length as the distance from the tip of a thumb to the first knuckle. Also tell students that a foot is about the length of a forearm (wrist to elbow) and a yard is about the length of both arms stretched out wide. Later, use the estimates in your whole-class directions and transition signals, such as saying, "Show me an inch if you're ready for the next step" or "Show me a centimeter if you agree with Taylor's statement."

Katie Smith, Park Lakes Elementary, Humble, TX

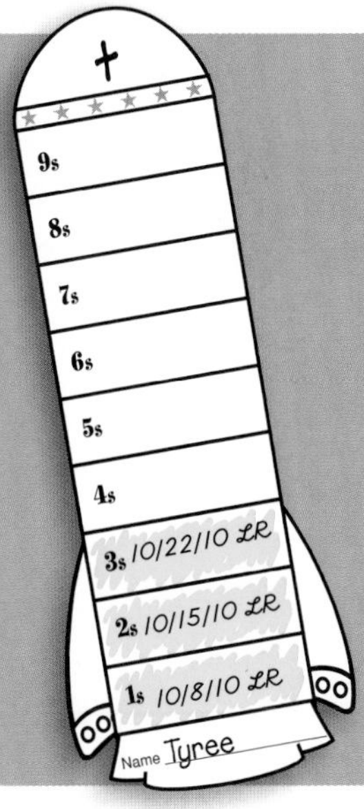
+
9s
8s
7s
6s
5s
4s
3s 10/22/10 LR
2s 10/15/10 LR
1s 10/8/10 LR
Name Tyree

Out of This World
Mastering basic facts

Take students on an exciting and rewarding trip toward fact fluency. First, make student copies of page 121 and cut apart the rocket patterns. Give each child a cutout; then direct him to write on the top of the rocket the operational symbol for the facts he will work on and, on the bottom, his name. Each time a student demonstrates mastery of a set of facts, write the date and your initials on the corresponding row. Then invite the child to color the row. Continue in this manner until the child has mastered each set of facts on his rocket. Then invite the student to visit a prize box before presenting him with a new rocket. Direct the student to program the rocket with a different operational symbol and encourage him to start mastering the facts.

Laureen Robben, North Mianus School, Riverside, CT

On the Right Track
Rounding numbers to the nearest ten

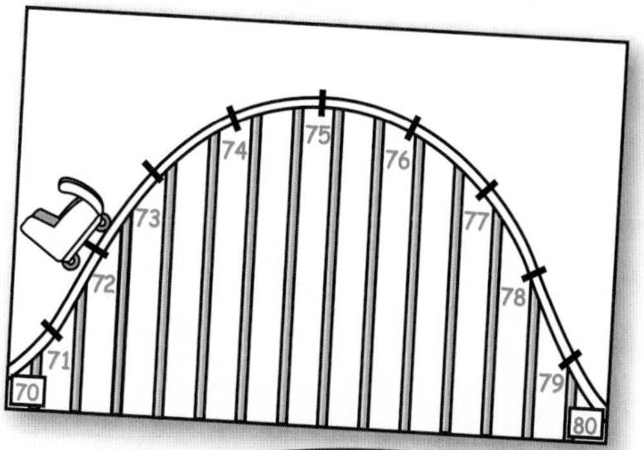
70
71
72
73
74
75
76
77
78
79
80

Accelerate students' understanding of rounding with this simple demonstration. In advance, make an enlarged copy of the roller coaster and car from page 122, laminate them, and cut them out. Use a dry-erase marker to label the track as shown. To begin, name a number on the left side of the track, such as 72. Demonstrate how the car moves up to that number on the track but can't get over the hill, so the number rounds down to the number at the left base of the hill. Then name a number on the right side of the track, such as 78. Demonstrate how that number is placed where the car can get enough speed to go over the hill so the number will, therefore, round up to the number at the right base of the hill. Erase the numbers and repeat with a new range.

Editor's Tip:
To display a rounding number line, make several copies of the roller coaster. Label the copies with successive number ranges and post them in a row.

Lisa Strieker, St. Paul Elementary, Highland, IL

Math Tips & Tools

Familiar Factories
Factors

Give each student a copy of the factory pattern on page 123 and direct him to write a product on the door. Instruct the child to write each of the product's factors in the space above the door; for each factor he writes, guide him to draw a rectangle (window) around it. Then have the child color the factory and cut it out. Post the cutouts on a board titled "Making Products at Factor Factories" or bind them in a book with the same title.

Betsy Lucas, Whiteville Elementary, Whiteville, TN

1
2
5
10
10

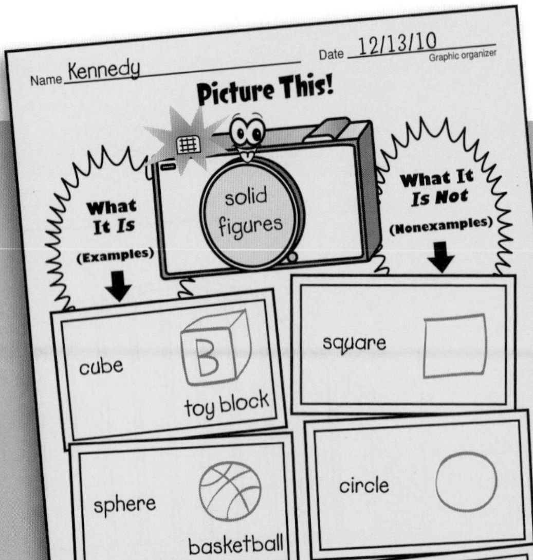

Name Kennedy
Date 12/13/10
Graphic organizer
Picture This!
What It Is (Examples)
solid figures
What It Is Not (Nonexamples)
cube
toy block
square
sphere
basketball
circle
rectangular prism
gift box
rectangle

Get the Picture?
Vocabulary, concepts

Help students capture the meanings of new terms and concepts with this flashy graphic organizer. Give each child a copy of page 124. Direct the student to write a term on the camera; then have her write or draw examples of the term in the left column. To complete the organizer, instruct her to show what the term does not mean in the right column.

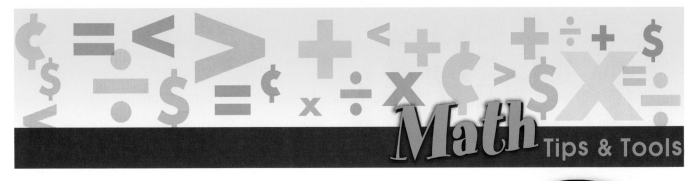

Math Tips & Tools

Starting Small
Rounding, front-end estimation

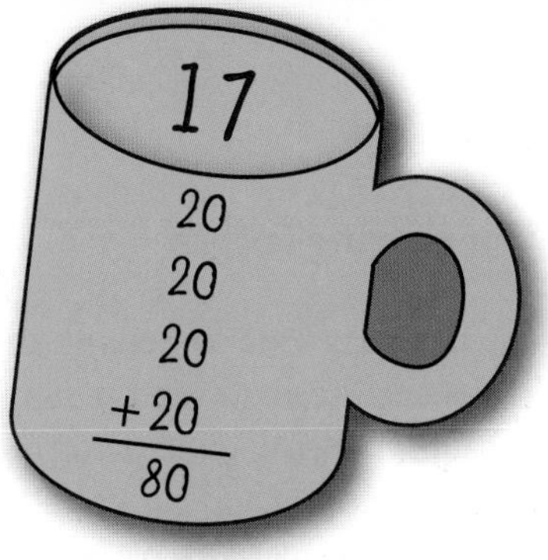
17
20
20
20
+20
80

To begin, show students an unopened bag of mini marshmallows and challenge them to guess how many are in the bag. Record their responses on the board; then give each student a sample of marshmallows and a copy of the mug pattern from page 123. Instruct each child to cut out the pattern, count her marshmallows, and write the number on the mug as shown. Next, divide students into small groups. Guide each child to round her total to the nearest ten and then write all her group's rounded numbers on the mug. Direct students to add the rounded numbers to find an estimate for their group. After each group shares its estimate, use the data to calculate a class estimate. Lead students to understand that determining a small estimate can help them find a larger one.

Laura Wagner, Austin, TX

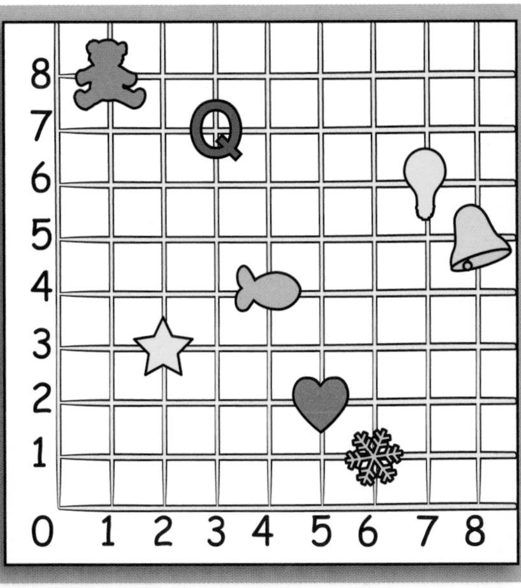
8
7
6
5
4
3
2
1
0 1 2 3 4 5 6 7 8
Q

Slide and Jump
Ordered pairs

In advance, use masking tape to make a grid on a plastic tablecloth. Then use a permanent marker to add numbers along each axis. Place different cutouts at various intersecting points on the grid. To begin, direct students to stand at their seats; then have them slide to the right and jump forward. Explain to students that when they use a coordinate grid, this is the sequence they will use to move. Then invite a child to the grid. Announce an ordered pair and have him slide right and jump forward to match the coordinates. Then have him tell the class whether there is a cutout at that location and, if so, tell what it is.

Barb Lavelle, Birch Primary, North Olmsted, OH

Attention, Please!
Multiplication facts

Jan. 7, 2011
6 x 7 = 42

Start each math lesson with a special fact announcement. Give one student a multiplication flash card and have him read the fact aloud. Then direct each child to write the fact in his math journal. Conduct your math lesson as planned; then wrap up your math time by having students say the day's fact aloud. **To extend the activity after division has been introduced,** have each student record the related division fact under the multiplication fact.

adapted from an idea by Katy Jones, Knowlton Elementary, Stroudsburg, PA

Editor's Tip:
Need a task for an early finisher? Direct her to review facts from the past week or month.

Math Tips & Tools

$15\frac{1}{2}$ in.
40 cm

Hats Off
Measuring length

Luck has little to do with this hands-on activity! To start, have each student use art supplies to create a paper leprechaun. Then, using the pattern on page 125 as a template, have him trace and cut out a leprechaun hat. Next, instruct the child to measure his leprechaun's height in centimeters and inches; then have him write the measurements on the hat. If desired, also have the student convert each measurement to another unit, such as feet. Display the leprechauns with the title "Hats Off to St. Patrick's Day" and place the hats, a supply of pushpins, and a ruler nearby. Invite students to visit the display, measure each leprechaun, and pin on the matching hat.

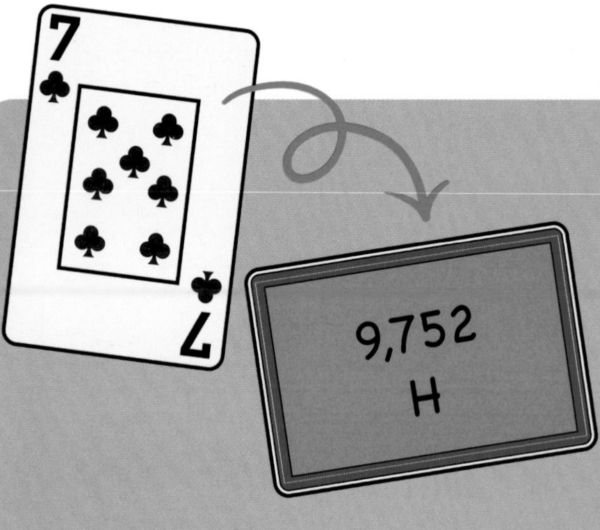
9,752
H

Quick Check
Identifying place value

To set up this center activity, gather the single-digit cards from a worn deck of playing cards. Program the back of each single-digit card with a multidigit number that includes the card's numeral. Next, write O, T, H, TH, or TTH *(ones, tens, hundreds, thousands,* or *ten thousands)* to correspond with the placement of the numeral in the programmed number. A student identifies which numeral is in the programmed place and then turns the card to check.

Math Tips & Tools

Top and Bottom
Recognizing parts of a fraction

Keep students in tune with numerators and denominators with this catchy jingle!

Sharla Fultz, Pyron Elementary, Clarksville, AR

The Fraction Jingle
(sung to the tune of "The Wheels on the Bus")

The numerator is the top number,
Top number, top number.
The numerator is the top number
In a fraction.

The numerator tells how many parts,
How many parts, how many parts.
The numerator tells how many parts are
In a fraction.

The denominator is the bottom number,
Bottom number, bottom number.
The denominator is the bottom number
In a fraction.

The denominator tells the total parts,
The total parts, the total parts.
The denominator tells the total parts
In a fraction.

Colorful Clocks
Telling time

Recycle a Twister game mat into a whole-class math game your students will want to play again and again! On each circle, draw a clockface with a different time. Refer to the mat as you write on index cards one review question for each time. To play, place the mat on the floor and divide the class into four teams. Assign a classroom supply—such as pencils, rulers, glue sticks, and math books—for each team and have the group bring six of the items to the mat. In turn, ask each team a question. If the team answers correctly, direct it to place one of its items on the matching clockface. If the team answers incorrectly, invite the next team to answer the question. The first team to have six items on the mat wins.

Colleen Dabney, Williamsburg, VA

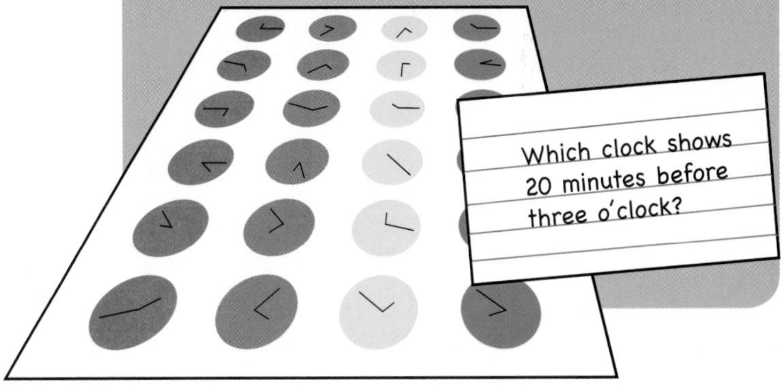
Which clock shows 20 minutes before three o'clock?

Quotient Queen
Using division vocabulary

Quotient Queen
I am the answer to a division problem!
quotient
divisor
dividend

Introduce your students to computation royalty and improve their knowledge of division-related terms at the same time! Have each child personalize a copy of the quotient queen pattern from page 126. Remind students that the answer to a division problem is called a quotient and that it is placed on the top line of the division sign (the queen's throne). Have the student tape her copy to her desktop or in her math journal. **To follow up the activity**, have each child complete a copy of the practice sheet at the bottom of page 126.

Patricia Syner, Edmond, WV

Math Tips & Tools

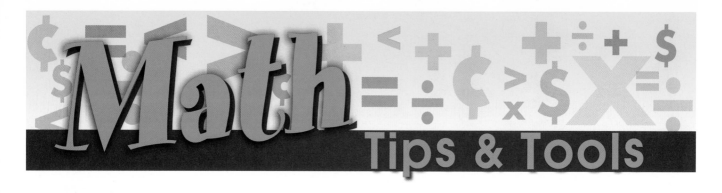

In Formation
Division readiness

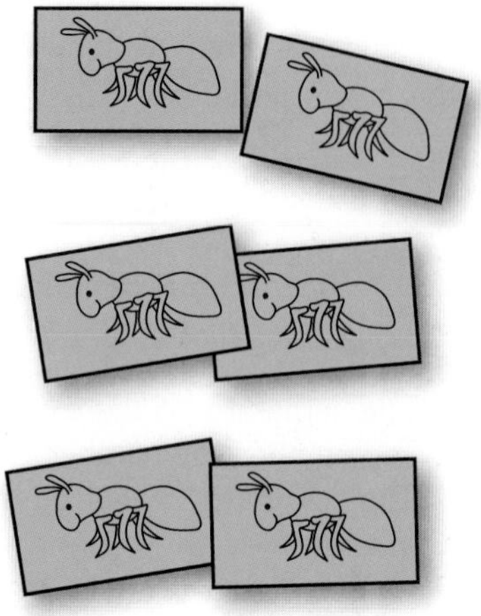

Lead your troops to a better understanding of equal sharing and remainders with this hands-on activity. To begin, instruct each child to cut apart the ants from a copy of page 127. Choral-read the poem "The Ants Go Marching" and then revisit the second stanza. Direct students to move their ant cutouts to show them paired in groups of two. Discuss the number of pairs and how this relates to equal sharing and division. Repeat with the third, fourth, sixth, and eighth stanzas, instructing students to manipulate their ants accordingly. Reread the fifth, seventh, and/or ninth stanzas to introduce remainders, having students group the ants and guiding them to understand that the ungrouped ants are known as remainders. **To extend the activity**, have each child write on a sheet of 11" x 17" paper an equal-sharing word problem about the ants. Then have him glue the ants to his paper to show the answer.

Carolyn Burant, St. John Vianney School, Brookfield, WI

Off the Charts!
Identifying measurement units

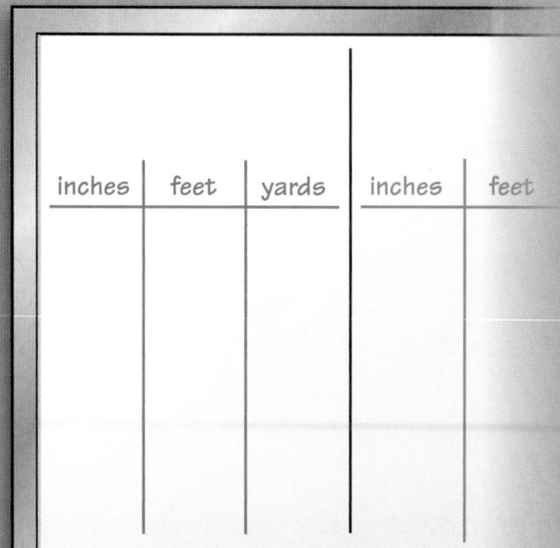
inches
feet
yards
inches
feet

Challenge students to race against the clock as they play this fast-paced game. On the board, draw and label two three-column charts with the headers shown. Assign one chart to each team. Set a timer for five minutes and give the first player on each team a marker. Direct each student to write the name of an object in the column that best names how to measure it; then have the child pass the marker to the next player. Play continues until the timer goes off. Review the words and award one point for each object that is correctly placed on the chart.

To make the game easier, cut out pictures from magazines. Put the pictures and tape near the board. If a child is unable to think of an item to write on the board, she tapes the top picture in the corresponding column.

To vary the game, use different units of measure such as ounces, pounds, tons; minutes, hours, days; cups, quarts, gallons; or centimeters, meters, kilometers.

Cynthia Wicks, Eastwood Elementary, Roseburg, OR

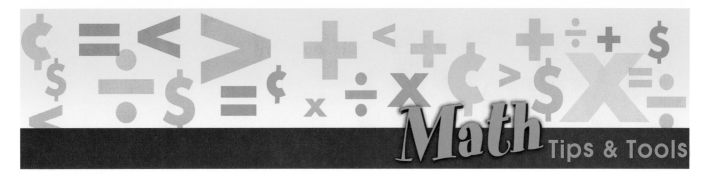

Math Tips & Tools

Get Specific
Identifying types of triangles

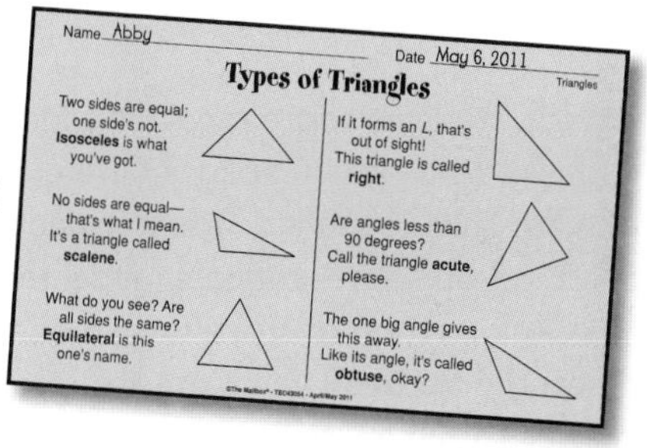
Name Abby Date May 6, 2011

Types of Triangles Triangles

Two sides are equal; one side's not. **Isosceles** is what you've got.

No sides are equal—that's what I mean. It's a triangle called **scalene**.

What do you see? Are all sides the same? **Equilateral** is this one's name.

If it forms an *L*, that's out of sight! This triangle is called **right**.

Are angles less than 90 degrees? Call the triangle **acute**, please.

The one big angle gives this away. Like its angle, it's called **obtuse**, okay?

This quick activity is sure to help students broaden their plane-shape vocabulary! To begin, give each child a copy of the rhyme at the top of page 128. Practice reciting the rhyme as a whole group. Then, if desired, assign each of six small groups a stanza to read. After students are familiar with the characteristics of each type of triangle, have each child draw a picture of the matching triangle next to its stanza.

Marsha Joyner, Davis Elementary, Marietta, GA

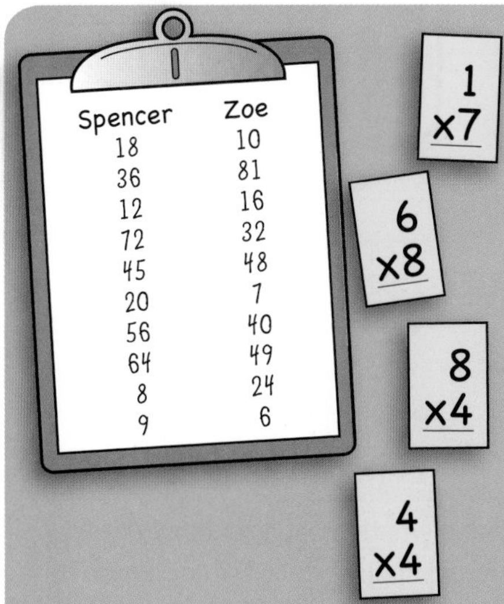

Spencer
18
36
12
72
45
20
56
64
8
9
Zoe
10
81
16
32
48
7
40
49
24
6
1 x7
6 x8
8 x4
4 x4

Practice Alfresco
Reviewing basic facts

Take advantage of warmer spring days by setting up this partner activity during recess. In advance, write the names of different student pairs on each of a supply of papers. Stack the papers on a clipboard. Next, place on level ground ten flash cards in a zigzag path and put the clipboard, the rest of the flash cards, and a pencil near the start of the path. To begin, Student 1 jumps from flash card to flash card, calling out the answer before moving to the next card. Student 2 jots down each answer in order on a sheet of paper. After Student 1 reaches the end of the path, the students turn over each flash card to check the answers. They put down ten new cards in a similar path and switch roles. When both students have had a turn, they move their paper to the bottom of the stack and inform the next pair of students that it is their turn.

adapted from an idea by Corrine Kemper, Brookville Elementary, Brookville, TN

Parts of a Rainbow
Identifying and comparing unit fractions

1/2
1/3
1/4
1/6
1/8
1/12

To prepare this demonstration, write each fractional amount shown on a piece of masking tape and attach each piece to a different one-cup container. Squeeze food coloring into each container, making a different color for each one. Fill each container with a fraction of water that matches its label; then tightly secure a lid on each container. Place the containers in a line, keeping the taped side away from the class. Use students' input to order the containers from most liquid to least. Next, invite students to name the fraction represented in each container. Turn the containers to show the fractions and share this rule with students: For unit fractions, a smaller denominator means a larger fraction. Then have each child color and label a copy of the bottom of page 128, cut it out, and tape it in her math journal or on her desk.

Editor's Tip:
Use two tablespoons and two teaspoons of water to make ⅙ cup. Use two tablespoons for ⅛ cup and four teaspoons for 1⁄12 cup.

Jess Fisher, John F. Kennedy Elementary, Winooski, VT

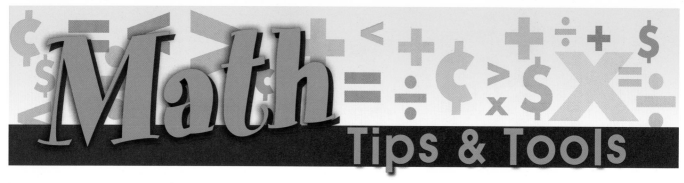

Math Tips & Tools

Make the Connection
Multiplication readiness

Help students relate repeated addition with multiplication with this small-group activity. Give each group a container of math links. Present a repeated addition problem, such as 3 + 3 + 3, and have students model the problem using the links. Ask a group to share their model with the class and reveal the answer. Then share that their answer is also the answer to the multiplication problem 3 x 3. Explain that the multiplication sign can be read as *groups of* and—since they made three groups, or links, of three—they modeled the multiplication problem too. Present other repeated addition problems for the groups to model and have them name the answers and the corresponding multiplication problems.

Jess started his homework at 6:35. He worked for 35 minutes. When did he finish his homework?
Time
Solve for End Time (↓) or Beginning Time (↑)
Minutes
6:35
Janelle
Time
Solve for End Time (↓) or Beginning Time (↑)
Minutes
0
6:35
5
6:40
10
6:45
15
6:50
20
6:55
25
7:00
30
7:05
35
7:10

It's About Time
Elapsed time

To introduce this strategy, post a copy of the word problem and the chart shown. Direct each student to copy the column heading onto a sheet of lined paper. Read the problem aloud; then have students determine whether the problem is looking for a beginning time or an ending time. Since it is looking for an ending time, guide each child to write the initial time in the left column. Next, have the child draw an arrow pointing down in the second column to show that she is solving for the end time. In the last column, guide the child to write increments of five minutes on each line until she reaches the amount of time passed in the problem *(35 minutes)*. Then, for each increment, have her write the corresponding time in the first column until she solves the problem. Repeat with different sample problems until students can complete the chart independently.

To solve for the beginning time, have the child write the time from the problem at the bottom of the left column and draw an arrow pointing up. **To solve a problem that asks the child to find the elapsed time between two events**, instruct the child to write the starting time at the top of the left column and the ending time at the bottom of the same column.

Terry Healy, Marlatt Elementary, Manhattan, KS

Math Tips & Tools

Spill the Beans
Mixed numbers and equivalent fractions

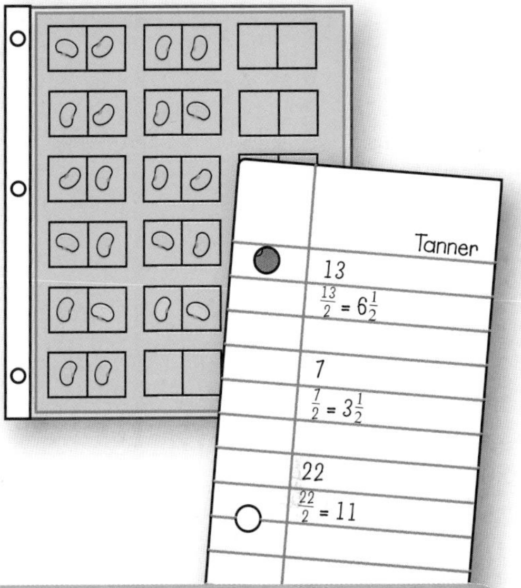

Tanner
13
$\frac{13}{2} = 6\frac{1}{2}$
7
$\frac{7}{2} = 3\frac{1}{2}$
22
$\frac{22}{2} = 11$

Reveal the truth about equal amounts with this simple center. Place a copy of the sorting sheet from page 129 in a plastic page protector. Put the sheet at a center with a cup of dried beans, a variety of different-size spoons, and a supply of paper. To complete the center, a student scoops a spoonful of beans and carefully pours them onto his workspace. He counts the beans and writes the total on his paper. Then the child writes an improper fraction to show the total divided into halves. He sorts the beans onto the mat until they are all placed, counts the number of complete and incomplete sets, and then writes the equivalent number or mixed number. The student returns the beans to the cup, chooses a different spoon, and repeats the steps.

Laura Wagner, Austin, TX

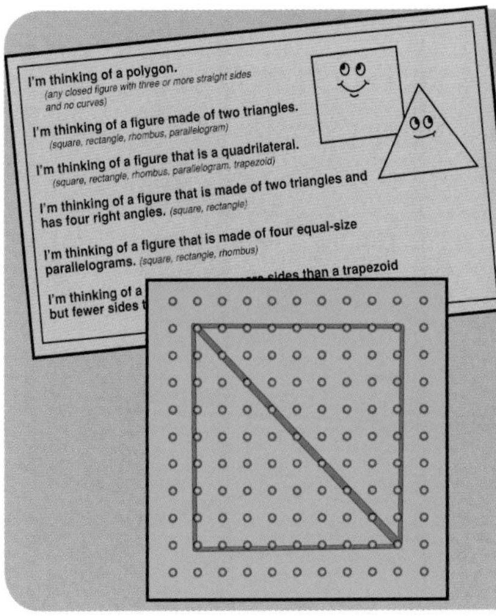

I'm thinking of a polygon.
(any closed figure with three or more straight sides and no curves)
I'm thinking of a figure made of two triangles.
(square, rectangle, rhombus, parallelogram)
I'm thinking of a figure that is a quadrilateral.
(square, rectangle, rhombus, parallelogram, trapezoid)
I'm thinking of a figure that is made of two triangles and has four right angles. (square, rectangle)
I'm thinking of a figure that is made of four equal-size parallelograms. (square, rectangle, rhombus)

Mind Readers
Attributes of geometry

With this guessing game, there's more than one possible answer! Give each student a Geoboard and a supply of rubber bands. Read a clue from the top of page 130 aloud and have each child use one or more rubber bands (depending on the clue) to create a matching shape. Invite a few students to share their creations, name the resulting figure, and explain which part of the clue led them to make that shape. Continue with the other clues. **As an alternative**, white-out the answers on a copy of the clues from page 130 and then make a class supply of the sheet. Challenge students to solve each clue, listing as many possible figures as they can.

Heather Wynne, Tobyhanna Elementary, Pocono Pines, PA

Right on Target
Basic facts

9
7

Toss your students some math practice with this activity for two. Use a permanent marker to label the fronts and backs of each of eleven beanbags with different numbers from zero to ten. Place the beanbags and a calculator in a bucket and place a hula hoop (target) a short distance away on the floor. Player 1 stands at the bucket while Player 2 stands at the target. Player 1 takes two beanbags from the bucket and tosses them into the target. Player 2 reads the numbers and uses them to say and solve a math fact; then Player 1 checks the problem on the calculator. If a beanbag doesn't make it in the target, Player 2 looks at the numbers on that beanbag and chooses one to use in his math fact. Students continue until one beanbag remains in the bucket; then they switch places.

Editor's Tip:
Don't have a hula hoop? Use masking tape to mark off a target area on the floor. Need beanbags? Fill resealable plastic bags with dried beans and seal the bags with packing tape.

Shannon Scott, McBride Elementary, Springfield, MO

Clock Strips

Use with "School-Home Link" on page 106.

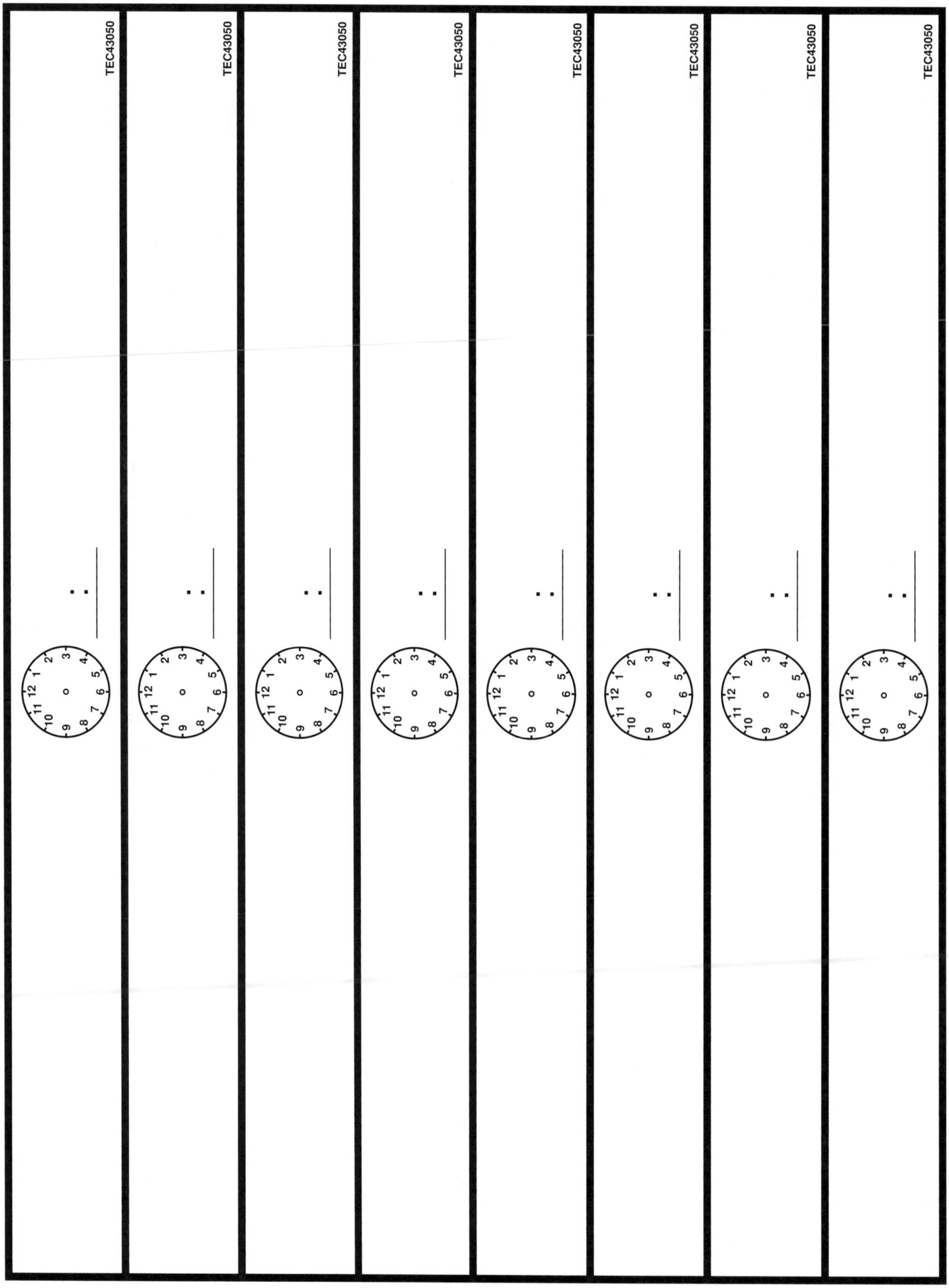
TEC43050
TEC43050
TEC43050
TEC43050
TEC43050
TEC43050
TEC43050
TEC43050

Berry Cards and Grid

Use with "'Berry' Cool" on page 107.

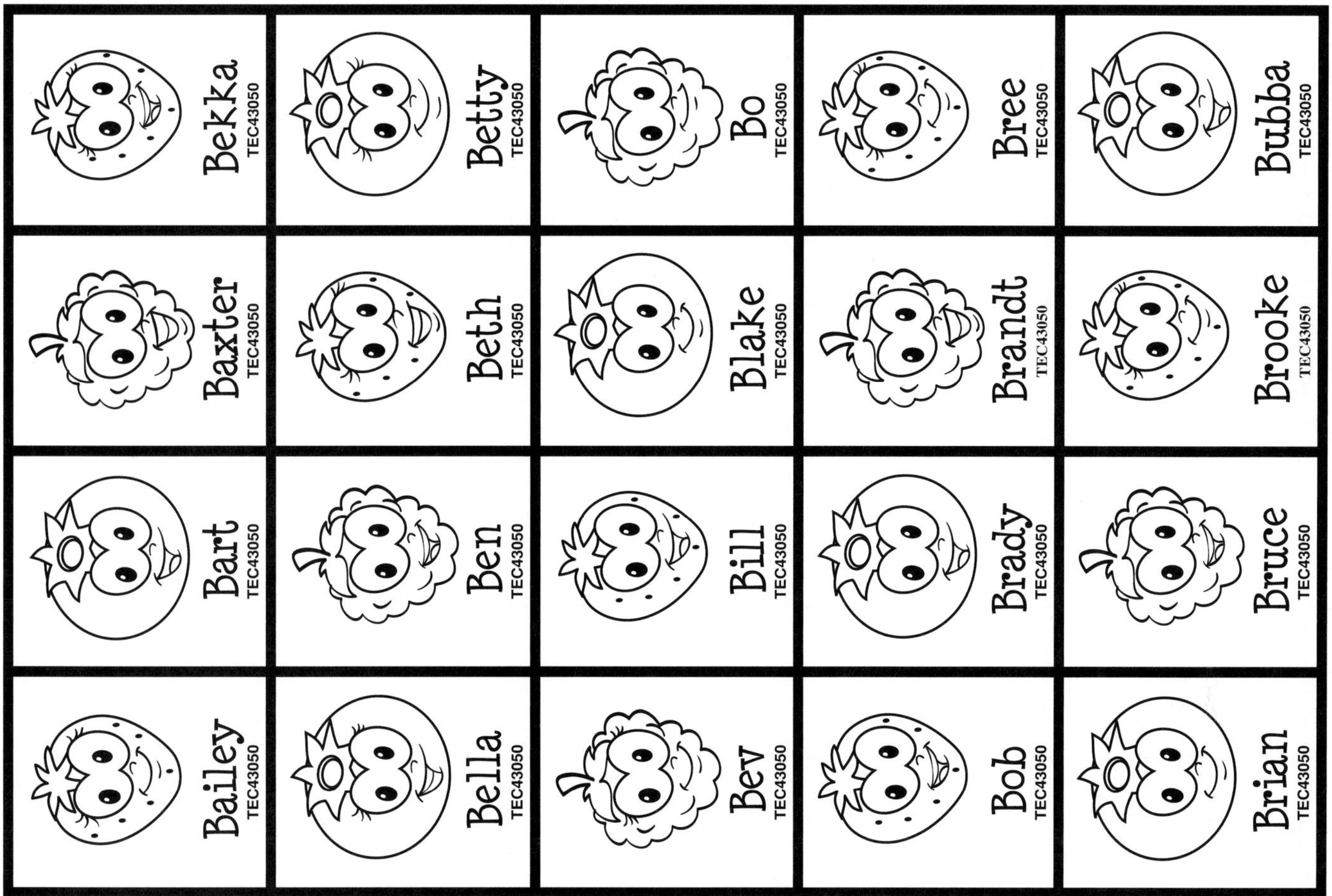
Bekka TEC43050
Betty TEC43050
Bo TEC43050
Bree TEC43050
Bubba TEC43050
Baxter TEC43050
Beth TEC43050
Blake TEC43050
Brandt TEC43050
Brooke TEC43050
Bart TEC43050
Ben TEC43050
Bill TEC43050
Brady TEC43050
Bruce TEC43050
Bailey TEC43050
Bella TEC43050
Bev TEC43050
Bob TEC43050
Brian TEC43050

	eighth			twentieth
			fifteenth	
		tenth		
first				TEC43050

Name ____________________ Date ____________________

Comparing numbers

Number-Sense Fun

	Numbers	Group's Expression	My Expression
A.			
B.			
C.			
D.			
E.			
F.			
G.			
H.			

is greater than

 Note to the teacher: Use with "In the Cards" on page 108.

Rocket Patterns

Use with "Out of This World" on page 109 and "Number Patterns Are a Blast!" on page 273.

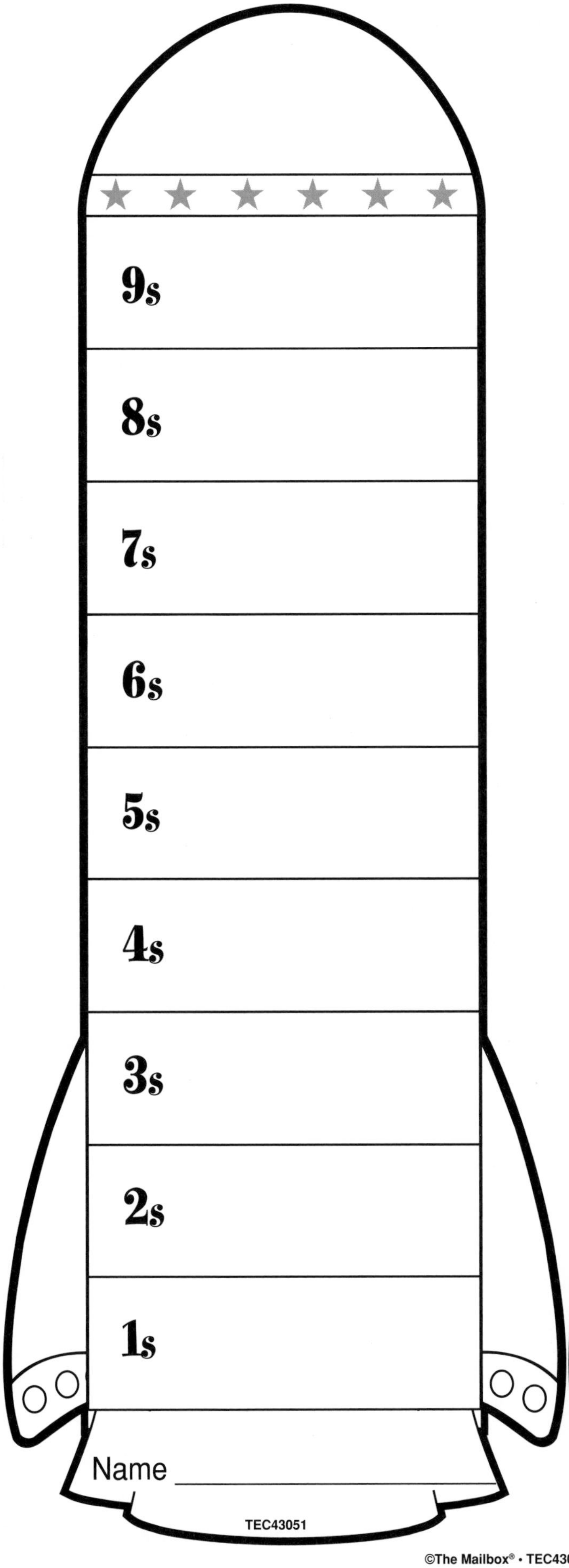
9s
8s
7s
6s
5s
4s
3s
2s
1s
Name
TEC43051

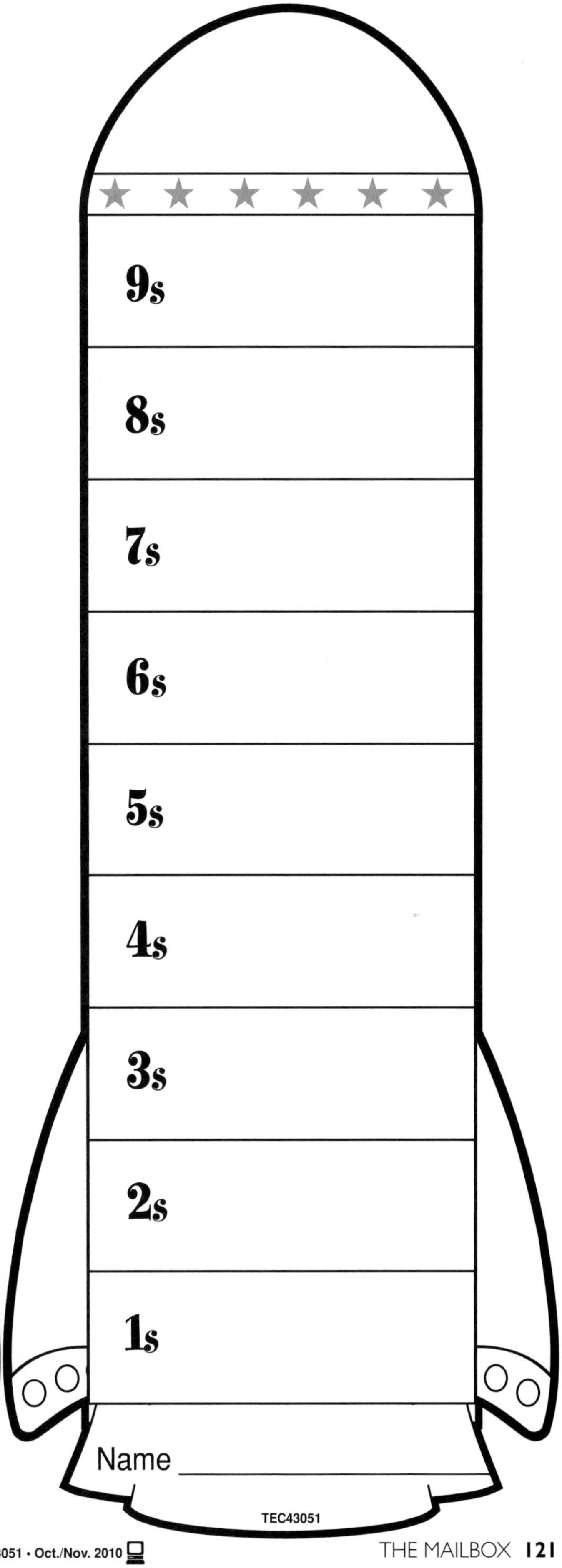
9s
8s
7s
6s
5s
4s
3s
2s
1s
Name
TEC43051

Roller Coaster and Car Patterns

Use with "On the Right Track" on page 109.

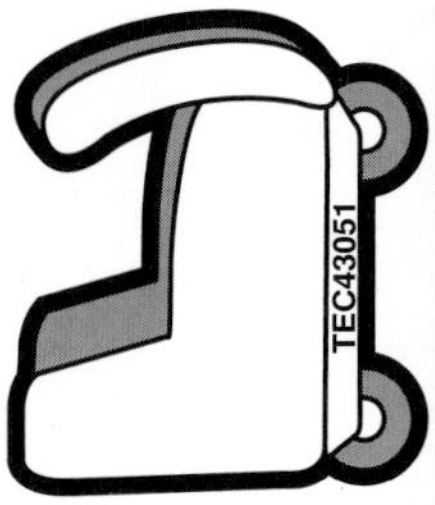
TEC43051

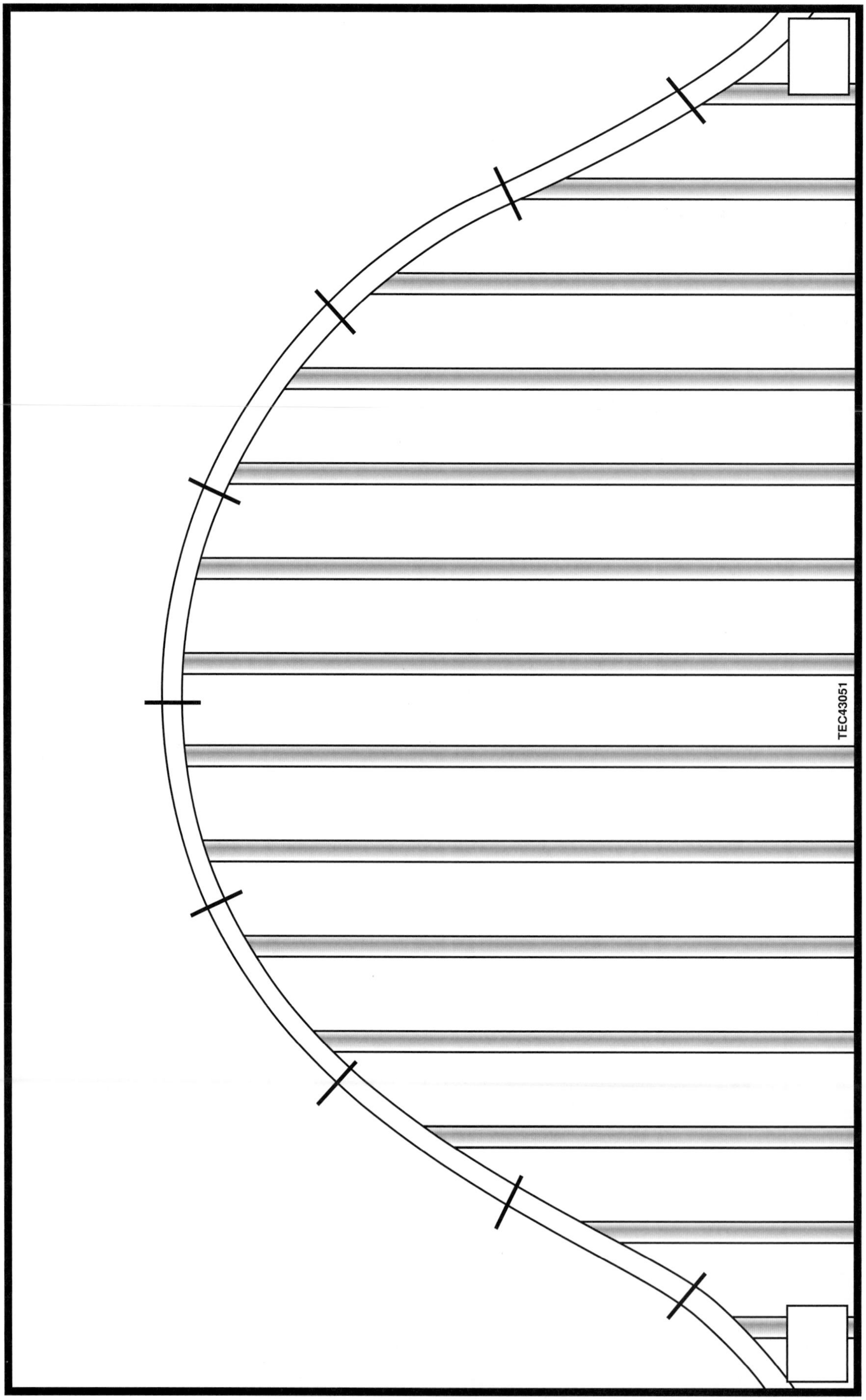
TEC43051

Factory Pattern

Use with "Familiar Factories" on page 110.

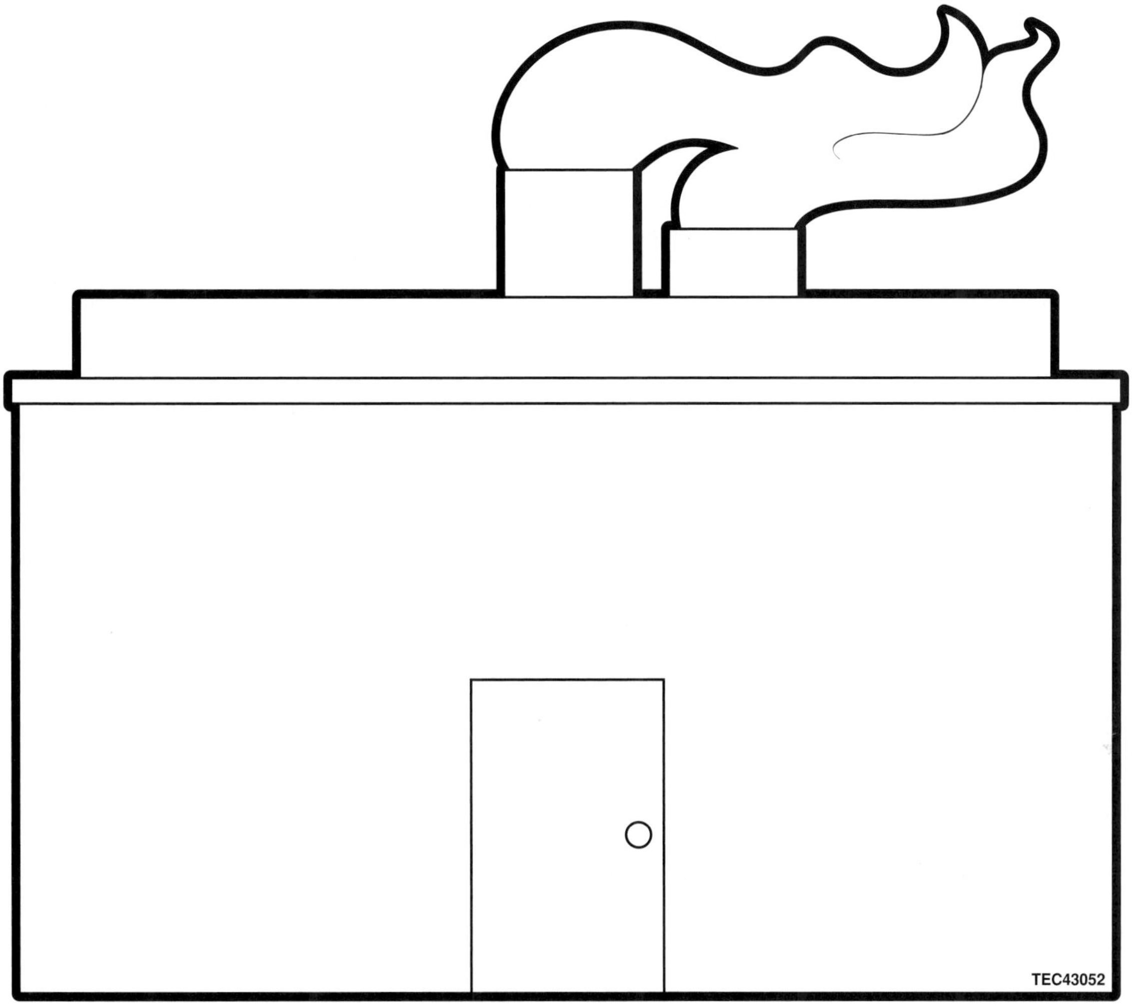
TEC43052

Mug Pattern

Use with "Starting Small" on page 111.

TEC43052

Name ____________________ Date ____________________

Graphic organizer

Picture This!

What It *Is*

(Examples)

What It *Is Not*

(Nonexamples)

©The Mailbox® • TEC43052 • Dec./Jan. 2010–11

 Note to the teacher: Use with "Get the Picture?" on page 110.

Leprechaun Hat Pattern

Use with "Hats Off" on page 112.

TEC43053

Quotient Queen Pattern and Practice Sheet

Use with "Quotient Queen" on page 113.

Quotient Queen
I am the answer to a division problem!
quotient
divisor
dividend
TEC43053

Name ______________________ Date ______________

Division

Crowning the Quotient Queen

Divide.

Draw a crown around each quotient.

A. $5\overline{)30}$ (quotient: 6; -30; 0)

B. $8\overline{)24}$

C. $2\overline{)16}$

D. $3\overline{)12}$

E. $6\overline{)42}$

F. $3\overline{)27}$

G. $4\overline{)16}$

H. $6\overline{)36}$

I. $9\overline{)72}$

J. $7\overline{)14}$

K. $8\overline{)32}$

L. $5\overline{)45}$

M. $3\overline{)15}$

Ant Cards

Use with "In Formation" on page 114.

TEC43054

TEC43054

TEC43054

TEC43054

TEC43054
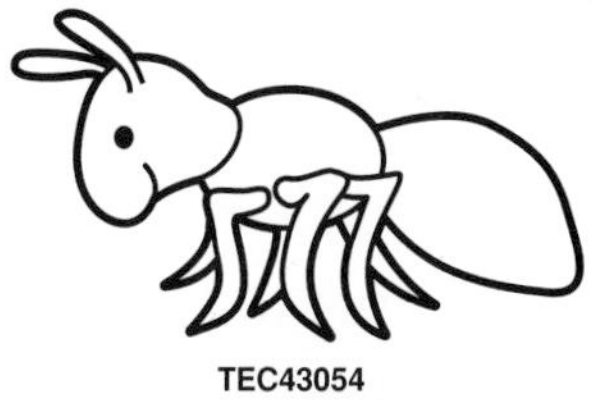
TEC43054

TEC43054

TEC43054

TEC43054

TEC43054

TEC43054

TEC43054

TEC43054

TEC43054

TEC43054

TEC43054

TEC43054

TEC43054

TEC43054

TEC43054

TEC43054

TEC43054

TEC43054

TEC43054

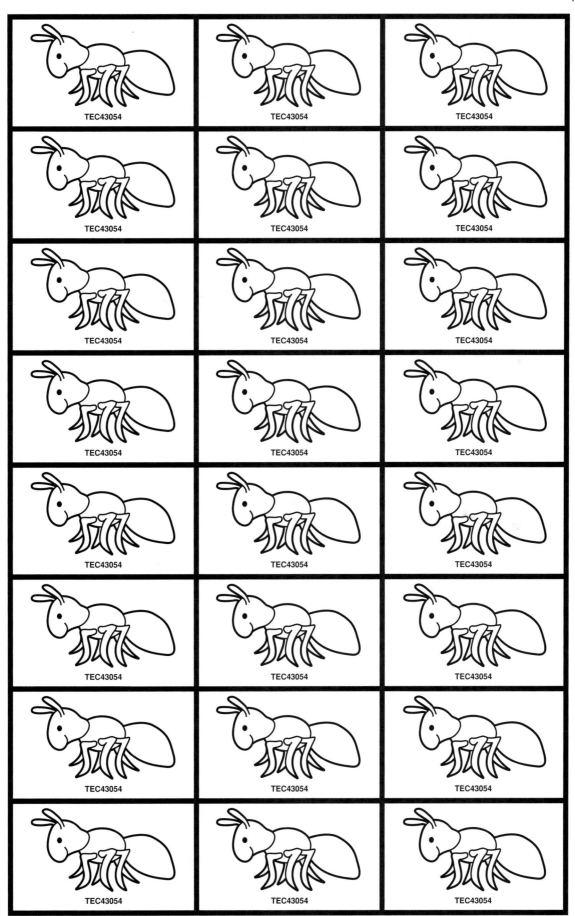

Name________________________________ Date ____________________

Triangles

Types of Triangles

Two sides are equal;
one side's not.
Isosceles is what
you've got.

No sides are equal—
that's what I mean.
It's a triangle called
scalene.

What do you see? Are
all sides the same?
Equilateral is this
one's name.

If it forms an **L**, that's
out of sight!
This triangle is called
right.

Are angles less than
90 degrees?
Call the triangle **acute**,
please.

The one big angle gives
this away.
Like its angle, it's called
obtuse, okay?

Name________________________________ Date ____________________

Unit fractions

Parts of a Rainbow

Color your paper to look like the cups.

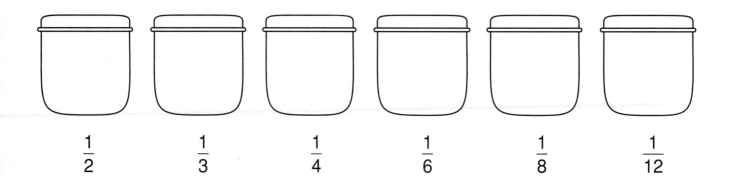

$\frac{1}{2}$ $\frac{1}{3}$ $\frac{1}{4}$ $\frac{1}{6}$ $\frac{1}{8}$ $\frac{1}{12}$

For unit fractions, a smaller denominator means a larger fraction.

Note to the teacher: Use the top half of the page with "Get Specific" on page 115 and the bottom half with "Parts of a Rainbow" on page 115.

Note to the teachers: Use with "Spill the Beans" on page 117.

Plane Shape Clues

Use with "Mind Readers" on page 117.

I'm thinking of a polygon.
(any closed figure with three or more straight sides and no curves)

I'm thinking of a figure made of two triangles.
(square, rectangle, rhombus, parallelogram)

I'm thinking of a figure that is a quadrilateral.
(square, rectangle, rhombus, parallelogram, trapezoid)

I'm thinking of a figure that is made of two triangles and has four right angles. *(square, rectangle)*

I'm thinking of a figure that is made of four equal-size parallelograms. *(square, rectangle, rhombus)*

I'm thinking of a figure that has more sides than a trapezoid but fewer sides than an octagon. *(pentagon, hexagon, heptagon)*

TEC43055

Name ______________________ Date ______________

Multiplication

Ready to Relax

Multiply.

A. 8 x 3 = ____ B. 9 x 7 = ____ C. 5 x 5 = ____

D. 9 x 9 = ____ E. 4 x 4 = ____ F. 3 x 7 = ____ G. 1 x 9 = ____

H. 9 x 3 = ____ I. 7 x 6 = ____ J. 8 x 8 = ____ K. 7 x 4 = ____

L. 7 x 5 = ____ M. 4 x 9 = ____ N. 9 x 6 = ____

O. 3 x 3 = ____ P. 5 x 2 = ____ Q. 2 x 9 = ____

Home,
"Tweet"
Home

Bonus: Circle each problem with an even product.

Math

Mind Builders

Mind Builder 1

Write three different facts for each sum.

10 11 13 14

Write three different facts for each difference.

5 6 7 9

TEC43050

Mind Builder 2

Write and solve five addition problems. Add the bold number to each of the other numbers.

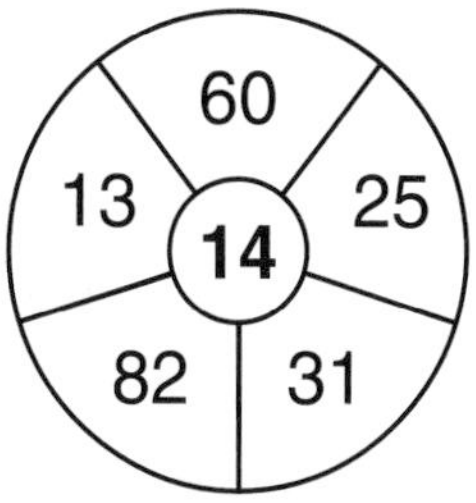

60
13
25
14
82
31

TEC43050

Mind Builder 3

a = short letter

k = tall letter

g = long letter

Make a tally chart to show the number of short, tall, and long lowercase letters in the alphabet.

TEC43050

Mind Builder 4

Would you rather have eight nickels or five dimes? Explain.

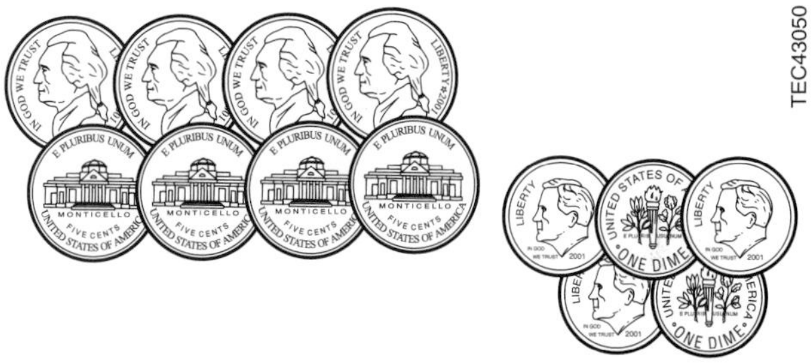

TEC43050

Mind Builder 5

Use the numbers below to make six different three-digit numbers.

4 1 7

Round each number you made to the nearest ten.

TEC43050

Mind Builder 6

Draw the next three clocks in the pattern.

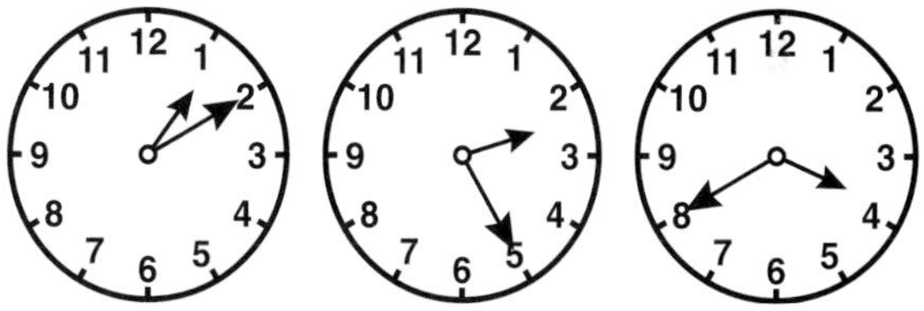

TEC43050

Mind Builder 7

Write and answer three questions about the graph.

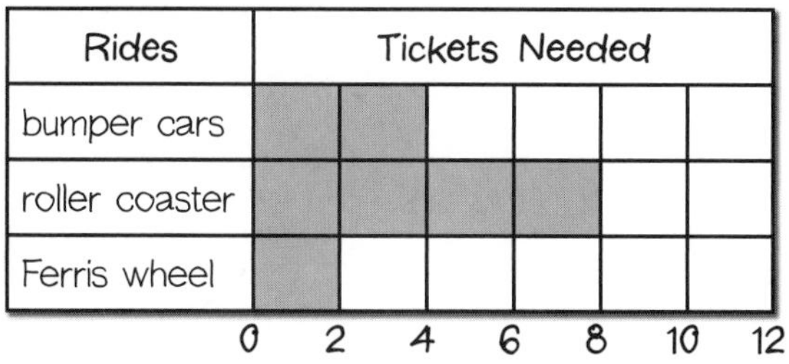

Rides
Tickets Needed
bumper cars
roller coaster
Ferris wheel
0 2 4 6 8 10 12

TEC43050

Mind Builder 8

List each number with a "5" in the hundreds place.

5,163	8,459	1,597
4,507	2,548	5,042
6,135	2,536	4,593

Rewrite the numbers listed from least to greatest.

TEC43050

Note to the teacher: Give each student a copy of this page (or one card at a time) to work on during free time. Have the student solve the problems on a separate sheet of paper.

Math

Mind Builders

Mind Builder 1

Draw lines across (—), up or down (|), and diagonally (╳) to make eight three-digit numbers. Write the numbers in order from least to greatest.

3	1	2
5	0	4
8	6	9

TEC43051

Mind Builder 2

Tell how to use skip-counting to find the number of

- ☐ fingers on 8 hands
- ☐ tires on 6 bicycles
- ☐ sides on 5 triangles
- ☐ toes on 7 people

TEC43051

Mind Builder 3

If you can use only three of these coins, which amount cannot be made?

IN GOD WE TRUST
LIBERTY
2001
1998

16¢ 21¢ 36¢ 41¢ 45¢

TEC43051

Mind Builder 4

Use the numbers to make ten different addition problems. Then solve.

	24	
12	31	43
	50	

TEC43051

Mind Builder 5

Copy and complete the chart.

4,361	
A. one less	
B. one thousand more	
C. one hundred less	
D. ten more	

TEC43051

Mind Builder 6

How is a number written in standard form (985) the same as a number written in expanded form (900 + 80 + 5)? How are the forms different?

TEC43051

Mind Builder 7

5 2 6

Use these numbers to write six different three-digit numbers. Round each number you make to the nearest ten.

TEC43051

Mind Builder 8

Write the time for _____.

12
1
2
3
4
5
6
7
8
9
10
11

A. 20 minutes later
B. 30 minutes before
C. 1 hour before
D. 35 minutes later
E. 2 hours later

TEC43051

How to use Give each student a copy of this page (or one card at a time) to work on during free time. Have the student solve the problems on his own paper.

Math

Mind Builders

Mind Builder 1

Copy.

_____ > 413 _____ < 341

_____ < 143 _____ > 134

_____ = 314 _____ < 314

Fill in each blank with a number.
Use only 1, 4, and 3 in each number.

TEC43052

Mind Builder 2

It was 45°F on Monday and 42°F on Tuesday. It is 39°F on Wednesday. If this pattern continues, will it be cold enough for snow by Saturday? Tell how you know.

TEC43052

Mind Builder 3

Which shape has a line of symmetry? Explain how you know.

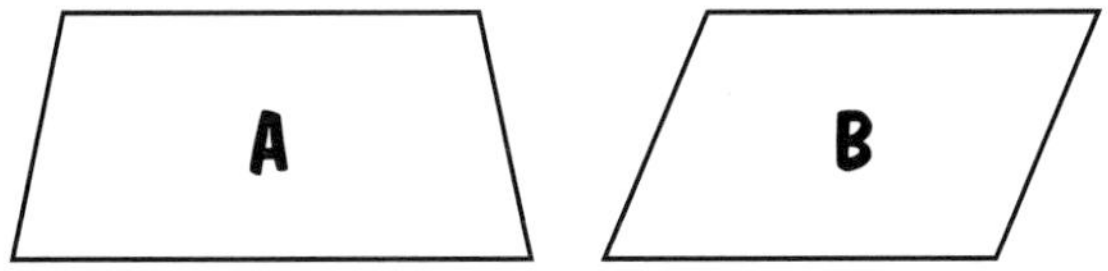
A
B

TEC43052

Mind Builder 4

Draw and label four squares.

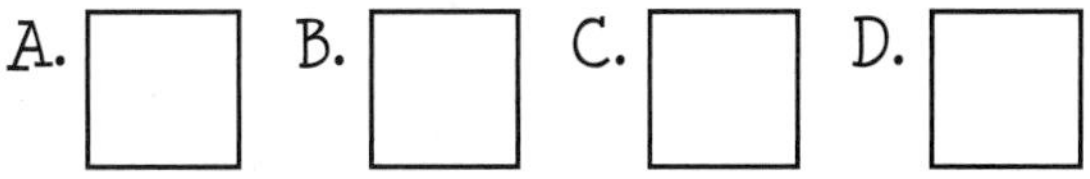
A.
B.
C.
D.

Draw a line or lines to show the following:

A. 1 square = 2 rectangles
B. 1 square = 4 squares
C. 1 square = 2 triangles
D. 1 square = 3 triangles

TEC43052

Mind Builder 5

Copy. Write the value of the underlined digit.

A. 3,$\underline{1}$27
B. $\underline{1}$,640
C. 7,9$\underline{1}$5
D. $\underline{1}$0,382
E. 4,59$\underline{1}$

TEC43052

Mind Builder 6

Write 8 multiplication problems.
Use the grid.
Only use factors that touch.

4	9	5
7		3
6	4	8

$$\begin{array}{r} 4 \\ \times 9 \\ \hline 36 \end{array}$$

TEC43052

Mind Builder 7

Find the change if you pay for each item with a $10 bill.

A. 
$4.59

B.  $6.88

C. 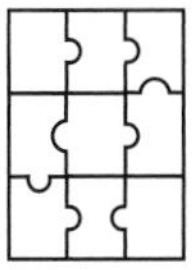 $5.37

D.  $3.24

TEC43052

Mind Builder 8

1,281	6,512
5,457	1,368

A. Add the two even numbers.
B. Add the two odd numbers.
C. Subtract the two even numbers.
D. Subtract the two odd numbers.

TEC43052

How to use Give each student a copy of this page (or one card at a time) to work on during free time. Have the student solve the problems on his own paper.

Math

Mind Builders

Mind Builder 1

Use the digits to write six three-digit numbers for each rule:

A. Show "5" in the tens place.
B. Show "2" in the hundreds place.
C. Show "6" in the ones place.

1 6 5 2

TEC43053

Mind Builder 2

Copy the chart.
List five items found in your desk.
Measure and write.

Items	Inches	Centimeters

TEC43053

Mind Builder 3

Write each total amount.
Use a **$** and **.**.

A. 3 quarters, 5 dimes
B. 1 half-dollar, 2 quarters, 3 nickels
C. 6 quarters, 7 pennies
D. 1 half-dollar, 2 quarters, 5 dimes, 2 nickels

TEC43053

Mind Builder 4

Find the value of △.

□ + 5 = 6 + 2
8 − 1 = 2 + ○
○ − □ = △?

TEC43053

Mind Builder 5

Multiply each number in a □ by a number in a ○. Write 16 facts.

□ 8 ○ 3 □ 9 ○ 7
○ 6 ○ 2 □ 5 □ 4

TEC43053

Mind Builder 6

If you traced the faces of solid figures, which figures would have these shapes?

A. square B. circle
C. triangle D. rectangle

TEC43053

Mind Builder 7

Write 3 or more sentences about the spinner. Use the terms.

most likely
least likely
impossible

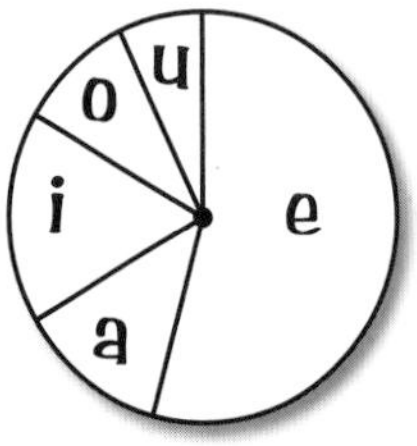

o
u
i
e
a

TEC43053

Mind Builder 8

Picture each time shown on an analog clock. Name the type of angle made by the clock hands. Write *acute, obtuse,* or *right.*

A. 3:00 B. 1:10 C. 5:00
D. 4:15 E. 2:35 F. 10:00
G. 11:20 H. 9:00 I. 12:05

TEC43053

How to use Give each student a copy of this page (or one card at a time) to work on during free time. Have the student solve the problems on his own paper.

Mind Builder 1

Fill in the missing numbers on the number line.

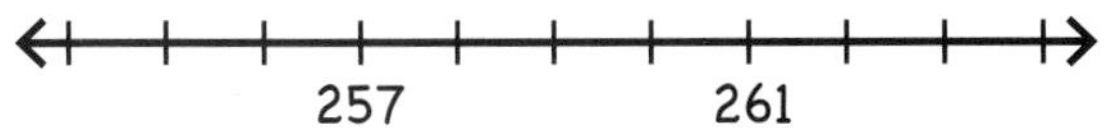
257
261

List eight number sentences that use these numbers and the symbols <, >, or =.

TEC43054

Mind Builder 2

Find each sum.

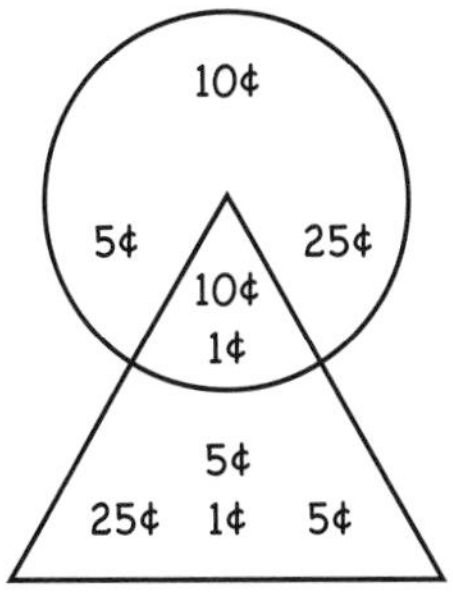
10¢
5¢
25¢
10¢
1¢
5¢
25¢
1¢
5¢

A. in the ○
B. in the △
C. in all
D. in the ○ but not the △
E. in the △ but not the ○

TEC43054

Mind Builder 3

Suppose you put these letters in a bag.

B	A	N	A	N	A

If you were to pull out one letter, name the *most likely* outcome, the *least likely* outcome, and an *impossible* outcome.

TEC43054

Mind Builder 4

List ten different three-digit numbers.
In each number, underline the digit in the tens place.
Next to each number, write the number that is 10 more.

TEC43054

Mind Builder 5

Copy the boxes.

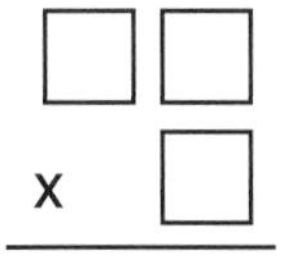
x

Write three different numbers.

6 4 3 8 7 1 9 2

Multiply. Repeat five times.

TEC43054

Mind Builder 6

Show three different ways to find this quotient.

$$18 \div 6 =$$

Use words, pictures, or number sentences.

TEC43054

Mind Builder 7

$\frac{1}{2}$ $\frac{2}{4}$ $\frac{3}{5}$ $\frac{4}{8}$

Which fraction does not belong? Why? Draw pictures to support your answer.

TEC43054

Mind Builder 8

Use cups, pints, and quarts to show six different ways to make one gallon.

TEC43054

How to use Give each student a copy of this page (or one card at a time) to work on during free time. Have the student solve the problems on his own paper.

Math

Mind Builders

Mind Builder 1

If June 30 falls on a Wednesday, what are the dates of each Friday in July?

July				
S	M	Tu	W	Th

TEC43055

Mind Builder 2

Explain how these three figures are alike and different.

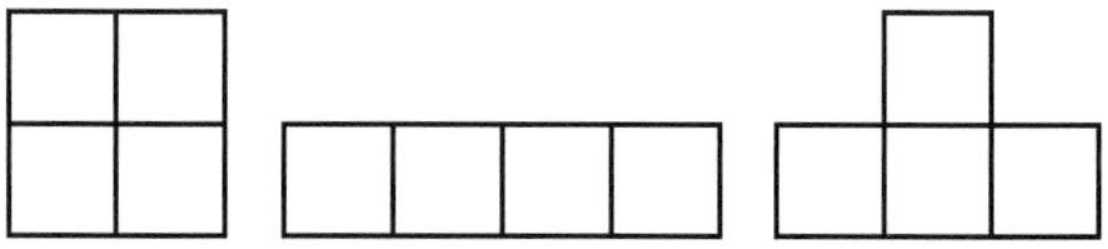

A. B. C.

TEC43055

Mind Builder 3

The day's high temperature is 93°F.
Describe what you might wear and do on a day like this.

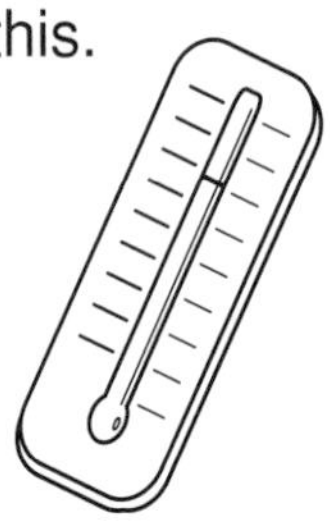

TEC43055

Mind Builder 4

Copy and complete the pattern.
Write the rule.
Then write a different number pattern that follows the same rule.

615, 610, 605, __, __, __

TEC43055

Mind Builder 5

Which shapes will look exactly the same after a flip, turn, and slide?

TEC43055

Mind Builder 6

Write the missing symbols to make each number sentence true.

(2 □ 4) □ 3 = 2

(10 □ 2) □ 4 = 20

TEC43055

Mind Builder 7

Fill in the blanks.
Write each number from the grid one time.

48	2	1
5		9
4	3	6

__ ÷ __ = 8

__ – __ = 8

__ x __ = 8

__ + __ = 8

TEC43055

Mind Builder 8

Using six or fewer coins, show five different ways to make $1.20.

$1.20

TEC43055

How to use Give each student a copy of this page (or one card at a time) to work on during free time. Have the student solve the problems on a separate sheet of paper.

Name ____________________ Date ____________

Number sense

Doggie ID

Read the clues in order.
Write each dog's name on the matching tag.

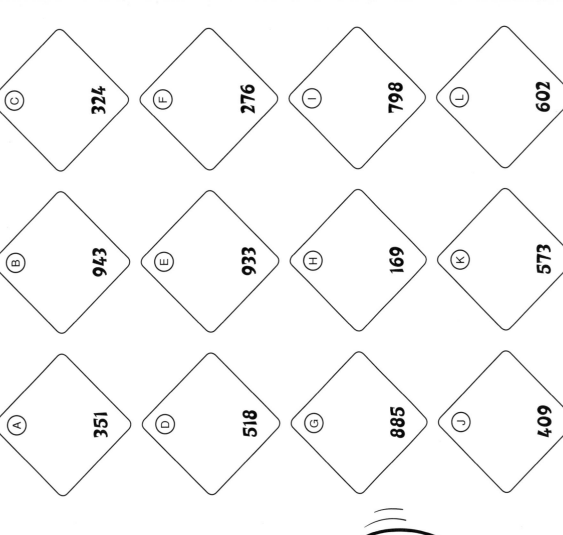

Clues

- **Max** has the tag with the smallest number.
- **Duke** has the tag with the number that is two away from 800.
- **Pepper** has the tag with six ones.
- **Lady** has the tag with three even digits.
- **Bella** has the tag with the same number in the tens and ones places.
- **Rover** has the tag with two tens.
- **Rocky** has the tag with the largest number.
- **Champ** has the tag with three odd digits. The sum of the digits is 9.
- **Lucky** has the tag with four hundreds.
- **Spot** has the tag with the number that is more than the number on **Princess**'s tag but less than the number on **Daisy**'s tag.

Bonus: Write three more clues that describe the number on Max's tag.

(A) 351	(B) 943	(C) 324
(D) 518	(E) 933	(F) 276
(G) 885	(H) 169	(I) 798
(J) 409	(K) 573	(L) 602

Name ______________________ Date ______________

Rounding to the nearest hundred

Rootin'-Tootin' Roundup!

Round each number to the nearest hundred.
Use the number line.

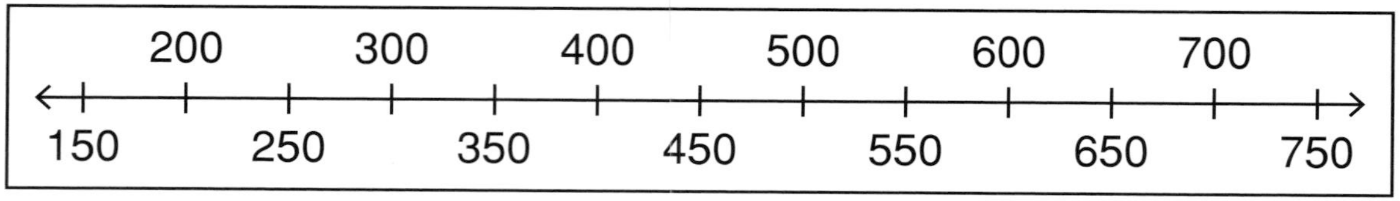
200 300 400 500 600 700
150 250 350 450 550 650 750

Circle each number that is rounded up!

A. 361 ________ B. 629 ________

C. 507 ________ D. 284 ________

E. 445 ________ F. 572 ________

G. 193 ________ H. 738 ________

I. 338 ________ J. 209 ________

K. 494 ________ L. 657 ________

M. 370 ________ N. 264 ________

O. 535 ________ P. 176 ________

Q. 610 ________ R. 749 ________

Bonus Box: Round each number to the nearest hundred. 112 _____ 768 _____
Tell how you decided to round up or round down for each number.

Name ____________________ Date ____________

Addition strategies: basic facts

School of Fish

Add.
Color by the code.

Color Code
doubles = yellow
near doubles = pink
sum of 10 = orange

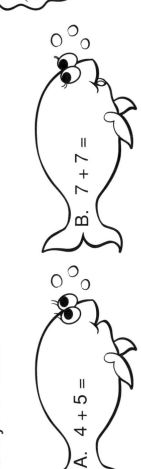

A. 4 + 5 =
B. 7 + 7 =
C. 4 + 6 =
D. 7 + 3 =
E. 9 + 9 =
F. 6 + 6 =
G. 4 + 4 =
H. 8 + 7 =
I. 1 + 9 =
J. 9 + 8 =
K. 2 + 8 =
L. 8 + 8 =
M. 5 + 6 =
N. 9 + 1 =
O. 7 + 6 =

Bonus Box: Add. 7 + 3 + 8 = ☐. Describe the strategy you used.

Name ______________________________ Date ____________________

Determining reasonable estimates

Hot on the Trail

Color the best estimate for each sum. Follow the trail to find out which rabbit left the tracks.

A. 43 + 51 =	60	70	80	90
B. 18 + 27 =	30	40	50	60
C. 63 + 29 =	60	70	80	90
D. 26 + 22 =	30	40	50	60
E. 34 + 33 =	50	60	70	80
F. 81 + 12 =	70	80	90	100
G. 12 + 11 =	10	20	30	40
H. 39 + 24 =	60	70	80	90
I. 57 + 14 =	60	70	80	90
J. 44 + 37 =	60	70	80	90
K. 68 + 31 =	70	80	90	100
L. 13 + 28 =	20	30	40	50

Which rabbit did it?
Circle the rabbit.

Bonus Box: Write to explain how you found the estimate for problem A.

Name ____________________ Date ____________

Anchors Aweigh!

Multiply.
Color each product.

A. 7 x 8 = ____ B. 6 x 8 = ____ C. 8 x 8 = ____

D. 5 x 2 = ____ E. 5 x 5 = ____ F. 3 x 9 = ____

G. 3 x 8 = ____ H. 2 x 7 = ____ I. 4 x 4 = ____

J. 6 x 7 = ____ K. 7 x 7 = ____ L. 9 x 5 = ____

M. 9 x 9 = ____ N. 3 x 4 = ____ O. 3 x 7 = ____

P. 3 x 3 = ____ Q. 7 x 5 = ____ R. 6 x 9 = ____

S. 4 x 7 = ____ T. 5 x 8 = ____ U. 9 x 8 = ____

V. 8 x 4 = ____ W. 3 x 6 = ____ X. 6 x 6 = ____

1	30	7	9	60	11	29
88	23	52	10	3	69	8
13	25	40	45	42	16	50
75	4	84	48	17	55	62
24	63	44	18	74	38	36
27	22	5	81	26	2	28
32	72	34	12	20	14	54
19	35	56	21	49	64	6

Name ______________________________ Date ______________

Fractions: parts of a whole

Follow the Signs

Write the fraction for the shaded parts of each sign.

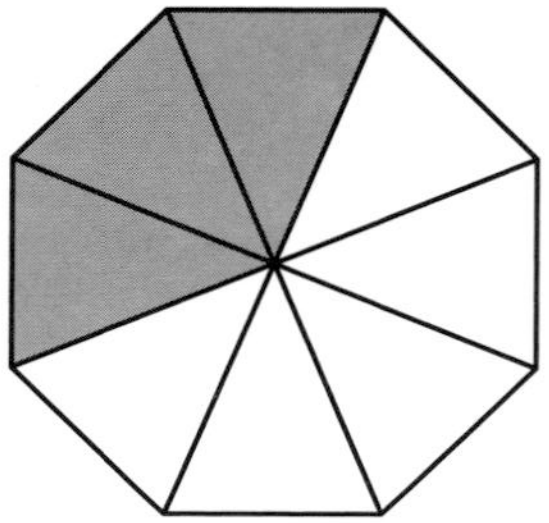

A. ______

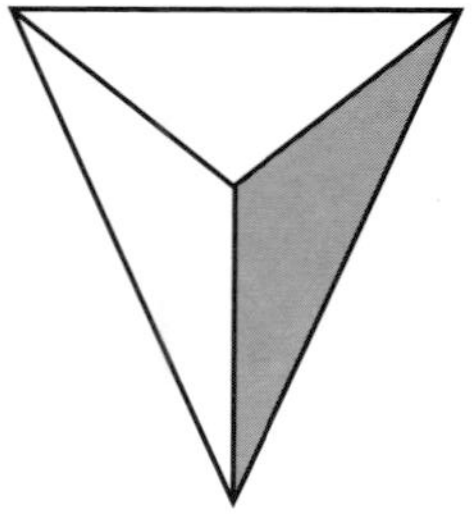

B. ______

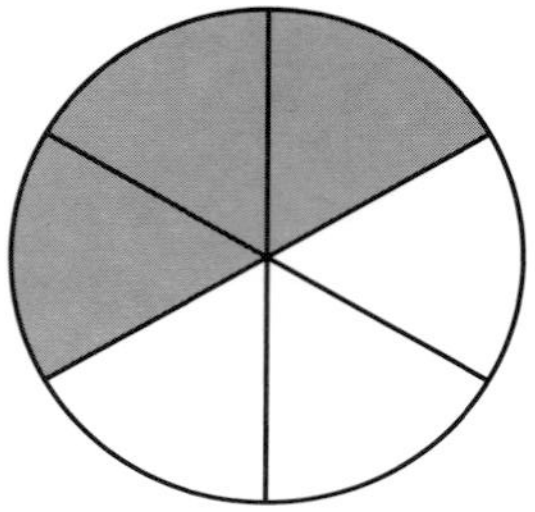

C. ______

D. ______

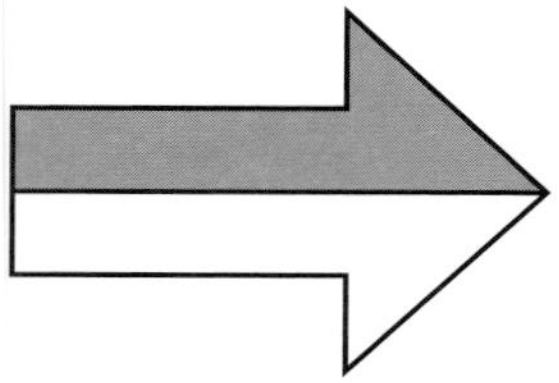

E. ______

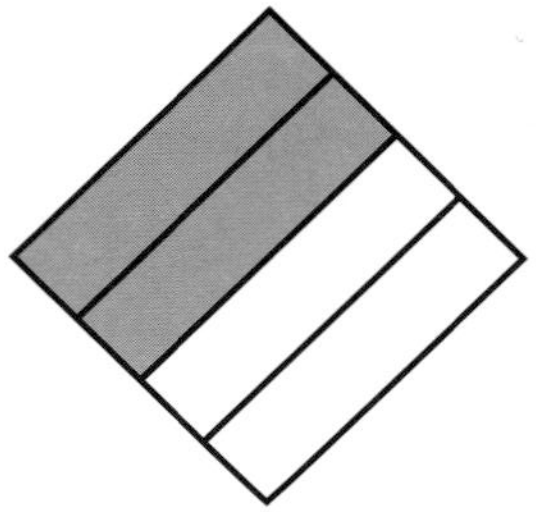

F. ______

Bonus: For each sign, write the fraction for the unshaded part.

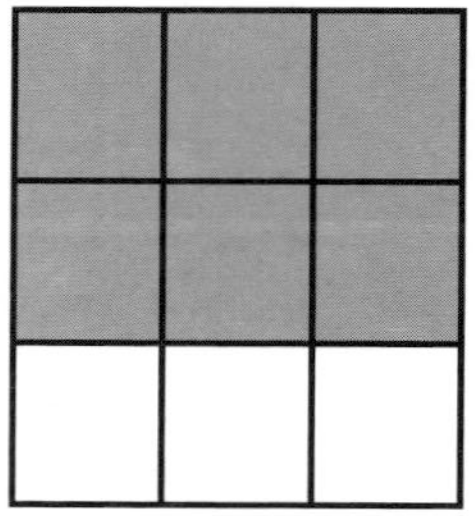

G. ______

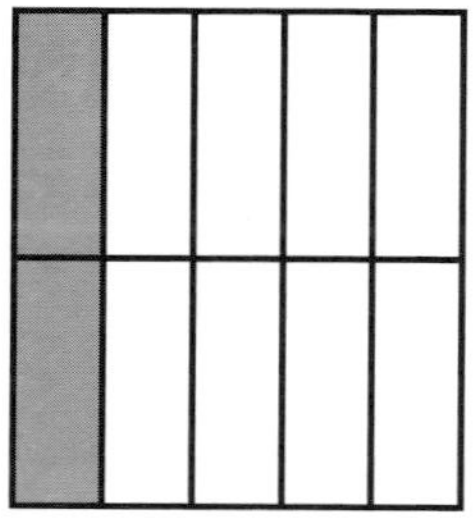

H. ______

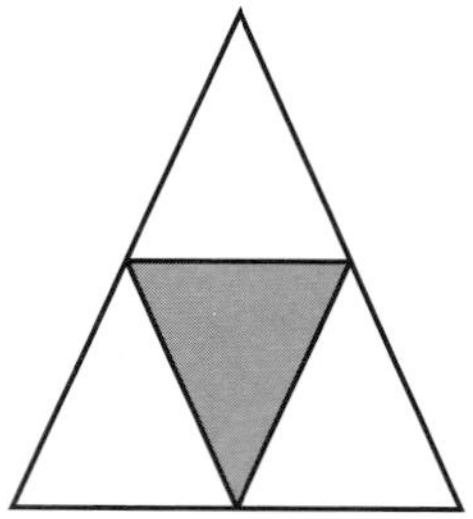

I. ______

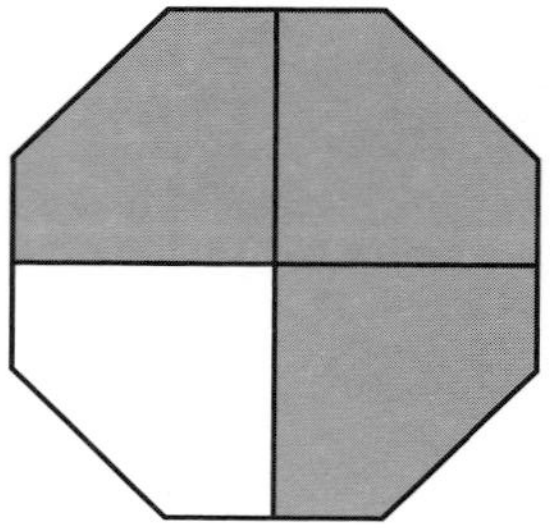

J. ______

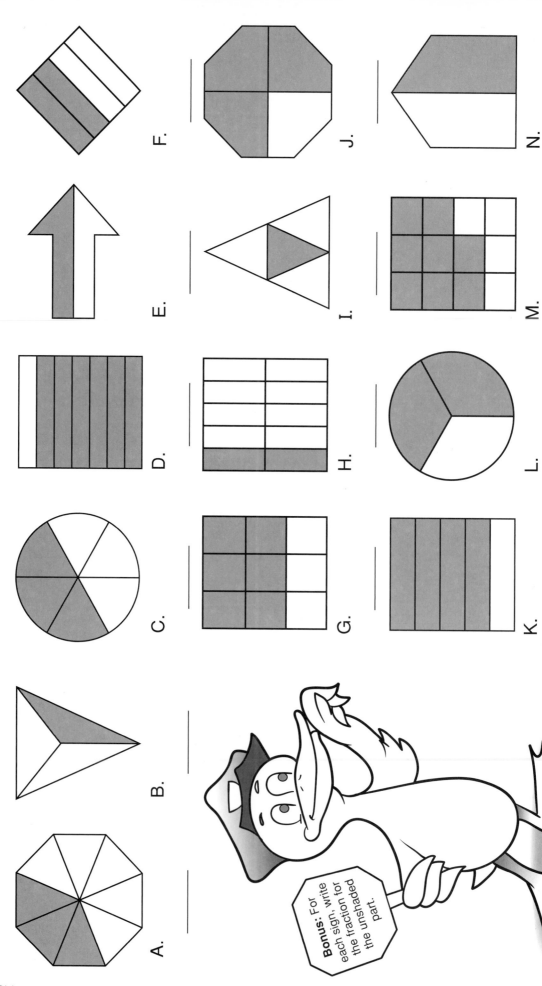

K. ______

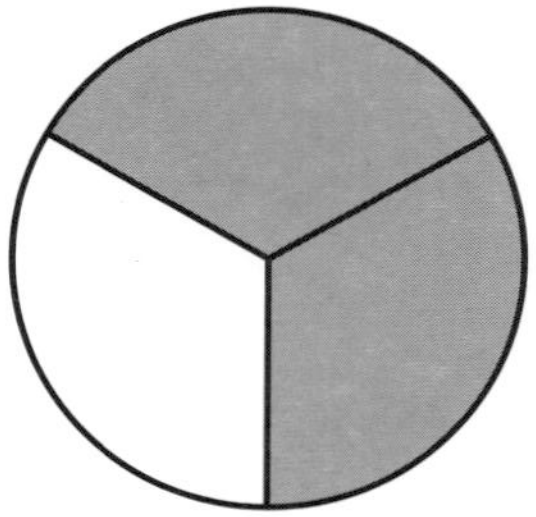

L. ______

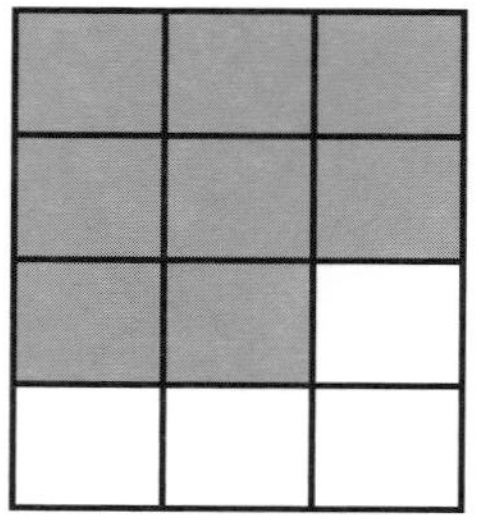

M. ______

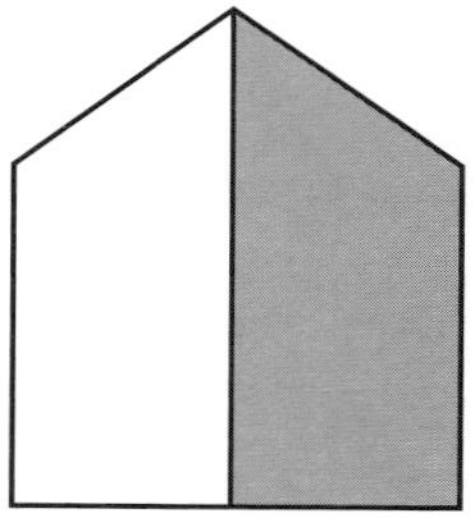

N. ______

Name ____________________ Date ____________

Pizza by the Slice

Add or subtract.
Lightly color the slice with the correct answer.

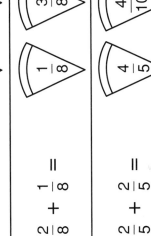

A. $\frac{1}{4} + \frac{2}{4} =$ $\frac{3}{8}$ $\frac{3}{4}$	B. $\frac{6}{8} - \frac{3}{8} =$ $\frac{3}{8}$ $\frac{3}{0}$
C. $\frac{5}{7} - \frac{1}{7} =$ $\frac{4}{7}$ $\frac{3}{7}$	D. $\frac{2}{10} + \frac{4}{10} =$ $\frac{6}{10}$ $\frac{5}{10}$
E. $\frac{2}{3} - \frac{1}{3} =$ $\frac{1}{3}$ $\frac{3}{3}$	F. $\frac{3}{7} + \frac{3}{7} =$ $\frac{6}{14}$ $\frac{6}{7}$
G. $\frac{2}{6} + \frac{3}{6} =$ $\frac{5}{12}$ $\frac{5}{6}$	H. $\frac{4}{5} - \frac{2}{5} =$ $\frac{2}{5}$ $\frac{3}{5}$
I. $\frac{2}{8} + \frac{1}{8} =$ $\frac{1}{8}$ $\frac{3}{8}$	J. $\frac{4}{6} - \frac{3}{6} =$ $\frac{2}{6}$ $\frac{1}{6}$
K. $\frac{2}{5} + \frac{2}{5} =$ $\frac{4}{5}$ $\frac{4}{10}$	L. $\frac{1}{3} + \frac{1}{3} =$ $\frac{2}{6}$ $\frac{2}{3}$
M. $\frac{3}{4} - \frac{2}{4} =$ $\frac{1}{4}$ $\frac{1}{8}$	N. $\frac{7}{10} - \frac{4}{10} =$ $\frac{3}{10}$ $\frac{3}{7}$

Bonus: Write three fractions about the pizza above. Then use two of the fractions in a story problem. Include the answer.

Name ______________________ Date ______________

Money, using a table

At the Coffee Shop

Write each amount.
Answer each question.

	Small	Medium	Large
Coffee	50¢	65¢	80¢
Tea	55¢	70¢	85¢
Cocoa	60¢	75¢	90¢

A. Lara has ________¢.

Can Lara buy a small cocoa? ________

B. Lou has ________¢.

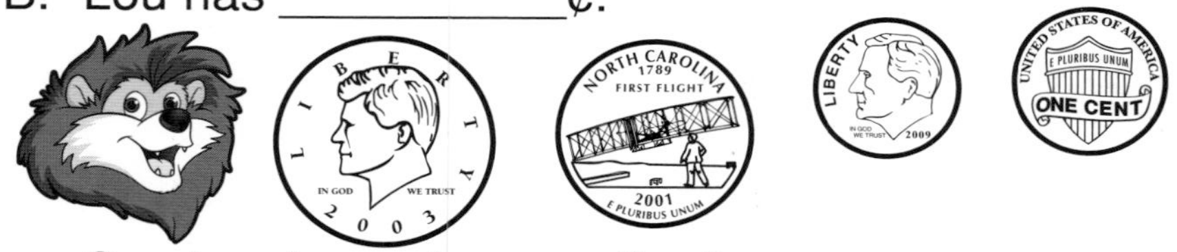

Can Lou buy a large coffee? ________

C. Luke has ________¢.

Can Luke buy a medium coffee? ________

D. Louisa has ________¢.

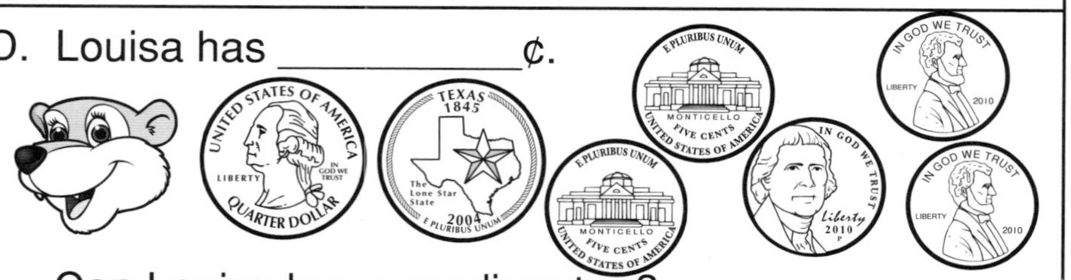

Can Louisa buy a medium tea? ________

E. Lexie has ________¢.

Can Lexie buy a large tea? ________

F. Leo has ________¢.

Can Leo buy a medium cocoa? ________

Name ______________________________ Date ____________________

Reading a calendar

On the Menu

Read.

September Lunch Menu

Lunches are served with a choice of one fruit, one vegetable, and milk.

Mon.	Tues.	Wed.	Thurs.	Fri.
		1 pizza	2 taco	3 grilled cheese
6 Labor Day No school!	7 hot dog	8 chicken nuggets	9 fish sticks	10 pizza
13 **breakfast for lunch:** pancakes	14 pizza	15 hot dog	16 taco	17 fish sticks
20 hamburger	21 chicken nuggets	22 fish sticks	23 pizza	24 grilled cheese
27 **breakfast for lunch:** pancakes	28 hot dog	29 taco	30 chicken nuggets	

Use the lunch menu to answer the questions.

1. On which date is grilled cheese first served? ____________________

   How many school lunches are there before grilled cheese is served again? ____

2. What is for lunch on September 9? ____________________

   What is on the menu one week earlier? ____________________

3. When are pancakes first served for lunch? ____________________

   What is on the menu two school days later? ____________________

4. Which lunch is served most often? ____________________

   How many lunches are there between the first time this food is served and the last time it is served? __________

Bonus Box: Why are Sunday and Saturday not on the menu? Explain.

Name ______________________ Date ______________

Linear measurement

Perfect Putting

Measure to the nearest inch.
Write the total length of each path.

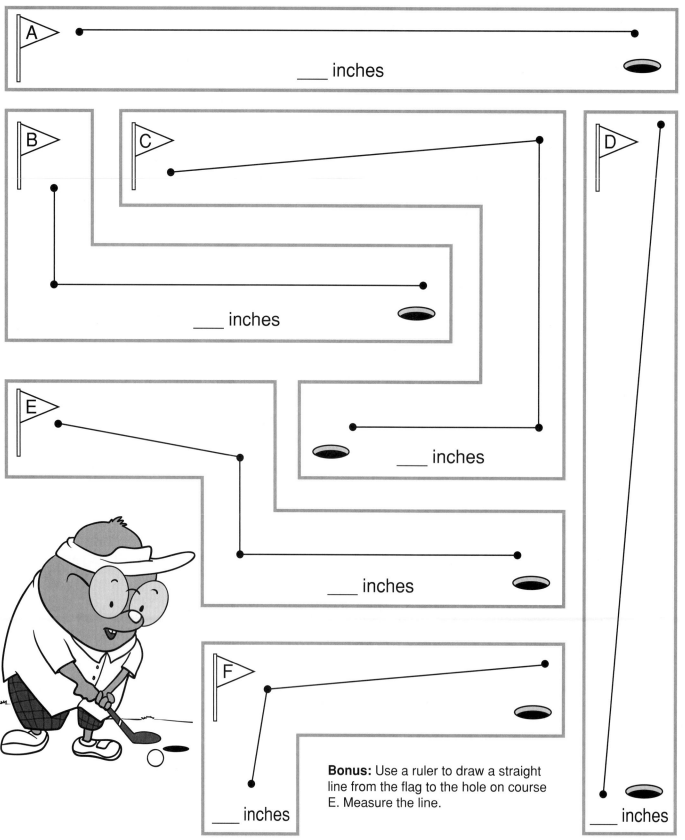

A

___ inches

B

___ inches

C

___ inches

D

___ inches

E

___ inches

F

___ inches

Bonus: Use a ruler to draw a straight line from the flag to the hole on course E. Measure the line.

More or Less?

Directions:

1. Take the cards out of the envelope.
2. Sort the cards by weight.
3. Complete the recording sheet.

Less Than One Pound
More Than One Pound

 penny TEC43054	 stamp TEC43054	 dog TEC43054
 soap TEC43054	 chip TEC43054	 bike TEC43054
 die TEC43054	 hammer TEC43054	 chair TEC43054
 macaroni TEC43054	 computer TEC43054	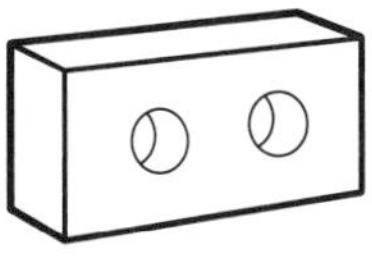 brick TEC43054

How to use Copy the mat and cards on construction paper and make student copies of page 148. Cut apart the mat and cards. Then glue the mat to a 6" x 9" (or larger) envelope and place the cards inside. Put the envelope and copies of page 148 at a center.

Name________________________ Date ____________

Comparing weights

More or Less?

Write the word for each picture below its matching weight.

Less Than One Pound	More Than One Pound
______	______
______	______
______	______
______	______
______	______
______	______
______	______
______	______

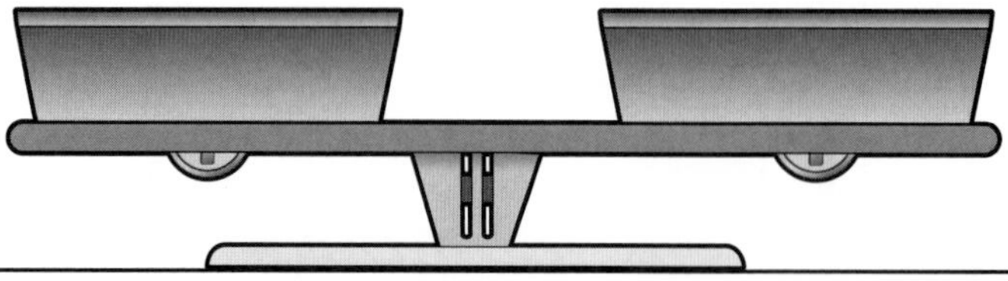

Bonus: Write your own examples on the four unused lines.

Note to the teacher: Use with the center mat and cards on page 147.

Name ______________________ Date ______________

Problem solving

Underground Gamers

Solve.
Label each answer.

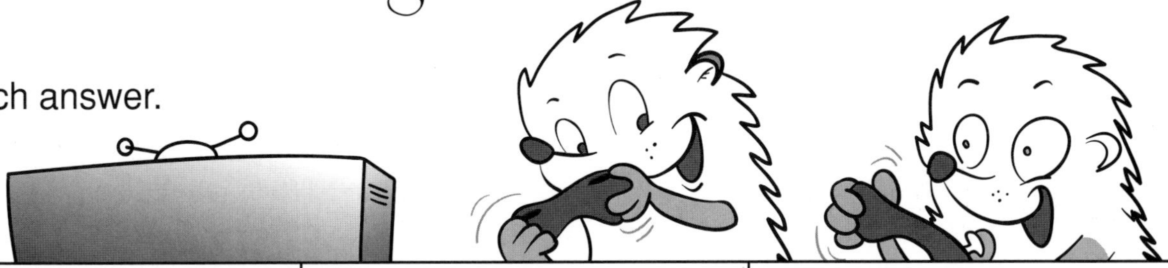

A. Grayson scores 75 points the first time he plays *Worm Warriors*. The next time he plays, he scores 125 points. By how many points does his score improve?

B. Greta likes to play *Soil Soldiers*. Each time she digs up a rock, she earns 10 extra points. If she digs up 10 rocks in one game, how many extra points does she earn?

C. Grayson and Greta play *Shadow Chasers*. Grayson scores 92 points. Greta scores 108 points. How many points do they score altogether?

D. Each time Greta plays *Burrow Guards*, she gets a lower score. Her first score is 808 points and her second score is 558 points. What is the difference between the two scores?

E. Each time Grayson escapes the gardener in *Garden Games*, he earns 50 extra points. In his last game, he escapes the gardener 7 times. How many extra points does he earn?

F. Greta teaches Grayson how to play *Groundhog Hero*. Her high score is 236. His high score is 214. How many points do they score in all?

G. Grayson scores 2,300 points in *Herbivore Helper*. He scores 1,850 points playing *Shadow Chasers*. How many more points does he score in *Herbivore Helper*?

H. Greta plays *Worm Warriors* for 4 hours. She scores 150 points each hour. How many points does she score playing *Worm Warriors*?

I. Grayson challenges Greta to a game of *Soil Soldiers*. Grayson scores 364 points. Greta scores 22 more points than Grayson. How many total points do they score?

Bonus: Look at the problems and the answers. Describe any patterns you see. (Hint: Look across rows and down columns.)

Name ______________________ Date ______________

Unit costs

"Sew" Many Choices

Solve each problem.
Write the unit cost on the matching tag.

A. Sadie buys 3 yards of starred fabric. She pays $6.00. What is the cost for 1 yard?	B. Sadie buys 6 yards of striped fabric. She pays $18.00. What is the cost for 1 yard?
C. Sadie spends $8.00 on 2 yards of moon fabric. What is the cost for 1 yard?	D. The total is $24.00 for 4 yards of rainbow fabric. What is the cost for 1 yard?
E. The total is $15.00 for 3 yards of heart fabric. What is the cost for 1 yard?	F. Sadie spends $12.00 on 4 yards of spaceship fabric. What is the cost for 1 yard?
G. Sadie buys 5 yards of baseball fabric for $20.00. What is the cost for 1 yard?	H. The total is $4.00 for 2 yards of ice cream fabric. What is the cost for 1 yard?

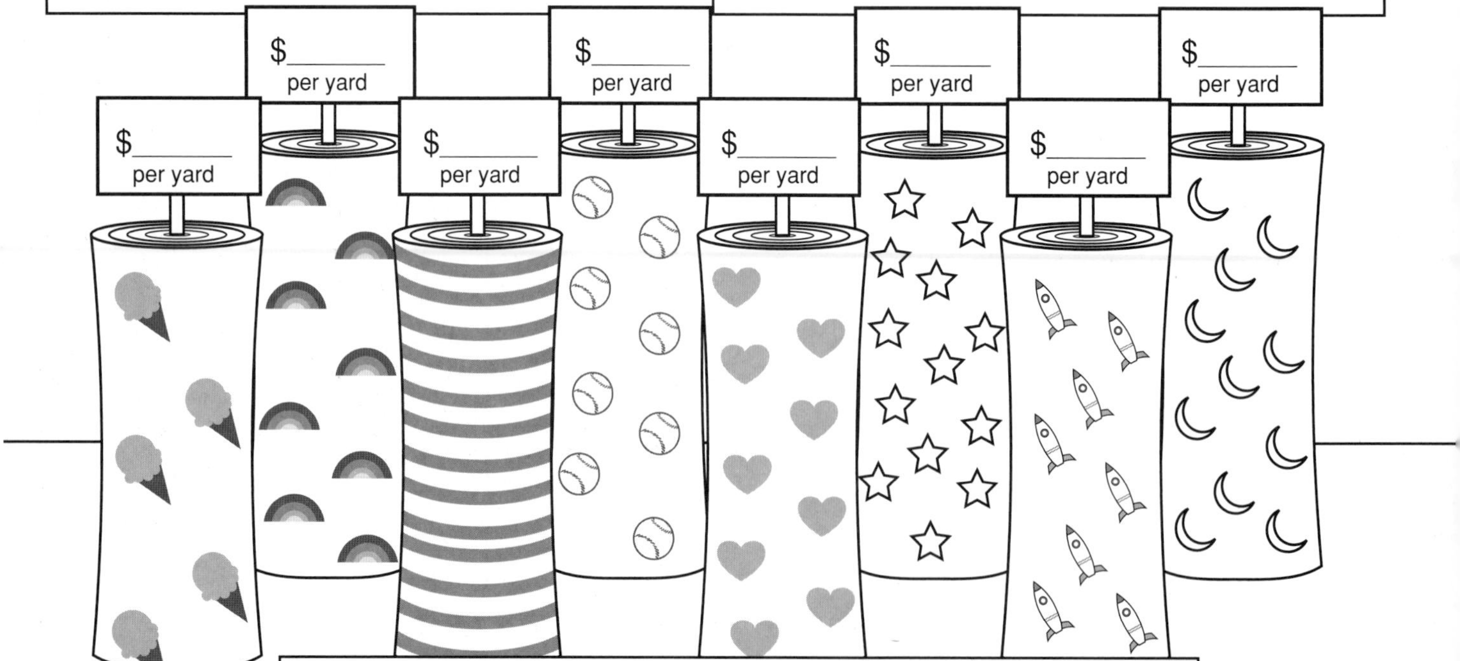
$______ per yard
$______ per yard
$______ per yard
$______ per yard
$______ per yard
$______ per yard
$______ per yard
$______ per yard

Bonus: Which costs more: 3 yards of striped fabric or 2 yards of heart fabric?

SCIENCE

Simply Science

In Other Words
Weather

Help students make connections to weather-related vocabulary. To start, direct each student to fold a sheet of paper in half, as shown, and then fold it in half two more times. Guide him to unfold the paper back to the first fold and then cut through the top layer of paper to make four flaps. Instruct the student to copy onto each flap the sentence starter shown and insert a different weather-related term at the beginning of each sentence. The child chooses an item with similar characteristics for the second blank in each sentence and then finishes each sentence. To complete the activity, each student illustrates the weather word and the related item on the space under the flap.

Chelsea Forbus LaVere, Chesapeake, VA

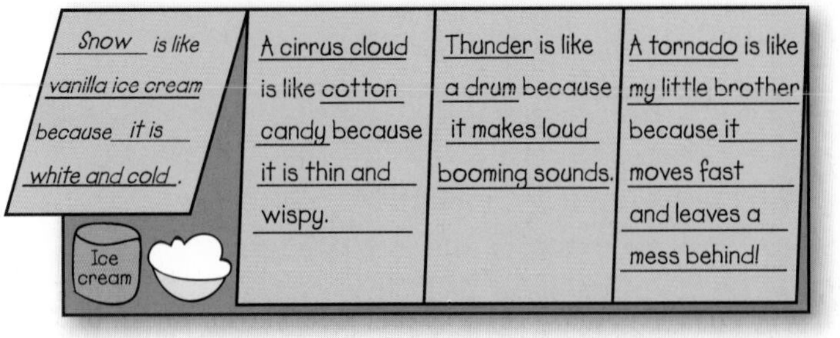
Snow is like vanilla ice cream because it is white and cold.
A cirrus cloud is like cotton candy because it is thin and wispy.
Thunder is like a drum because it makes loud booming sounds.
A tornado is like my little brother because it moves fast and leaves a mess behind!
Ice cream

______ is like ______ because ______.

Scientific Inquiry
Name Kassidy
1
2
3
4

A Bright Idea
Scientific inquiry

To shed some light on the steps involved in a scientific investigation, direct each child to cut apart the booklet pages from a copy of page 158. Next, have the student hole-punch each circle and stack the pages in order. Then help the child secure the pages together with a metal ring. Instruct the student to keep her booklet with her science journal and to refer to it as she conducts classroom investigations.

Simply Science

Playing Around With Science
Forces and motion

Make your school's playground the setting for this partner activity. In advance, program a supply of index cards each with the name of a different piece of playground equipment. On the playground, give each student duo a card. Direct the pair to sketch the matching piece of equipment on the card and then mark with an arrow the direction the equipment moves. Take the class back inside, draw a chart as shown, and have each pair tape its card in the matching column. Discuss the results.

Stephanie Brachtenbach, Harmony Elementary, Overland Park, KS

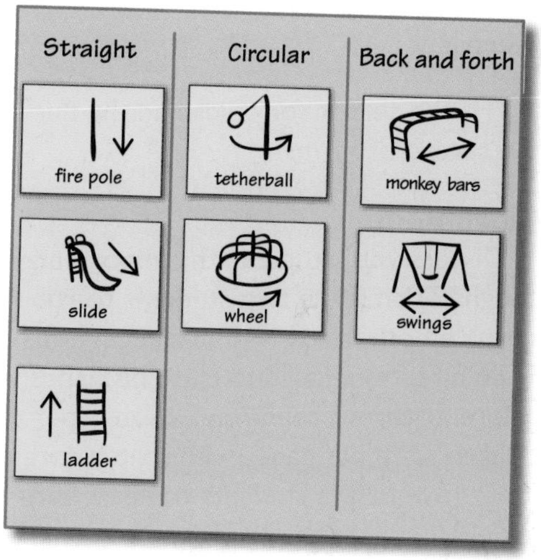

Straight
Circular
Back and forth
fire pole
tetherball
monkey bars
slide
wheel
swings
ladder

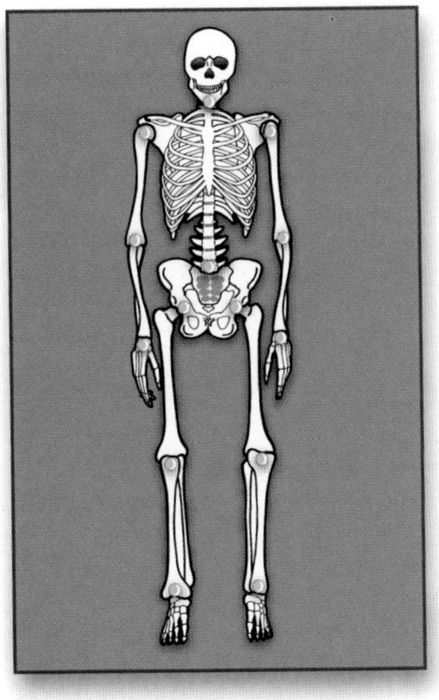

Assembly Required!
Human skeleton

Challenge students to learn more about their bodies and how they move with this hands-on activity. Give each student duo or small group a copy of the bone patterns on page 159 and 14 brads. Have students cut apart the bones and assemble the skeleton using the brads. Use the completed projects to discuss the different types of joints; then have students locate the joints on their paper skeletons.

Jennifer Cooper, Park Hills Elementary, Hanover, PA

Now You See Me, Now You Don't
Animal camouflage

For this simple demonstration, have each student draw a picture of an animal and cut it out. While your class has their eyes closed, choose one child to hide his animal on a surface in the classroom. Then have the students open their eyes and try to spot the camouflaged animal. Repeat until each child has had a chance to play.

Sima Silverstein, Bais Rivka Elementary, Brooklyn, NY

Simply Science

Healthy Habits
Germs

'Tis the season for colds and the flu—use these quick activities to remind students to control the spread of germs!

Clean Routine

Discuss with students the importance of hand washing, especially after a child sneezes or coughs. Then invite two students to rub a thin layer of shortening (body oils) on their hands and sprinkle both hands with nutmeg (germs). Have both students show their hands to the class. Then direct one child to rinse his hands with water but no soap before drying his hands on a clean paper towel. Instruct the other child to wash her hands with soap before drying them on a clean paper towel. Have students compare their hands and their paper towels; then lead the class to understand that using soap makes hand washing more effective in killing germs.

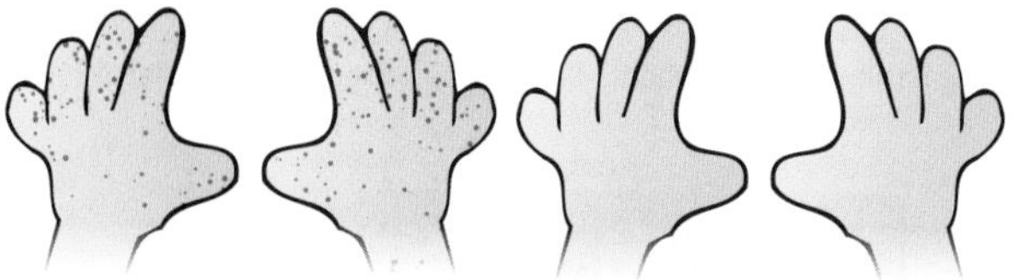

Watch Your Sneeze, Please!

Invite a child to hold a sheet of paper in front of his face. Fake a sneeze and, as you do, use a plant mister to spray water onto the paper. Have the child show his classmates the paper; then discuss with students how this spread of germs could be avoided. Discuss methods such as using tissues or sneezing into one's elbow.

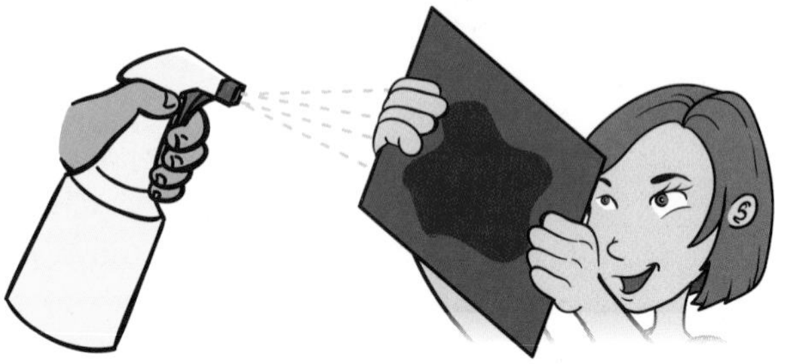

Rockin' Out
Properties of rocks

Your junior geologists are sure to remember ways to identify and categorize rocks when they sing this catchy tune!

Bridgett Smith, Bray Elementary, Cedar Hill, TX

Rock Properties Song
(sung to the tune of "Row, Row, Row Your Boat")

Many different rocks
Have different properties.
Hardness, *(softly knock forehead with fist)*
Texture, *(rub fingers together)*
Color, *(make a rainbow arch with index finger)*
Luster *(shield eyes with hand)*
Are some properties.

Simply Science

Ripple Effects
Exploring sound waves

To demonstrate the rippling movement of sound waves, engage students in one or more of the following activities:

- **S-T-R-E-T-C-H:** Have two students hold the ends of an outstretched Slinky toy. Ask one student to push her end up and down to send a simulated sound wave to the other end.
- **Domino Dance:** Set up a row of dominoes close together. Have a student push over the first domino. Direct students to watch the line of dominoes to see how a sound wave travels.
- **Waves of Water:** Fill a 9" x 13" pan with 1½ inches of water. Place a small paper slip on the surface of the water at one end of the pan. At the other end, have a student drop a penny into the water. Instruct students to observe the ripples produced by the penny and how they affect the paper.

Loads of Understanding
Using a lever

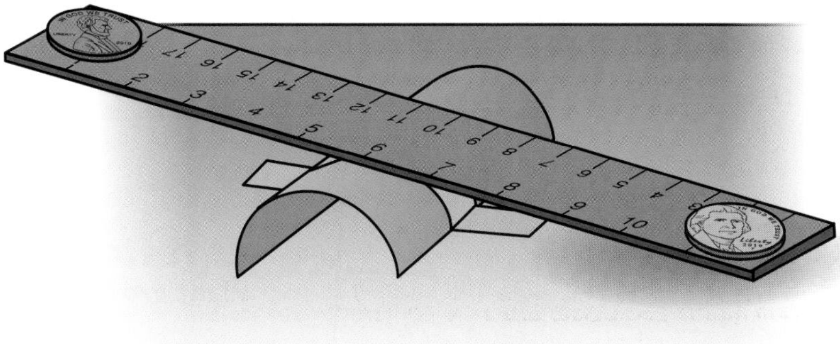

Balance hands-on practice with simple-machine vocabulary during this partner activity. To prepare, cut a supply of cardboard tubes in half lengthwise, making enough so each duo has one half. To start the activity, direct each pair to lay the tube's cut edges on a work surface and secure it with a piece of masking tape. Tell students that they have created the fulcrum of the lever. Next, guide each duo to balance a ruler (lever) atop the fulcrum. Explain that because there is equal force at each end of the lever, it balances when the middle of the lever rests on the fulcrum. Then have each pair place a nickel on one end of the lever and a penny on the other. Lead students to conclude that the load is now unequal because the heavier nickel creates greater force. Challenge students to rebalance the load without moving the coins. Students will discover that by repositioning the lever so the heavier load is closer to the fulcrum, they can balance the load.

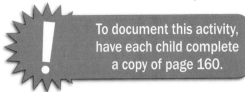

! To document this activity, have each child complete a copy of page 160.

Simply Science

Out of This World
Objects in the sky

The Sun
a star
enormous
not a planet

With these stellar activities, students' understanding really shines!

To make a mobile, instruct a child to label a paper plate as shown and decorate it to look like the sun. Next, have the student write on an index card a fact about the sun, using the letter s from the word *sun*. Direct him to trace the s with a marker; then have the child punch a hole in the plate and one in the card. Guide him to feed a length of yarn through each hole and tie off the ends. Have the student repeat the steps with different facts for the other two letters in the word *sun*.

To demonstrate how objects in the sky orbit, provide each student with three sugar cookies: one large (sun), one medium (Earth), and one small (moon). Instruct the child to use yellow icing to cover the sun, blue and green icing to cover Earth, and white icing to cover the moon. Have the student place the cookies on a sheet of black paper, showing their positions relative to each other. Then lead students to move Earth around the sun and move the moon around Earth.

Caryn Fuiten, Garfield Montessori Magnet School, Decatur, IL

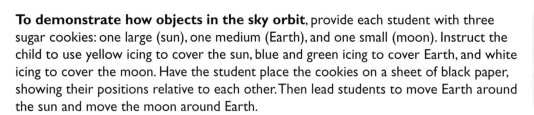

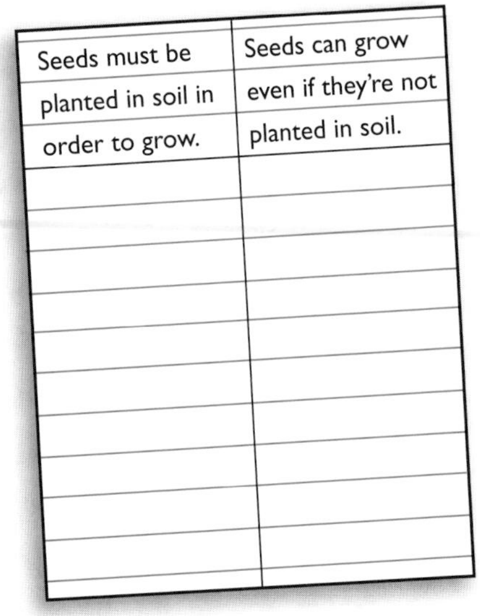
Seeds must be planted in soil in order to grow.
Seeds can grow even if they're not planted in soil.

Is It Really Needed?
Plant growth

Do seeds need soil to grow? Challenge students to find the answer with this hands-on investigation. First, write the two statements shown on a sheet of chart paper and have each student write her name under the statement she agrees with. Next, soak a pine cone or a corn cob in water, place it in a pan, and sprinkle it with grass seeds. Put the pan near a window and use a water mister to keep the seeds moist. When the seeds sprout, guide students to refer to the statements and, if needed, have them reevaluate their ideas. If desired, challenge students to name other soil-free settings where seeds might grow and have them test the settings to find out.

Marie E. Cecchini, West Dundee, IL

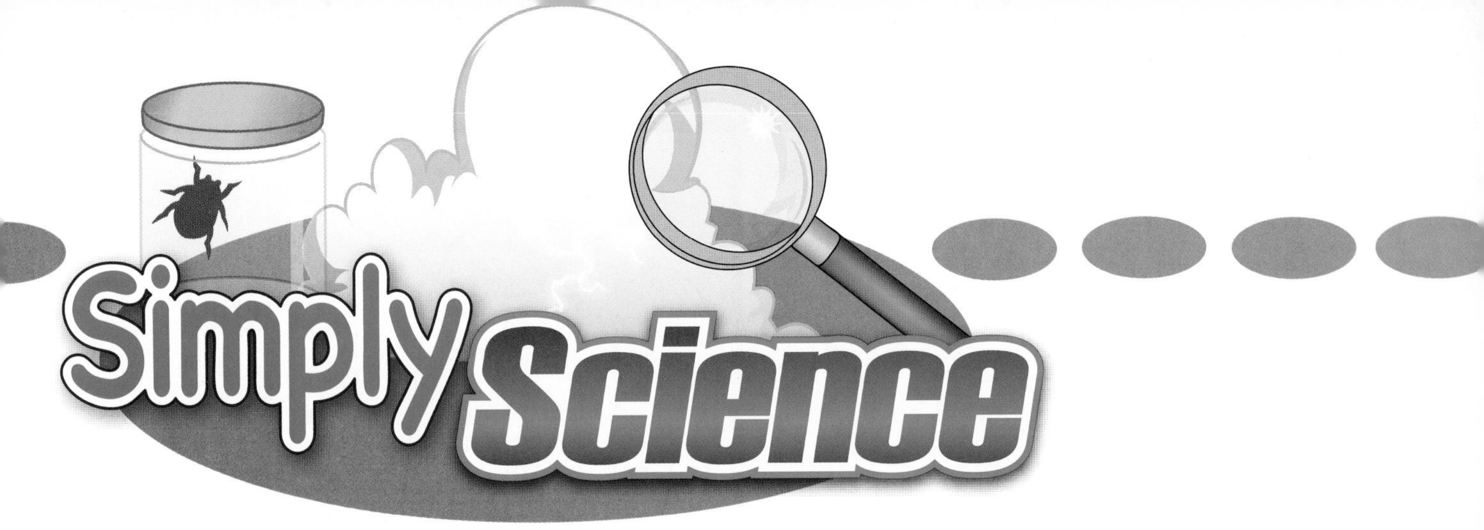

Simply Science

Cookie Connections

Types of rocks

Here are a few sweet activities to help your students identify rocks! As a basic review, give each group a sandwich cookie, a chocolate chip cookie, or a brownie. Direct each group to determine which rock its treat represents and why. Provide time for each group to share its ideas. Then, for independent practice with each type of rock, have students complete the following activities.

For sedimentary rocks, remind students that a sandwich cookie represents a sedimentary rock because it is made up of layers. Give each child a sandwich cookie and challenge him to separate the "minerals" found in each layer and explain his results.

For metamorphic rocks, remind students that the minerals that make up a metamorphic rock "morph" together to create a new mineral, similar to when a chocolate chip cookie is made. Then tell students the ingredients used to make chocolate chip cookies. Give each child a cookie and challenge her to separate all the ingredients (minerals) from the cookie into piles and explain her results.

For igneous rocks, remind students that these rocks are formed when hot magma cools and hardens, similar to how a brownie is made. Also remind students that igneous rocks can be intrusive or extrusive. Give each child a brownie and challenge him to draw and label a diagram of the brownie as if it were an igneous rock, indicating areas of intrusive or extrusive "rocks."

Kelli Higgins, P. L. Bolin Elementary, East Peoria, IL

What Sharp Teeth You Have

Animal adaptations

This catchy song serves as a simple reminder of carnivorous dinosaurs' traits.

Carnivore Song

(sung to the tune of "Row, Row, Row Your Boat")

Sharp, sharp are my teeth. I'm a carnivore.
Meat, meat is all I eat; I need nothing more.
I am a dinosaur and a carnivore.
I chase my food on my two feet: I don't use all four.

Veronica Botts, Hammond Elementary, Odessa, FL

Science Booklet

Use with "A Bright Idea" on page 152.

Scientific Inquiry

Name ____________________

Ask questions.
?

1

Plan an investigation.

2

Use tools to gather data.

3

Think. Then explain your data.

4

Tell others what you found and what you think about it.

5

Skeleton Patterns

Use with "Assembly Required!" on page 153.

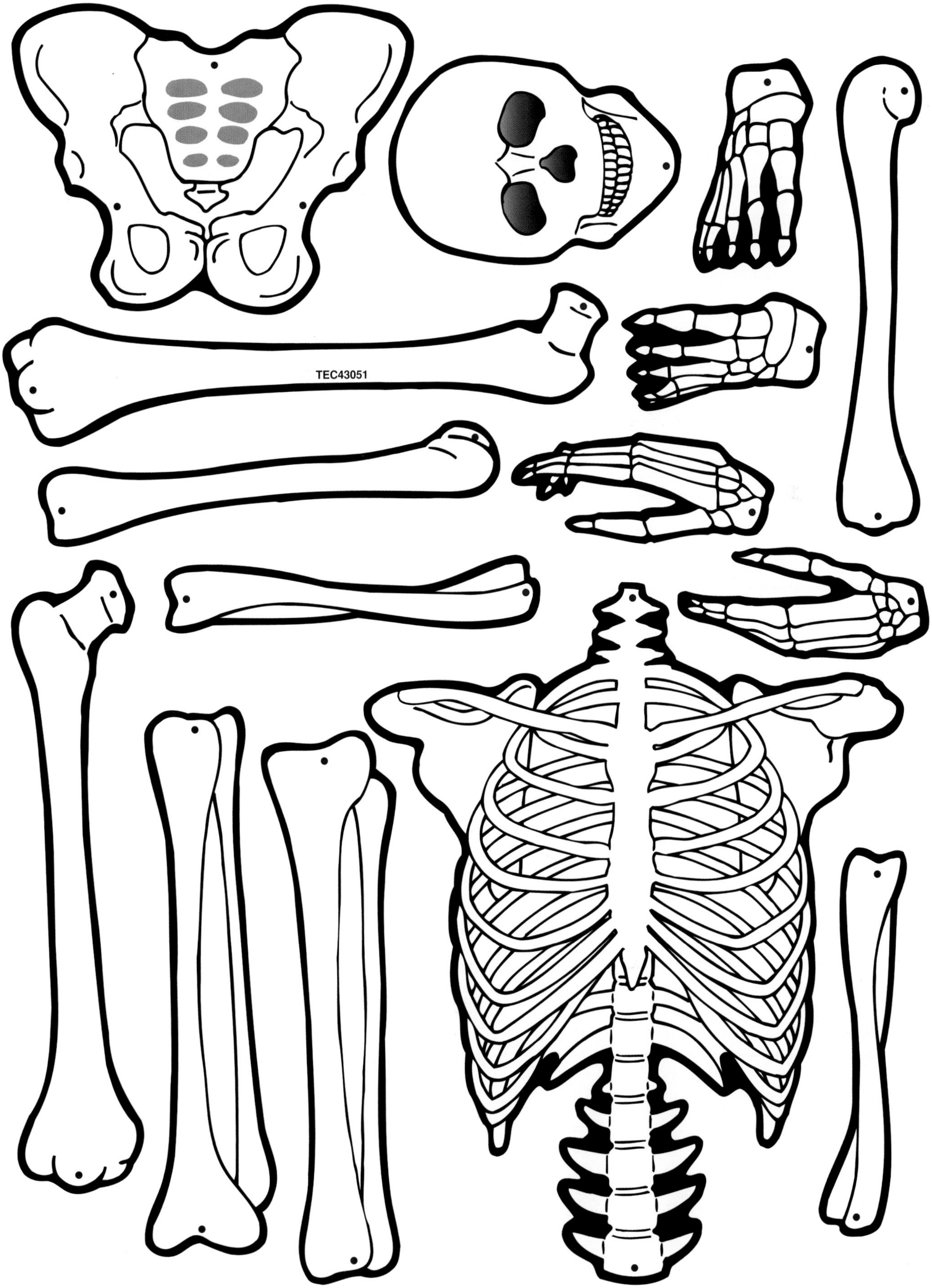
TEC43051

Name ______________________ Date ______________

Simple machines: lever

Loads of Fun!

Before

Draw and write to explain how you set up the activity.

Words to Know

balance fulcrum lever

During

Draw and write to explain what you did.

1	2	3

After

Describe what you learned about using a lever.

Note to the teacher: Use with "Loads of Understanding" on page 155.

Patterns in the Sky

Name ______________________________

Directions to make a booklet:

1. Color the booklet pages.
2. Cut apart the booklet pages.
3. Stack the pages in order.
4. Staple the pages together.

Patterns in the Sky
Name
2
3
4

When you look at the sky, what do you notice about how the sun, stars, and moon move? Do you see patterns?

1

The sun is a star. Each day, it looks as though the sun rises in the east and sets in the west. Is the sun really moving? No! The earth spins. This motion makes the sun look as though *it* is moving in the same pattern each day.

2

Other stars can be seen at night. Stars in groups make patterns called constellations. Constellations can also look as though they move from season to season. Like the sun, the stars don't move—the earth does.

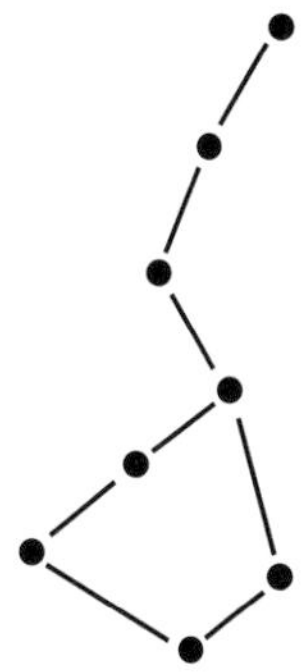

3

Each night of the month, the moon looks a little different. What we see of the moon is part of a pattern that happens about every 28 days. This pattern is known as the moon's phases.

4

How to use Make a copy of this page for each student. Then lead him to follow the directions above.

Insect Life Cycles

Name ____________________

Every living thing goes through a **life cycle**. This is when a living thing changes, grows, and makes offspring. Insects go through one of three kinds of life cycles. They are known as **simple growth**, **incomplete metamorphosis**, and **complete metamorphosis**.

1

Simple Growth

When the insect hatches from its egg, it looks like an adult, only smaller. The insect grows bigger until it is an adult.

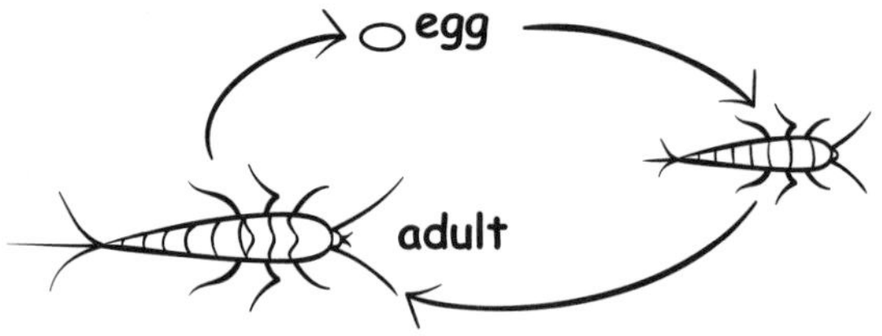
egg
adult

The silverfish is an example. The firebrat is another example.

2

Incomplete Metamorphosis

When the insect hatches from its egg, it may look like its parents (like katydids) or it may look very different from its parents (like dragonflies). The young insect (nymph) will eat and grow, but it will not go through a pupal stage. Often it will not have wings until it is an adult.

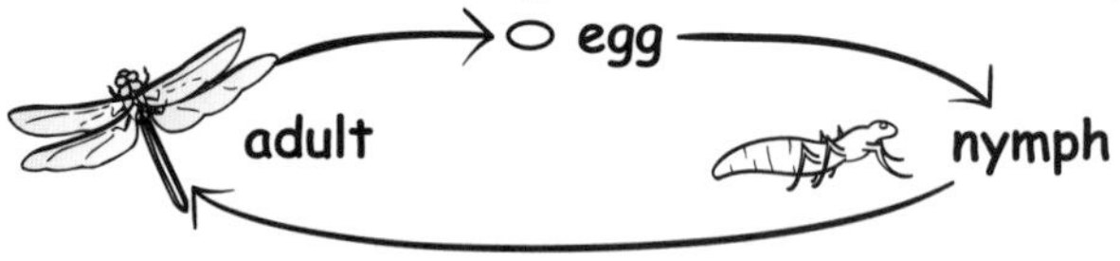
egg
adult
nymph

The dragonfly is an example. So are grasshoppers and cockroaches.

3

Complete Metamorphosis

When the insect hatches from its egg as a larva, it looks very different than the adult. The larva spends a lot of time eating but then doesn't eat at all as a pupa.

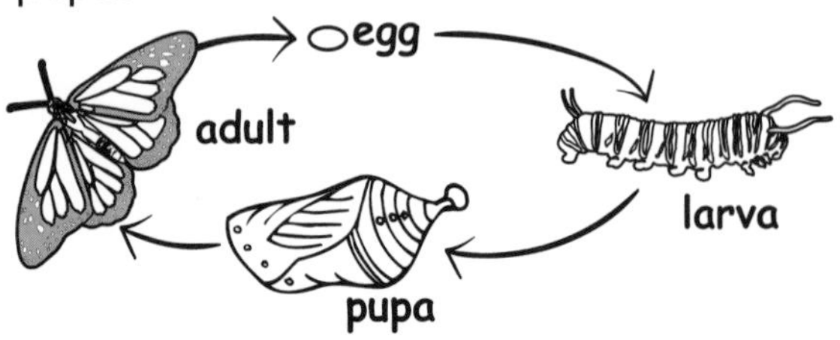
egg
adult
larva
pupa

The butterfly is an example. So are flies and bees.

4

Fun Facts

- Metamorphosis means "change."
- *Larva* is one. *Larvae* is more than one.
- *Pupa* is one. *Pupae* is more than one.
- When it is a nymph, an insect will **molt** four to eight times. This means it will shed its exoskeleton (outer covering) and replace it with a larger one.
- Larvae of many insects have their own names. Larvae of butterflies and moths are called **caterpillars**. Fly larvae are called **maggots,** and beetle larvae are called **grubs**. Larvae of mosquitoes are called **wrigglers**.
- An insect's pupa stage can take from four days to many months.

5

How to use Have each student cut apart the booklet pages from a copy of this page. Have him order the pages and staple them together to make a booklet.

SOCIAL STUDIES

Exploring Social Studies

Where in the World?
Map Skills

What better way to help students learn about the earth's continents and oceans than by having them make their own globes? In advance, gather for each child a copy of the continent patterns on page 170, a four-inch Styrofoam sphere, blue paint, a paintbrush, four blank circular stickers, a black marker, crayons, and glue. To create a globe, have each student paint the sphere blue and allow it to dry. Next, direct him to color the continents green, cut them out, and glue them in the appropriate locations on the sphere. Then have him label each sticker with the name of an ocean and instruct him to place them on his sphere. Finally, guide the child to use a black marker to draw a line around the globe to represent the equator. If desired, have the student insert a craft stick into the bottom of the globe, stuff tissue paper into a small cup, and then insert the stick into the cup to make a stand.

Sima Silverstein, Beth Rivkah Elementary, Brooklyn, NY

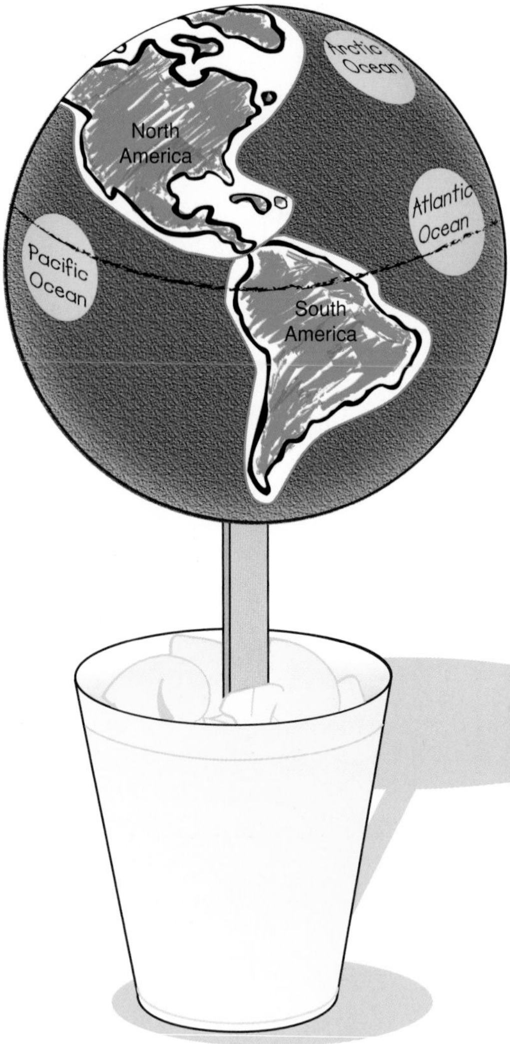
Arctic Ocean
North America
Atlantic Ocean
Pacific Ocean
South America

River!

Mold It!
Landforms

Here's an activity your students will love to get their hands on! To start, give each student a fist-size piece of molding clay. Call out a landform–such as *mountain, hill, island, river,* or *continent*–and have each student mold her clay into a matching model. As each child completes the model, check her work for accuracy. Then announce another landform. **To extend the activity,** have small groups of students work together to create landscapes made up of several different landforms. Challenge each child to write a description of the landscape her group created.

Chelsea Forbus LaVere, Chesapeake, VA

Exploring Social Studies

SECRET!
fire department

Top Secret
Government services

In advance, write a government service on each paper strip in a supply, and place each strip in a different envelope labeled as shown. Give each small group of students an envelope, index cards, and a large sheet of paper. Direct students to quietly read the services listed inside their envelopes; then have each child illustrate a related image on an index card. When students are finished, instruct each group to write the name of its service across the top of its paper and then cover it with a piece of paper. Then have each group member glue his index card to the paper. Provide time for each group to share its project and challenge classmates to determine the service. Use the completed projects to lead a discussion about why these services are important to communities and their citizens. Then post the projects around the room.

Stephanie Brachtenbach, Harmony Elementary, Overland Park, KS

911

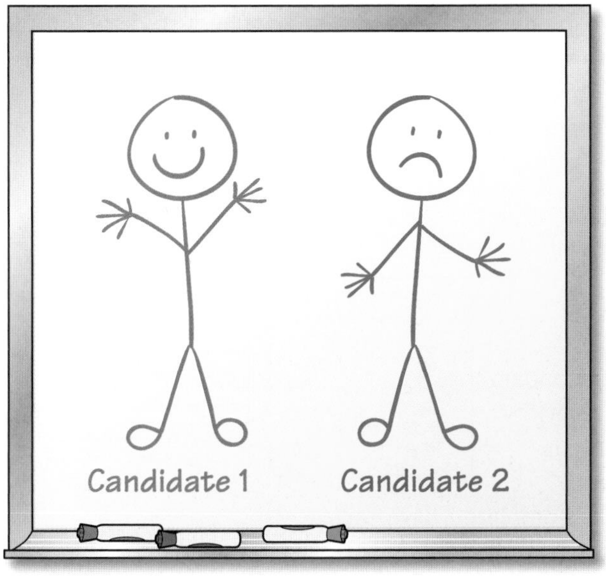
Candidate 1
Candidate 2

Conflicting Candidates
Voting

To begin, draw and label two stick figures on the board. Show Candidate 1 smiling and show Candidate 2 frowning. Tell students that these two candidates want to be in charge of your school. Then have each student vote for one on a slip of scrap paper (ballot). Collect the ballots and have a student tally the votes on the board. Announce the winner; then tell students that Candidate 1 wants ten-hour school days, no lunch choices in the cafeteria, and no recess, while Candidate 2 wants to make learning fun, will provide choices when possible, and will make recess longer. Ask students to consider their original choices; then discuss with students the importance of knowing the candidates' plans before voting.

Cynthia Wicks, Eastwood Elementary, Roseburg, OR

Exploring Social Studies

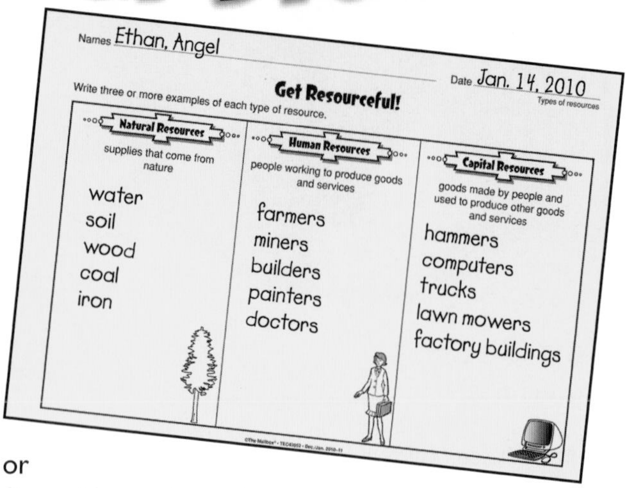

Names Ethan, Angel

Date Jan. 14, 2010

Types of resources

Get Resourceful!

Write three or more examples of each type of resource.

Natural Resources	Human Resources	Capital Resources
supplies that come from nature	people working to produce goods and services	goods made by people and used to produce other goods and services
water	farmers	hammers
soil	miners	computers
wood	builders	trucks
coal	painters	lawn mowers
iron	doctors	factory buildings

Sort Them Out

Types of resources

Give each student pair a copy of page 171. After reviewing the different types of resources, challenge each duo to list three or more examples of each. Provide time for partners to share their lists with another pair; then have each duo share one example with the rest of the class.

Chelsea Forbus LaVere, Chesapeake, VA

Bald eagle!
bird

Quick on the Draw

American symbols

To set up this fun class game, write the name of a different American symbol on each of a supply of index cards and then place the cards in a container. (If desired, include an image of the symbol on each card.) To play, a student from Team 1 takes a card and draws a picture of the named symbol. If a player from his team correctly identifies the symbol in the first minute, award two points to the team; then invite a player from the next team to take a turn. If the symbol is not correctly identified in the first minute, direct the child to write one common noun to describe the symbol before he continues to draw for one more minute. If the team identifies the symbol before time expires, award one point. If the team still can't identify the symbol, have the student return the card to the container. The team with the most points wins.

Juli Engel, Tyler, TX

Sharing the Past

Community changes over time

Here's a timesaving way to introduce students to primary and secondary sources while learning about your school's community. Invite long-term citizens of your community to speak to groups of students and share artifacts, such as photos or newspaper clippings. Take a photo of each speaker as he presents his information. When the presentations are completed, have each student write a paragraph describing what she learned from her presenter, noting how the community has changed and how it has stayed the same. Print the photos and post them in a column. Then display the paragraphs by their corresponding photos for students to review.

Terry Healy, Marlatt Elementary, Manhattan, KS

Exploring Social Studies

Meaningful Musical Chairs
Scarcity

Use the classic party game to connect meaning to this economics term. To begin, review the rules of the game. Provide time for students to play a few rounds; then ask how the game compares to product scarcity. Lead students to understand how the chairs are like scarce products—since there aren't enough for everyone, one player (consumer) each round will be left without one. Further explain that just as a student might feel frustrated when he can't find a chair during the game, being left without a desired product can frustrate a consumer too.

Chelsea Forbus LaVere, Chesapeake, VA

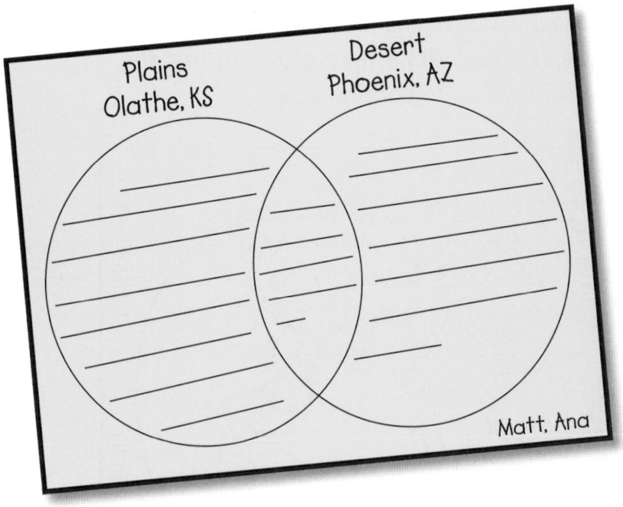
Plains
Olathe, KS
Desert
Phoenix, AZ
Matt, Ana

Comparing Here to There
Role of a community's physical environment

To begin this partner activity, have each duo research a different biome to determine how people have adapted to living there. Direct students to explore the kinds of shelters, clothing, and food found in their biome. Then have students use their research to create a Venn diagram that compares and contrasts the area researched to their own. **As an alternative,** encourage students to draw overlapping outlines that represent shelter for each community instead of drawing circles.

Stephanie Brachtenbach, Harmony Elementary, Olathe, KS

Exploring Social Studies

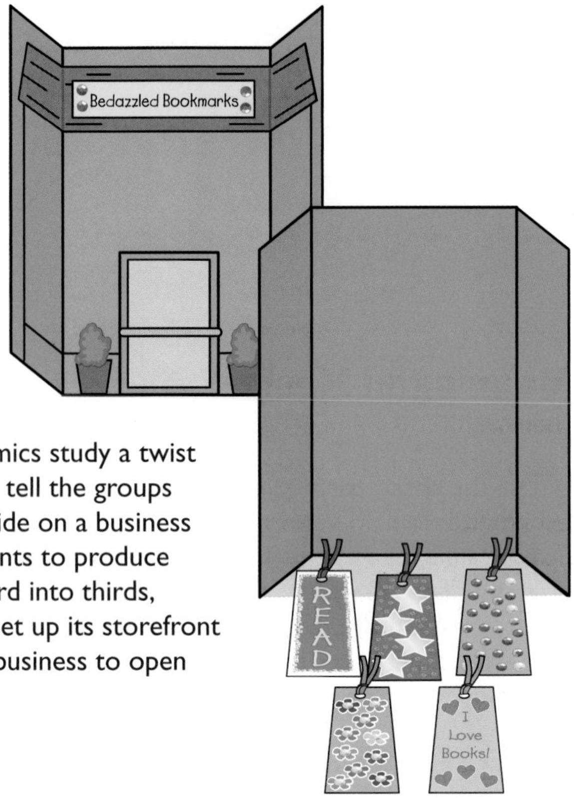
Bedazzled Bookmarks
READ
I Love Books!

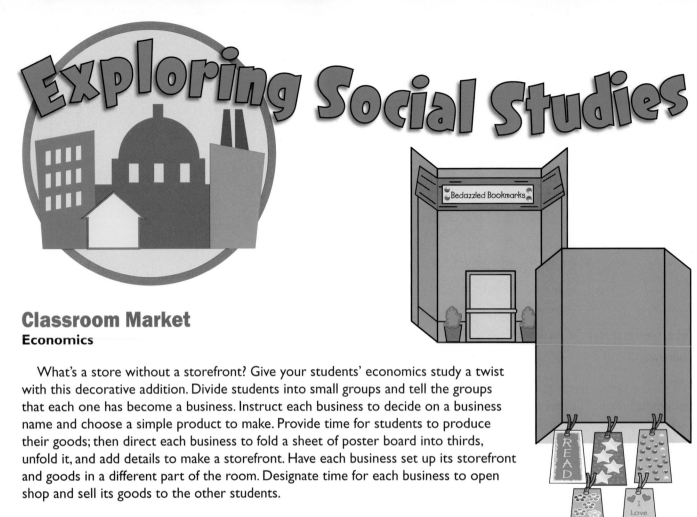

Classroom Market
Economics

What's a store without a storefront? Give your students' economics study a twist with this decorative addition. Divide students into small groups and tell the groups that each one has become a business. Instruct each business to decide on a business name and choose a simple product to make. Provide time for students to produce their goods; then direct each business to fold a sheet of poster board into thirds, unfold it, and add details to make a storefront. Have each business set up its storefront and goods in a different part of the room. Designate time for each business to open shop and sell its goods to the other students.

Casey Avery, Hobbton Elementary, Newton Grove, NC

Travel the World
Continents, map skills

It's not time for vacation just yet, but with this easy-to-prepare activity, students can visit well-known landmarks around the world. Cut apart a copy of the landmark cards from page 172, hole-punch each one, and attach the cards to a metal ring. Place the cards at a center with reference materials and student copies of a world map. A child writes the name of each continent on a map. Then she uses reference materials to determine on which continent each landmark is found and writes its corresponding number near the continent's name. **To make the activity more challenging**, the student writes the landmark's number where it would be located on the continent.

Brenda Liffengren, Faribault, MN

Taj Mahal
12

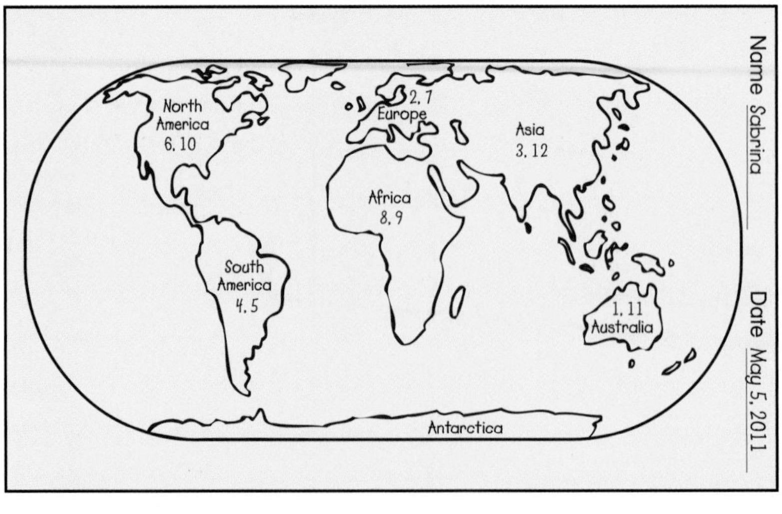
Name Sabrina
Date May 5, 2011
North America 6, 10
Europe 2, 7
Asia 3, 12
Africa 8, 9
South America 4, 5
1, 11 Australia
Antarctica

Exploring Social Studies

A Common Culture

Patriotism

With Independence Day just around the corner, get students thinking about the unique qualities of the USA. To start, have each student complete a copy of the organizer on page 173. Next, have the child use the organizer to write a description of what makes the USA unique. Then have the child make an abstract art piece that uses paper cutouts of red, white, and blue rectangles and stars. Post the descriptions and artwork on a display. **As an alternative**, have students use what they've learned about another country's culture and compare it to the United States in their writing.

Dawn Maucieri, Signal Hill Elementary, Dix Hills, NY

Name
Date
Across the 50 States
Complete the web.
Foods
Holidays
United States of America
Other:
Sports

From Here to There

Map scale

Send students on a trip to an imaginary town with this partner activity. Give each pair a sheet of graph paper; then post a map scale on the board. (Match the scale to the type of graph paper, using centimeters or inches.) Instruct students to draw buildings and roads on the graph paper to create a map. Remind them to label the map, include a key, and copy the assigned map scale. Then have them write four or more questions about their map on a separate paper, listing at least two questions that involve the map scale. Place each map and question set side by side in plastic page protectors and put the page protectors in a thin binder. Set the binder at a center. Direct students to choose a map and answer the corresponding questions.

adapted from an idea by Christa Caffrey
Fairview Elementary, High Point, NC

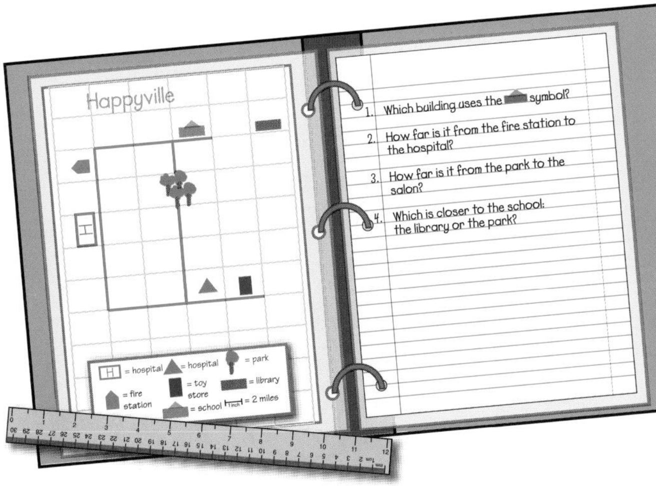
Happyville
1. Which building uses the symbol?
2. How far is it from the fire station to the hospital?
3. How far is it from the park to the salon?
4. Which is closer to the school: the library or the park?
= hospital
= hospital
= park
= fire station
= toy store
= library
= school
= 2 miles

Continent Patterns

Use with "Where in the World?" on page 164.

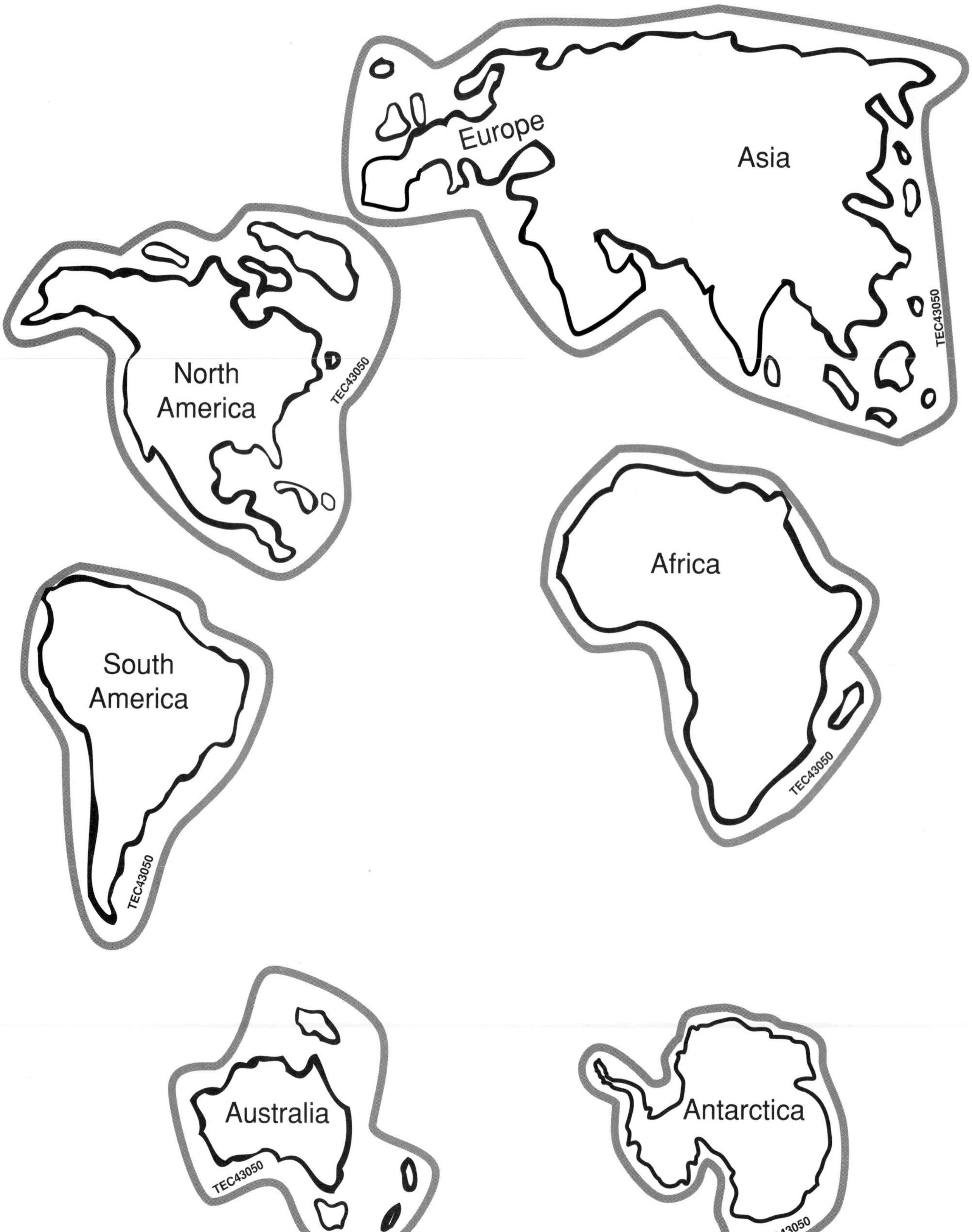
Europe
Asia
TEC43050
North
America
TEC43050
Africa
TEC43050
South
America
TEC43050
Australia
TEC43050
Antarctica
TEC43050

Names ____________________ Date ____________

Get Resourceful!

Write three or more examples of each type of resource.

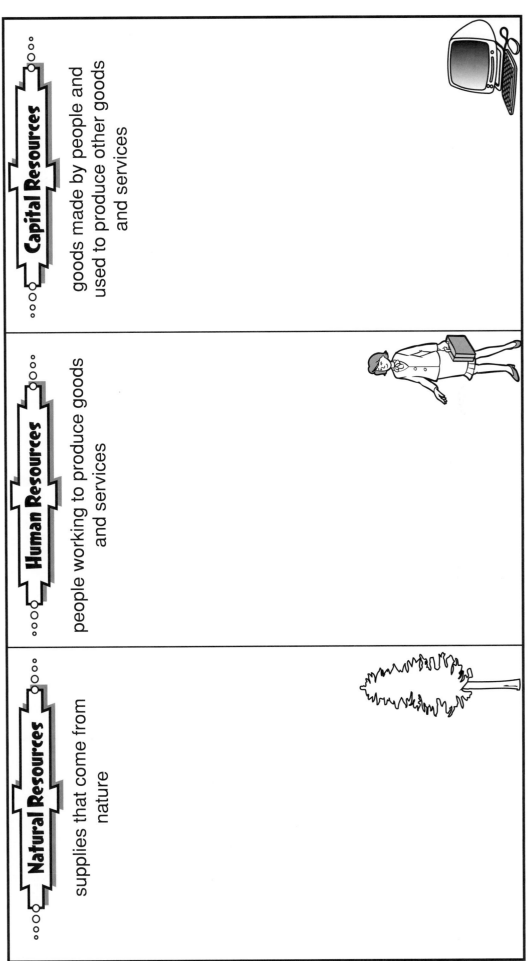

Natural Resources	Human Resources	Capital Resources
supplies that come from nature	people working to produce goods and services	goods made by people and used to produce other goods and services

Note to the teacher: Use with "Sort Them Out" on page 166.

Landmark Cards

Use with "Travel the World" on page 168.

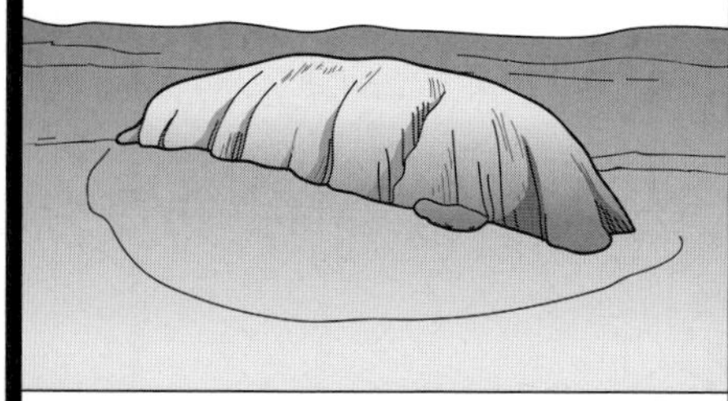

Uluru (Ayers Rock) 1

TEC43054

Eiffel Tower 2

TEC43054

Great Wall of China 3

TEC43054

Iguaçú Falls 4

TEC43054

Machu Picchu 5

TEC43054

Mount Rushmore 6

TEC43054

Parthenon 7

TEC43054

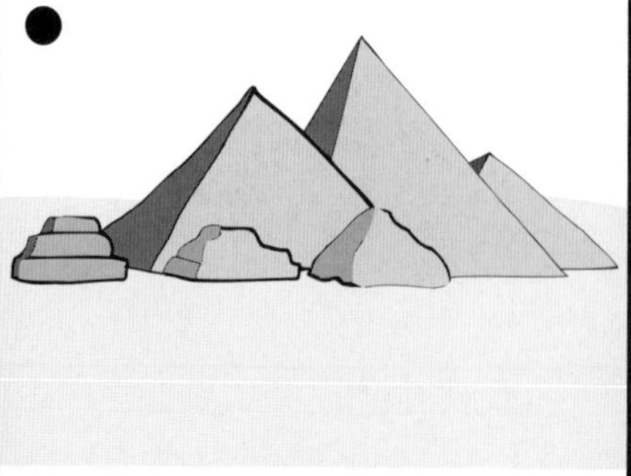

Pyramids at Giza 8

TEC43054

Great Sphinx at Giza 9

TEC43054

Statue of Liberty 10

TEC43054

Sydney Opera House 11

TEC43054

Taj Mahal 12

TEC43054

Name ____________________ Date ____________________

Graphic organizer: United States of America

Across the 50 States

Complete the web.

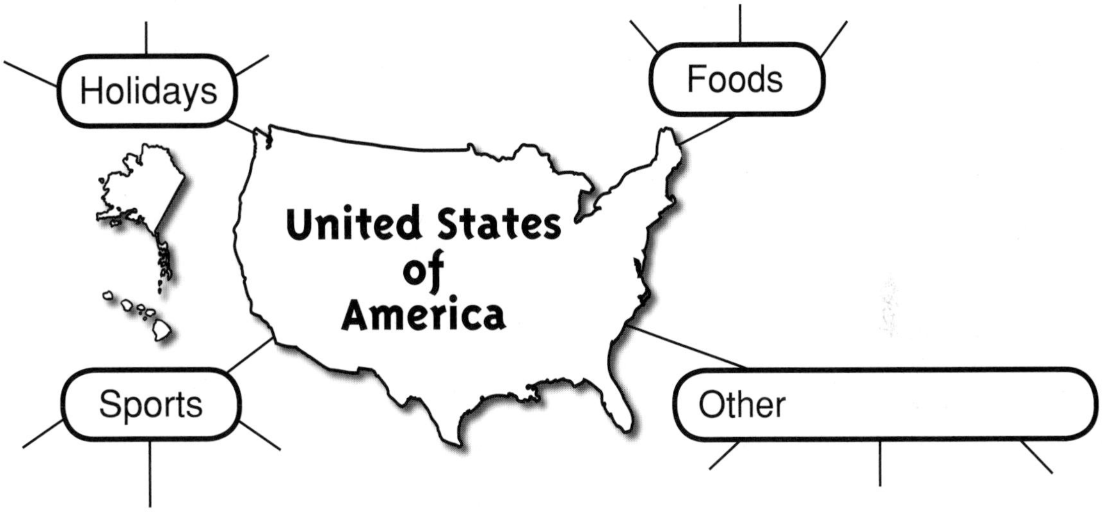
Holidays
Foods
United States of America
Sports
Other

The USA is special because

1. ____

2. ____

3. ____

Note to the teacher: Use with "A Common Culture" on page 169.

Prompts for Social Studies

Citizenship

Describe a good citizen. Tell what he or she does to help the community.

I Voted

Community Laws

What would happen if your community had no laws? Write three or more effects.

SPEED LIMIT 55
DO NOT ENTER
STOP

Community Leaders

List five traits you think a good community leader should have. Then rank the traits from 1 to 5. Tell why you think the trait you ranked as number 1 is the most important.

1.
2.
3.
4.
5.

Physical Environments

How would being near a river help a community grow? Explain.

Time and Change

People who are your grandparents' ages did not have computers when they were in school. How do you think their lives were different?

How to use Have each child staple a copy of this page in her writing journal. Or cut copies into sections and distribute only one prompt at a time to students.

Prompts for Social Studies

Geography

Think of a place you like to go. What landforms do you find there?

Write a riddle about this place. Include one or more clues that tell about the landforms. Be sure to write the answer too!

Resources

What resources are important to your community? Why? What can the citizens of your community do to maintain these resources?

Economics

Damon bought flowers for Valentine's Day at Rosemont Flower Shop. Then he bought candy from the Love Park Sweet Shoppe. After that, he stopped by Lou's Barber Shop to get a haircut. Then he took his mom to lunch at the Foo-Foo Café, where he gave her the flowers and candy.

What goods are described above? What services are named?

Community Changes

A+
Movers

Suppose a lot of people moved to your community. How would this affect your community? (Hint: Think of the good and bad results.)

Historic Figures

Describe someone who lived long ago and made a difference in his or her community. Then tell how his or her work affects people today.

Sojourner Truth

How to use Have each child staple a copy of this page in his writing journal. Or cut copies in sections and distribute only one prompt at a time to students.

Prompts for Social Studies

Maps and Globes

How are maps and globes alike? How are they different?

Geography

List landforms and bodies of water that are found on Earth. Draw a star next to those that are found in your local community.

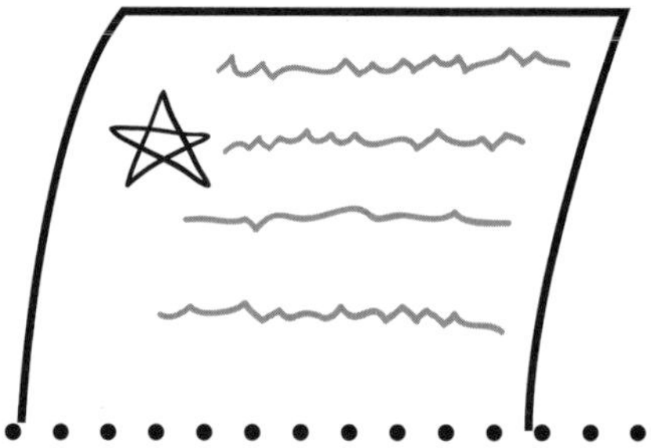

Physical Environment

How might cutting down an area of trees help a community? How might it hurt a community?

Economy

Does your community make more money during one season than during the others? Explain.

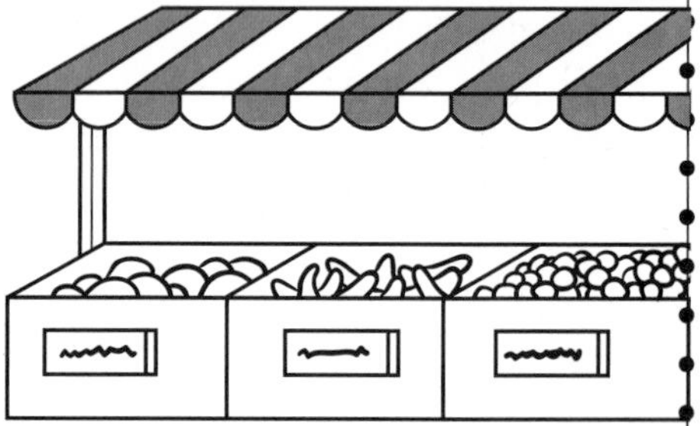

Technology

How does technology at school make your work easier? Give examples.

Choose a real-world job. How does technology make the job easier? Give examples.

How to use Have each child staple a copy of this page in his writing journal. Or cut copies in sections and distribute only one prompt at a time to students.

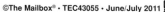

Learning Centers

Learning Centers

Flipping for Words
High-frequency words

Materials:
5 or more pairs of cards, each pair labeled with a different high-frequency word
paper

A child labels his paper with the headings shown. Then he places the cards facedown in columns on his workspace. The student turns over two cards, reads the words, and then writes them in the appropriate column. If the words match, he sets the cards aside. If the words do not match, he turns the cards over. The child continues until all matches have been made.

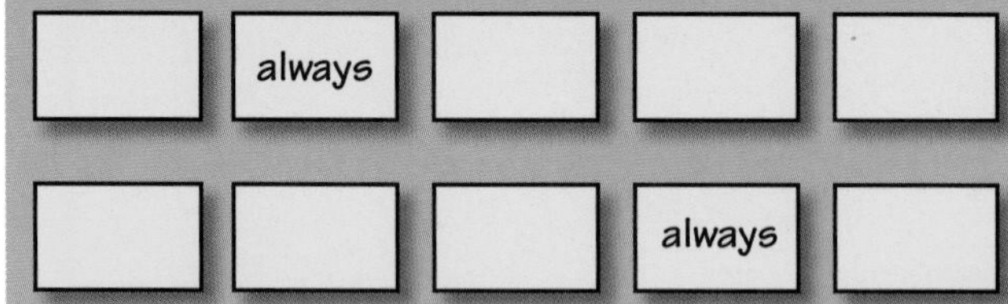
always
always

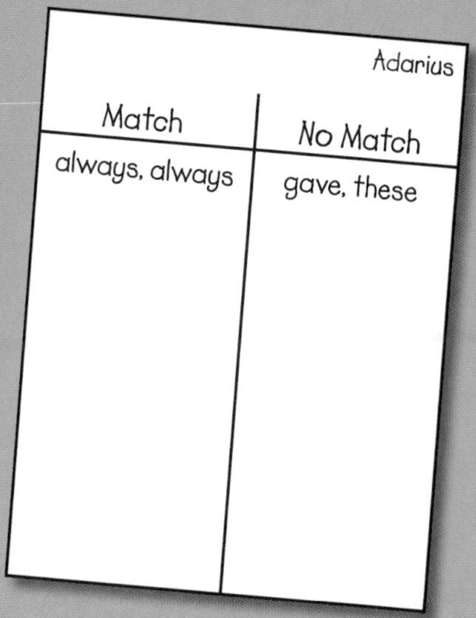
Adarius
Match
No Match
always, always
gave, these

Getting It Right
Editing for capitalization

Materials:
sentence strips labeled with sentences, some without capitalization
copy of the letter cards from page 190, cut apart
clothespins

A student reads a sentence. If it needs to be capitalized, she uses a clothespin to clip the corresponding letter card in place. If it does not need capitalization, she sets the sentence aside. The child continues in this manner until all the sentences are correctly capitalized.

To have students also edit for punctuation, write some sentences without punctuation marks and include copies of the punctuation cards from page 190 with the materials.

Editor's Tip:
For added fun, use students' names in the sentences.

Blake went to Phoenix this summer.
We are happy Maria joined our class on september 15.
A
M
S

Any Way You Slice It
Number sense

Materials:
student copies of the pizza pattern on page 191
resealable plastic bags
crayons
scissors

A child writes a number on one pizza slice; then, on each of the other slices, he writes or draws a different way to represent the number. He cuts apart the slices and puts them in a bag.

To extend the activity at another time, combine the contents of two bags that feature different numbers. A student sorts the slices to make two separate number pizzas.

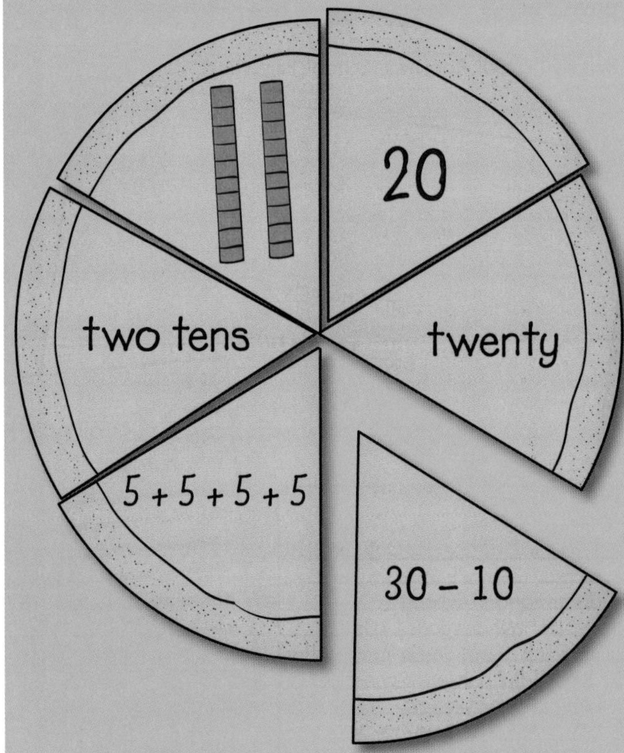
20
two tens
twenty
5 + 5 + 5 + 5
30 – 10

Put Two and Two Together
Commutative property of addition

Materials:
2 pom-poms
portion of a hundred chart (use the upper left quarter for practice without regrouping)
paper

A student drops the pom-poms on the number chart. She uses the two numbers the pom-poms land on to write an addition sentence. Then she switches the order of the numbers to write a second addition sentence. She repeats the steps until she has ten or more pairs of problems, or as time allows.

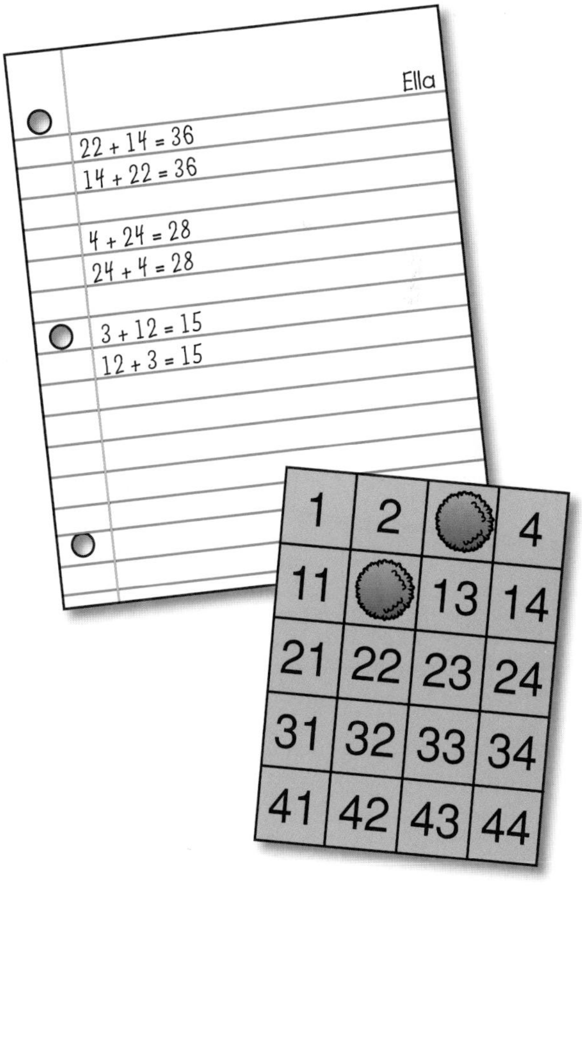
Ella
22 + 14 = 36
14 + 22 = 36
4 + 24 = 28
24 + 4 = 28
3 + 12 = 15
12 + 3 = 15
1 2 4
11 13 14
21 22 23 24
31 32 33 34
41 42 43 44

Learning Centers

Football Fun
Spelling

Materials:
2" x 11" paper strip, folded as shown to a make a football
10 or more word cards
die

For this partner activity, students stack the cards facedown. Player 1 rolls the die and Player 2 takes the corresponding number of cards from the stack. Player 2 reads each word to Player 1, who spells each word aloud. For each correctly spelled word, Player 1 earns one flick of the paper football—he flicks the football across a desktop, aiming to score a touchdown (six points) by getting the football to hang over the desk's edge without falling off. After Player 1 scores a touchdown or uses all his tries, he returns the cards to the bottom of the stack and Player 2 takes a turn in the same manner. The player with more points at the end of play wins.

Georgia Menzinger, Astatula Elementary School for the Arts
Astatula, FL

twice

To make a football:
1. Fold the right corner toward the left side to make a triangle. Then fold the paper down.
2. Continue folding until another whole triangle cannot be made (about seven times).
3. Tuck the leftover paper inside the open pocket.

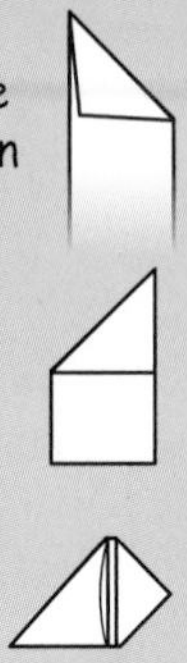

Contact a Character
Writing friendly letters

Materials:
list of familiar story characters
large envelope labeled with a fictitious address, as shown
paper clips
paper

At this center, a child writes a friendly letter to a character from the list, including the name of a story the character is in and at least one question. When she completes her letter, the student places it inside the envelope. If time allows, she reads a letter written by a classmate and prepares a friendly-letter response from the character's viewpoint. The child paper-clips her letter to the original before placing it back in the envelope.

Barclay Marcell, Roosevelt School, Park Ridge, IL

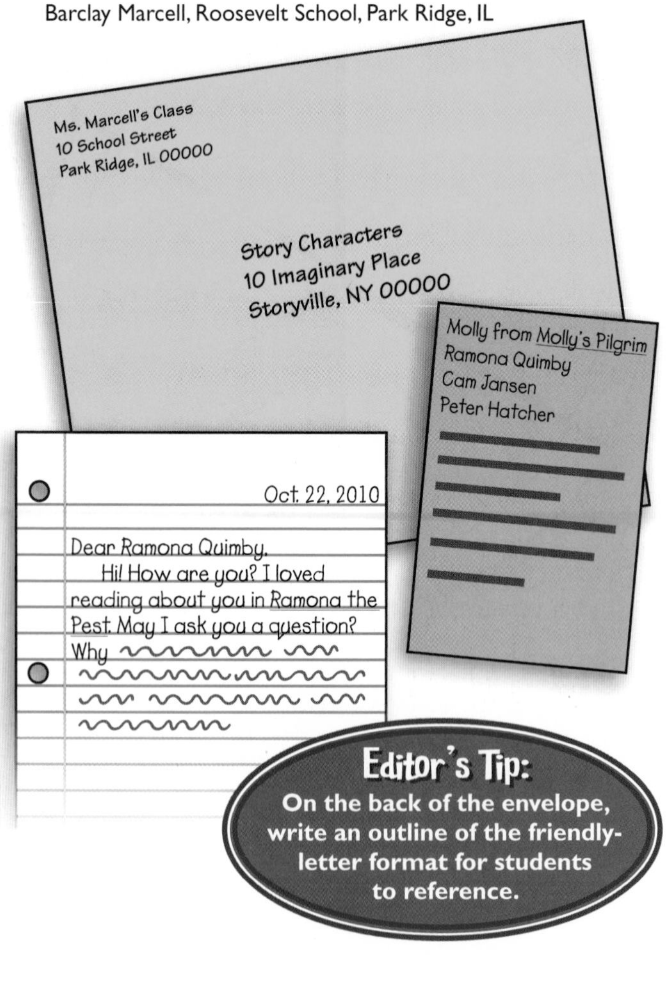
Ms. Marcell's Class
10 School Street
Park Ridge, IL 00000
Story Characters
10 Imaginary Place
Storyville, NY 00000
Molly from Molly's Pilgrim
Ramona Quimby
Cam Jansen
Peter Hatcher
Oct. 22, 2010
Dear Ramona Quimby,
Hi! How are you? I loved reading about you in Ramona the Pest. May I ask you a question?
Why

Editor's Tip:
On the back of the envelope, write an outline of the friendly-letter format for students to reference.

It's "Plane" to See

Identifying plane shapes, recording data

Materials:

copy of the cards on page 192
student copies of the recording sheet on page 192
crayons

A child chooses a card, identifies the shapes used to make the picture, and finds the number of each shape used. Next, he writes on his recording sheet a title that includes the name on the card. Then he labels the *y*-axis of his graph with the names of the shapes shown on his card and labels the *x*-axis to best represent the number of shapes. The student uses the crayons to color the graph; then he writes and answers two questions about it. **To make the activity easier,** set out recording sheets already programmed with titles and shapes to match each card. A student visiting the center simply refers to the corresponding card to complete the graph on the matching recording sheet.

Kelly J. Smith
Ocean Springs, MS

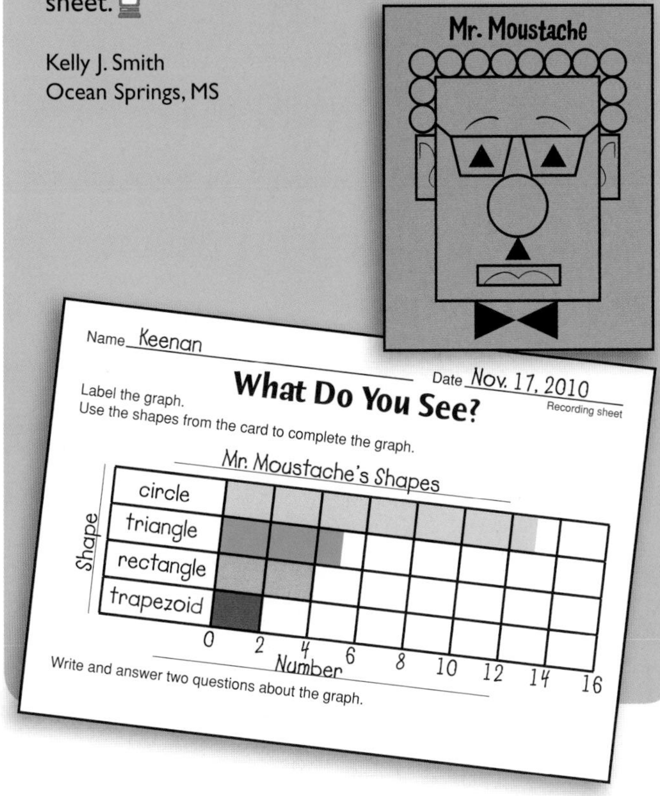

Mr. Moustache
Name Keenan
Date Nov. 17, 2010
What Do You See?
Recording sheet
Label the graph.
Use the shapes from the card to complete the graph.
Mr. Moustache's Shapes
Shape
circle
triangle
rectangle
trapezoid
0 2 4 6 8 10 12 14 16
Number
Write and answer two questions about the graph.

Field Trip!

Elapsed time

Materials:

copy of page 193
orange paper
scissors

A student uses the orange paper to cut out two large pumpkin shapes. She uses the schedule from a copy of page 193 to write on each shape a different problem involving elapsed time. Then she turns each shape over to write the problem's matching answer and an explanation of how she solved it.

Ms. Sun's class just finished lunch. How long will it be before they leave the farm?
Victoria
How long will Mr. Brown's class be at the farm?
Victoria
Field Trip!
Use the schedules to write two word problems. Each problem should use elapsed time. Show each answer and how you solved it.
Like this!
How long was Ms. Black's class at the farm before they ate lunch?
2 hours 15 minutes.
They arrived at 9:45.
From 9:45 to 10:45 is one hour.
From 10:45 to 11:45 is another hour.
From 11:45 to 12:00 is 15 minutes.
Field Trip Schedule
Friendly Farm
Ms. Black's Class
Arrive 9:45
Apple orchard 10:00–10:45
Pumpkin patch 11:00–11:45
Lunch 12:00–12:45
Corn maze 1:00–1:45
Leave 2:00
Ms. Sun's Class
Arrive 9:45
Corn maze 10:00–10:45
Apple orchard 11:00–11:45
Pumpkin patch 12:00–12:45
Lunch 1:00–1:45
Leave 2:00
Mr. Brown's Class
Arrive 9:45
Pumpkin patch 10:00–10:45
Lunch 11:00–11:45
Corn maze 12:00–12:45
Apple orchard 1:00–1:45
Leave 2:00

Learning Centers

Goody Bag

Forms of *have*

Materials:
bag filled with catalog pictures of toys and gifts
die code shown
die
paper

Editor's Tip:
Put the pictures in a Christmas stocking.

A child takes a picture from the bag and rolls the die. He refers to the die code; then he writes a sentence using the corresponding verb and the name of the object. The student underlines the verb form of *have* and then sets the cutout aside. He repeats the steps four or more times. When he's finished, he returns the pictures to the bag.

Roland
12/10/10
We have two computers in our house.
My sister had a bake set when she was little, but my mom sold it in a yard sale.

Die Code
1 or 4 = have
2 or 5 = has
3 or 6 = had

Catchy Beginnings

Introductory sentences

Materials:
class supply of the cards from page 194, cut apart
baseball mitt
glue
lined paper

Lay the cards in the mitt. A student selects a card from the mitt and glues it onto her paper. She reads the prompt and continues writing the story as time allows.

Danielle Ambrosio, Knollwood School, Piscataway, NJ

Have I got a story to tell you! It all started when...
Every student in the room was as quiet as a mouse. Here's why.
Have you ever had ants in your pants? Well, I have!
GLUE

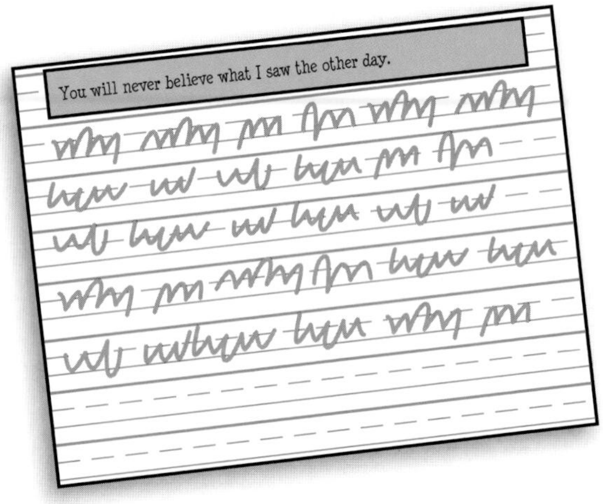
You will never believe what I saw the other day.

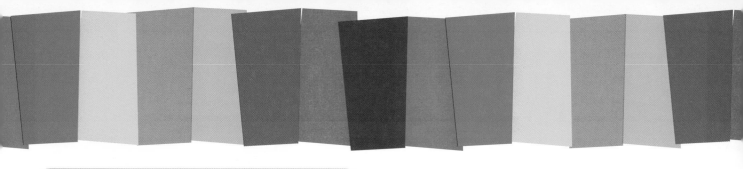

Charged Up!
Comparing and ordering fractions

Materials:
copy of the cards from page 195, cut apart
paper

To compare fractions, a child stacks the cards facedown. He turns over the top two cards and determines which fraction amount is greater. The student writes a matching expression or sentence on his paper. He places the cards to the side and continues until all the cards have been used.

To order fractions, a student places the cards facedown in three rows. He turns over one card from each row and then orders them from least to greatest. The child writes the ordered fractions on his paper. Then he turns the cards facedown and repeats the steps five or more times.

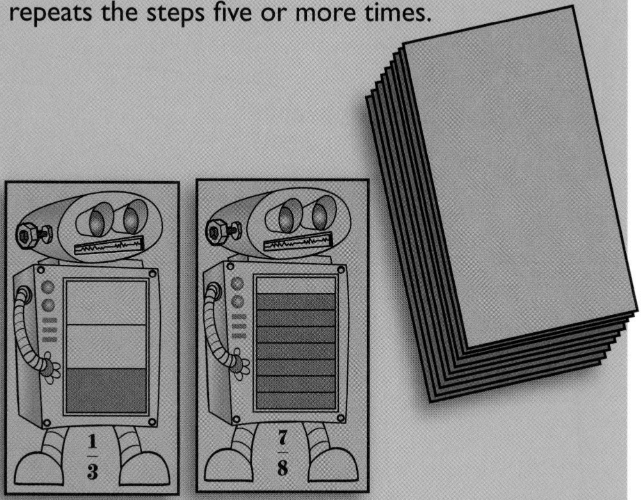
1/3
7/8

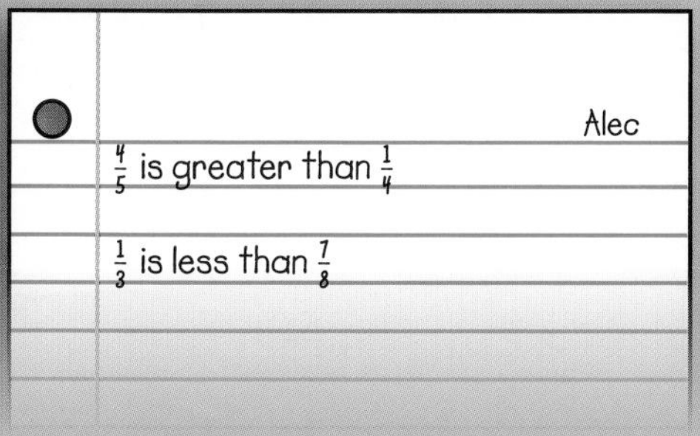
Alec
4/5 is greater than 1/4
1/3 is less than 7/8

Building a Snowman
Number sense

Materials:
paper

Here's a fun partner game that is played much like Hangman. First, Player 1 makes a game mat by folding a sheet of paper in half and unfolding it. She draws on the left side of the mat one blank for each digit of a number she is thinking of. Then she divides the right side into sections, one section for each place value of her number, and writes the digits 0–9 in each section.

To play, Player 2 names a place value and a digit. If the digit is found in the named place, Player 1 writes it on the matching line and crosses it off the matching section. If it is not found in the named place, Player 1 crosses the digit off the matching section and then draws one part of a snowman. Play continues until Player 2 identifies the number or the snowman is complete.

Cynthia Wicks, Eastwood Elementary, Roseburg, OR

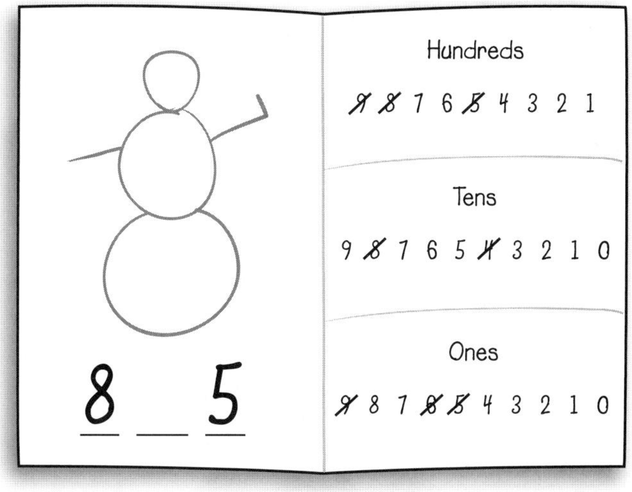
8 _ 5
Hundreds
9 8 7 6 5 4 3 2 1
Tens
9 8 7 6 5 4 3 2 1 0
Ones
9 8 7 8 5 4 3 2 1 0

Learning Centers

Heart to Heart
Identifying homophones

Materials:
paper heart, programmed with six homophone pairs
candy or paper hearts

A child reads the words, and when he finds a homophone pair, he covers both words with matching colored hearts. The student continues until all the pairs are matched. Then, one pair at a time, he removes the hearts and lists the homophone pairs on his paper. **To vary the activity,** program the heart with synonym pairs or antonym pairs instead.

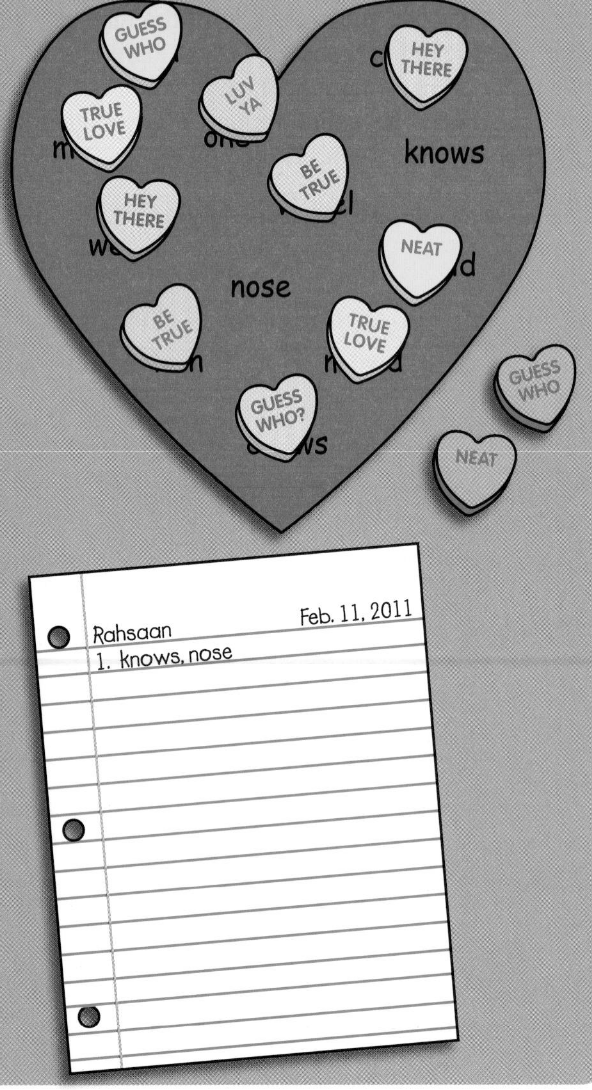

GUESS WHO
HEY THERE
LUV YA
TRUE LOVE
knows
BE TRUE
HEY THERE
NEAT
nose
BE TRUE
TRUE LOVE
GUESS WHO
GUESS WHO?
NEAT
Rahsaan
Feb. 11, 2011
1. knows, nose

Meet the Presidents
Comparing and contrasting

Materials:
copy of the cards from page 196, cut apart

A student reads each paragraph, noting the boldfaced words. Then she divides her paper into three columns and labels it as shown. She compares and contrasts the presidents, writing the boldfaced words in the corresponding columns.

Cyndi Stumpf, Ellen T. Briggs Elementary, Lake Hopatcong, NJ

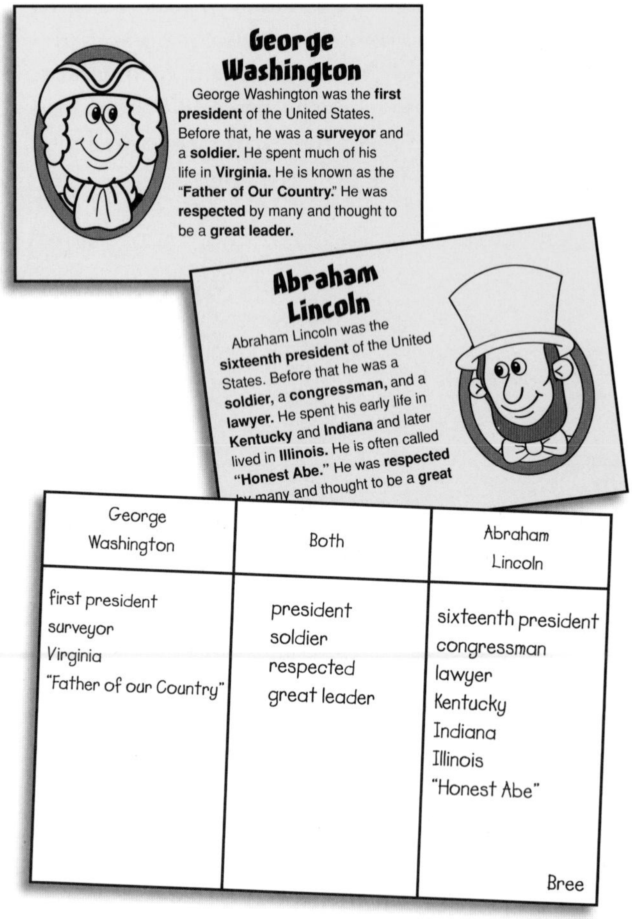

George Washington
George Washington was the **first president** of the United States. Before that, he was a **surveyor** and a **soldier.** He spent much of his life in **Virginia.** He is known as the **"Father of Our Country."** He was **respected** by many and thought to be a **great leader.**
Abraham Lincoln
Abraham Lincoln was the **sixteenth president** of the United States. Before that he was a **soldier,** a **congressman,** and a **lawyer.** He spent his early life in **Kentucky** and **Indiana** and later lived in **Illinois.** He is often called **"Honest Abe."** He was **respected** by many and thought to be a **great**
George Washington
Both
Abraham Lincoln
first president
surveyor
Virginia
"Father of our Country"
president
soldier
respected
great leader
sixteenth president
congressman
lawyer
Kentucky
Indiana
Illinois
"Honest Abe"
Bree

"Plane" to See

Spelling, drawing plane shapes

Materials:
copy of the shape key on page 197
spelling list

A student numbers his paper and writes each spelling word, skipping a line between each word. Then he refers to the shape key to draw the matching shape around the word's number. **To vary the activity,** the child creates a chart, labeling each section with a different shape. He sorts the words according to the number of letters and writes each one in the corresponding section.

Brooke Beverly, Dudley Elementary, Dudley, MA

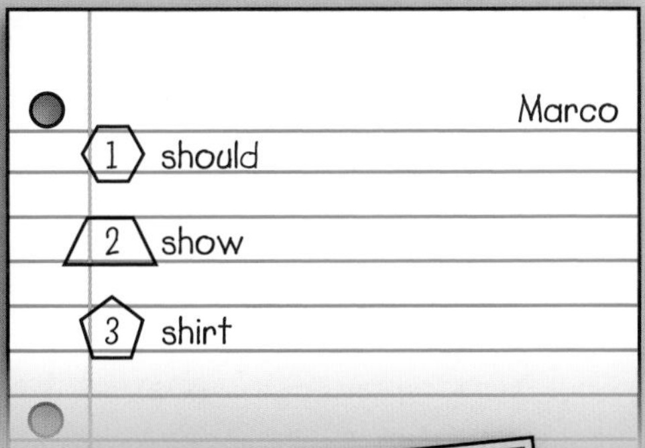

Marco
1 should
2 show
3 shirt

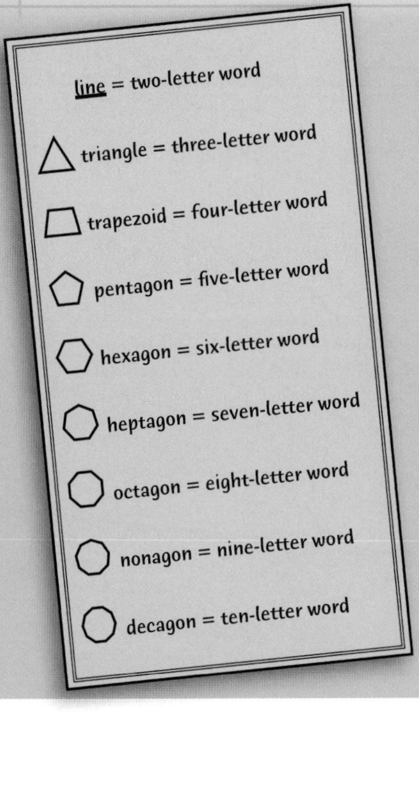

line = two-letter word
triangle = three-letter word
trapezoid = four-letter word
pentagon = five-letter word
hexagon = six-letter word
heptagon = seven-letter word
octagon = eight-letter word
nonagon = nine-letter word
decagon = ten-letter word

Book-Buying Binge

Adding and subtracting money

Materials:
book order form
student copies of the recording sheet on page 197, programmed with a budget amount

Based on the budget, a child selects books she would like to purchase and writes the item numbers on her recording sheet. Next, she determines the cost of her books and calculates the change. If the student is over budget, she edits her book choices. If the child is under budget, she finds additional purchases and recalculates her spending.

Tomekia Darrisaw, Diamond Lakes Elementary, Hephzibah, GA

Name Morgan
Date March 7, 2011
Recording sheet
Let's Shop!
My budget: $15.00
Goods to Buy
Total Amount Spent (Add the prices.)
My Change (Subtract the total from the budget.)
68
42
50
$3.99
$5.95
+ $4.99
$14.93
$15.00
- $14.93
$0.07
Book Club

Editor's Tip:
If you have enough order forms, have the student cut out and glue the selected books to the first section of the recording sheet.

Learning Centers

By the Dozen
Contractions

Materials:
student copies of the recording sheet on page 198
12 plastic eggs
permanent marker

To prepare, use a permanent marker to program half of an egg with the first word part of a contraction. Then label another half with the second word part and its apostrophe. Repeat 11 more times and store all the egg halves in a basket. A student matches two egg halves to make a contraction and completes the first row of the recording sheet. He sets the egg aside and continues until he makes 12 contractions.

Erin Killian, Liberty Drive Elementary, Thomasville, NC

was
he
could
n't
's
'll
was n't

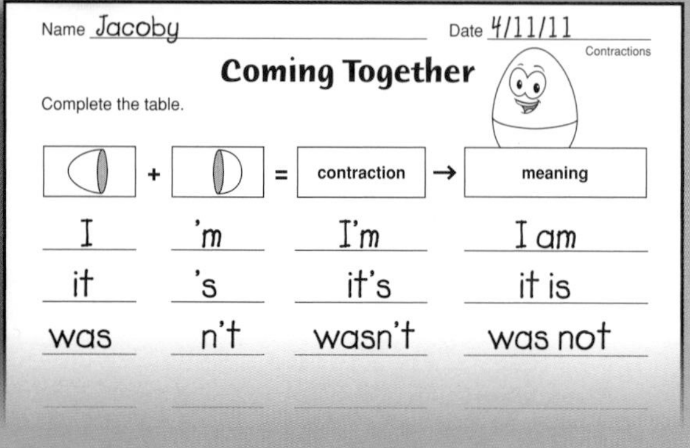

Name Jacoby   Date 4/11/11
Contractions

Coming Together

Complete the table.

+	=	contraction →	meaning
I	'm	I'm	I am
it	's	it's	it is
was	n't	wasn't	was not

Students in Bloom
Main idea and details

Materials:
drawing paper
crayons

A child writes in the middle of her paper a sentence that includes her name and an important personal trait. Then she uses a crayon to draw a circle around the sentence. Next, the child writes four sentences that support and provide more information about her trait. She uses a different-colored crayon to draw a petal around each of these sentences. If time allows, the student uses her organizer to write a description.

Heather Schumacher, Coronado Village Elementary, Universal City, TX

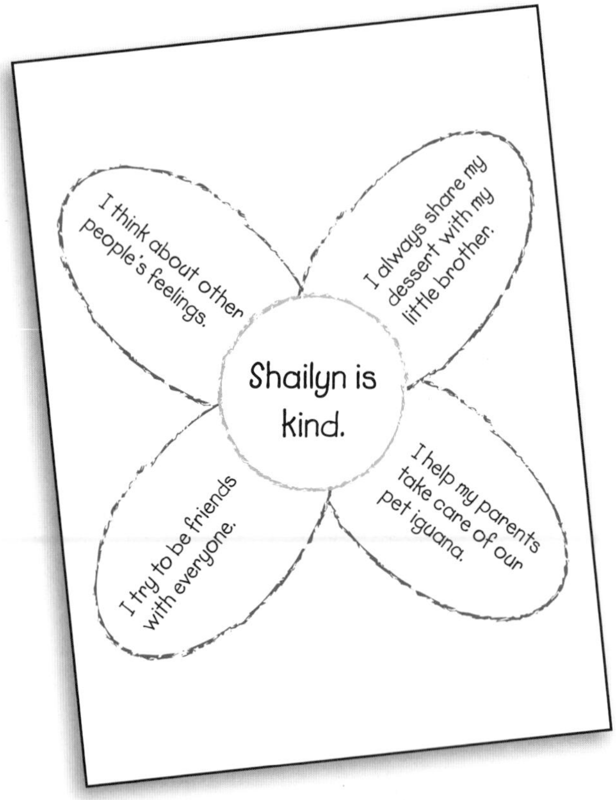
I think about other people's feelings.
I always share my dessert with my little brother.
Shailyn is kind.
I try to be friends with everyone.
I help my parents take care of our pet iguana.

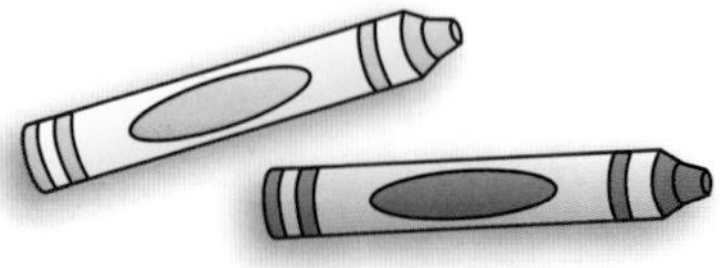

Rain, Rain...
Organizing data

Materials:
copy of the cloud patterns on page 199, cut out
envelope, labeled as shown
graph paper
crayons

Place the clouds in the envelope; then set the envelope with the graph paper and crayons. A student takes five clouds from the envelope and graphs the data on his paper. Then he turns the paper over and writes four or more questions about the data. If desired, have the student include the answers.

David Green, North Shore Country Day School, Winnetka, IL

Cities and Their Yearly Rainfall in Inches
Soggyport
38 inches

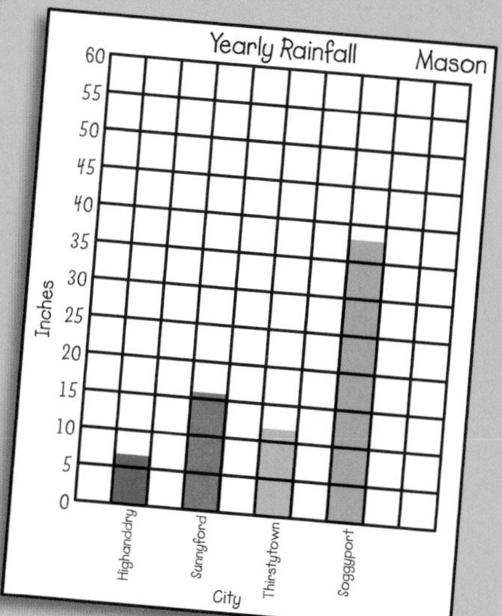
Yearly Rainfall
Mason
60
55
50
45
40
35
30
25
20
15
10
5
0
Inches
Highanddry
Sunnyford
Thirstytown
Soggyport
City

Something in Common
Relating multiplication and division

Materials:
beans
multiplication flash cards (facts to 10)
20 paper circles
file folder

For this partner activity, the students place the file folder between themselves and set the other materials within reach of both players. To begin, Player 1 takes a flash card and reads the multiplication problem aloud. She uses the circles (sets) and beans to model the problem. The student restates the problem with its answer. Then Player 2 states a related division fact and creates a model of his fact with the circles and beans. When he is finished, students remove the file folder and compare the models. Then students alternate roles.

Barbara Duran, Dorris Jones Elementary, Rockwall, TX

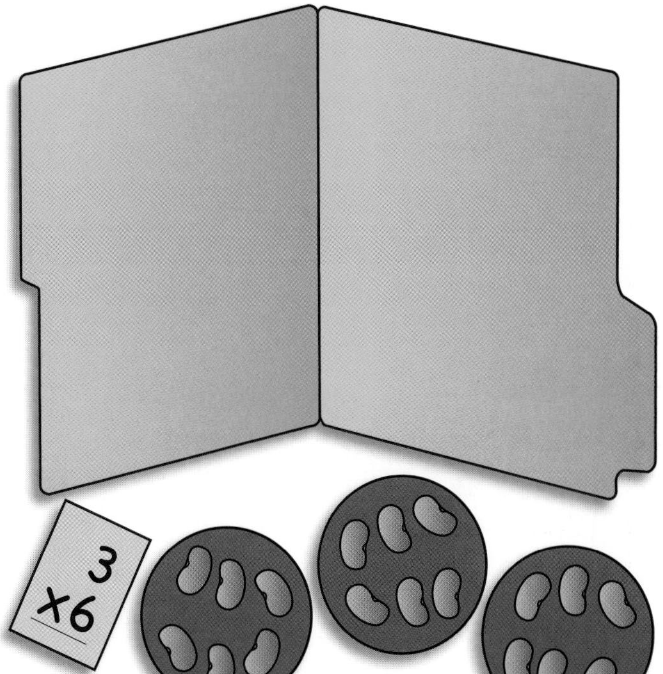
3
x6

Learning Centers

Super Sounds Sleuth

Vowel sounds and spelling patterns

Materials:
student copies of page 200, preprogrammed with a vowel sound and vowel spellings
supply of student books

A student uses his prior knowledge, as well as words found in the books provided, to list as many examples for each vowel spelling as he can. **To vary the activity**, write words with the matching sound on a supply of index cards. A child sorts the cards by vowel spelling and then records the words under the matching headings on his paper.

Tracey Stuart, Oregon, WI

Name Mack
Date June 3, 2011
Super Sounds Sleuth
Your Assignment
Find words with the /ā/ sound, as in trail and play
a_e
ace sale tale whale snake ate tape gale
ay
play stay today clay tray
ai
trail train aid pail rail rain
eigh
neighbor weigh sleigh neigh
ey
they whey
How many examples can you list?
ei
vein reins
ea
great steak bear break

Uppercase or Lowercase?

Proper and common nouns, capitalization

Materials:
2 cards with the headings shown
cards with uncapitalized nouns
blank paper

A child lays out the heading cards to begin two columns. For each noun card, she determines whether the word should be capitalized as a proper noun or written as a common noun; then she places the card in the corresponding column. After the student sorts all the cards, she labels a paper with the headings. Then she writes the words as she sorted them, adding capital letters where needed. **To extend the activity**, the child draws a star next to any word that could be considered a proper noun or a common noun, depending on how it is used. Then she writes two sentences for one starred word, using the word as a common noun in one sentence and a proper noun in the other.

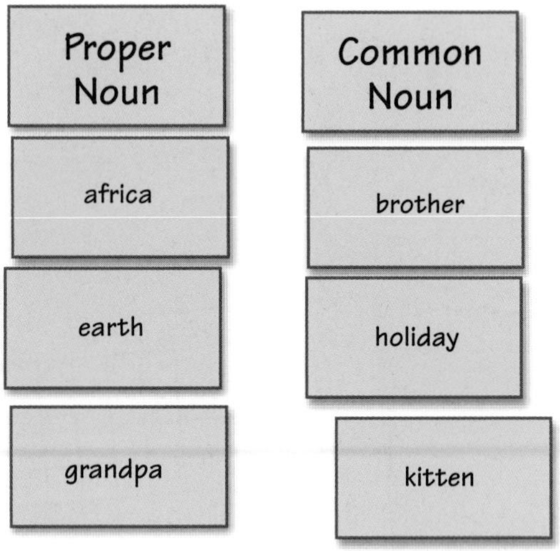

Proper Noun
Common Noun
africa
brother
earth
holiday
grandpa
kitten

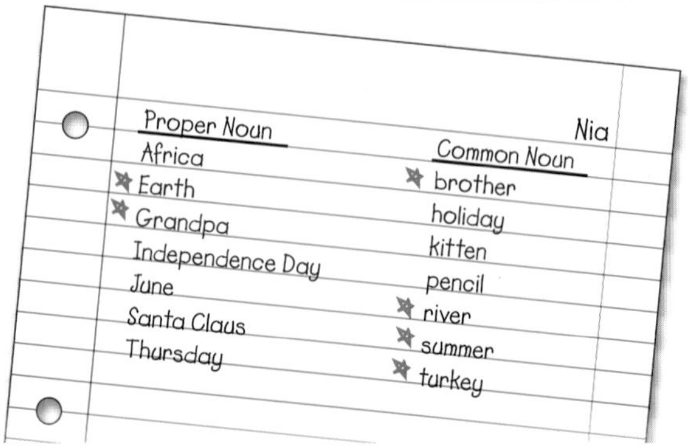

Proper Noun
Nia
Common Noun
Africa
Earth
Grandpa
Independence Day
June
Santa Claus
Thursday
brother
holiday
kitten
pencil
river
summer
turkey

Measurement Match-Up

Perimeter and area

Materials:

copy of the cards on page 201, cut out and separated into two stacks (shapes, measurements)
centimeter ruler
paper

A child takes a card from the shape stack; then he finds the perimeter and area of the shape on the card. Next, the student locates the measurement card with the matching perimeter and area. Then the child selects another card and repeats the process as time allows or until the measurements have been found for each card.

Jennifer Cripe, James Bilbray Elementary, Las Vegas, NV

H.
Perimeter =
10 cm
Area =
6 sq.cm

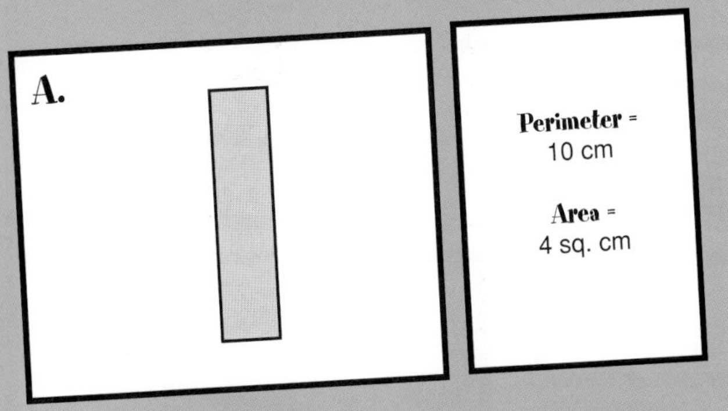
A.
Perimeter =
10 cm
Area =
4 sq. cm

Lure Them In

Comparing numbers

Materials:

3 containers, labeled as shown
fish cutout, labeled with a number
worm cutouts (patterns on page 201), each labeled with a different problem

A child lays the worms facedown on her workspace. She turns over a worm, solves the problem, and determines whether the answer is greater than, less than, or equal to the number on the fish. Then she places the worm in the corresponding container and repeats the process until all the worms have been sorted. **For an easier version**, label each worm with just a number.

13 + 6
less than <
greater than >
equal to =

56
7 × 8

Capital Letter and Punctuation Cards

Use with “Getting It Right” on page 178.

A TEC43050	B TEC43050	C TEC43050	D TEC43050	E TEC43050	F TEC43050	G TEC43050	H TEC43050	I TEC43050	J TEC43050
K TEC43050	L TEC43050	M TEC43050	N TEC43050	O TEC43050	P TEC43050	Q TEC43050	R TEC43050	S TEC43050	T TEC43050
U TEC43050	V TEC43050	W TEC43050	X TEC43050	Y TEC43050	Z TEC43050	. TEC43050	, TEC43050	! TEC43050	? TEC43050

Pizza Pattern

Use with “Any Way You Slice It” on page 179.

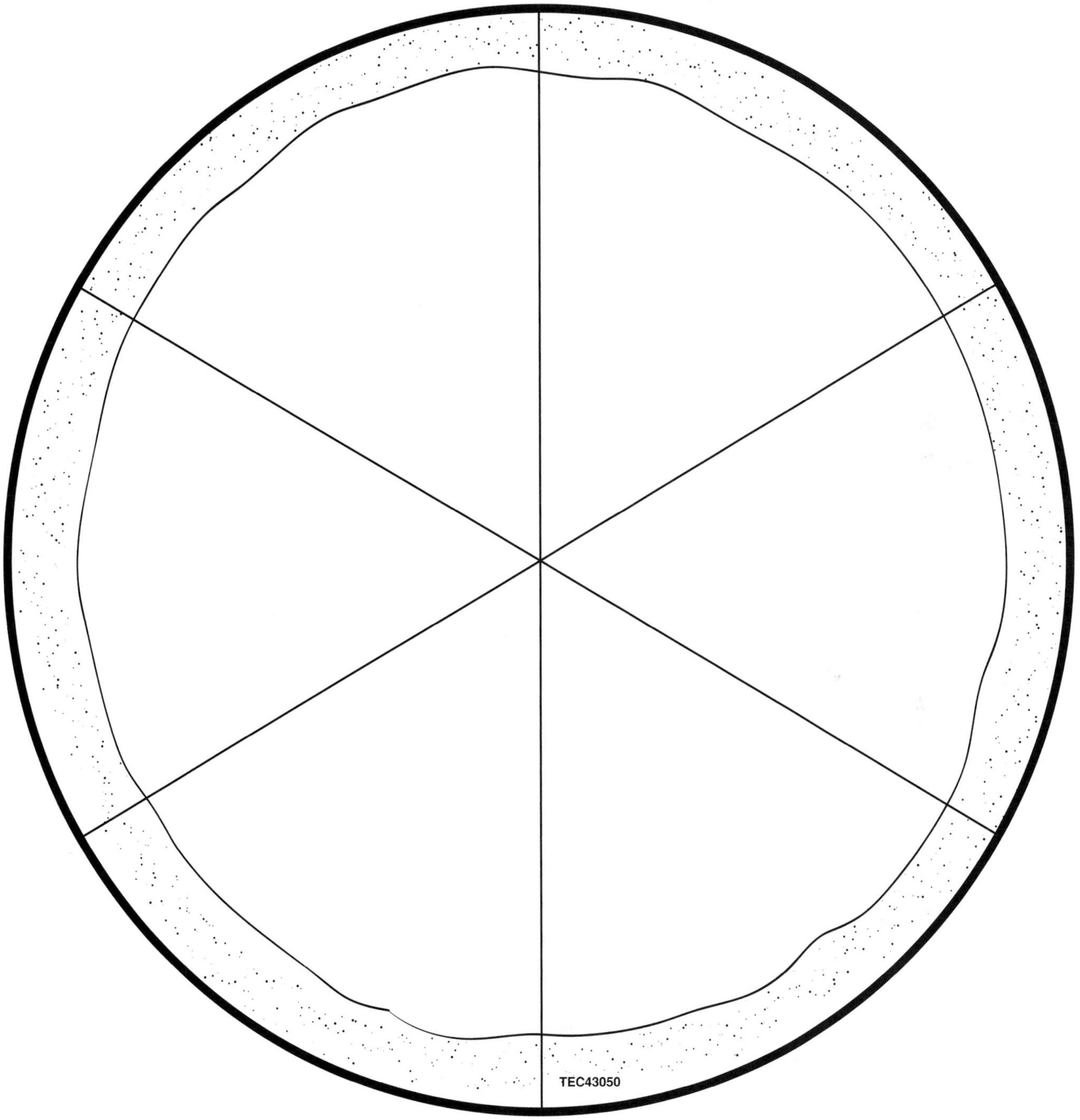

TEC43050

Shape Cards and Recording Sheet

Use with "It's 'Plane' to See" on page 181.

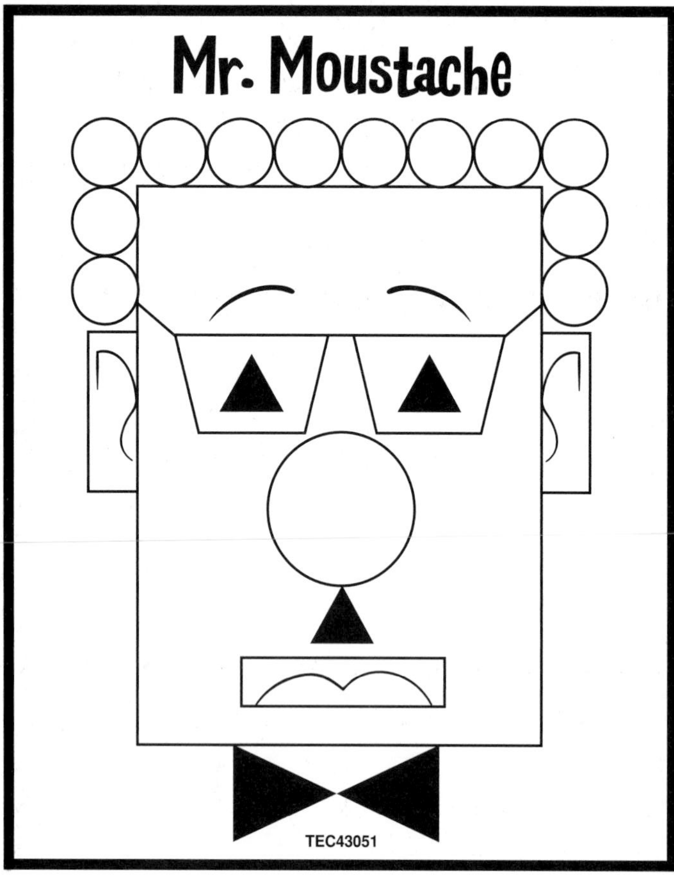
Mr. Moustache
TEC43051

Ms. Matchy-Matchy
TEC43051

Name ______________________________ Date ______________

Recording sheet

What Do You See?

Label the graph.
Use the shapes from the card to complete the graph.

____

____

Write and answer two questions about the graph.

Field Trip!

Use the schedules to write two word problems.
Each problem should use elapsed time.
Show each answer and how you solved it.

Like this!

How long was Ms. Black's class at the farm before they ate lunch?

2 hours 15 minutes.
They arrived at 9:45.
From 9:45 to 10:45 is one hour.
From 10:45 to 11:45 is another hour.
From 11:45 to 12:00 is 15 minutes.

Field Trip Schedule
Friendly Farm

Ms. Black's Class		Ms. Sun's Class		Mr. Brown's Class	
Arrive	9:45	Arrive	9:45	Arrive	9:45
Apple orchard	10:00–10:45	Corn maze	10:00–10:45	Pumpkin patch	10:00–10:45
Pumpkin patch	11:00–11:45	Apple orchard	11:00–11:45	Lunch	11:00–11:45
Lunch	12:00–12:45	Pumpkin patch	12:00–12:45	Corn maze	12:00–12:45
Corn maze	1:00–1:45	Lunch	1:00–1:45	Apple orchard	1:00–1:45
Leave	2:00	Leave	2:00	Leave	2:00

Note to the teacher: Use with "Field Trip!" on page 181.

Sentence Cards

Use with "Catchy Beginnings" on page 182.

Whack! The ball went flying out toward left field.	TEC43052
"Psst...did you hear that?"	TEC43052
Go ahead. Call me a bookworm because I love to read!	TEC43052
Do you want to hear a funny story?	TEC43052
You will never believe what I saw the other day.	TEC43052
"That is the coolest thing ever!"	TEC43052
Did you know that a penguin can walk as fast as a human? That's not all!	TEC43052
3, 2, 1...Happy New Year!	TEC43052
Have you ever had ants in your pants? Well, I have!	TEC43052
Kerplunk! That's the sound I heard when...	TEC43052
Busy as a beaver—that's how I would describe my _____ every day.	TEC43052
Every student in the room was as quiet as a mouse. Here's why.	TEC43052
I have something in common with President George Washington—he loved ice cream and so do I!	TEC43052
Have I got a story to tell you! It all started when...	TEC43052

Fraction Cards

Use with "Charged Up!" on page 183.

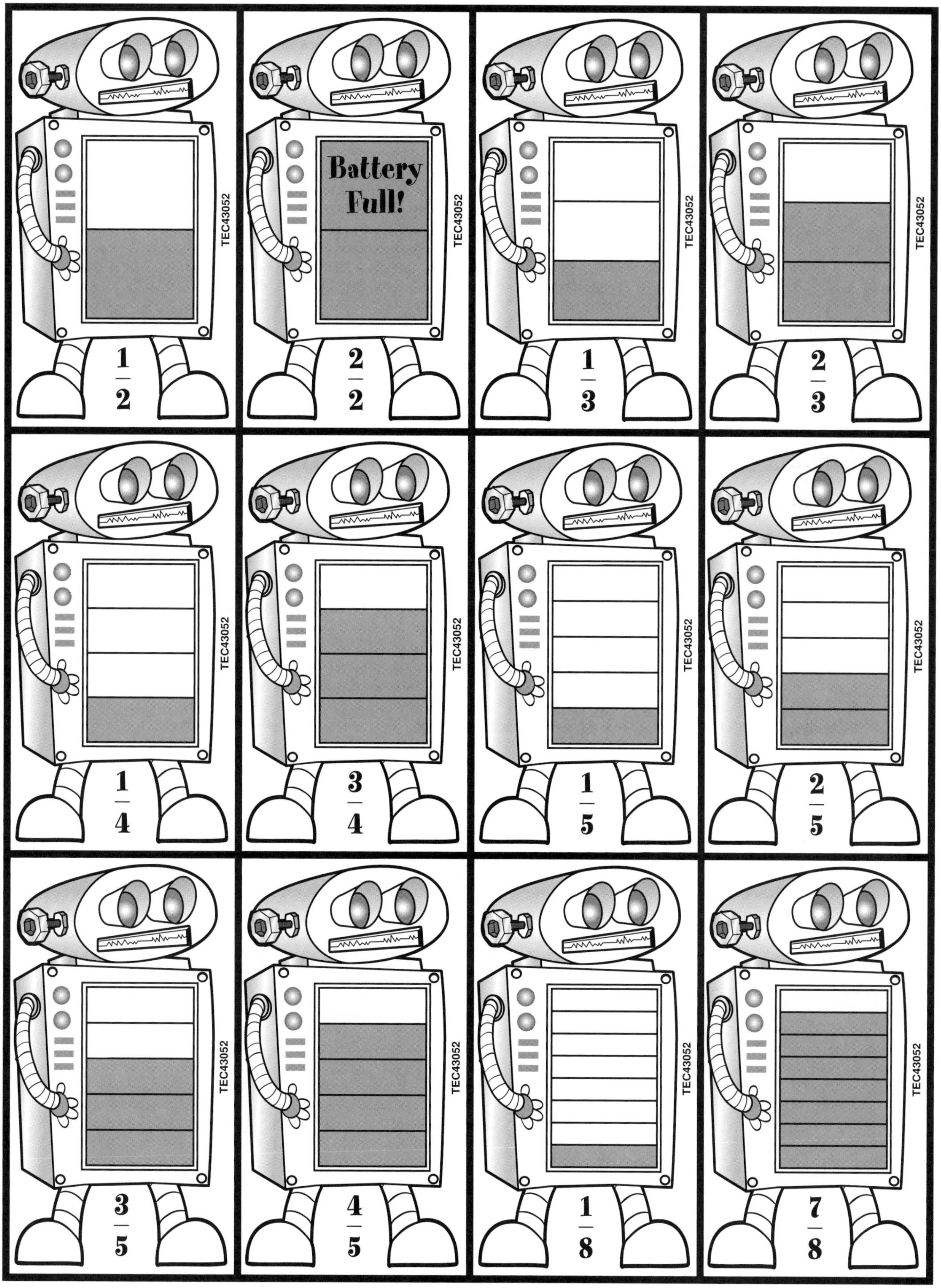
1/2
TEC43052
Battery Full!
2/2
TEC43052
1/3
TEC43052
2/3
TEC43052
1/4
TEC43052
3/4
TEC43052
1/5
TEC43052
2/5
TEC43052
3/5
TEC43052
4/5
TEC43052
1/8
TEC43052
7/8
TEC43052

Paragraph Cards

Use with "Meet the Presidents" on page 184.

George Washington

George Washington was the **first president** of the United States. Before that, he was a **surveyor** and a **soldier.** He spent much of his life in **Virginia.** He is known as the "**Father of Our Country.**" He was **respected** by many and thought to be a **great leader.**

Abraham Lincoln

Abraham Lincoln was the **sixteenth president** of the United States. Before that he was a **soldier,** a **congressman,** and a **lawyer.** He spent his early life in **Kentucky** and **Indiana** and later lived in **Illinois.** He is often called "**Honest Abe.**" He was **respected** by many and thought to be a **great leader.**

Shape Key

Use with "'Plane' to See" on page 185.

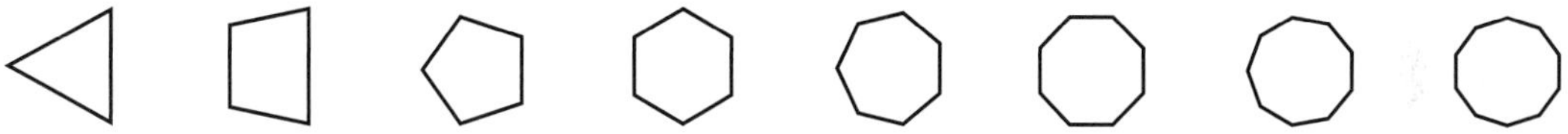

- line = two-letter word
- triangle = three-letter word
- trapezoid = four-letter word
- pentagon = five-letter word
- hexagon = six-letter word
- heptagon = seven-letter word
- octagon = eight-letter word
- nonagon = nine-letter word
- decagon = ten-letter word

TEC43053

Name ______________________ Date ______________

Recording sheet

Let's Shop!

My budget: $.

Goods to Buy	**Total Amount Spent** (Add the prices.)	**My Change** (Subtract the total from the budget.)

Note to the teacher: Use with "Book-Buying Binge" on page 185. Program the students' spending budget before copying.

Name ______________________________ Date ________________

Coming Together

Complete the table.

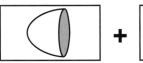

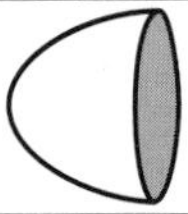	+	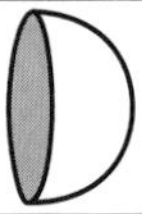	=	contraction	→	meaning

Bonus: Choose three or more contractions. Write each contraction in a different sentence.

The Mailbox® • TEC43054 • April/May 2011

Note to the teacher: Use with "By the Dozen" on page 186.

Use with "Rain, Rain..." on page 187.

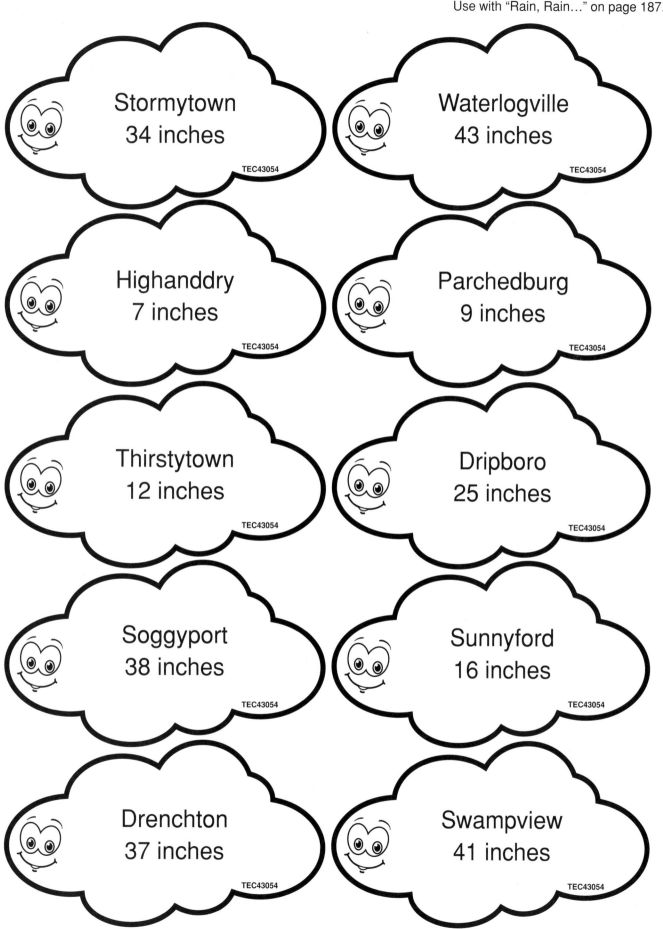

Stormytown
34 inches
TEC43054

Waterlogville
43 inches
TEC43054

Highanddry
7 inches
TEC43054

Parchedburg
9 inches
TEC43054

Thirstytown
12 inches
TEC43054

Dripboro
25 inches
TEC43054

Soggyport
38 inches
TEC43054

Sunnyford
16 inches
TEC43054

Drenchton
37 inches
TEC43054

Swampview
41 inches
TEC43054

Name ______________________________ Date ________________

Super Sounds Sleuth

Your Assignment Find words with the ________ sound, as in ____________________ ____________________.		

How many examples can you list?

 Note to the teacher: Use with "Super Sounds Sleuth" on page 188.

Perimeter and Area Cards

Use with "Measurement Match-Up" on page 189.

A.

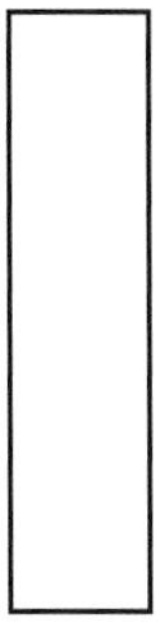

TEC43055

Perimeter =
10 cm

Area =
4 sq. cm

TEC43055

B.

TEC43055

Perimeter =
8 cm

Area =
4 sq. cm

TEC43055

C.

TEC43055

Perimeter =
14 cm

Area =
12 sq. cm

TEC43055

D.

TEC43055

Perimeter =
12 cm

Area =
9 sq. cm

TEC43055

E.

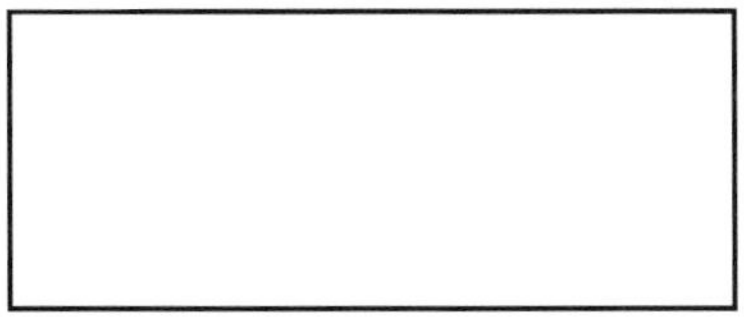

TEC43055

Perimeter =
14 cm

Area =
10 sq. cm

TEC43055

F.

TEC43055

Perimeter =
12 cm

Area =
8 sq. cm

TEC43055

G.

TEC43055

Perimeter =
10 cm

Area =
6 sq. cm

TEC43055

H.

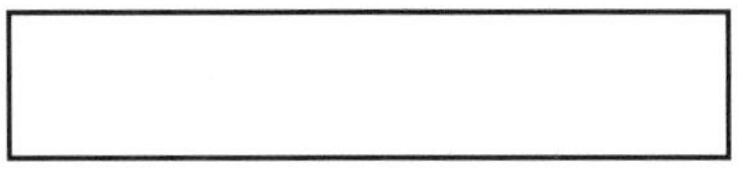

TEC43055

Perimeter =
12 cm

Area =
5 sq. cm

TEC43055

Worm Patterns

Use with "Lure Them In" on page 189.

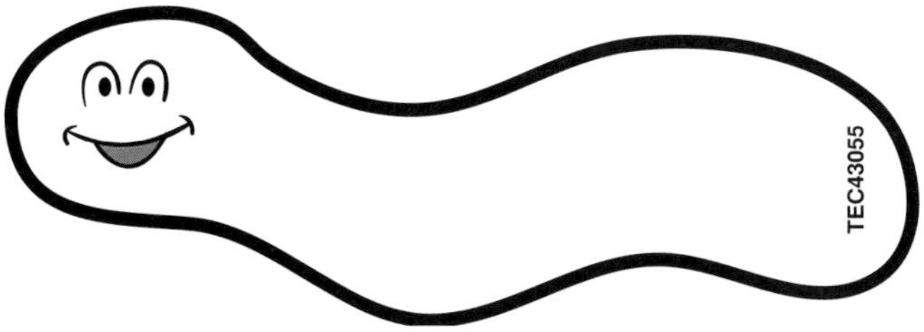
TEC43055

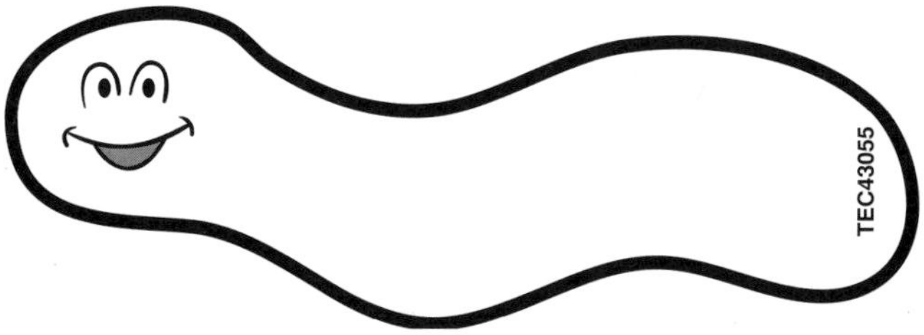
TEC43055

Measuring Me

What You Need

Unifix cubes

paper clips

2 sheets of paper

What You Do

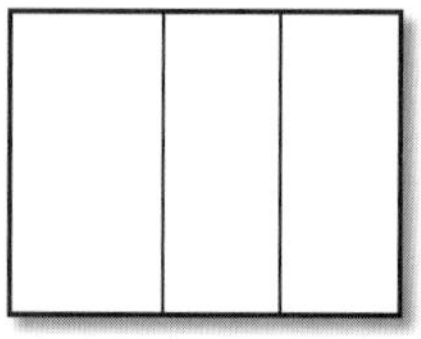

1. Draw 2 lines.

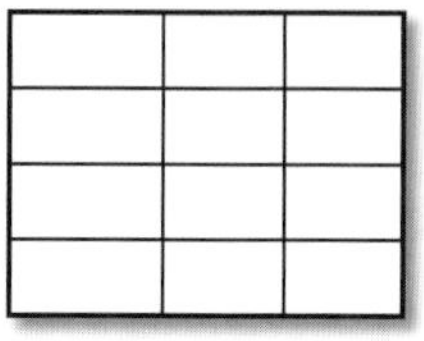

2. Draw 3 more lines.

3. Copy the words.

	cubes	paper clips
width of my hand		
length of my hand		
length of my ring finger		

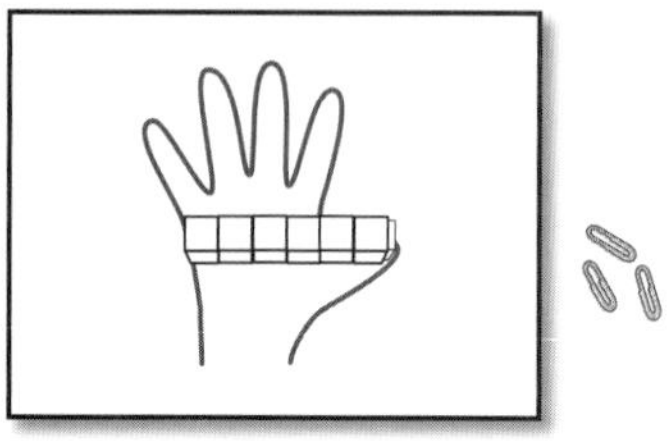

4. Trace your hand on the second paper.

5. Use cubes and paper clips to complete the chart.

	cubes	paper clips
width of my hand	6	
length of my hand		
length of my ring finger		

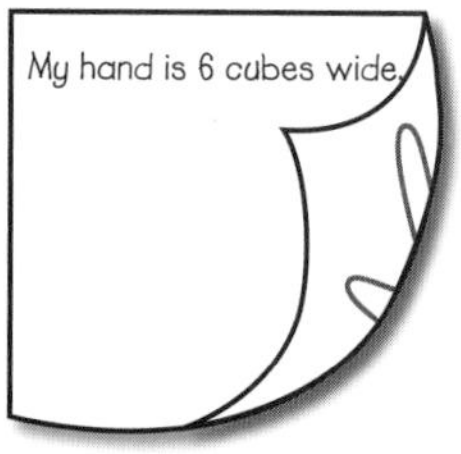
My hand is 6 cubes wide.

6. On the back of the second paper, write 4 or more sentences about the chart.

Step-by-step center: Copy this activity card and put it in a plastic page protector for durability. Then put the activity card and the needed materials at a center.

Give Me Details!

What You Need

die
lined paper

What You Do

Code

Roll 1 = A–D	Roll 4 = M–P
Roll 2 = E–H	Roll 5 = Q–T
Roll 3 = I–L	Roll 6 = U–Z

1. Roll the die.
   Look at the code.

2. Choose a subject that begins with a letter you rolled. Write a three-word sentence about the subject.

   The dog barked.

3. Rewrite the sentence to tell *how.*

   The dog barked.
   The dog barked loudly.

4. Rewrite the sentence to tell *when.*

   The dog barked.
   The dog barked loudly.
   Last night, the dog barked loudly.

5. Rewrite the sentence to tell *why.*

   The dog barked.
   The dog barked loudly.
   Last night, the dog barked loudly.
   Last night, the dog barked loudly when it saw the cat.

6. Repeat Steps 1–5 two more times.

Step-by-step center: Copy this activity card and put it in a plastic page protector for durability. Then put the activity card and the needed materials at a center.

In the News

What You Need

newspaper
glue
highlighter
paper
scissors

What You Do

1. Fold in half 2 times. Unfold. Copy.

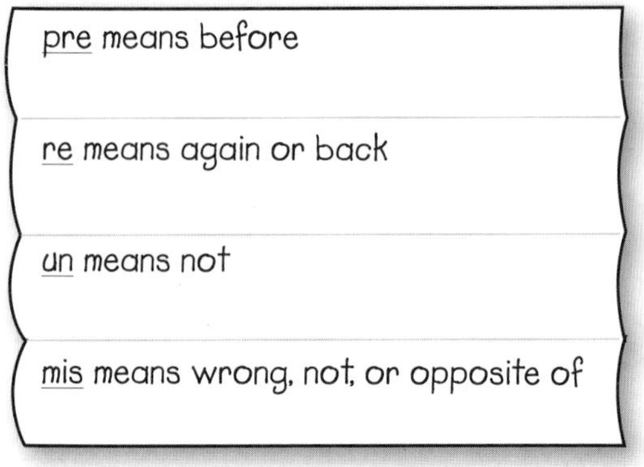

pre means before
re means again or back
un means not
mis means wrong, not, or opposite of

2. Find a word with the prefix *pre.* Cut out the sentence or headline.

Sports
Preseason Favorites Out of Playoff Picture

3. Highlight the word. Glue.

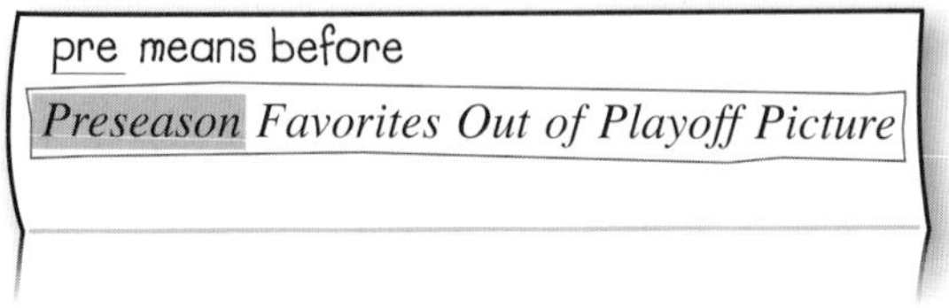

pre means before
Preseason Favorites Out of Playoff Picture

4. Write the meaning of the highlighted word.

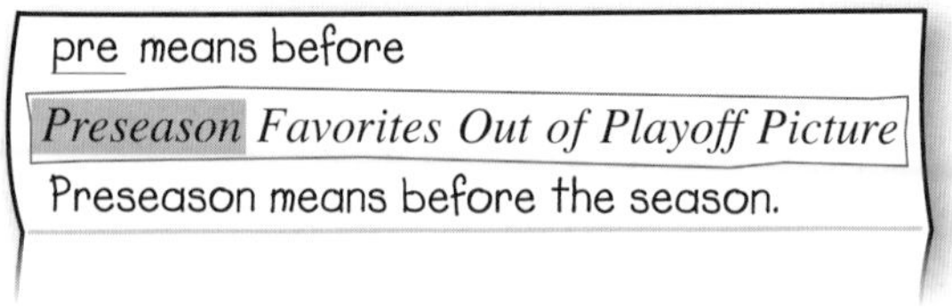

pre means before
Preseason Favorites Out of Playoff Picture
Preseason means before the season.

5. Repeat Steps 2–4 for the other prefixes.

Step-by-step center: Copy this activity card and put it in a plastic page protector for durability. Then put the activity card and the needed materials at a center.

New and Improved!

What You Need

pattern blocks

paper

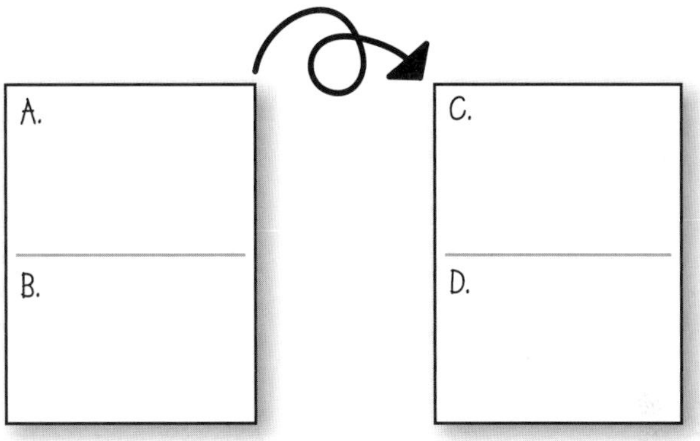
A.
B.
C.
D.

What You Do

1. Draw a line on each side. Label each section.

2. Trace 2 blocks. Label the drawing to tell how many shapes and sides.

A.
2 shapes
8 sides

3. Arrange the same blocks to make 1 shape. Trace. Label.

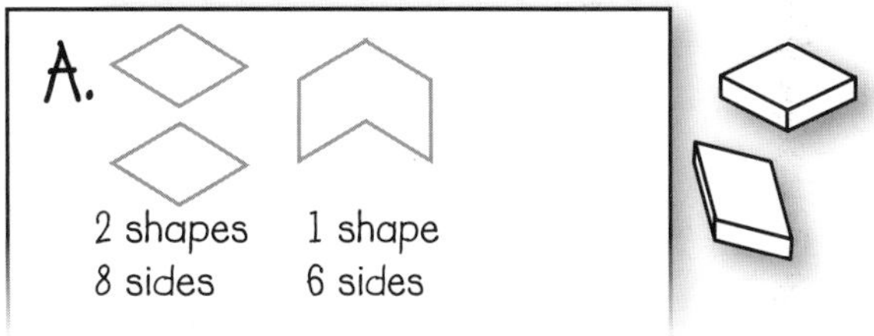
A.
2 shapes
8 sides
1 shape
6 sides

4. Rearrange the blocks to make a different shape. Trace. Label.

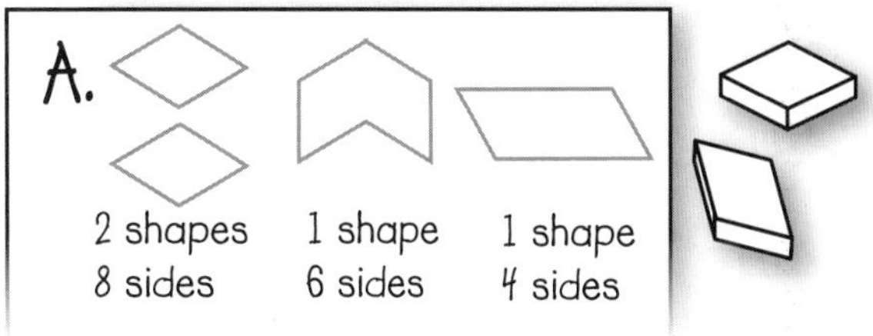
A.
2 shapes
8 sides
1 shape
6 sides
1 shape
4 sides

5. Repeat Steps 2–4. Use 2 blocks in section B, 3 blocks in section C, and 3 blocks in section D. Vary the blocks you use in each section.

Step-by-step center: Copy this activity card and put it in a plastic page protector for durability. Then put the activity card and the needed materials at a center.

What Are the Chances?

What You Need

2 2 2 2 2 2
4 4 4 4 6 6

sanitized egg carton with each section labeled as shown
pom-pom
blank paper

What You Do

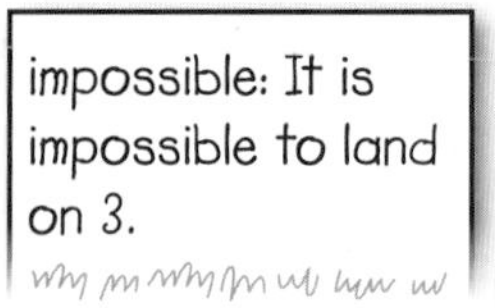
impossible: It is impossible to land on 3.

1. Write a sentence about the numbers in the carton. Use each term.

impossible	certain	likely	unlikely

2. Make a chart as shown.

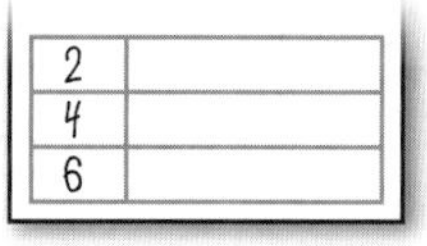
2
4
6

3. Put the pom-pom in the carton.

2 2 2 2 2
4 4 4 4 6 6

4. Close the lid and shake the carton.

5. Open the lid. Draw a tally mark to show where the pom-pom landed.

2 2 2 2 2 2
4 4 4 6 6

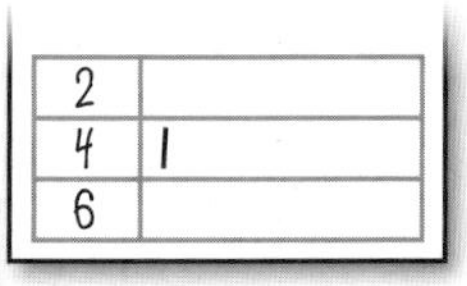
2
4 |
6

6. Repeat Steps 4 and 5 nineteen more times.

7. Write a sentence about your results.

Step-by-step center: Copy this activity card and put it in a plastic page protector for durability. Then put the activity card and the needed materials at a center.

SEASONAL

Celebrate the Season!

Getting to Know You
Using a Venn diagram

Establish a classroom of friends with this partner activity. To begin, guide the class to brainstorm questions, like the ones shown, that students can use to get to know a new classmate. Write each question on the board. Next, pair students and direct each child to ask his partner each listed question and record her answers on a sheet of paper. Then have each pair use its answers to complete a Venn diagram on a separate paper, decorating each circle to look like the matching student.

Karen Bryan King, Park Village Elementary, San Diego, CA

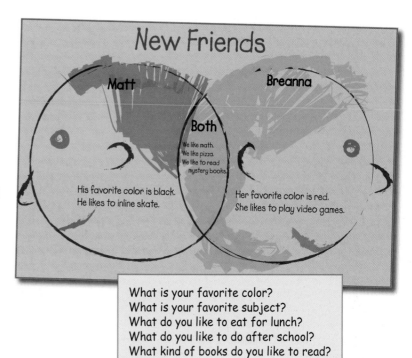

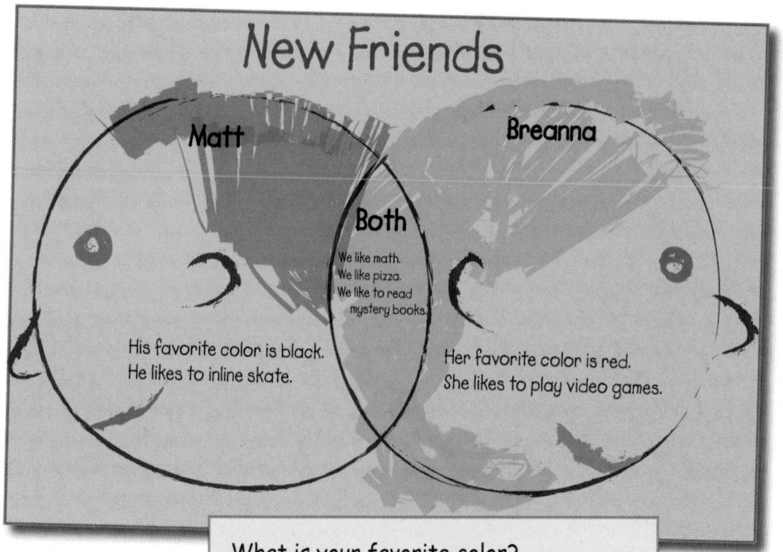
New Friends
Matt
Breanna
Both
We like math.
We like pizza.
We like to read mystery books.
His favorite color is black.
He likes to inline skate.
Her favorite color is red.
She likes to play video games.

What is your favorite color?
What is your favorite subject?
What do you like to eat for lunch?
What do you like to do after school?
What kind of books do you like to read?

Double-Duty Desktags
Presenting information

With this simple back-to-school idea, students create personalized nametags and introduce themselves to their new classmates. First, instruct each child to write her name on a sentence strip; then have her draw a picture of something she values next to her name. After a brief practice period, invite each child to introduce herself to the class, share her desktag, and explain why she values the item she drew. Then collect each tag, laminate it for durability, and mount it on the matching student's desk.

Allie

Sue Kelly, Baldwin Elementary, Manassas, VA

What Do You Do?
Writing questions and statements

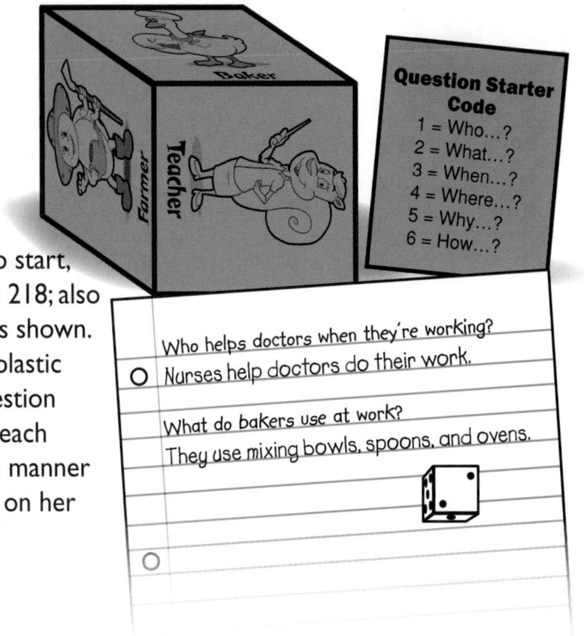
Baker
Farmer
Teacher
Question Starter Code
1 = Who...?
2 = What...?
3 = When...?
4 = Where...?
5 = Why...?
6 = How...?
Who helps doctors when they're working?
Nurses help doctors do their work.
What do bakers use at work?
They use mixing bowls, spoons, and ovens.

Roll into an interactive Labor Day discussion with this fun activity. To start, provide each student pair with a copy of the pattern and code on page 218; also give each pair a plastic die. Guide students to assemble the paper die as shown. Next, have each child take a turn tossing the paper die and rolling the plastic die. Each partner refers to the code to write on a sheet of paper a question about the laborer that was rolled. Then students exchange papers and each child writes an answer to her partner's question. Duos continue in this manner as time allows. To extend the activity, each child illustrates the answers on her original paper.

Carolyn Burant, St. John Vianney, Brookfield, WI

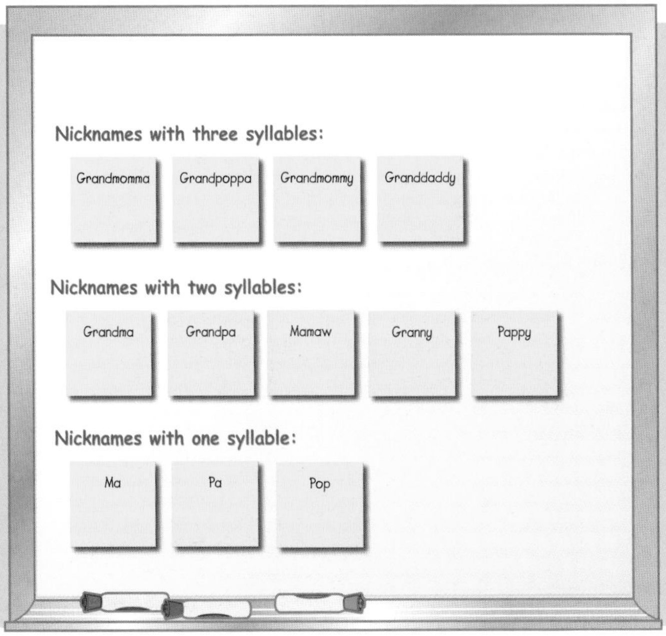
Nicknames with three syllables:
Grandmomma
Grandpoppa
Grandmommy
Granddaddy
Nicknames with two syllables:
Grandma
Grandpa
Mamaw
Granny
Pappy
Nicknames with one syllable:
Ma
Pa
Pop

Grand Names and Nicknames
Sorting and classifying

Recognize National Grandparents' Day (the first Sunday after Labor Day) and find out what your students call their grandparents. First, instruct students to write their nicknames for each grandparent or grandpal on a separate sticky note. Then invite them to place the notes on the board. Put students into small groups and have each group write a set of rules for sorting the names. Provide time for each group to share their rules. If desired, have the class choose a preferred sorting method; then use it to post the results on a display titled "Our Grand Grandparents."

Laura Johnson, South Decatur Elementary, Greensburg, IN

Language Lingo
Using a dictionary

Kick off National Hispanic Heritage Month (September 15–October 15) with this word-definition matching game. To prepare, cut apart a copy of the word cards on page 219; then give one card and one blank index card to each child. Have the student locate his word in a dictionary and then copy the word's definition onto the index card. Collect the word cards and redistribute each one, being careful not to give any card to the student who originally had it. Provide time for each child to research his new word in the dictionary. To play, one child stands and reads his word. The student with the matching definition stands, reads aloud the definition from her card, and then reads aloud her word card. Play continues until all the words and definitions are matched.

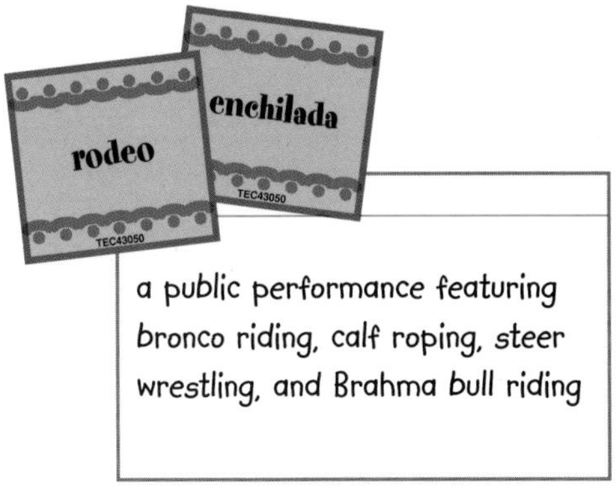
enchilada
TEC43050
rodeo
TEC43050
a public performance featuring bronco riding, calf roping, steer wrestling, and Brahma bull riding

Laura Wagner, Austin, TX

Celebrate the Season!

A Slice of a Story
Book sharing

In honor of National Pizza Month (October), invite students to sink their teeth into this post-reading activity! Have each child program a copy of page 220 with his name and information about a book he has read. Next, direct the student to color the pizza pattern, cut it out, and glue it on a paper plate. Post each plate on a display titled "A Slice of a Story."

Anita Heinzelman
Ozaukee Elementary
Fredonia, WI

Editor's Tip:
Dress up the display by using a red and white disposable tablecloth for the background.

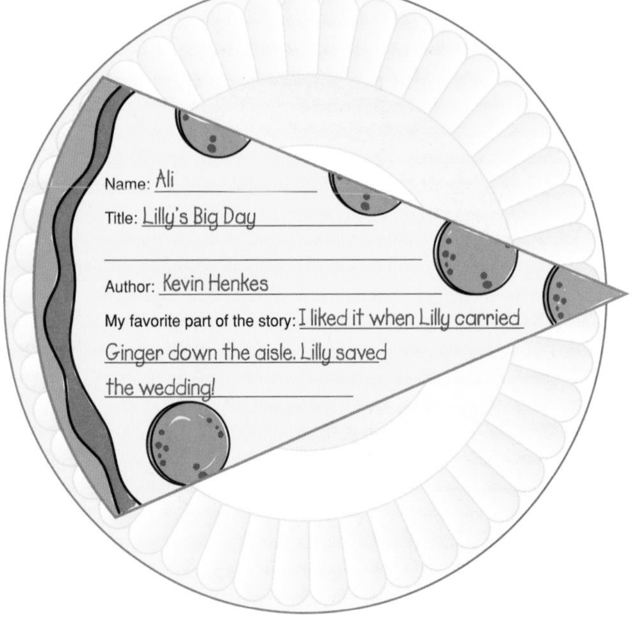
Name: Ali
Title: Lilly's Big Day
Author: Kevin Henkes
My favorite part of the story: I liked it when Lilly carried Ginger down the aisle. Lilly saved the wedding!

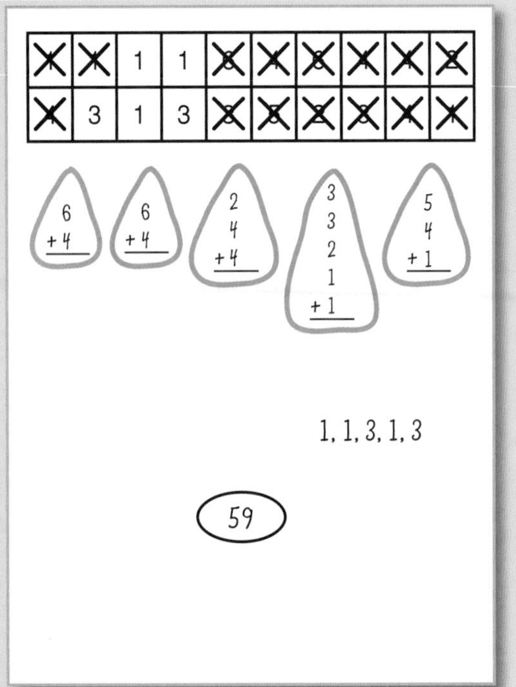
1, 1, 3, 1, 3
59

Sweet Sums
Addition, logical reasoning

Candy-corn shapes make this Halloween-themed partner game a real treat! Give each student pair a die and two sheets of paper. To play, each child draws a grid with two rows and ten columns on her paper. Players take turns rolling the die and writing each number rolled on her grid until each grid is filled. Next, each student refers to her numbers to write addition problems with sums of ten. She crosses out each number as she uses it and then uses an orange crayon to draw a candy-corn shape around the problem. When she cannot make any more sums of ten, she writes the unused numbers below her candy-corn shapes. Then she adds the sets of ten and the unused numbers to find her total score. The player with more points wins the game.

Cynthia Wicks, Eastwood Elementary, Roseburg, OR

Spooky Cave Dwellers
Contractions

Word Bank	
had	is
not	will

To begin, write the word bank shown. Then have each student trim a sheet of construction paper into a cave shape. On the cave, the child writes one word from the word bank and then sets the cave cutout aside. Next, he uses a copy of the bat pattern on page 221 to make five cutouts from black construction paper. He uses a white crayon to draw facial features on each bat and then places each bat upside down on his desk. The child combines the word from his cave with another word to make a contraction and then writes the contraction in the center of the bat. He folds the wings inward and writes each word that makes the contraction on a wing. The child repeats the steps with the remaining bats, making a new contraction each time. Finally, he uses a hole puncher to make three or more holes on the cave and a hole on each bat. He attaches each bat to the cave with a length of yarn to complete the mobile.

adapted from an idea by Angela Shelton, Sarah Smith Elementary, Atlanta, GA

not
will
not
don't
isn't
have
not
didn't

November 8, 1621
Dear Friends,

Thankful Thoughts
Writing a thank-you note

Celebrate the Thanksgiving holiday by sharing several nonfiction books on the topic with the class. Have students discuss the Pilgrims' first year in America. Lead them to brainstorm ways that the Wampanoag Indians helped the Pilgrims adjust to their new home and list each idea on the board. Next, ask each child to imagine she is a Pilgrim living in America in 1621. Have the child write a note to the Wampanoag Indians thanking them for the help they gave the Pilgrims. **To vary the activity,** encourage students to write a thank-you note to their parents or another adult for the help they have received this year.

Laura Johnson, South Decatur Elementary, Greensburg, IN

Feasting on Solutions
Addition and subtraction

This easy-to-prepare center strengthens your students' computation skills. Program numbered cards with appropriate math problems and then place them in a large soup pot. Display the pot, a ladle, and an answer key on a holiday-themed placemat. A student uses the ladle to stir the cards in the pot and then takes one. He copies the problem, solves it, and then repeats the steps until he has solved all the problems. The child returns the cards to the pot and then checks his answers against the key.

Eric
④ 1,275
+ 982
2,257
④ 1,275 + 982 =

Celebrate the Season!

Trimmed With Tinsel
Measuring

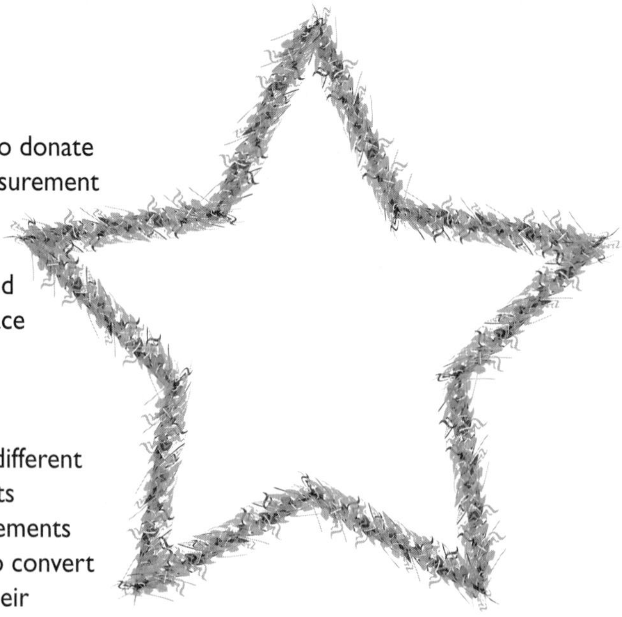

Add a little sparkle to your math activities! Encourage parents to donate tinsel garland to your class. Use different lengths of garland as measurement manipulatives for small groups.

Estimating and measuring length: Display the pieces of garland and have students estimate each length. Remove the pieces and place them in various locations around the room. Direct small groups to move to each piece and have them find the actual measurements.

Converting measurements: Instruct each group to measure a different piece of garland using an assigned unit. Invite each group to share its measurement with the class, and have each child write the measurements on a sheet of paper. After each group has shared, direct students to convert each measurement to another unit and write the conversion on their papers.

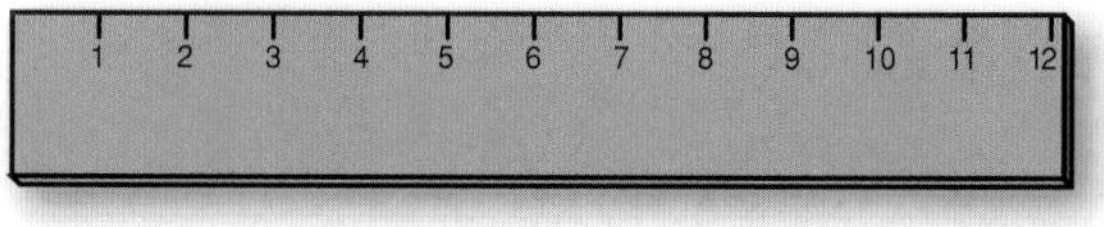
1 2 3 4 5 6 7 8 9 10 11 12

Introducing perimeter: Using pieces at least two feet long, have each group determine the length of its garland piece. Then instruct the group to shape the piece into a closed figure with straight lines. Guide each group to measure the sides of the closed figure, record each length, and then add the sides together. Direct students to compare their initial measurements to the total and then lead the class in a discussion of how perimeter is the distance around a figure.

adapted from an idea by Ann Blake
Coquitlam River Elementary, Port Coquitlam, British Columbia, Canada

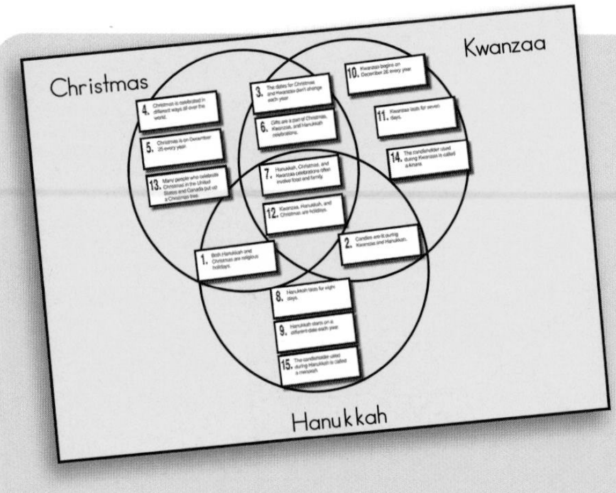
Christmas
Kwanzaa
Hanukkah

A Trio of Winter Holidays
Using a Venn diagram

Students learn about Kwanzaa, Hanukkah, and Christmas at this partner center. Use a paper plate to trace three overlapping circles (Venn diagram) on a large sheet of paper. Label the Venn diagram as shown. Next, cut apart a copy of the holiday fact cards on page 222 and place them in a resealable bag. Put the bag and student copies of the recording sheet on page 222 near the Venn diagram. Students read the facts on the cards and place each one in the corresponding section of the Venn diagram. When the duo is satisfied with the cards' placement, have each child complete the recording sheet by writing the number of each card in the corresponding Venn diagram section.

Holiday Meals
Exploring traditions, using alphabetical order

This New Year's activity serves double duty, providing practice with both social studies and language arts skills. Begin by telling students that many New Year's traditions around the world involve food; then share the facts shown. Next, invite each student to bring a copy of a recipe from home that represents a dish his family likes to eat on New Year's Eve or New Year's Day. Have each child highlight the ingredients needed to make the dish. Then instruct him to write the highlighted words in alphabetical order on a sheet of paper. Provide time for students to share their recipes and ingredient lists with the class.

Michelle Bayless
Zushi, Japan

Antonio
bacon
black-eyed peas
cheese
chicken broth
hot pepper sauce
onion
parsley
rice
tomato

A tradition in Spain is to eat 12 grapes in 12 seconds at midnight. Each grape eaten means a happy month in the year ahead.

In Greece, St. Basil's cake is served. A coin is baked inside the cake, and whoever gets the slice with the coin will be very lucky in the coming year.

One tradition in the southern United States is to eat a dish made of black-eyed peas and ham hocks. Eating the peas is believed to lead to a plentiful year.

Editor's Tip:
If a child's family doesn't have a traditional dish, encourage him to bring a recipe for any favorite dish.

Wonderful Work
Analyzing text

I wonder why
Dr. King

Build knowledge of Martin Luther King Jr. with this reading-based idea. To begin, direct each child to cut out the dove patterns from a copy of page 223. Then read aloud a favorite nonfiction text about Dr. King. Periodically stop reading and invite each child to write an "I wonder" statement about Dr. King on one of the doves. Tell students that if the answer is later revealed in the reading, they should write it on the back of the dove. After reading, invite students to share what they learned and direct students who did not discover an answer to trace their dove outlines with a crayon. Post the doves on a display and challenge students to use reference materials to find answers for the doves traced with crayon.

Barclay Marcell, Roosevelt School, Park Ridge, IL

Just Getting Warmed Up
Naming adjectives

Work out the winter wiggles while building students' vocabularies. Seat students in a circle and then teach them a simple movement pattern, such as *tap knees, clap, clap*. Give a student a winter-related object, such as a mitten or a picture of a sled, and have her start the pattern. At the end of the pattern, guide the child to name an adjective to describe the item and then pass it to the student on her right. Challenge each child to name a different adjective to describe the item as it gets passed around the circle.

Striped.

Laura Wagner, Austin, TX

Celebrate the Season!

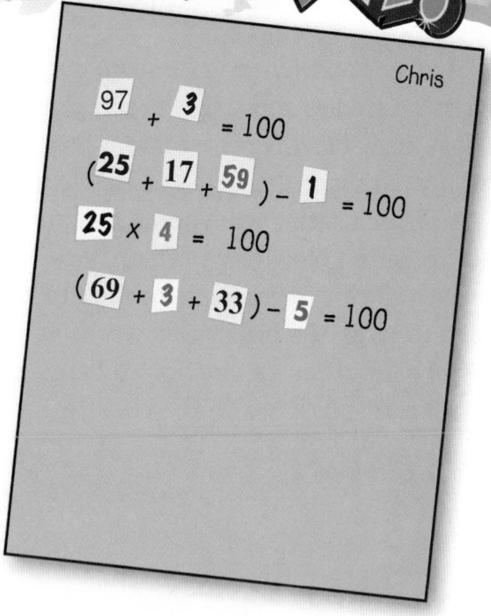
Chris
97 + 3 = 100
(25 + 17 + 59) − 1 = 100
25 × 4 = 100
(69 + 3 + 33) − 5 = 100

Clip and Calculate
Computation

This activity for the 100th day is a cut above the rest! To begin, have each child cut out numbers from various newspaper sections, such as weather listings, sports pages, and grocery flyers. Then have him glue the numbers on a sheet of paper to make number sentences that each equal 100. **For an added challenge,** specify the number of numerals each student must use in his sentences or require students to use only numbers from winter sports scores.

Michelle Bayless, Zushi, Japan

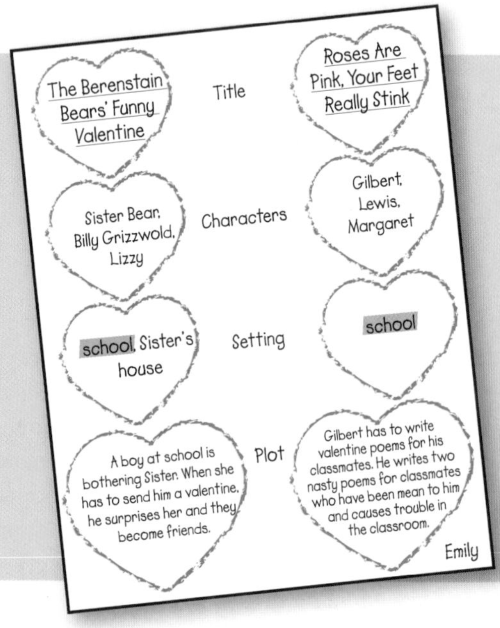
The Berenstain Bears' Funny Valentine
Title
Roses Are Pink, Your Feet Really Stink
Sister Bear, Billy Grizzwold, Lizzy
Characters
Gilbert, Lewis, Margaret
school, Sister's house
Setting
school
A boy at school is bothering Sister. When she has to send him a valentine, he surprises her and they become friends.
Plot
Gilbert has to write valentine poems for his classmates. He writes two nasty poems for classmates who have been mean to him and causes trouble in the classroom.
Emily

Heart to Heart
Comparing story elements

Use Valentine's Day stories to inspire students to take a closer look at literature. To begin, have each child cut out a copy of the heart templates from page 224 and trace them to make a graphic organizer as shown. Next, read aloud a Valentine's Day–themed story and lead students to fill in the first column of the organizer. Repeat the steps with a second story; then direct students to highlight any story elements the two stories have in common.

Laura Johnson, South Decatur Elementary, Greensburg, IN

Join the Facts
Using conjunctions, historic figures

Mix in facts about Presidents' Day, Black History Month (February), or Women's History Month (March) as you reinforce sentence-writing skills! Guide students to use reference materials to find facts about two notable historic figures, such as George Washington and Abraham Lincoln or Dr. King and Rosa Parks. Next, make a chart on the board, listing a different conjunction in each column. Direct each student to write on an index card a sentence that links facts about both figures with a conjunction. Then have him trace the conjunction with a marker. Instruct the child to write a second sentence that uses a different conjunction on another card. Provide time for each student to share his sentences aloud and then have him tape each one under the matching conjunction on the chart.

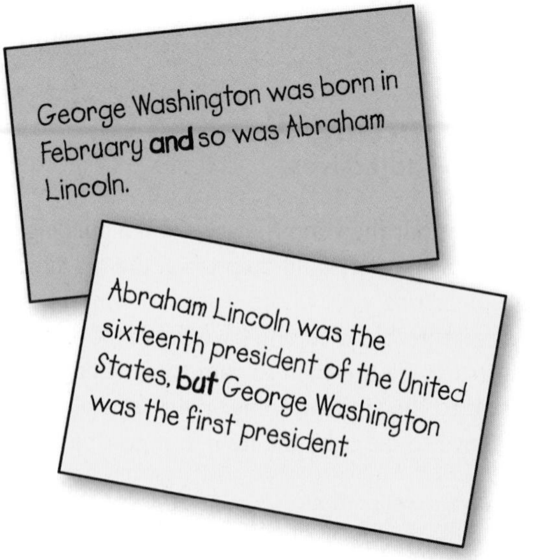
George Washington was born in February **and** so was Abraham Lincoln.
Abraham Lincoln was the sixteenth president of the United States, **but** George Washington was the first president.

Stephanie Brachtenbach, Harmony Elementary, Olathe, KS

A Gift From Lucky Leprechaun

Matter, mixtures

Boost students' observation skills with this activity that's just right for St. Patrick's Day. To prepare, gather several clear containers with tight-fitting lids. Pour four tablespoons of instant pudding mix (magic powder) into each container. To begin, give each small group a container and ½ cup of milk. Also give each student a copy of the recording sheet on page 225 and a plastic spoon. Next, explain to the class that a leprechaun named Lucky left some magic powder for their activity. Provide time for groups to follow the directions on the recording sheet, with each child writing her own observations; then lead students in a discussion of their results.

Dawn Courtney, Orvis Risner Elementary, Edmond, OK

MILK

Editor's Tip:
Show *physical change* by adding a few drops of green food coloring to the milk before pouring it.

Blooming With Spring Words
daisy
baseball
butterflies
buzzing bees
fluttering wings
bunnies hop
tennis
playing at the park
fishing
frogs

Prompting Spring

Brainstorming writing topics

Prepare students to write all season long with these individual word banks. Direct each child to color and cut out a copy of the word bank cover on page 224. Then have her glue the pattern on the front of a folded sheet of construction paper. Next, lead the class to brainstorm spring words and phrases as you list the ideas on the board. Instruct each child to copy on the inside of her folded paper a variety of words she hopes to use in future writings. Then have her slip the word bank inside her journal, where it will be ready for her when she needs ideas.

Laura Johnson
South Decatur Elementary
Greensburg, IN

Celebrate the Season!

Sweet Figures of Speech
Writing similes

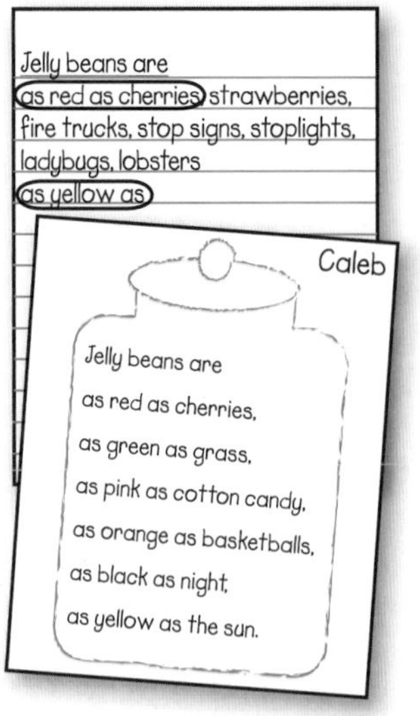

Jelly beans are
as red as cherries, strawberries,
fire trucks, stop signs, stoplights,
ladybugs, lobsters
as yellow as
Caleb
Jelly beans are
as red as cherries,
as green as grass,
as pink as cotton candy,
as orange as basketballs,
as black as night,
as yellow as the sun.

Colorful spring candies are the inspiration for this figurative language activity. To begin, give each group a small container of jelly beans and a sheet of paper. Direct the group to title the paper as shown. Then guide the group to write one jelly bean color and list items that are the same color. Have students repeat the steps with the remaining jelly bean colors. Finally, have each child refer to his group's list as he writes on a sheet of paper a simile for each jelly bean color. If desired, direct the child to decorate his paper to look like a candy jar.

Pat Hart, W. S. Freeman Elementary, Troy, IL

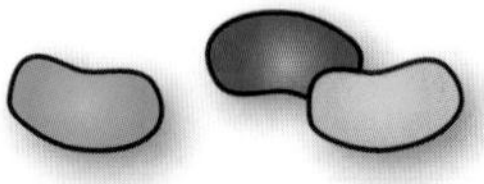

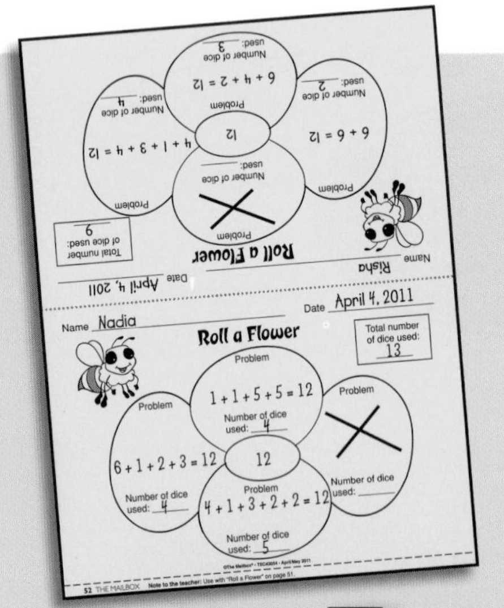

Name Nadia
Date April 4, 2011
Roll a Flower
Total number of dice used: 13
Problem
1 + 1 + 5 + 5 = 12
Number of dice used: 4
6 + 1 + 2 + 3 = 12
12
4 + 1 + 3 + 2 + 2 = 12
Number of dice used: 5

Roll a Flower
Addition

Math skills bloom when students play this partner game. Give each student pair a copy of the gameboard on page 226. To begin, Player 1 rolls three dice and adds the numbers rolled. Each player writes the sum in the center of her flower. Next, Player 1 rolls five dice. She uses all or some of the numbers to make an addition sentence that equals the sum in the flower's center. Then she writes the problem on one petal and records the number of dice she used. If she is unable to make a problem, she marks an X on a petal, and her turn ends. Players take turns rolling five dice until each player has had four turns. Then each student writes the total number of dice she used to make her problems. The player who uses more dice is the winner!

Cynthia Wicks, Eastwood Elementary, Roseburg, OR

To Name a Few
Cause and effect

Happy Mother's Day!
I ♡ you, Mom!
Because my mom washes my clothes
I have clean clothes to wear to school
When my mom hugs me it makes me smile
My mom helps me with my homework
As a result, I learn more in school
Love, Jack

Students acknowledge some of the things their moms do with this easy-to-make Mother's Day card. Put at a center copies of the card on page 227 and crayons. Direct each student to complete the three flowers with cause-and-effect statements about his mother or another special female. Have the child fold his paper in half to make a card and then use crayons to add desired details.

adapted from an idea by Carolyn Burant, St. John Vianney School, Brookfield, WI

Celebrate the Season!

Round of Applause
Main idea and details

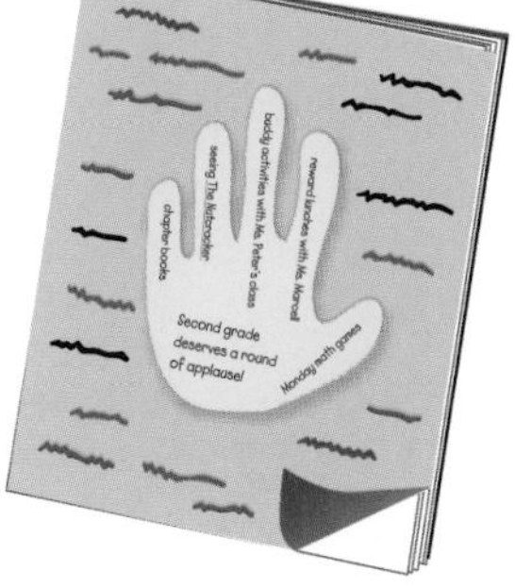

Second grade deserves a round of applause!

Give a cheer for the end of the year as students create personalized keepsakes. First, have each child trace his hand on a sheet of paper and cut the tracing out. Instruct him to label the palm with a main idea, such as one from the list shown. Then have the student write a different detail on each digit. Next, direct him to use his handprint planner to write a paragraph. Copy all students' paragraphs for each child. To make a book, have each child fold a large sheet of construction paper in half (covers), glue his handprint planner to the front cover, place his copies of the paragraphs between the covers, and staple along the left side. As an added touch, provide time for each student to sign his classmates' book covers.

____ grade deserves a round of applause!
I loved ____ grade!
I learned so much this year.
There were more good times this year than I can count on one hand!

Barclay Marcell, Roosevelt Elementary, Park Ridge, IL

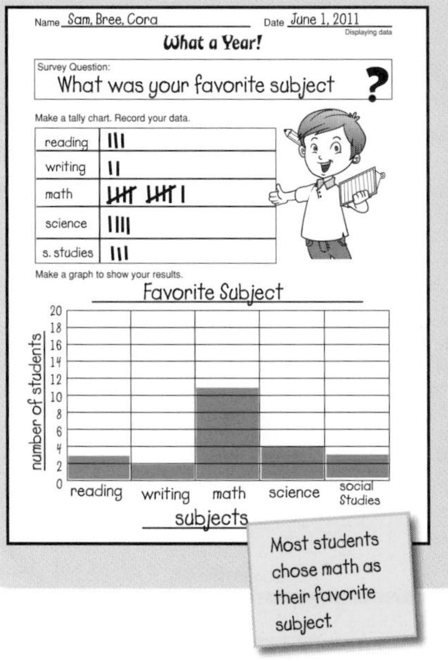

Name Sam, Bree, Cora
Date June 1, 2011
Displaying data
What a Year!
Survey Question:
What was your favorite subject ?
Make a tally chart. Record your data.
reading |||
writing ||
math 𝍸 𝍸 |
science ||||
s. studies |||
Make a graph to show your results.
Favorite Subject
number of students
0 2 4 6 8 10 12 14 16 18 20
reading writing math science social Studies
subjects
Most students chose math as their favorite subject.

Looking Back
Displaying data

Reflect on the highlights of the school year with this group activity. To start, challenge each group to generate three multiple-choice survey questions related to the school year. Provide time for students to share their questions with the rest of the class; then have each group select a different question. Direct each group's members to write the question on a copy of page 228, survey each classmate, and record the data on the same page. Instruct students to graph the results on the bottom of the page. Finally, have each group member write a different statement about the data on a small sticky note. Title a display "Looking Back" and post each group's sticky notes next to its data sheet. Keep the board displayed for next year's students to review, but change the title to read "Looking Ahead."

Laura Wagner, Austin, TX

Editor's Tip:
To add color to the display and to keep the groups' items organized, give each group its own color of sticky notes.

Sweet Beginnings
Sequencing, timelines

1295 Some believe Marco Polo brought a recipe for a frozen treat that is like sherbet from a trade visit to China.
1660 Ice cream was at first a very special treat that only the wealthy could enjoy. In this year, people in Europe who were not royalty were able to buy ice cream.
1774 Ice cream was first served in what would become the United States of America.
1790 President George Washington spent almost $200 during the summer on ice cream.
1851 A man named Jacob Fussell started the first ice cream plant. In this building, large amounts of ice cream were made for sale.
1904 During the World's Fair in St. Louis, Missouri, ice cream cones were served for the first time.
The Early History of Ice Cream

Students scoop up interesting facts about ice cream with this activity. To begin, a student cuts out the scoop patterns from a copy of page 229. Next, she orders the scoops from the earliest event to the most recent. Then the child makes an ice cream cone or sundae. **To make an ice cream cone**, she glues the scoops together in a column. Then she glues them to a paper cone shape and writes on the cone a title for the timeline. **To make a sundae**, she orders the scoops side-by-side, glues them to a paper dish shape, and writes on the dish a title for the timeline.

Kelli Jones, East Clayton Elementary, Clayton, NC

Die Pattern and Code

Use with "What Do You Do?" on page 209.

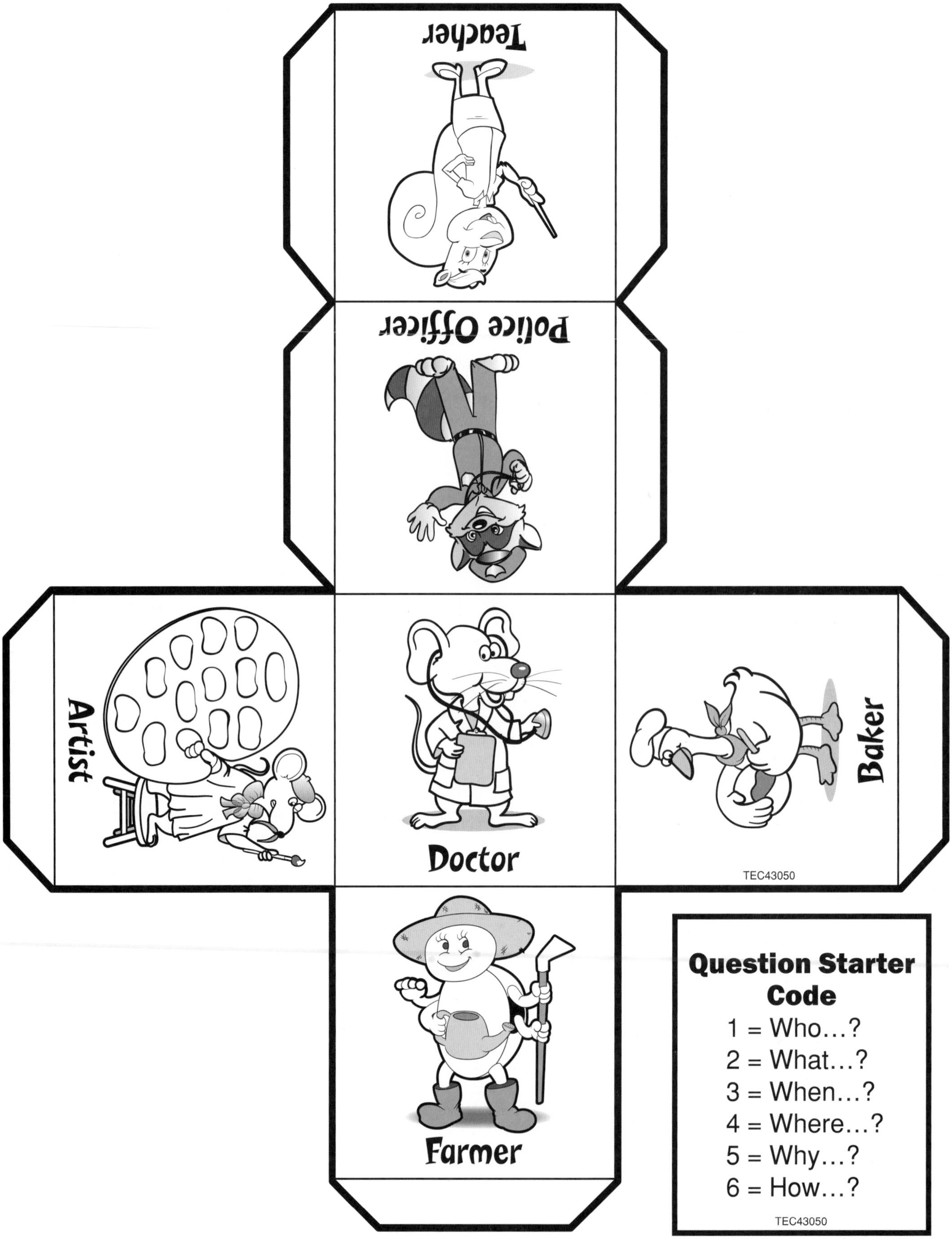
Teacher
Police Officer
Artist
Doctor
Baker
TEC43050
Farmer

Question Starter Code

1 = Who…?
2 = What…?
3 = When…?
4 = Where…?
5 = Why…?
6 = How…?

TEC43050

Word Cards

Use with “Language Lingo” on page 209.

cilantro TEC43050	piñata TEC43050	savvy TEC43050	cigar TEC43050	guacamole TEC43050	mosquito TEC43050
oregano TEC43050	barracuda TEC43050	salsa TEC43050	tobacco TEC43050	burrito TEC43050	renegade TEC43050
guerrilla TEC43050	vanilla TEC43050	enchilada TEC43050	hurricane TEC43050	patio TEC43050	rodeo TEC43050
ranch TEC43050	lariat TEC43050	cafeteria TEC43050	lasso TEC43050	alligator TEC43050	mustang TEC43050
tornado TEC43050	tamale TEC43050	adios TEC43050	bronco TEC43050	cargo TEC43050	taco TEC43050

Pizza Pattern

Use with “A Slice of a Story” on page 210.

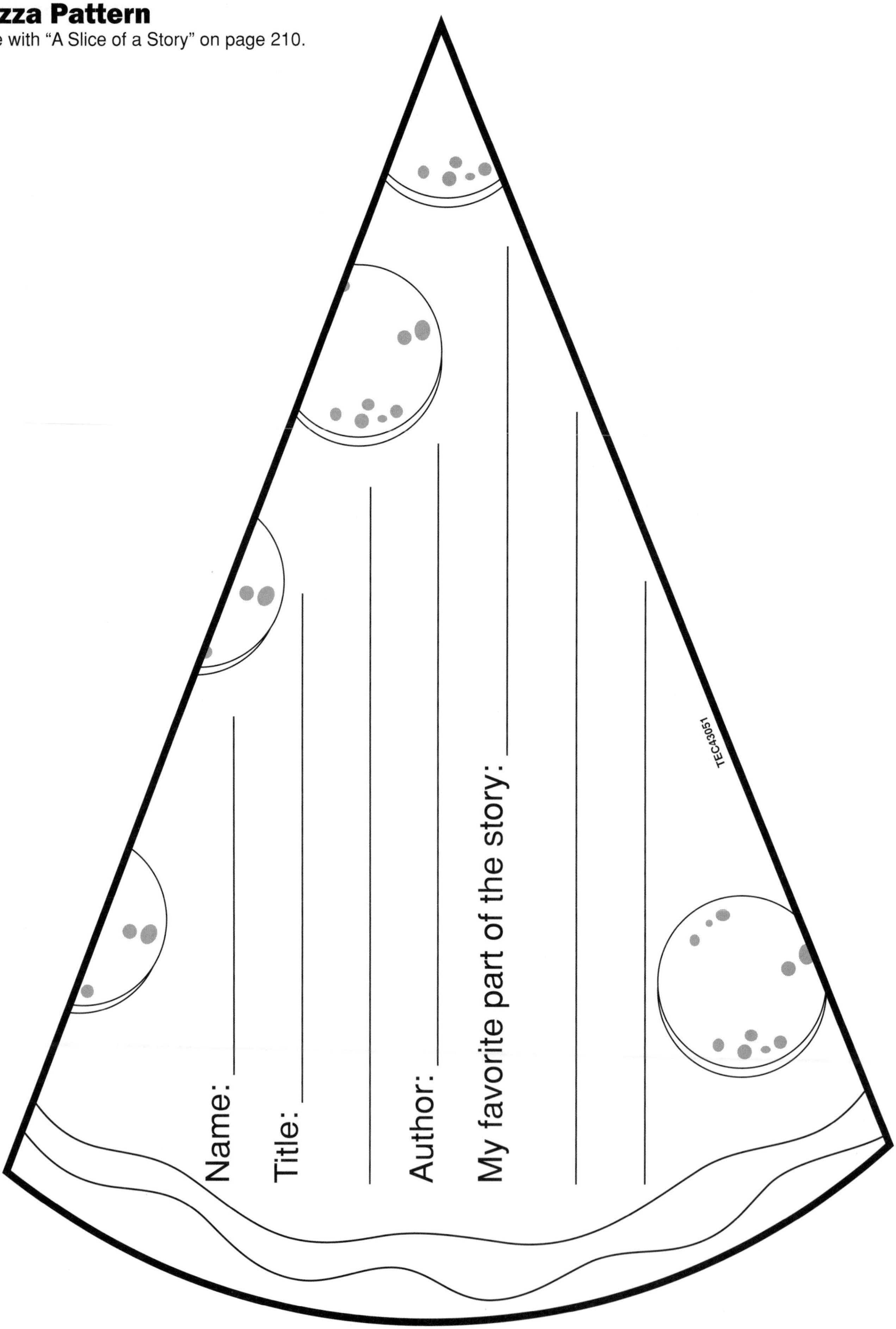
Name:
Title:
Author:
My favorite part of the story:
TEC43051

Bat Pattern

Use with "Spooky Cave Dwellers" on page 211.

TEC43051

Holiday Fact Cards and Recording Sheet

Use with "A Trio of Winter Holidays" on page 212.

1. Both Hanukkah and Christmas are religious holidays. TEC43052	**2.** Candles are lit during Kwanzaa and Hanukkah. TEC43052	**3.** The dates for Christmas and Kwanzaa don't change each year. TEC43052
4. Christmas is celebrated in different ways all over the world. TEC43052	**5.** Christmas is on December 25 every year. TEC43052	**6.** Gifts are a part of Christmas, Kwanzaa, and Hanukkah celebrations. TEC43052
7. Hanukkah, Christmas, and Kwanzaa celebrations often involve food and family. TEC43052	**8.** Hanukkah lasts for eight days. TEC43052	**9.** Hanukkah starts on a different date each year. TEC43052
10. Kwanzaa begins on December 26 every year. TEC43052	**11.** Kwanzaa lasts for seven days. TEC43052	**12.** Kwanzaa, Hanukkah, and Christmas are holidays. TEC43052
13. Many people who celebrate Christmas in the United States and Canada put up a Christmas tree. TEC43052	**14.** The candleholder used during Kwanzaa is called a *kinara.* TEC43052	**15.** The candleholder used during Hanukkah is called a *menorah.* TEC43052

Name ______________________________ Date ________________

Venn diagram

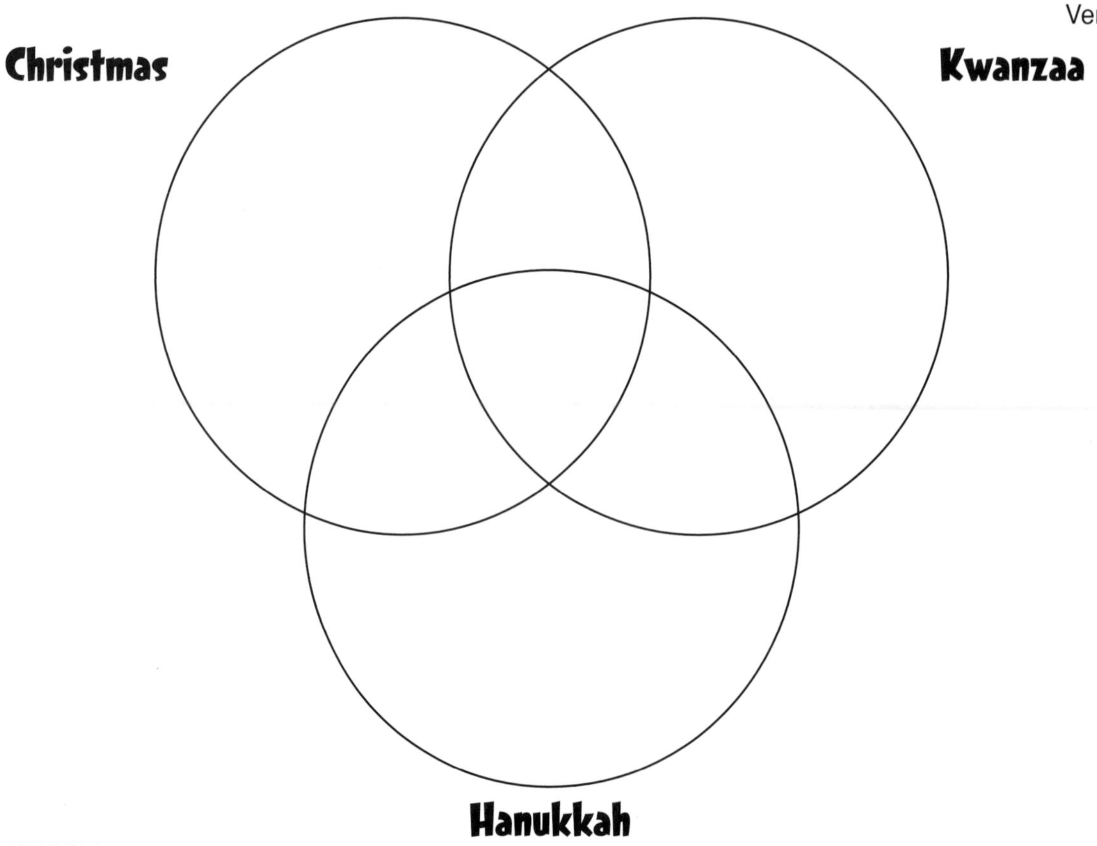
Christmas
Kwanzaa
Hanukkah

TEC43052

TEC43052

Heart Patterns

Use with "Heart to Heart" on page 214.

TEC43053
TEC43053
TEC43053
TEC43053

Word Bank Cover

Use with "Prompting Spring" on page 215.

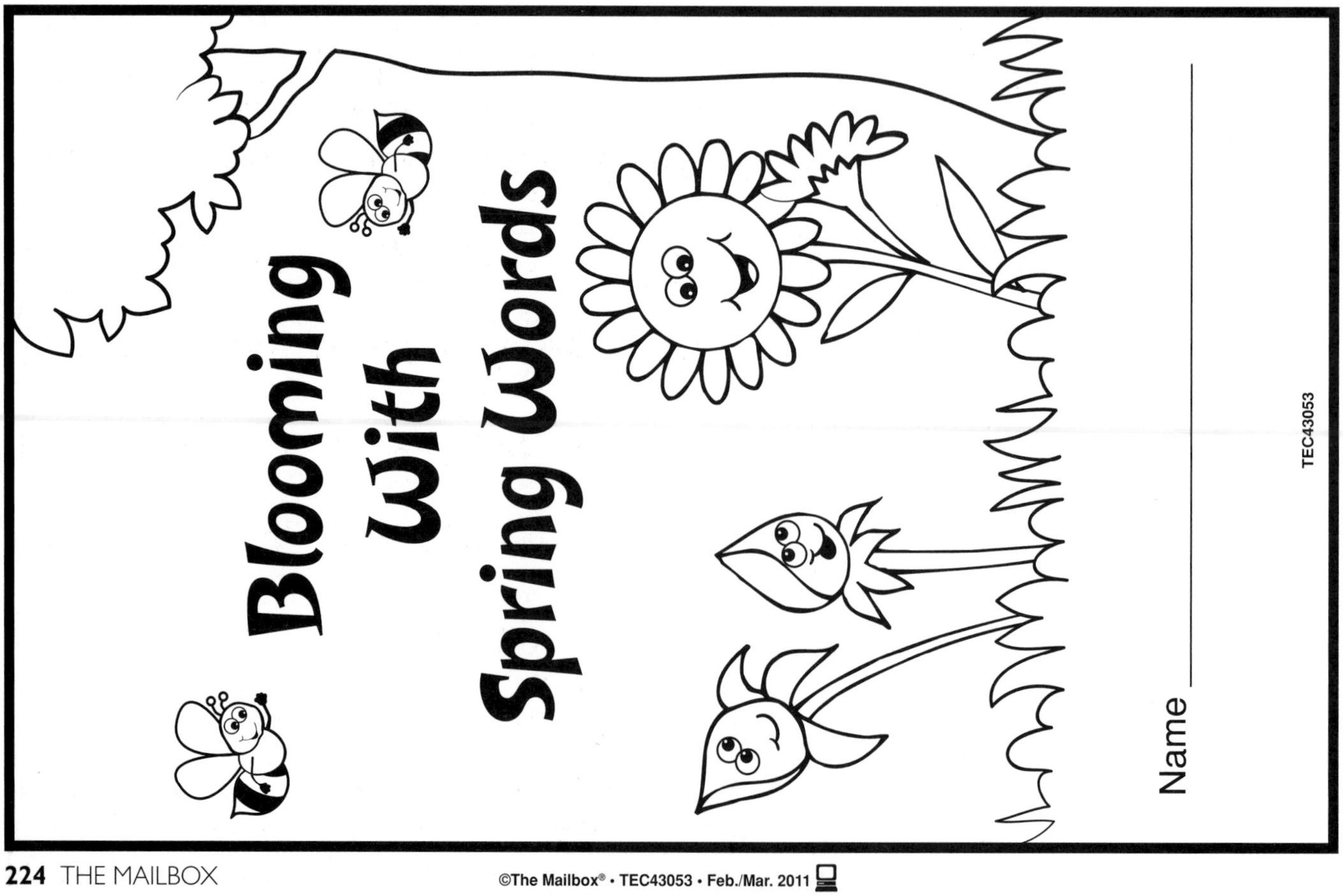
Blooming
With
Spring Words
Name
TEC43053

Name ______________________________ Date ____________________

Matter

Thanks, Lucky!

Follow the directions and answer the questions.
Use the word bank.

1. Describe the powder. ______________________________

____

____

Add the milk. Put the lid on tightly. Shake the container for at least two minutes. Remove the lid and look at the mixture.

2. How did the mixture change? ______________________________

____

____

3. Why do you think the mixture did or did not change? ______________________________

____

____

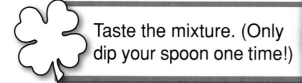

Taste the mixture. (Only dip your spoon one time!)

Word Bank

dry	lumpy
sweet	smooth
cold	thick
warm	wet
liquid	solid
gas	bad

Do you believe in leprechauns?

4. How does it taste? ______________________________

____

____

____

Bonus: What happens when matter gets mixed together?

Note to the teacher: Use with "A Gift From Lucky Leprechaun" on page 215.

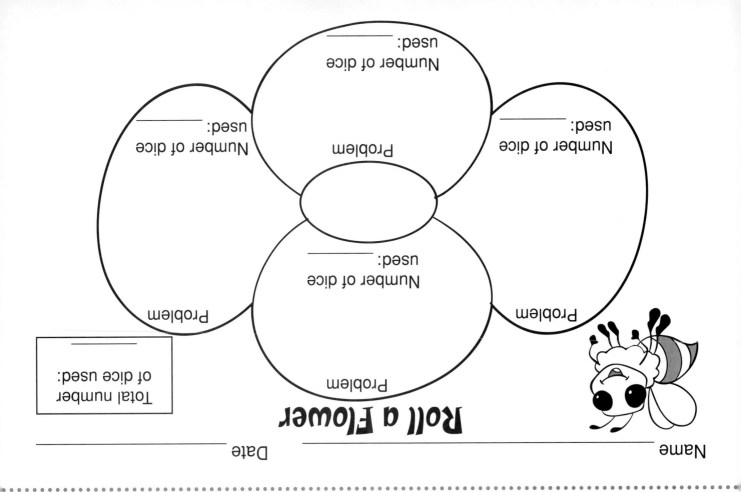

Name ____________ Date ____________

Roll a Flower

Total number of dice used: ________

Problem

Number of dice used: ________

Problem

Number of dice used: ________

Problem

Number of dice used: ________

Problem

Number of dice used: ________

Problem

Number of dice used: ________

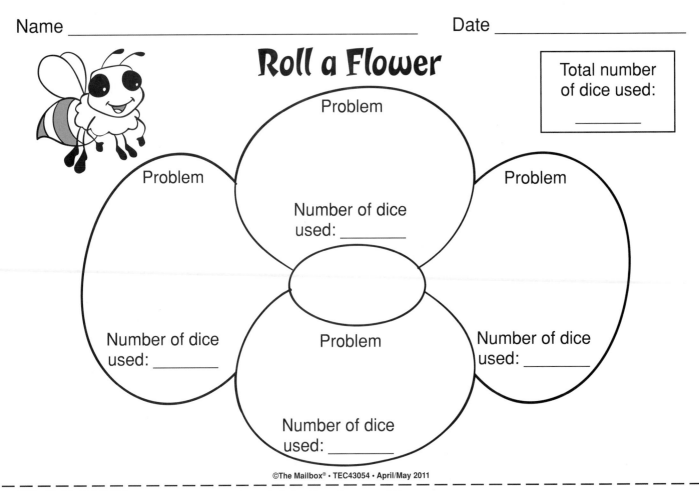

Name ______________________________ Date ________________

Roll a Flower

Total number of dice used: ________

Problem

Number of dice used: ________

Problem

Number of dice used: ________

Problem

Number of dice used: ________

Problem

Number of dice used: ________

Problem

Number of dice used: ________

 Note to the teacher: Use with “Roll a Flower” on page 216.

Because my mom ______________

____

______________________________,

I ____________________________

______________________________.

When ______________

____

______________________________,

____

______________________________.

____

______________________________.

As a result, ______________

____

______________________________.

Note to the teacher: Use with “To Name a Few” on page 216.

Name ______________________ Date ______________

Displaying data

What a Year!

Survey question:

Make a tally chart. Record your data.

Make a graph to show your results.

 Note to the teacher: Use with “Looking Back” on page 217.

Ice Cream Scoops

Use with "Sweet Beginnings" on page 217.

1904
During the World's Fair in St. Louis, Missouri, ice cream cones were served for the first time.

TEC43055

1295
Some believe Marco Polo brought a recipe for a frozen treat that is like sherbet from a trade visit to China.

TEC43055

1851
A man named Jacob Fussell started the first ice cream plant. In this building, large amounts of ice cream were made for sale.

TEC43055

1660
Ice cream was at first a very special treat that only the wealthy could enjoy. In this year, people in Europe who were not royalty were able to buy ice cream.

TEC43055

1790
President George Washington spent almost $200 during the summer on ice cream.

TEC43055

1774
Ice cream was first served in what would become the United States of America.

TEC43055

Language Arts Activity Cards

Cut out the cards. Use them as center or free-time activities.

Categorizing and classifying words

Around the Classroom

Sort the words into two or more groups.
Label each group.

backpacks	crayons	papers
board	desks	pencils
books	door	rug
chairs	flag	students
clock	globe	teacher

TEC43050

Compound words

My Fun Grandpa

Write eight or more compound words shown in the picture.

TEC43050

What's for Lunch?

Choose a topic sentence.
Write three detail sentences.

I like to buy my lunch at school.
Lunch is better when you bring it from home.
VITAMIN D MILK

TEC43050

Using a dictionary

It's Apple Season!

Find each word in a dictionary.
Write each word and the page number you found it on.

apple
cider
core
fruit
harvest
orchard
pioneer
rose
seed
wilderness

TEC43050

Subtraction

Sport Star

Write each problem.
Use the code.
Solve.

18 – ⚽ = ___	13 – ⚾ = ___	16 – 🏀 = ___	15 – 🏈 = ___
16 – 🏈 = ___	17 – 🏀 = ___	14 – ⚽ = ___	12 – ⚾ = ___
14 – 🏀 = ___	15 – ⚾ = ___	13 – 🏈 = ___	17 – ⚽ = ___

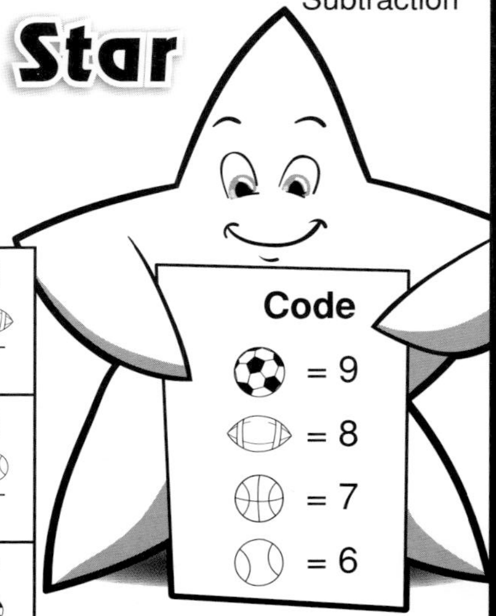

Code
⚽ = 9
🏈 = 8
🏀 = 7
⚾ = 6

TEC43050

Odd and even numbers

Snacktime!

Write to a friend.
Tell how to find out whether a number is odd or even.

TEC43050

Ordering numbers

Pick a Puzzle

List the numbers from least to greatest.
Write the list again. Add five more numbers that come between the smallest number and the largest number.

- 1,082 pieces
- 982 pieces
- 1,002 pieces
- 1,209 pieces
- 1,028 pieces

TEC43050

Graphs

Tools They Love

Read the pictograph.
Make a bar graph that shows the same data.
Then write two sentences about the data.

Our Favorite Art Supplies	
Crayons	🧍🧍
Markers	🧍🧍🧍🧍🧍🧍
Colored pencils	🧍🧍🧍 half 🧍
🧍 = 2 students	

TEC43050

Language Arts Activity Cards

How to use Cut out the cards. Use them as center or free-time activities.

Adding *-ed*

Feasting on Words

Rewrite the words.
Add *ed* to each one.
If you dropped the silent *e,* circle the word.

bake	care	clean	gobble	munch	place
pull	scrape	store	thank	wash	wipe

TEC43051

Writing a friendly letter

Fall Favorites

Write a letter to a friend or family member.
Describe two of your favorite things about fall.

Date
Greeting,
Body
Closing,
Signature

TEC43051

Alphabetical order

Outdoor Chores

Copy each list.
Finish four more words in each list.
Be sure the words are in ABC order.

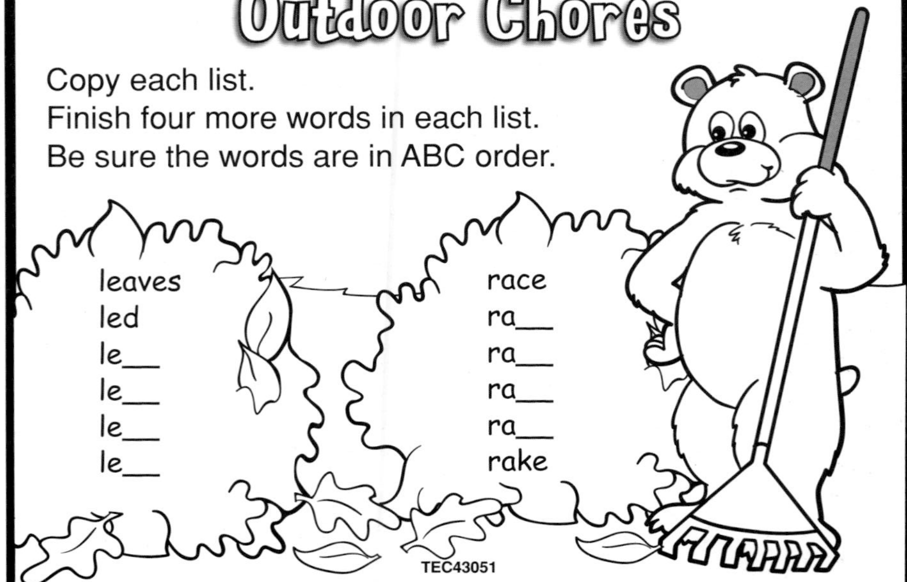

leaves	race
led	ra___
le___	ra___
le___	ra___
le___	ra___
le___	rake

TEC43051

Similes

The Pumpkin Patch

A simile compares two different things using the word *like* or *as*.
Write two or more similes about the objects in the pumpkin patch.

The crow is as black as night.

TEC43051

How to use Cut out the cards. Use them as center or free-time activities.

Number words

Bobbing for Numbers

Copy each number.
Write the word for each number.

94
39
76
110
61
45
52
18
100
83

TEC43051

Attributes of plane shapes

Who's Who?

Write the name of each shape.
Circle two shape names.
Tell how the two shapes are the same.
Tell how the two shapes are different.

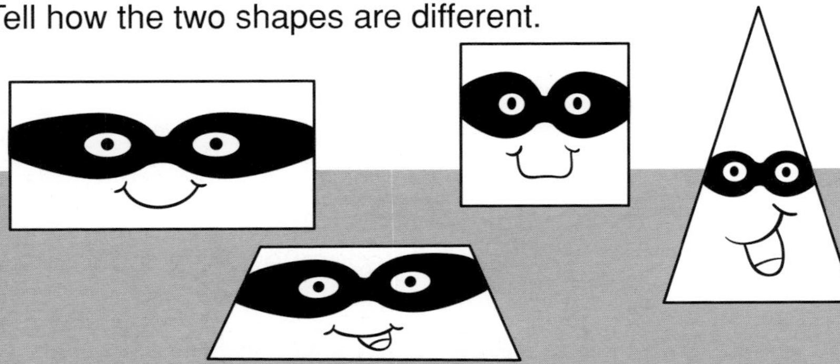

TEC43051

Patterns

In the Field

Write a pattern for each rule.
Use five or more numbers in each pattern.

A. Increase by five.

B. Decrease by eight.

C. Double the number.

D. Add 5, add 4, add 3, add 2, add 1.

TEC43051

Estimating sums

A Football Fan

Use the numbers to write ten different addition problems.
Estimate each sum.

108
872
346
108 + 872 = ?
110 + 870 = 980
513
251
629

TEC43051

Language Arts Activity Cards

How to use Cut out the cards. Use them as center or free-time activities.

Abbreviations

A Busy Lady

Copy the lists.
Use the abbreviation for each underlined word.

Things to Do Before Christmas:
- Read the elves' December newsletter.
- Buy 999 feet of gift wrap.
- Make thirty pounds of fudge.
- Find 25 Reindeer Road.
- Mend Mister Claus's suit.

Things to Do After Christmas:
- Plan a fancy dinner for January 1.
- Set up spa days (every Saturday).
- Visit Doctor Smith.
- Attend a party for Dasher Junior.
- Build a new workshop on Snow Street.

TEC43052

Contractions

On the Ice

Write five or more sentences about the picture.
Use a different contraction in each sentence.
Underline the contractions.

I don't think Bunny can skate today.

TEC43052

Guide words

Time for Snow!

Copy each set of guide words.
Write five or more words that would come between each set.

blizzard–buried
flake–frozen
silent–snowstorm

TEC43052

Paragraph writing

Winter Writing

Choose a topic sentence.
Use it to write a paragraph with three supporting details and a closing sentence.

Topic Sentences
- December is the best month!
- There are some important things to know when playing with a dreidel.
- Many holidays use candles in their celebrations.
- I should be allowed to stay up late on New Year's Eve.

TEC43052

Math Activity Cards

How to use Cut out the cards. Use them as center or free-time activities.

Symmetry

Let's Bake Cookies

Draw two rectangles (trays).
On one tray, show six or more different cookies that have symmetry.
On the other tray, show six or more different cookies that do not have symmetry.
Label each tray.

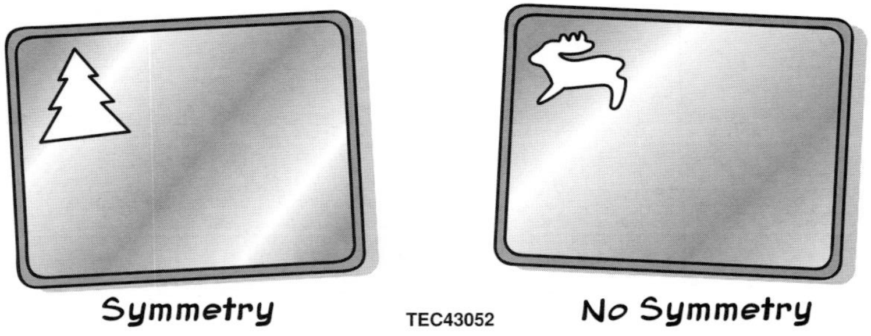
Symmetry
No Symmetry

TEC43052

Addition with regrouping

Gift Boxes Galore

Copy the problems.
Draw a box around the problem if it requires regrouping.
Write to tell how you know that you will regroup.
Then solve each problem to check.

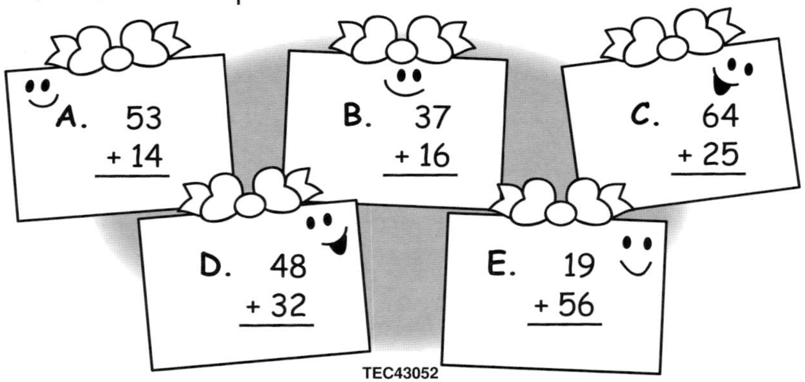
A. 53 + 14
B. 37 + 16
C. 64 + 25
D. 48 + 32
E. 19 + 56

TEC43052

Problem solving: money

A Chilly Day

You have $5.00 to spend.
Which three items can you buy?
List four sets.
For each set, solve to find your change.

Specials
coffee $0.75
spiced milk $1.10
tea with lemon $2.65
apple cider $2.80
hot cocoa $3.50

TEC43052

Weight

Weighing In

Make your paper look like the one shown.
Write two or more examples in each section.

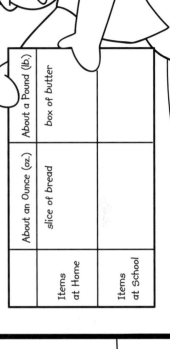

	About an Ounce (oz.)	About a Pound (lb.)
Items at Home	slice of bread	box of butter
Items at School		

TEC43052

How to use Cut out the cards. Use them as center or free-time activities.

Punctuation

The Right Fit

Write three examples for each punctuation mark shown.
Circle each mark.

. period
? question mark
! exclamation point
, comma

TEC43053

Adjectives

Important Leaders

Make a list of adjectives that describe a president.
Rewrite each sentence shown.
Add a different adjective from your list to each one.

1. George Washington was the president.
2. Abraham Lincoln was another president.
3. These men helped the United States.
4. We honor these leaders on Presidents' Day.

TEC43053

Writing book titles

Valuable Treasures

Choose five of your favorite books.
Write each title and author.

Remember to underline the book title!
The Lucky Leprechaun
by Tom O'Callaghan
The Lucky Leprechaun

TEC43053

Alliteration

Some Similar Sounds

Write the first letter of your first name.
Write a sentence that uses words that start with the same sound as that letter.
Then write a sentence using words with the first letter of your last name.

Silly Sarah sings for spring!

TEC43053

How to use Cut out the cards. Use them as center or free-time activities.

Subtraction with regrouping

Have a Heart

Write a top number.
Write a bottom number.
Subtract.
Repeat nine or more times.

Top Number	Bottom Number
90	59
82	47
71	38
63	25

TEC43053

Number sense

Honoring 100

List as many different ways as you can to show 100.

Happy 100th Day
100
50 + 50

TEC43053

Capacity

Question and Answer

Copy the quiz shown.
List nine more containers that hold liquid.
Make an answer key for your quiz.

Capacity Quiz
What is the best unit to use to measure the liquid in each container: cups, pints, quarts, or gallons?
1. **bathtub**

TEC43053

Algebraic expressions

Lucky Numbers

Copy each set.
Write numbers to make each set a true number sentence.

A. 19 + □ = □
B. □ – 10 = □
C. □ x □ = 36
D. 7 + □ = □ + □
E. □ – □ = 100 – □
F. □ x 8 = □ x □
G. 25 + □ > □
H. □ – □ < 150

TEC43053

Language Arts Activity Cards

How to use Cut out the cards. Use them as center or free-time activities.

Sequence words

In Training

Copy the topic sentence.
Explain how the tortoise prepared for the big race.
Use each of the words shown.

Topic Sentence
You may not know it, but the tortoise took many steps to prepare for his race against the hare.

First,
Next,
Then
After that,
Finally,

TEC43054

Varied sentence lengths

More and More

Write a sentence about the picture. Use three words.
Rewrite the sentence with four or five words.
Rewrite the sentence again. Use six or more words.

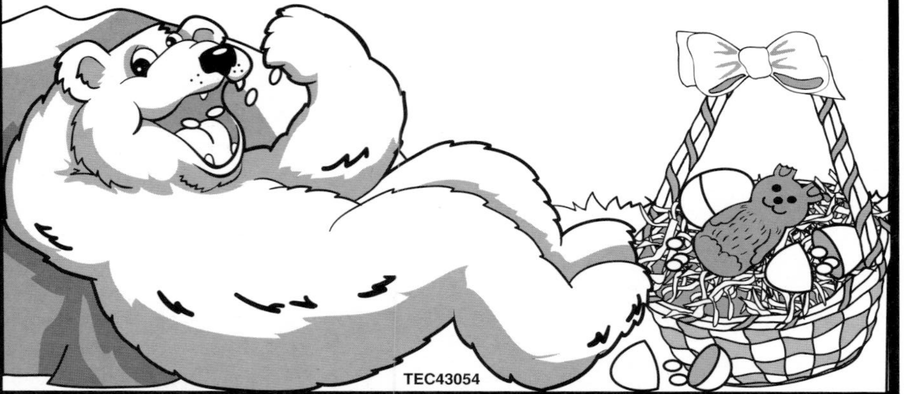

TEC43054

Writing couplets

Twice as Nice

Choose a topic. Write a couplet.

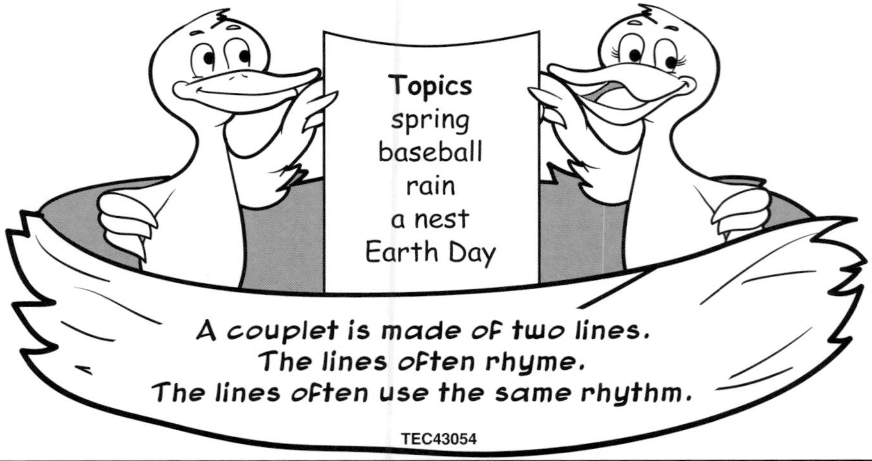
Topics
spring
baseball
rain
a nest
Earth Day
A couplet is made of two lines.
The lines often rhyme.
The lines often use the same rhythm.

TEC43054

Adverbs

Fun in the Sun

Copy the adverbs that tell *how*.
Choose five or more words.
Use each word in a different sentence.

gleefully	almost	happily
slowly	loudly	never
often	softly	proudly
swiftly	gently	brightly
bravely	closely	cheerfully

TEC43054

How to use Cut out the cards. Use them as center or free-time activities.

Skip-counting

Leapfrog!

Name and show five different ways Blaze Bullfrog can skip-count from zero to 80.

TEC43054

Three-dimensional shapes

Bird's-Eye View

Use blocks to make each building.
Draw each building from above.
Hint: Some buildings can be built several ways.

Library
2 cubes, 1 rectangular prism
Bank
1 rectangular prism
Fire Station
3 cubes
Beauty Parlor
1 rectangular prism, 1 cylinder
Grocery Store
1 cube, 1 rectangular prism

Library

TEC43054

Probability

Bunnies in a Burrow

Write three or more sentences about the bunnies.
Use a word from the word bank in each sentence.

It is possible to find a brown bunny in this burrow.

Word Bank
possible
impossible

TEC43054

Measuring length

Long and Short of It

Copy and complete the chart.

Tool	Items
Best measured with a ruler	
Best measured with a yardstick	
Best measured with a measuring tape	

TEC43054

Language Arts Activity Cards

How to use Cut out the cards. Use them as center or free-time activities.

Base words

Star of the Sea

Copy the words.
Circle each base word.

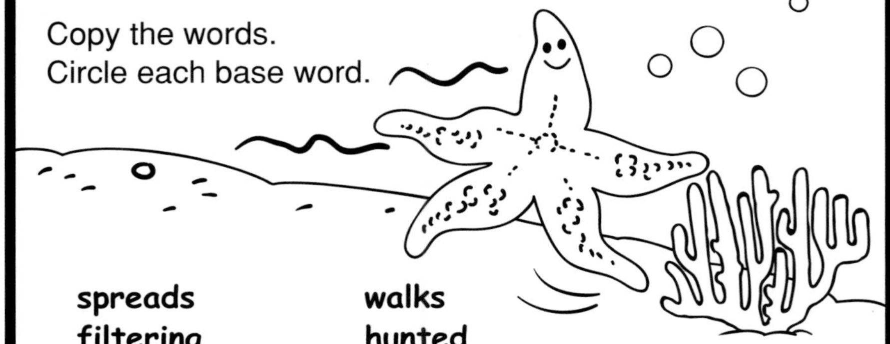

spreads
filtering
feeding
pointed
builds

walks
hunted
crawling
divides
passed

branched
attaching

TEC43055

Writing a list

Summer Rules!

Choose a summer setting.
Write a list of five or more rules to follow there.

- *summer camp*
- *at the pool*
- *on a family vacation*
- *traveling in the car with your family*
- *at an amusement park*
- *at a friend's house*

Camp
Dogwood

TEC43055

Pronouns: *I, me*

Personal Favorites

Think about what you like to do with your friends and family.
Write four or more sentences about these events using *I*.
Write four or more sentences using *me*.

Birds

My mom and I go bird-watching together. Will you help Dad and me make s'mores?

TEC43055

Writing a summary

All Wrapped Up

List the main events from the past week of school.
Use the list to write a summary of the week.

TEC43055

Math Activity Cards

How to use Cut out the cards. Use them as center or free-time activities.

Problem solving: make a list

Mix 'n' Match Milk Shakes

Look at the menu.
List the possible flavor pairings.
If you add another flavor, how many more pairings would you have?

Flavors *Pick Two!*

vanilla
chocolate
strawberry
mint
peanut butter
bubble gum

TEC43055

Writing fraction word problems

Pie Guys

Write three or more questions about the pies.
Include the answers.

What part of the cherry pie was eaten? $\frac{1}{2}$

TEC43055

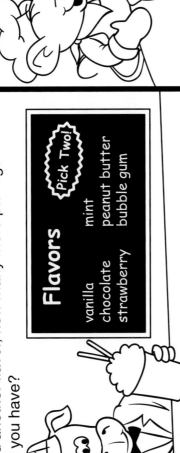

Inverse relationships

The Flip-Flops

For each pair of numbers, write a multiplication problem.
Then write the inverse.

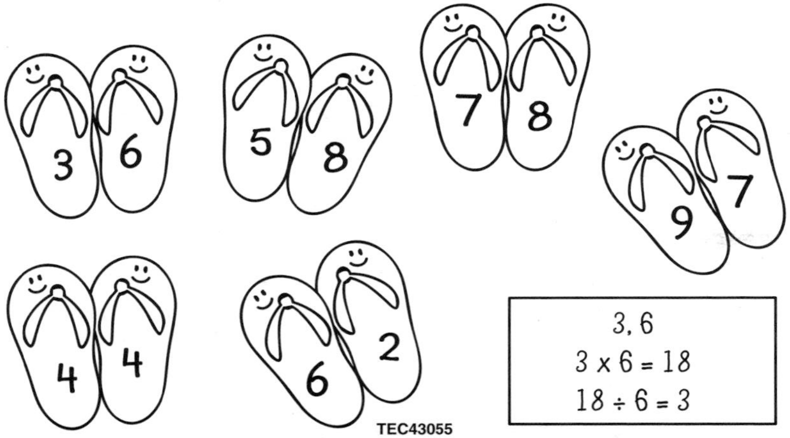
3 6
5 8
7 8
9 7
4 4
6 2

3, 6
$3 \times 6 = 18$
$18 \div 6 = 3$

TEC43055

Division

Afraid of the Dark

Write and solve ten or more division problems without remainders.
Use the numbers on the bear's blanket as the divisors.
Use the numbers on the tent as the dividends.

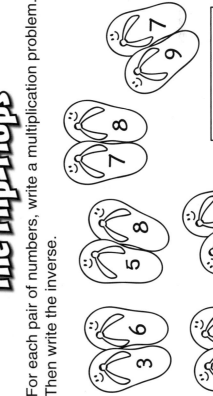

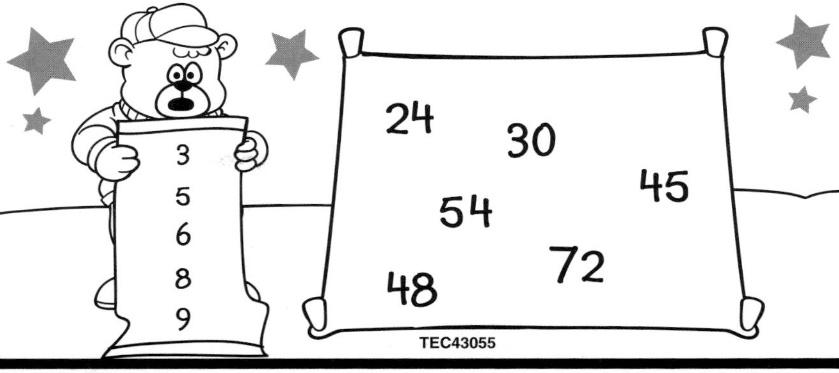
3
5
6
8
9
24
30
45
54
72
48

TEC43055

Name ______________________________ Date ______________

Patterns

Back-to-School

Read each problem.
Solve each one on the matching bus window.

1.	2.	3.	4.	5.

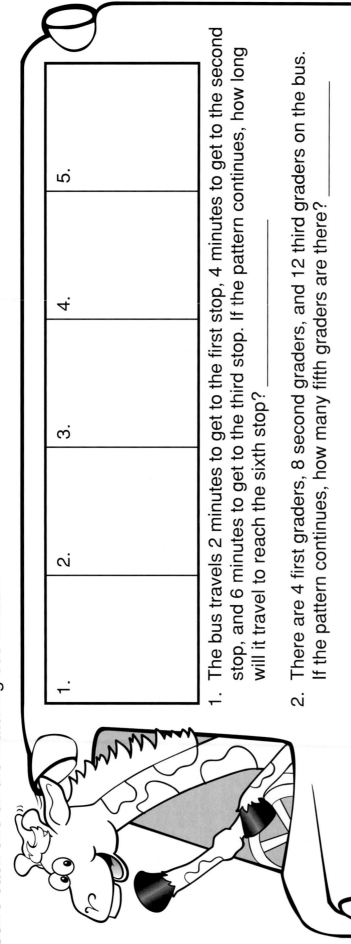

1. The bus travels 2 minutes to get to the first stop, 4 minutes to get to the second stop, and 6 minutes to get to the third stop. If the pattern continues, how long will it travel to reach the sixth stop? ________________

2. There are 4 first graders, 8 second graders, and 12 third graders on the bus. If the pattern continues, how many fifth graders are there? ___________

3. Five children get on the bus at each bus stop. How many children will be on the bus after 8 stops? ____

4. Every third window on the bus is open. Is the 11th window open or closed? ___________

5. At school, 2 girls get off the bus, followed by 1 boy. Then 2 more girls get off, followed by another boy. If the pattern continues, will the 13th child be a girl or a boy? ___________

Name ______________________ Date ______________

One-, two-, and three-syllable words

Labor Day Picnic

Use the code to color each square.

Code

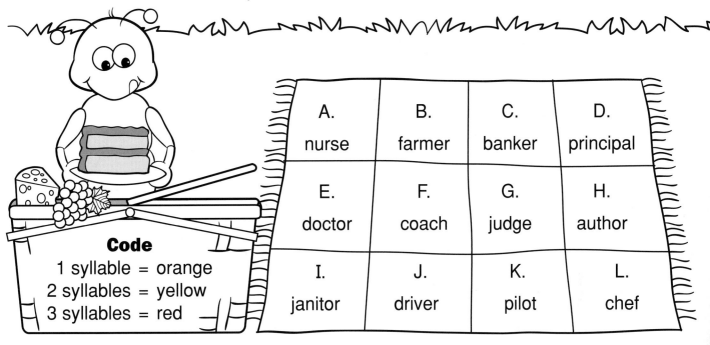

1 syllable = orange
2 syllables = yellow
3 syllables = red

A. nurse	B. farmer	C. banker	D. principal
E. doctor	F. coach	G. judge	H. author
I. janitor	J. driver	K. pilot	L. chef

Name ______________________ Date ______________

Two-, three-, and four-syllable words

At a Cookout

Sort the words.

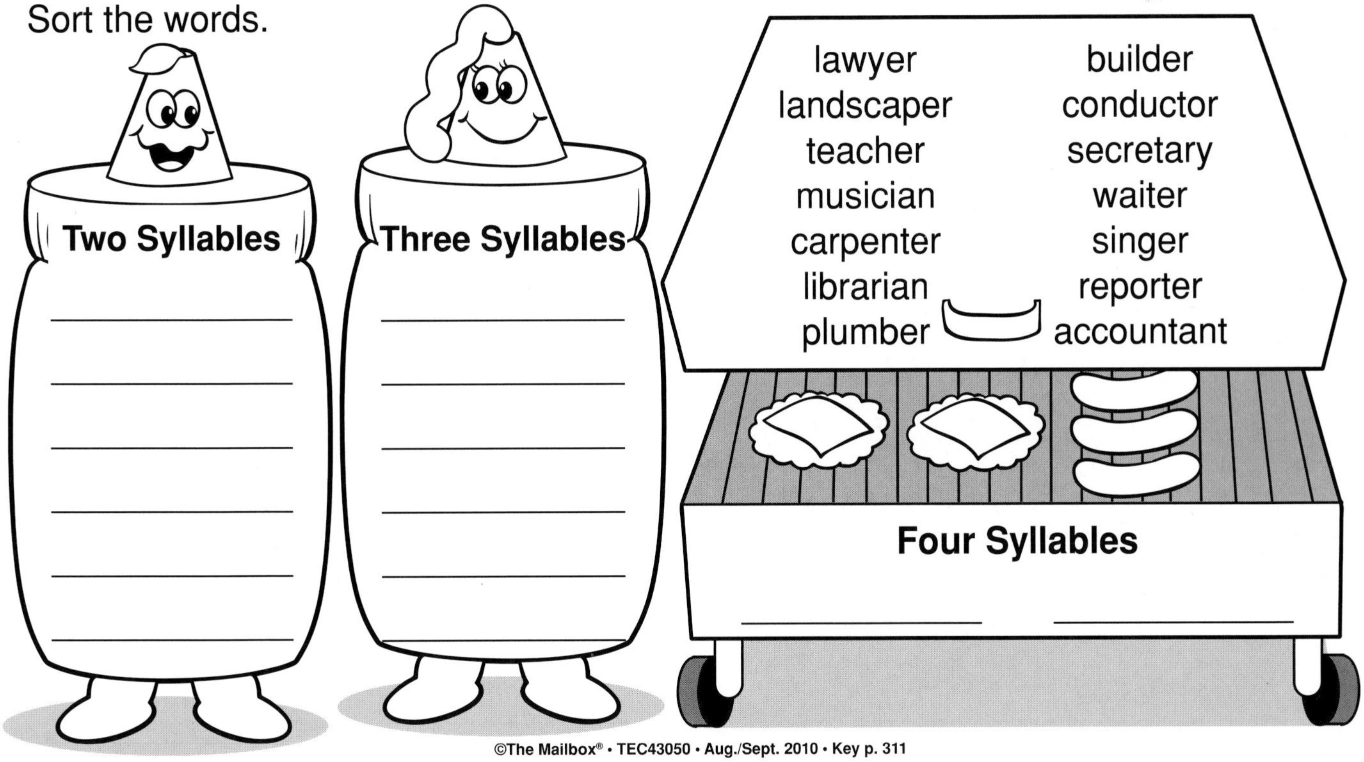
Two Syllables
Three Syllables
Four Syllables

lawyer	builder
landscaper	conductor
teacher	secretary
musician	waiter
carpenter	singer
librarian	reporter
plumber	accountant

Name ______________________ Date ______________

A Powerful Plan

Constitution Day is on September 17 in the United States.

Constitution (kon-sti-too-shun) is a pretty big word. Do you know what it means? A constitution is a statement that tells what a group of people believe in. The group may be a club or it might be a government. The constitution tells how the group will be run and how its leaders will be picked. It tells how rules or laws will be made. Often it is written down.

James Madison and Benjamin Franklin were two of the men who wrote the U.S. Constitution.

The Constitution of the United States was written in 1787. The men who wrote it wanted to set up a strong government for the country. The Constitution they wrote set up the three parts of government (called *branches*) that we still have today. The Constitution lists the key rights for American citizens. The basic laws of the U.S. are found in this written statement.

Write two facts about any constitution.

1. ______________________

____

____

2. ______________________

____

____

Write two facts about the U.S. Constitution.

1. ______________________

____

____

2. ______________________

____

____

Names ______________________ Date ______________

Ordering numbers

Trick or Treat!

Try to be the first player to place six number cards in order on your sidewalk.

 Player 1	smallest					largest

Directions for two players:

1. Cut apart the cards below. Stack them facedown.
2. When it is your turn, take the top card.
3. If it's a number card, place it on a blank space on your sidewalk or trade it for a card already in place. (Put the other card at the bottom of the stack).
4. Take turns drawing cards until one player has ordered six number cards. The student says, "Trick or treat!" and the other player checks the order. If the cards are ordered correctly, the game ends. If not, continue play until one student has six cards correctly ordered.

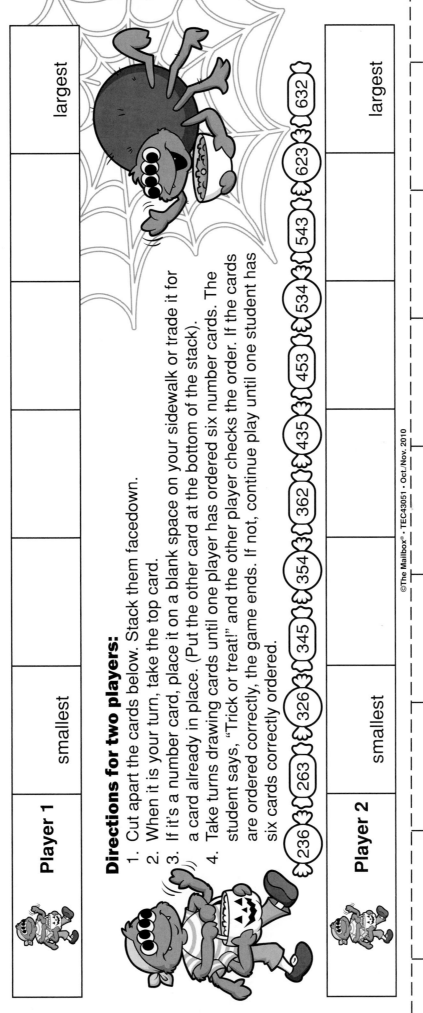

236 263 326 345 354 362 435 453 534 543 623 632

 Player 2	smallest					largest

326 TEC43051	632 TEC43051	453 TEC43051	543 TEC43051	534 TEC43051	435 TEC43051	Lose a turn. TEC43051
623 TEC43051	345 TEC43051	362 TEC43051	236 TEC43051	263 TEC43051	354 TEC43051	Lose a turn. TEC43051

How to use Give each duo a copy of this page.

Name ____________________ Date __________

Reading a diagram

An "A-maize-ing" Plant

Corn is also called maize. It is a plant with many uses. Corn grows in many parts of the world, but more corn is grown in the United States than anywhere else. A mature, or grown, corn plant found in the United States can be about eight feet tall. It has many parts.

Read the diagram.

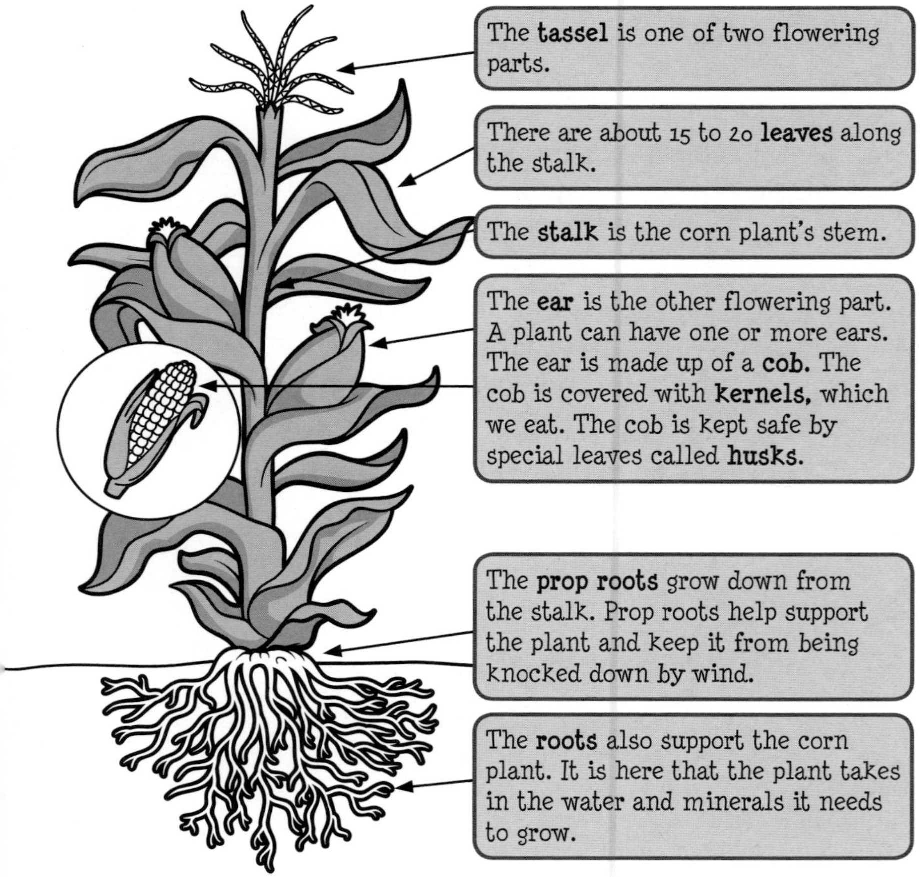
The **tassel** is one of two flowering parts.
There are about 15 to 20 **leaves** along the stalk.
The **stalk** is the corn plant's stem.
The **ear** is the other flowering part. A plant can have one or more ears. The ear is made up of a **cob**. The cob is covered with **kernels**, which we eat. The cob is kept safe by special leaves called **husks**.
The **prop roots** grow down from the stalk. Prop roots help support the plant and keep it from being knocked down by wind.
The **roots** also support the corn plant. It is here that the plant takes in the water and minerals it needs to grow.

Answer each question.

1. What special leaves keep the corncob safe? __________
2. What is found at the top of the stalk? __________
3. What is the name for the corn plant's stem? __________
4. What helps the corn plant during a windstorm? __________
5. What part of the corn plant do we eat? __________
6. About how many leaves grow on a corn plant? __________
7. Why do you think a corn plant needs two sets of roots? __________
8. How do you use corn? __________

Name ______________________ Date ____________

Capitalization

A Fine-Feathered Friend

Circle the nouns that should have capital letters.
Correctly write each circled noun on a feather.

corn

thursday

november

october

day

pie

mr. bradford

wednesday

family

friday

ms. feathers

december

Bonus Box: Write three or more sentences. Use a different circled noun from above in each sentence.

Name ______________________ Date ____________

Editing for capitalization

My Thanksgiving Plans

Draw lines (≡) under each letter that should be capitalized.

aunt bertie hosts Thanksgiving dinner every year. it is a hard job, because I have a big family. it takes some work to get everyone to her house in new jersey. I have cousins in maryland, florida, new york, and texas. my grandparents live in new mexico and maine. we have to start making travel plans in june just to make it all work out. But it is always worth it. We have tons of fun and eat lots of great food. Then on the friday after thanksgiving, we always start our christmas shopping. I love Thanksgiving at Aunt Bertie's house!

Did you draw 20 sets of lines?

Bonus Box: Write a paragraph about your Thanksgiving plans. Draw lines (≡) under each capital letter you use.

How to use Provide each student with a copy of the portion of the practice page that matches his learning needs.

Name______________________________ Date ______________________

Ordered pairs

A Snowy Scene

Mark each pair on the grid with a •.
Connect the • in order.

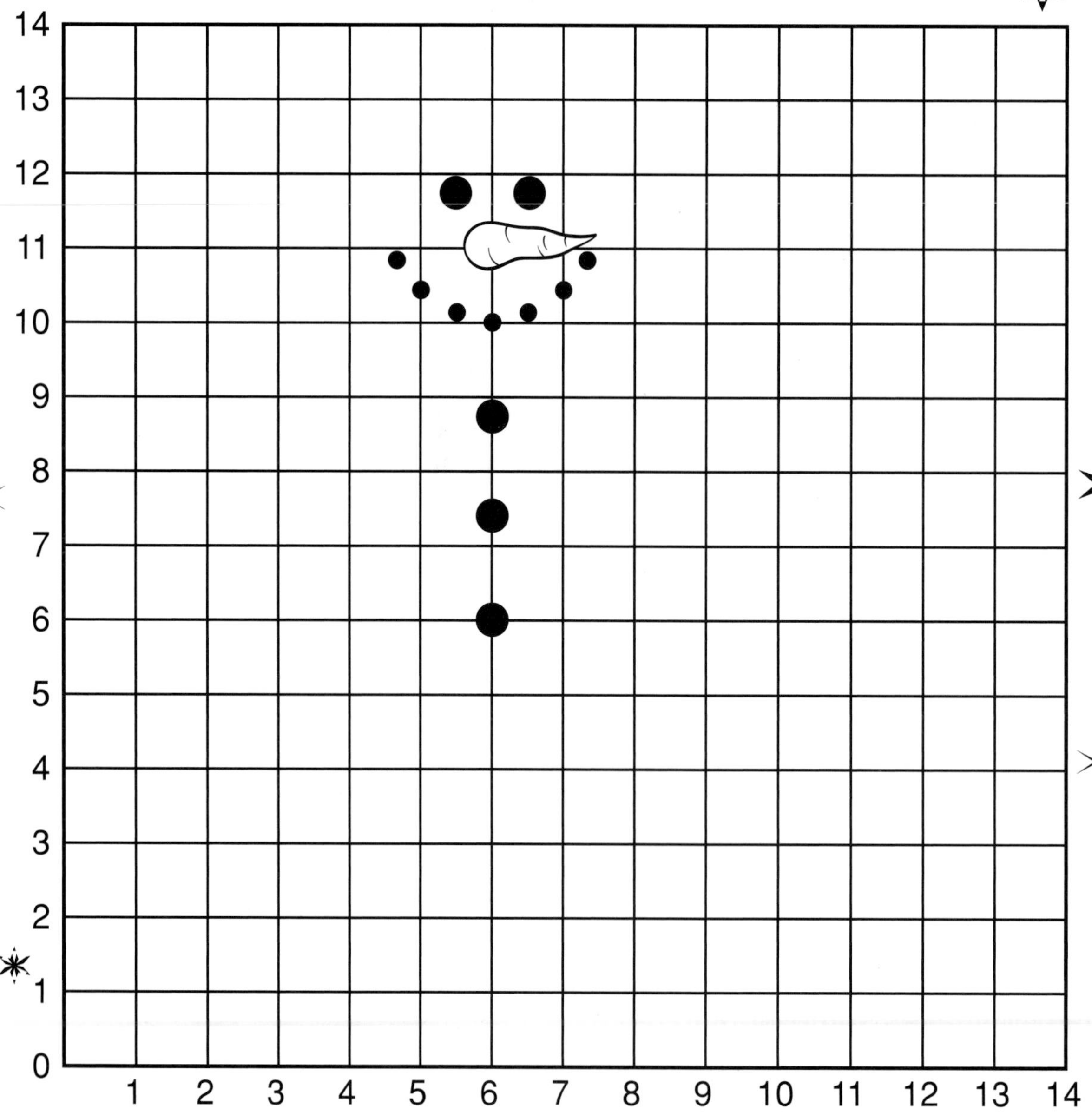
0 1 2 3 4 5 6 7 8 9 10 11 12 13 14
0 1 2 3 4 5 6 7 8 9 10 11 12 13 14

A. (4, 0)
B. (3, 2)
C. (3, 4)
D. (5, 6)
E. (4, 7)
F. (4, 9)
G. (5, 10)
H. (4, 11)
I. (4, 12)
J. (5, 13)
K. (7, 13)
L. (8, 12)
M. (8, 11)
N. (7, 10)
O. (8, 9)
P. (8, 7)
Q. (7, 6)
R. (9, 4)
S. (9, 2)
T. (8, 0)

Bonus: Add a • at (8, 8) and (11, 10). Draw a line to connect them. Then add a • at (4, 8) and (1, 9). Draw a line to connect them.

Name ____________________ Date ____________

Reading a thermometer

Trim the Tree

Write each temperature.
Color a matching ornament.

A. ____°F

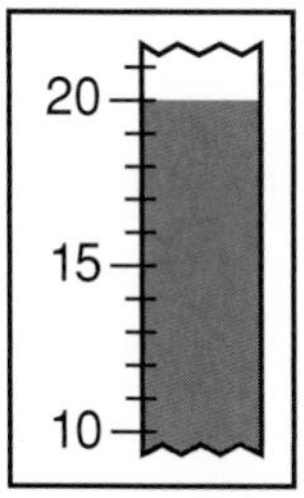
20
15
10

B. ____°F

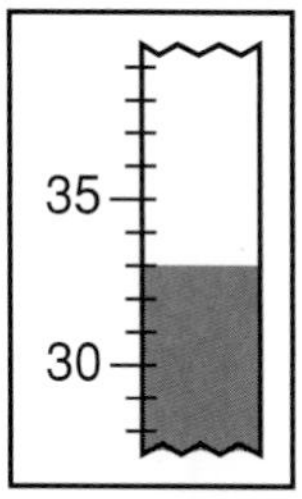
35
30

C. ____°F

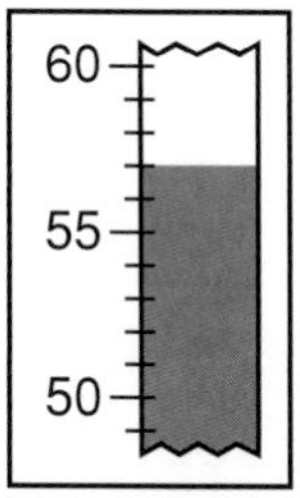
60
55
50

D. ____°F

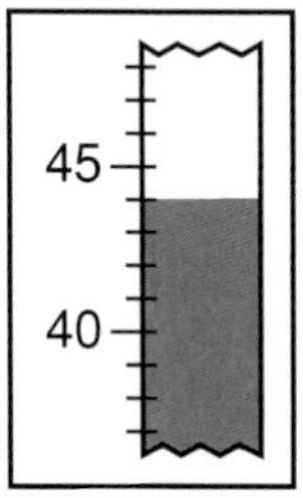
45
40

E. ____°F

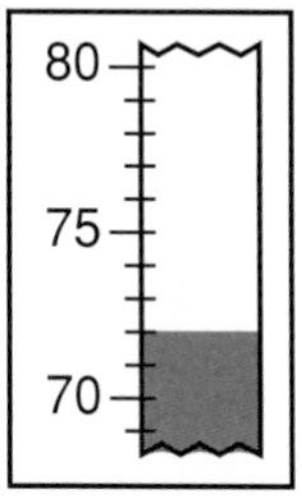
80
75
70

F. ____°F

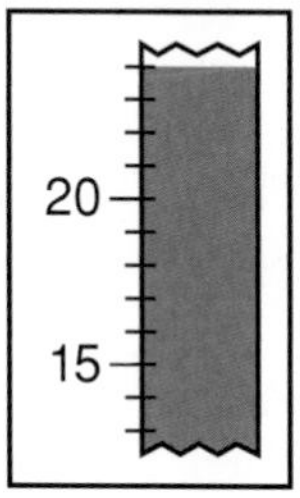
20
15

57°
44°
20°
24°
72°
33°

Bonus: Choose two temperatures from above. For each temperature, draw a picture of yourself playing outside. Show clothes you would wear for that temperature.

Name ____________________ Date ____________

Reading a thermometer

Pine Pals

Write each temperature.
Then write *cold, cool, warm,* or *hot.*

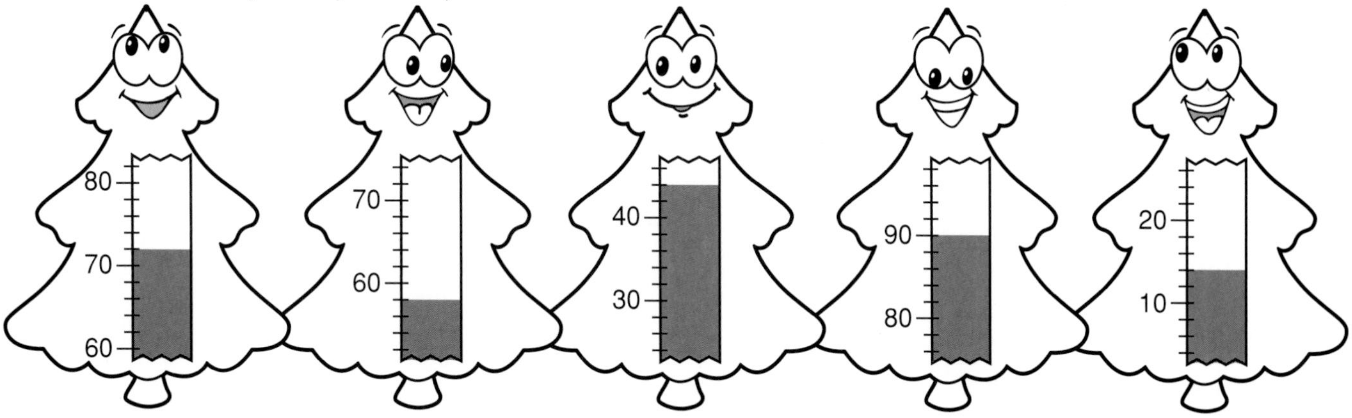
80
70
60
70
60
40
30
90
80
20
10

____°F ____°F ____°F ____°F ____°F

A. ________ B. ________ C. ________ D. ________ E. ________

Bonus: Write an explanation for a friend. Tell how to read a thermometer like the ones on this page.

How to use For each student, copy the portion of the practice page that matches his learning needs.

Name ______________________________ Date ______________

Martin Luther King Day, making inferences

Working for Equal Rights

Dr. King is only one of two Americans whose birthday is marked with a national holiday.

Martin Luther King Jr. was born in 1929. He was the middle child of three and his family lived in Atlanta, Georgia. That is also where Martin went to school. Martin worked hard in school. He skipped both ninth and twelfth grades. That means he was just 15 when he started college! After he finished college, he got more degrees from colleges in two other states. He even earned the title of doctor.

Dr. King spent the rest of his adult life working for equal rights. He felt that all people should be treated the same way. Dr. King led boycotts and marches to spread his message. This means he urged others to stop doing business with people who were unfair. He also gave speeches.

Dr. King's efforts made an impact on many. Even after he died, people wanted to continue his work for peace and equal rights.

Answer each question.
Then follow the directions.

1. Was Martin an only child? ____________ Draw a box around the words that make you think so.
2. Was Martin a good student? ____________ Draw a line under the words that make you think so.
3. Did Dr. King have goals? ____________ Draw an arrow next to the sentences that makes you think so.
4. Was Dr. King an important person in U.S. history? ____________ Draw a star next to the part or parts of the passage that make you think so.

Name ____________________ Date ____________________

Probability

Famous Faces

Study the cards.
Pretend the cards are placed in a bag and only one is drawn.
Complete each sentence using *more, less, equally, most,* or *least.*

1. I am ____________________ likely to draw a man or a woman.
2. I am ____________________ likely to draw a poet than an inventor.
3. I am ____________________ likely to draw an athlete than a poet.
4. I am ____________________ likely to draw an athlete.
5. I am ____________________ likely to draw a female athlete than a male athlete.
6. I am ____________________ likely to draw an athlete than an inventor.
7. I am ____________________ likely to draw a poet.
8. I am ____________________ likely to draw a male inventor or a female inventor.

Bonus: Cut out the cards. Put them in a bag. Test each statement above. For each statement that matches your result, draw a ☺.

Jack Johnson

athlete

Jackie Robinson

athlete

Wilma Rudolph

athlete

Phillis Wheatley

poet

Garrett Morgan

inventor

Madam C. J. Walker

inventor

Name ____________________ Date ____________

Reading a table

Lunar New Year

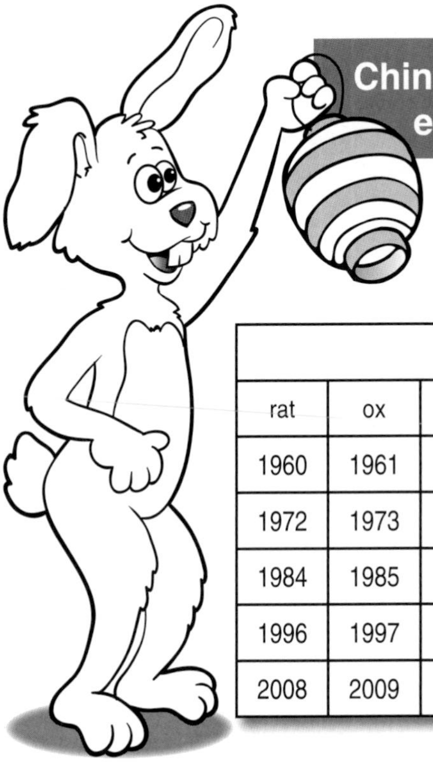

Chinese New Year falls in January or February. With each new year, a different animal is honored.

Study the table.
Answer the questions.

Animals and Their Years

rat	ox	tiger	rabbit	dragon	snake	horse	sheep	monkey	rooster	dog	pig
1960	1961	1962	1963	1964	1965	1966	1967	1968	1969	1970	1971
1972	1973	1974	1975	1976	1977	1978	1979	1980	1981	1982	1983
1984	1985	1986	1987	1988	1989	1990	1991	1992	1993	1994	1995
1996	1997	1998	1999	2000	2001	2002	2003	2004	2005	2006	2007
2008	2009	2010	2011	2012	2013	2014	2015	2016	2017	2018	2019

1. How many animals are shown in the table? ________
2. Which animal is shown after the ox? ________________
3. Which animal is shown before the horse? ________________
4. Which animal was honored in 2003? ________________
5. When will the monkey be honored next? ________________
6. Which animal will be celebrated in 2020? ________________

   How do you know? ________________________________

   ____

   ____
7. Which animal is shown for this year? ________________
8. How many years will it be before this year's animal is honored again? ________

   What year will that be? ____________

Bonus: Write and answer two or more questions about the table.

Name_______________________ Date_______________

Time to five minutes

Hand in Hand

Draw the hands to show each time.

A. 2:30

B. 6:15

C. 11:05

D. 9:25

E. 12:20

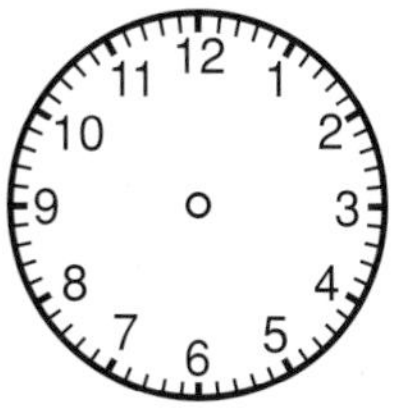
F. 3:40

G. 4:10

H. 1:45

Bonus: Lunch starts at 11:25. It ends 30 minutes later. Draw a clock to show each time.

Name_______________________ Date_______________

Time to one minute

Be My "Valen-time"

Write the time shown on each clock.

A. ___ : ___

B. ___ : ___

C. ___ : ___

D. ___ : ___

E. ___ : ___

F. ___ : ___

G. ___ : ___

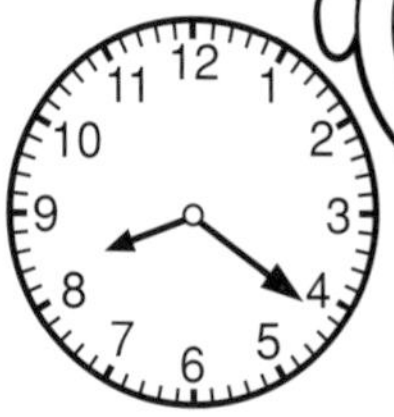
H. ___ : ___

Bonus: Add two minutes to each clock. Write the times.

How to use For each student, copy the portion of the practice page that matches his learning needs.

Name____________________ Date ____________

Measurement conversions

Seeds of Spring

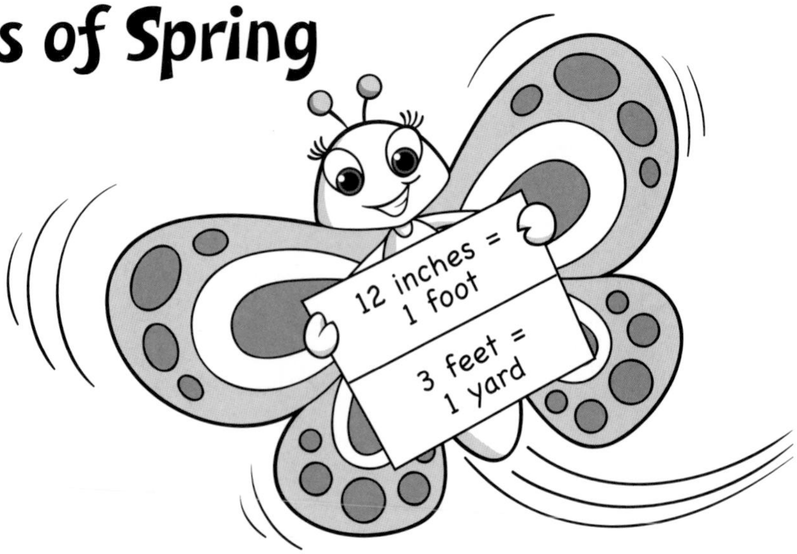
12 inches =
1 foot
3 feet =
1 yard

Complete each equation.
Cross off the matching number.

A. _____ feet = 60 inches

B. 1 foot = _____ inches

C. _____ feet = 36 inches

D. 2 feet = _____ inches

E. 8 feet = _____ inches

F. _____ feet = 84 inches

G. 4 feet = _____ inches

H. 6 feet = _____ inches

I. _____ yard = 3 feet

J. _____ yards = 18 feet

K. 7 yards = _____ feet

L. _____ yards = 6 feet

M. 9 yards = _____ feet

N. 5 yards = _____ feet

O. 3 yards = _____ feet

P. _____ yards = 24 feet

48
2
9
24
96
6
8
5

7	12
21	27
3	1
15	72

Bonus

Which is the longest length?
Explain how you know.

2 yards

5 feet

65 inches

Name______________________________ Date __________________

Division readiness

"Eggs-tra" Special Delivery

Circle to show equal groups.
Write the number of groups.

A. 12 ÷ 4 = *3*	
B. 9 ÷ 3 =	
C. 6 ÷ 3 =	
D. 8 ÷ 2 =	
E. 12 ÷ 2 =	
F. 10 ÷ 2 =	
G. 4 ÷ 2 =	
H. 12 ÷ 3 =	

Bonus: Draw a picture to solve 15 ÷ 3.

Name______________________________ Date __________________

Division

An Easter Artist

Divide.
Color by the code.

2 = blue	5 = yellow
3 = pink	6 = green
4 = purple	7 = orange

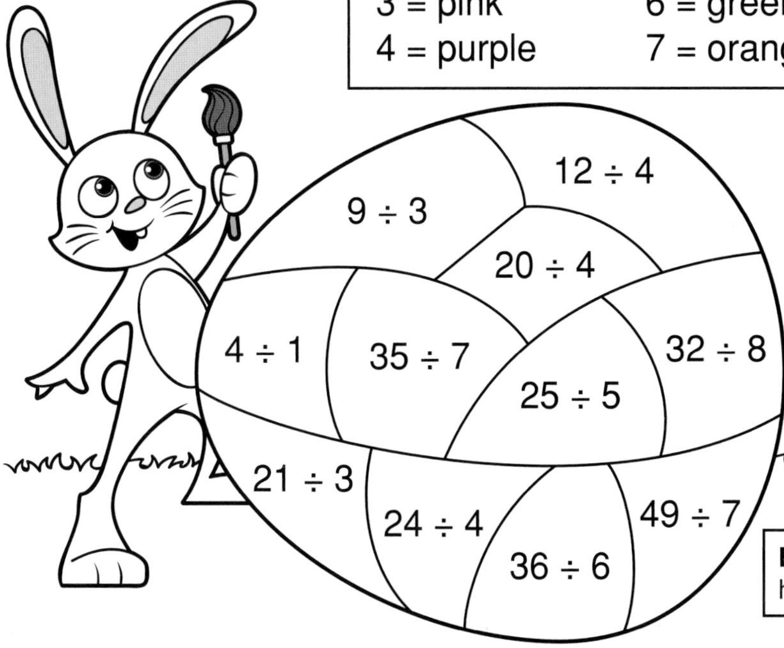
9 ÷ 3
12 ÷ 4
20 ÷ 4
4 ÷ 1
35 ÷ 7
32 ÷ 8
25 ÷ 5
21 ÷ 3
24 ÷ 4
49 ÷ 7
36 ÷ 6

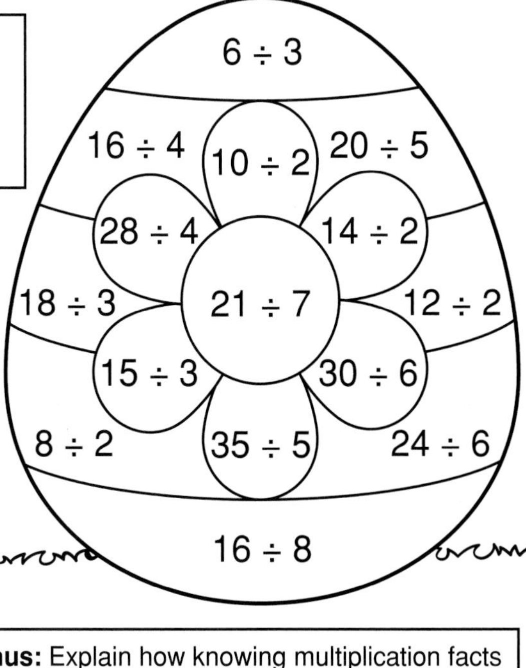
6 ÷ 3
16 ÷ 4
10 ÷ 2
20 ÷ 5
28 ÷ 4
14 ÷ 2
18 ÷ 3
21 ÷ 7
12 ÷ 2
15 ÷ 3
30 ÷ 6
8 ÷ 2
35 ÷ 5
24 ÷ 6
16 ÷ 8

Bonus: Explain how knowing multiplication facts helps you solve division problems.

Name ______________________ Date ______________

Parts of speech

Splashing Around City Pool

Outline each flag by the code.
Use the words to complete the passage.
(Your choices should make sense!)

Code
noun = red verb = blue adjective = yellow

stood
racers
big
one
day
cheered
cool
jumped
parents
City Pool
won
nervous
stretched
horn
sunny
sprinted

It was time for the ____________ (adjective) swim meet at ____________ (noun). What a beautiful ____________ (noun) it was! The warm, ____________ (adjective) morning was perfect for a race. Swimmers ____________ (verb) by the starting blocks. Some ____________ (verb) their arms and put on their goggles. Others ____________ (verb) up and down. The ____________ (noun) encouraged their ____________ (adjective) children with kind words.

Soon, the ____________ (noun) blew. The ____________ (noun) dived off the blocks. They ____________ (verb) through the ____________ (adjective) water. Everyone who watched from the pool deck ____________ (verb). Before long, ____________ (adjective) swimmer touched the wall. He ____________ (verb) the race!

Bonus: Write what happens next. Underline and label each noun, verb, and adjective you use.

Name ____________________ Date ____________

Using a table

Finders Keepers

Use the table to answer each question.

Shells Found			
seagull	Fri.	Sat.	Sun.
Sandy	43	75	62
Sonny	51	34	78
Shelly	29	65	67

A. Who found the most shells on Friday?

B. On which day did Sandy find fewer shells than her friends?

C. How many shells did Sonny find in all?

D. How many shells were found on Saturday?

E. How many shells did Shelly find on Saturday and Sunday?

F. On Friday, how many more shells did Sonny find than Shelly?

G. On Sunday, how many more shells did Shelly find than Sandy?

H. Who found the most shells in all?

I. How many more shells were found on Saturday than on Friday?

J. On which day were the fewest shells found?

Bonus: Explain how you would use the chart to find the answer to this question: Who found the most shells on Saturday?

Name ____________________ Date __________

Commas in a series

One Cool Cat

Color the correctly placed commas in each sentence.

1. Katie loves to run, jump, and hop, outside.
2. She cools off with treats, that are sweet, cold, and tasty.
3. Ice pops, ice cream, and fruit, are her favorite snacks.
4. Katie likes, orange, lime, or cherry ice pops.
5. She tops her ice cream, with sprinkles, whipped cream, and a cherry.
6. Katie knows it's better to snack on, watermelon, grapes, and pineapple.

Bonus: Write a sentence that names three of your favorite summer treats. Use commas.

Name ____________________ Date __________

Commas in dialogue

The Ice Cream Man!

Add a comma (^,) to each sentence.

MR. FROSTY

1. Carlos shouts "I hear Mr. Frosty!"
2. Kyle exclaims "There he is!"
3. Mr. Frosty asks "What would you like?"
4. "I'd like a cherry ice" Carlos answers.
5. Kyle asks "May I have a mint cone?"
6. "Here you go" Mr. Frosty says.
7. "Thank you" the boys reply.
8. Mr. Frosty smiles and says "Stay cool!"

Bonus: What would you order from Mr. Frosty? Write a sentence that uses dialogue.

 How to use Provide each student with a copy of the portion of the practice page that matches his learning needs.

Arts & Crafts

Arts & Crafts

A Show of Hands

Celebrate individuality in your classroom with this "handy" art project.

Materials for each student:

8½" x 11" sheet of white paper
black marker
crayons or colored pencils
pencil

Steps:

1. Use a pencil to trace your hand in the center of the paper. Rotate the paper any direction and trace your hand again, being sure to overlap the handprints.
2. Continue rotating the paper and tracing your hand until there are no large open spaces left on the paper.
3. Outline the handprints using a black marker.
4. Color each section. Alternate colors, making sure no touching sections are the same color.

Lara Daugherty, St. Margaret Mary School, Wichita, KS

Patriotic Citizens

In honor of Constitution Day and Citizenship Day (September 17), have each child make and wear an Uncle Sam hat of his very own.

Materials for each student:

copy of the hat pattern on page 265
clear glitter
red, white, and blue paint
paintbrush
sentence strip
scissors
tape

Steps:

1. Paint the background behind the stars blue. Paint the stars and every other stripe white. Then paint the bill and remaining stripes red.
2. Lightly sprinkle glitter on the wet paint and shake off the excess.
3. Allow the paint to dry.
4. Cut out the hat.
5. Tape the hat to each end of the sentence strip to make a band.

Arts&Crafts

Mosaic Pumpkin

Make this no-carve jack-o'-lantern to celebrate fall or Halloween!

Materials for each student:

pumpkin pattern from page 266
orange and yellow tissue paper scraps
8" x 10" waxed paper
black construction paper
orange and green crayons
glue
scissors

Steps:

1. Color and cut out the pumpkin pattern.
2. Trace the pattern on the waxed paper.
3. Cut small squares from the orange and yellow tissue paper. Glue the squares inside the traced area of the waxed paper. Overlap the pieces of tissue and alternate colors.
4. Glue the pumpkin pattern atop the waxed paper tracing. Trim away the extra waxed paper.
5. Cut two eyes, a nose, and a mouth from the black construction paper. Glue the pieces onto the tissue paper.

Jennifer L. Kohnke, St. Charles, IL

Hi, Mom & Dad!
I hope you like my best work!
Love,
Callie

My Best-Work Folder

Present this one-of-a-kind folder at parent conferences.

Materials for each student:

3" x 18" red construction paper strip
2 sheets skin-colored construction paper
pink construction paper
crayons
glue
scissors

Steps:

1. Trace a six-inch circle on one sheet of skin-colored paper. Decorate the circle so it looks like your head. Carefully cut around the drawing.
2. Trace each of your hands on the other sheet of skin-colored construction paper and cut the tracings out.
3. Cut a heart from the pink paper. Write a message on the heart and glue it in the middle of the red strip as shown.
4. Glue the head cutout to the red strip so it is above the heart. Then glue one hand at each end of the strip.
5. Place your best work samples in the center of the red strip and fold each arm over the work so the hands are crossed.

Karen Fouts, Honey Creek Elementary, Conyers, GA

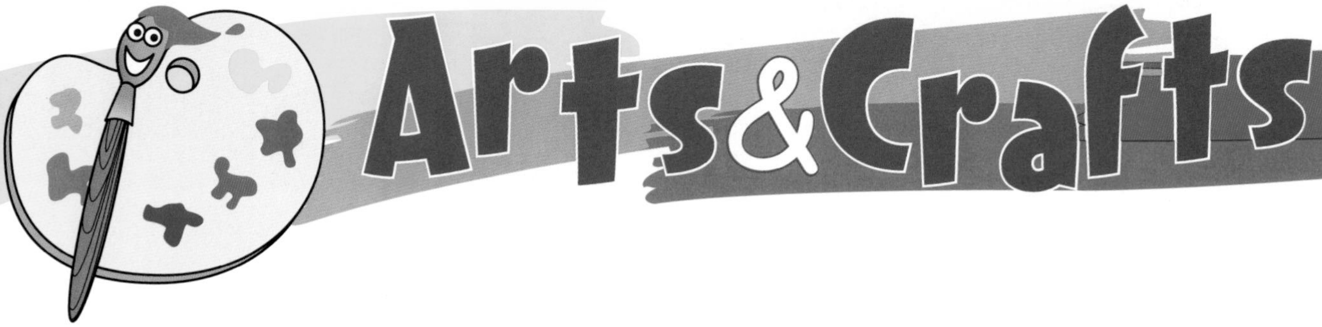
Arts&Crafts

The Red-Nosed Puppet

Have students use this adorable Rudolph puppet as they read their own holiday-related stories, or post them as part of an eye-catching display.

Materials for each student:

- two 8½" x 11" sheets of brown construction paper
- 2 cotton balls
- 1" red construction paper circle
- scissors
- stapler
- glue
- black marker

Steps:

1. Cut one sheet of brown construction paper in half. Roll one half into a cone shape and staple the ends together.
2. Trace and cut out two handprints (antlers) from the second sheet of brown construction paper. Staple the antlers to the cone.
3. Glue the red circle (nose) to the tip of the cone.
4. Use a permanent marker to draw a black dot on each cotton ball (eye). Glue the eyes on the cone.
5. To use the puppet, place your fingers inside the cone and your thumb underneath. Move your thumb to make the puppet talk.

Beverly McCormick, Hixon Elementary, Chattanooga, TN

There's "snow-body" like you!

Lighting Up Winter Days

Students add their personal touches to make these votive candles the perfect holiday gifts!

Materials for each student:

- copy of page 267
- clear or blue glass candleholder
- votive candle
- white acrylic craft paint
- paintbrush
- fine-tip permanent markers
- scissors
- crayons

Steps:

1. Paint your index finger with white paint.
2. Press your finger on the side of the candleholder.
3. Repeat Steps 1 and 2 two more times to make three snowmen.
4. After the paint dries, use markers to add eyes, a nose, a mouth, arms, and buttons to each snowman.
5. Place the candle inside the holder.
6. Cut out the card pattern. Color it and write a message to the person you plan to give the gift to.

Arts & Crafts

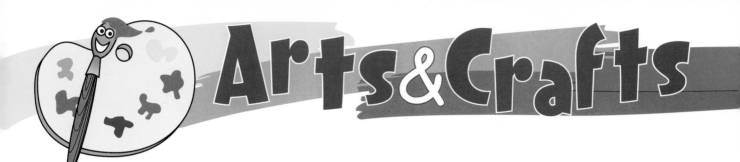

Love Bug Card Container

This cute valentine holder is made from a recycled cereal box!

Materials for each student:

copy of the love bug pattern on page 268
clean, empty cereal box
1" x 18" construction paper strip
construction paper
construction paper scraps
2 brass fasteners
hole puncher
scissors
crayons
glue

Steps:

1. Cut the flaps off the top of the cereal box. Cover the box with construction paper.
2. Color and cut out the love bug patterns.
3. Glue the love bug cutouts to the box.
4. Use construction paper scraps and crayons to decorate the box as desired.
5. To make a handle, hole-punch each side of the box. Then hole-punch each end of the paper strip. Use the brass fasteners to attach the strip to the box.

Rhesia Mitchell, Forestville Road Elementary, Knightdale, NC

Claire

Faces of March

After each student makes one of these adorable critters, you'll have a class set of projects to use for activities such as generating word lists, writing word problems, and organizing data.

Materials for each student:

tagboard template of a lion or lamb pattern from page 269
dessert-size paper plate
cotton balls (lamb)
tan (lion) or black (lamb) construction paper
paper scraps
crayons
scissors
glue

Steps to make a lion:

1. Color the plate.
2. Make one-inch cuts around the outside edge of the plate.
3. Trace the face template on tan construction paper and cut the tracing out.
4. Use paper scraps and crayons to add details.
5. Glue the face to the plate.

Steps to make a lamb:

1. Glue cotton balls on the plate.
2. Trace the face template on black construction paper and cut the tracing out.
3. Use paper scraps and crayons to add details.
4. Glue the face atop the cotton balls.

Editor's Tip:
These projects also look great on a display titled "March Brings Lions and Lambs."

Barb Lavelle, Birch Primary, North Olmsted, OH

Arts&Crafts

Rainy Day Forecast

Splish, splash! This colorful project showcases student writing.

Don't put your umbrellas away.
Rain is in the forecast today.
Big drops soon will begin to fall,
And rain will make the plants grow tall.
Daniel

Materials for each student:

12" x 18" sheet of colored construction paper
blue construction paper scraps
writing paper
paper towel
pipe cleaner
12" length of yarn
watercolors
water
paintbrush
glue
scissors

Steps:

1. Dip the paintbrush in water and then into one of the watercolors. Brush the paint onto the paper towel. Repeat this step with other colors.
2. When the paper towel is dry, glue one end of the pipe cleaner to the center of it. Then gently gather the edges of the paper around the pipe cleaner to form an umbrella. Tie the yarn around the umbrella and set it aside.
3. Write a rainy day poem on writing paper. Trim off any excess paper.
4. Cut raindrop shapes out of blue construction paper scraps.
5. Glue the umbrella, poem, and raindrops onto the construction paper.

Lou Smeja, Emerson Elementary, Elmhurst, IL

Happy
Mother's
Day

Editor's Tip:
For an inexpensive alternative, have each child plant a flower seed in a small cup of potting soil and place the cup in the gift box.

Mother's Day Garden

This lovely flowerbox makes a special gift that any mom or other loved one is sure to treasure.

Materials for each student:

copy of the fence and sign patterns on page 270
small potted plant
empty cube-shaped tissue box with the top third trimmed off
colorful magazine pages or gift wrap scraps
$3\frac{3}{4}$" x 17" blue construction paper strip
tissue paper
green marker or crayon
hole-puncher
glue
scissors

Steps:

1. Draw green plants on one side of the blue paper. Cover the box with the blue paper.
2. Hole-punch the magazine page or gift wrap. Glue the punched circles onto the plants to make flowers.
3. Cut out the fence and sign patterns.
4. Glue one fence pattern on each side of the box.
5. Glue the garden sign to the box. Add any other desired details.
6. Wrap the plant in tissue paper and put it in the box.

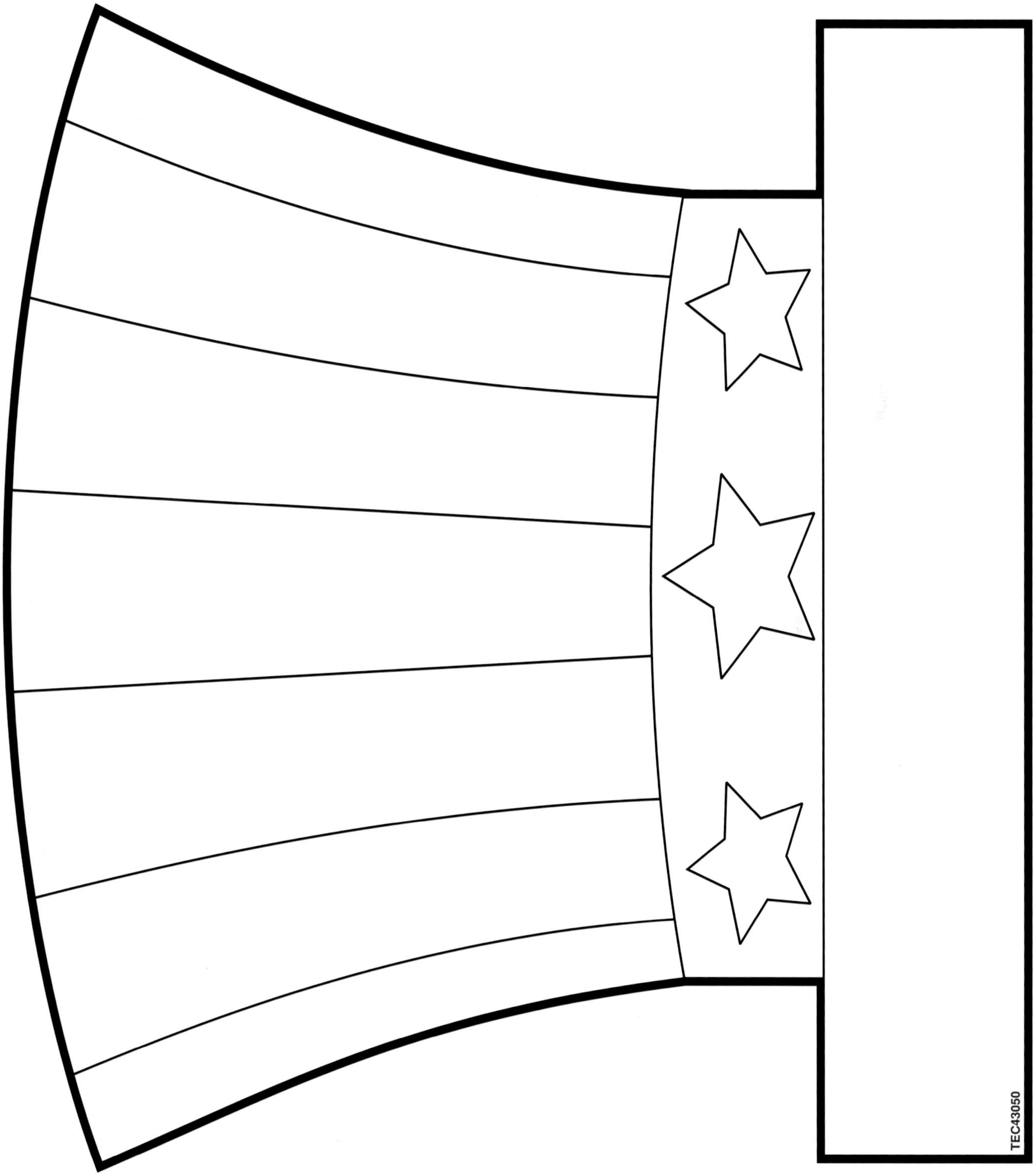
TEC43050

Pumpkin Pattern

Use with "Mosaic Pumpkin" on page 261.

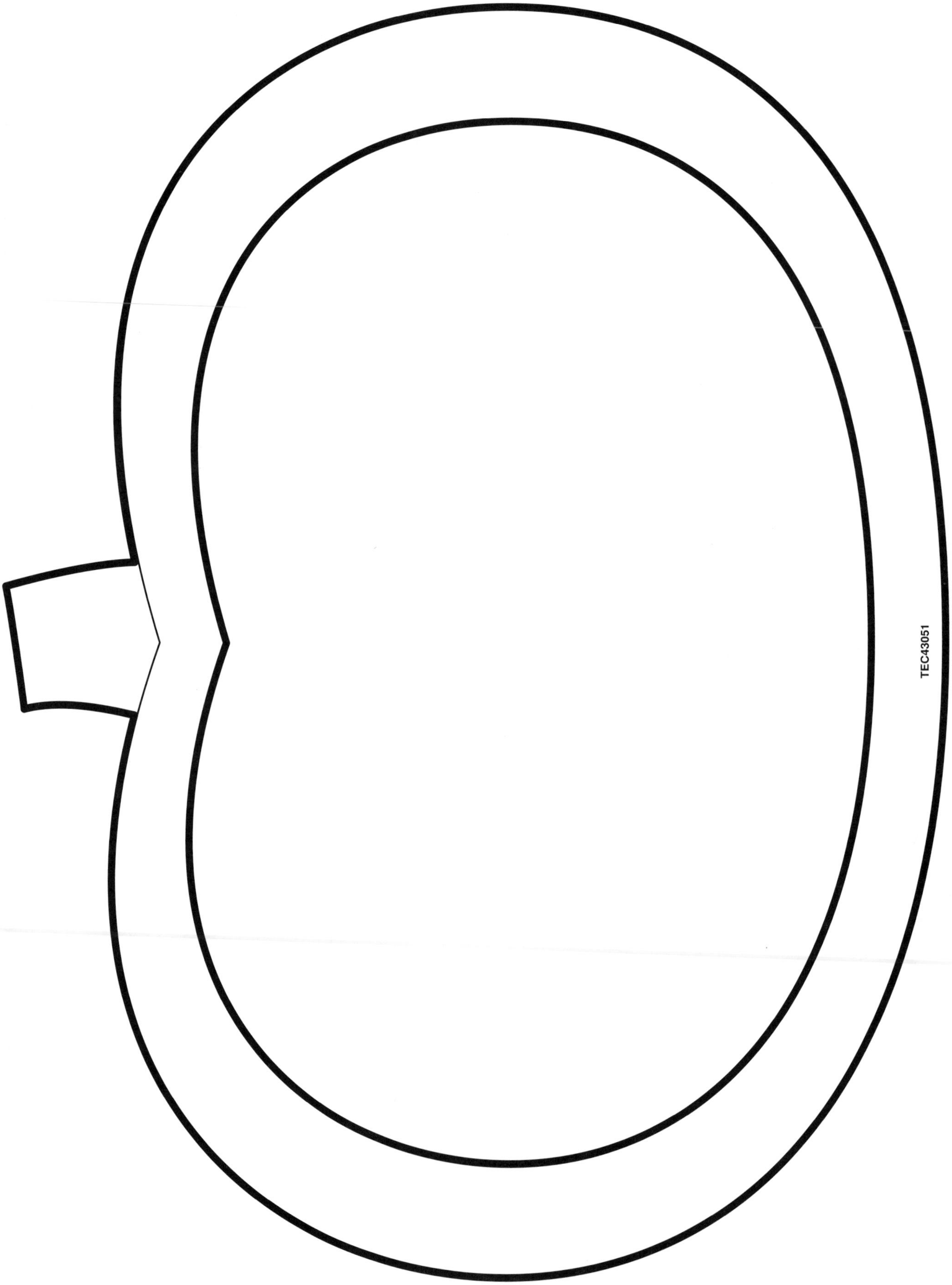
TEC43051

Card Pattern

Use with “Lighting Up Winter Days” on page 262.

There's
"snow-body"
like you!

Love Bug Pattern

Use with "Love Bug Card Container" on page 263.

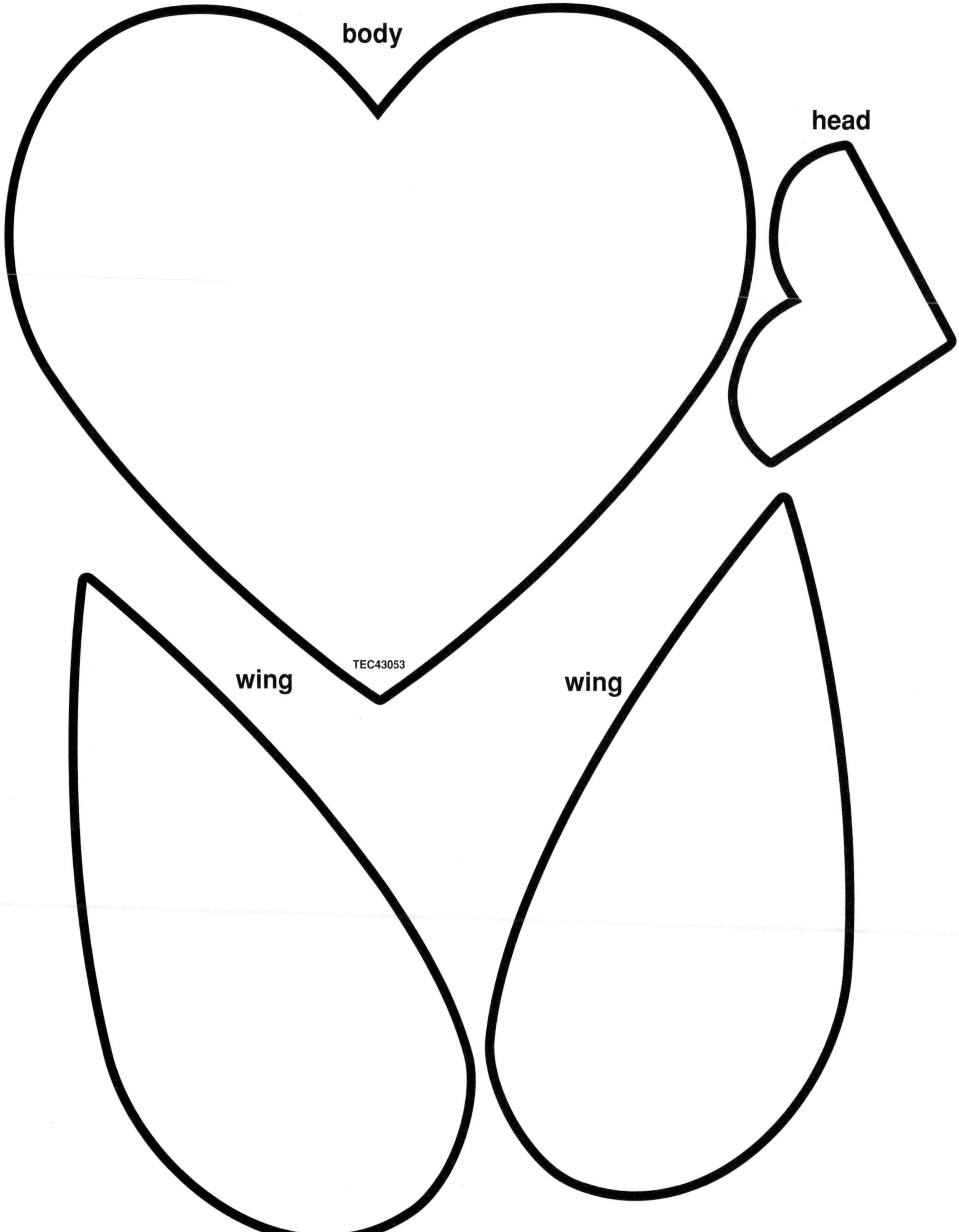
body
head
TEC43053
wing
wing

Lion and Lamb Patterns

Use with "Faces of March" on page 263.

lion

TEC43053

TEC43053

lamb

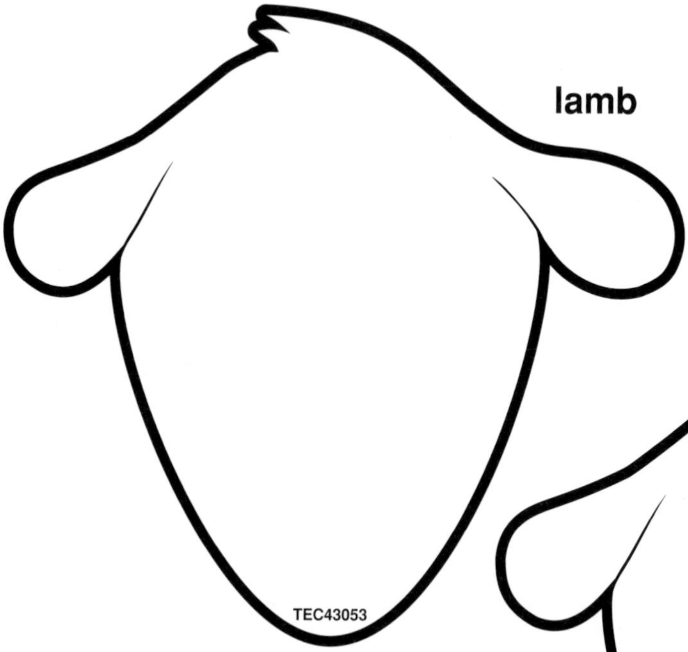
TEC43053

TEC43053

Fence and Garden Sign Pattern

Use with "Mother's Day Garden" on page 264.

TEC43054

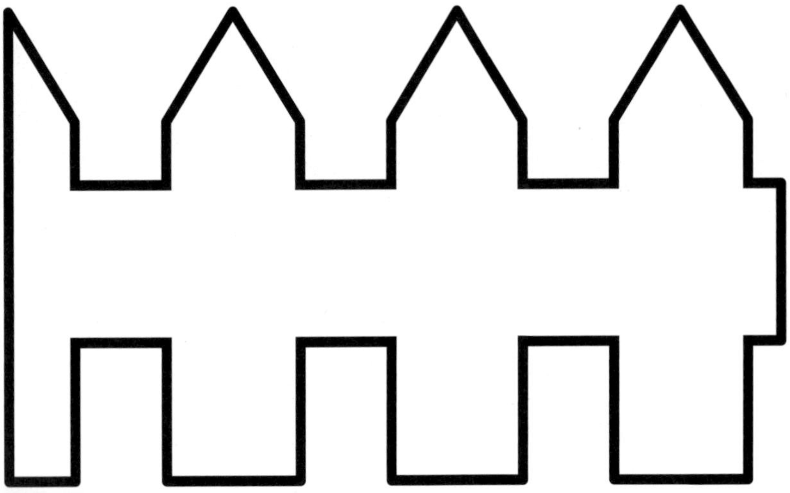

Happy
Mother's
Day

Classroom Displays

Classroom Displays

Looking Forward to a "Purr-fect" Year!
Brianna
Adalyn
Rosita
Kayla
Riley
Noah
Hannah
Tristen
Jasmine
Sean
Stella
Dominic

Welcome your students to the new school year! Post a large cat cutout on a board titled as shown. Then make a class supply of pawprint cutouts. Write each child's name on a different pawprint and post the pawprints as shown. If desired, take a photo of each student on the first day of school and glue the photos on the corresponding pawprints.

Karen Spano, Mount Sinai Elementary, Mount Sinai, NY

Swinging Through the Writing Process
Prewriting
Rough Draft
Editing
Revising
Publishing
Cooper
Mya
Hunter
Emma
Elijah
Jillian
Nolan
Victoria
Owen
Lacey
Destiny

To keep track of each student's writing progress, post this display within students' reach. First, staple brown or green yarn onto a board to create five vines. Next, label five paper leaf cutouts, each with a different step of the writing process, and staple one on each vine. Have each student personalize and cut out a copy of the monkey pattern on page 280. Then attach each monkey to the prewriting vine. When a student completes a step in the writing process, he moves his monkey to the next vine.

Brian Muffoletto, Eggert Road Elementary, Orchard Park, NY

Simplify your jobs chart with this cute display. To prepare, cover a board with blue paper as shown. Also post an enlarged copy of the fish tank pattern from page 281. Then have each child personalize and cut out a copy of the fish pattern from page 281. Attach the fish to the bottom of the board. To display the name of your helper each week, simply move the child's fish to the fish tank.

Katie Kolowski, Bolin Elementary, East Peoria, IL

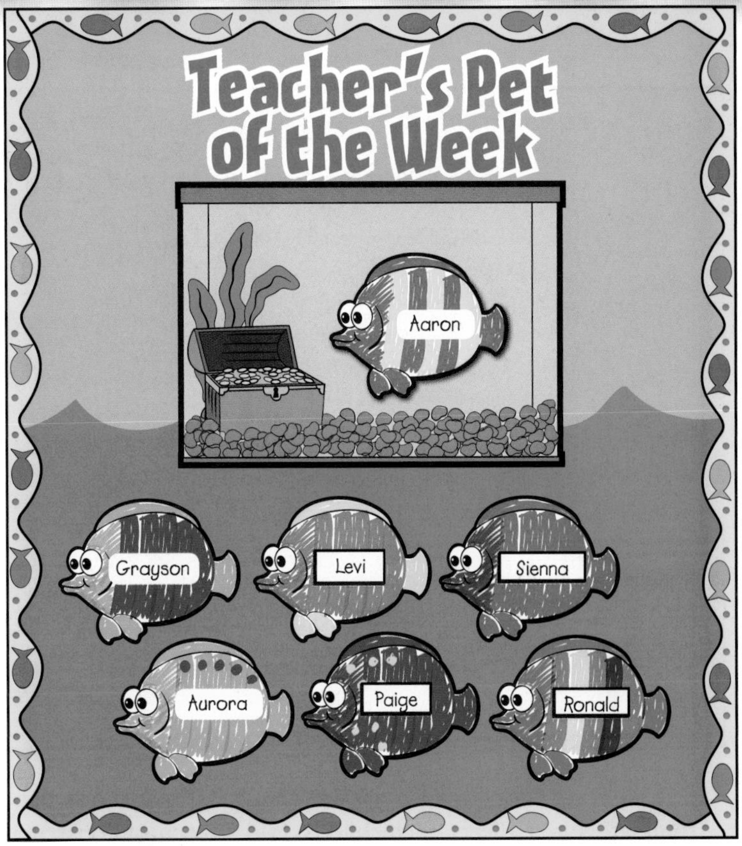
Teacher's Pet of the Week
Aaron
Grayson
Levi
Sienna
Aurora
Paige
Ronald

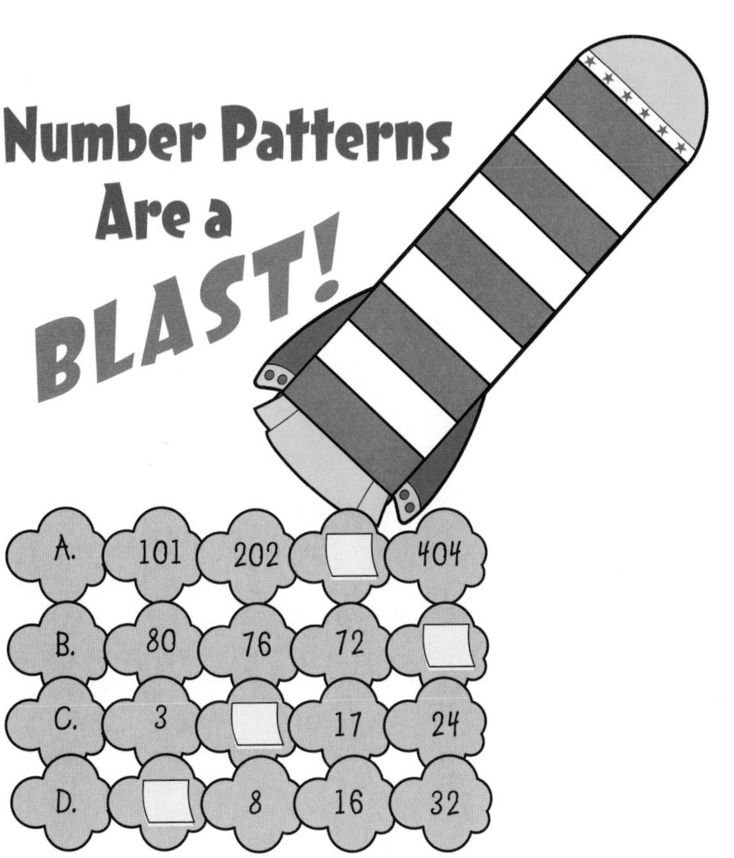
Number Patterns Are a BLAST!
A. 101 202 404
B. 80 76 72
C. 3 17 24
D. 8 16 32

Reinforce patterning skills with this interactive display! Trace an enlarged copy of the rocket pattern from page 121, cut it out, and post it with smoke cloud cutouts as shown. Label each row of clouds with a different letter and then program the cutouts with a number pattern. Cover one cutout in each row with a sticky note. When a student visits the display, he copies the number patterns on his paper and completes each one. Then he lifts each sticky note to check his work.

Colleen Dabney, Williamsburg, VA

Classroom Displays

Our Favorite Corny Jokes and Riddles
Nolan
Maya
Cal
Isla
Ben
Raul
What did the farmer say to the cows last night?
Riley
It's "pasture" bedtime!
Alex
Esme

Celebrate fall with a few giggles and grins. In advance, use the pattern on page 280 to make a candy corn template. Next, direct each child to fold a piece of construction paper in half, trace the template along the fold, and cut out the tracing while leaving the fold intact. Instruct each student to write his name and a joke or riddle on the top flap and then write the punch line inside the flap. Finally, have the child color his candy corn before posting it on the display.

Colleen Dabney, Williamsburg, VA

A Thankful Flock
School
Home
Food
Family
Friends
Addison is thankful for...
Oakes is thankful for...
Tristan is thankful for...
Ella is thankful for...
Payton is thankful for...

Give students a chance to share what they are thankful for this holiday season. Instruct each child to complete a copy of the turkey pattern on page 282, writing one thing she is thankful for on each feather. Then have the student color the turkey and cut it out. Invite each child to share her writing with the class and then post the turkey on the board.

Whitney Fisher, North Elementary, Morgantown, WV

Dominic
Maya
Grayson
Logan
Payton
Brooklyn
Seema
Aiden
Adalyn
Hot chocolate, hot chocolate,
I love you a lot.
I wish I could drink every last drop.
Hot chocolate, hot chocolate,
You're such a treat.
On a cold day, you just can't be beat!
Warmly Welcoming Winter

Give winter a warm welcome with this sweet display. Have each student write a winter-related poem on a marshmallow-shaped cutout. Then post the marshmallows above a large mug as shown.

Linda Skupski, Parma Community School, Parma, OH

Perched on Place Value
1
3
4
6
7
9
8
0
5
2
The Ten Thousands House
The Thousands House
The Hundreds House
The Tens House
The Ones House

To prepare this interactive display, make colored copies of the birdhouse on page 283 (one for each place value your students study) and cut a slit along each dotted line. Next, label each house with a different place value, post the birdhouses in order, and draw commas where needed. Then make five copies of the bird patterns on page 283 and program each with a number from 0 to 9. Use pushpins to attach the birds and insert a paper clip into each birdhouse's slit as shown. When students visit the display, direct them to move the birds to create numbers and then read and write them. **For a seasonal touch,** attach paper snow on each house during winter and remove it in spring.

Jennifer Schindler, Grundy County Elementary, Humphreys, MO

Classroom Displays

Luckily for Me...
Luckily for me, Elizabeth Blackwell became the first woman in the United States to get a medical degree. She made it possible for other women, like my mom, to become doctors.
Name Evan

Highlight contributions of influential women during Women's History Month (March) with this easy-to-prepare board. After providing research time, give each child a copy of the four-leaf clover pattern on page 284. The student completes the sentence, describing an important contribution of the woman he researched and how the contribution affects his life. Then the child cuts out his clover pattern and posts his project on a board titled as shown.

We're Springing Forward!
I read ten more books!
Kevia

Keep track of students' accomplishments with this colorful display! Each time a child achieves a milestone—such as mastering facts, reading a certain number of books, or making a desired score on a test—invite her to personalize a copy of the flower pattern on page 284. Then have her post it in a designated "garden area," such as along the floor. Before long, your classroom will be blooming with bright colors and proud students!

Kimberly Barnhill, North Highlands Elementary
Shreveport, LA

Classroom Displays

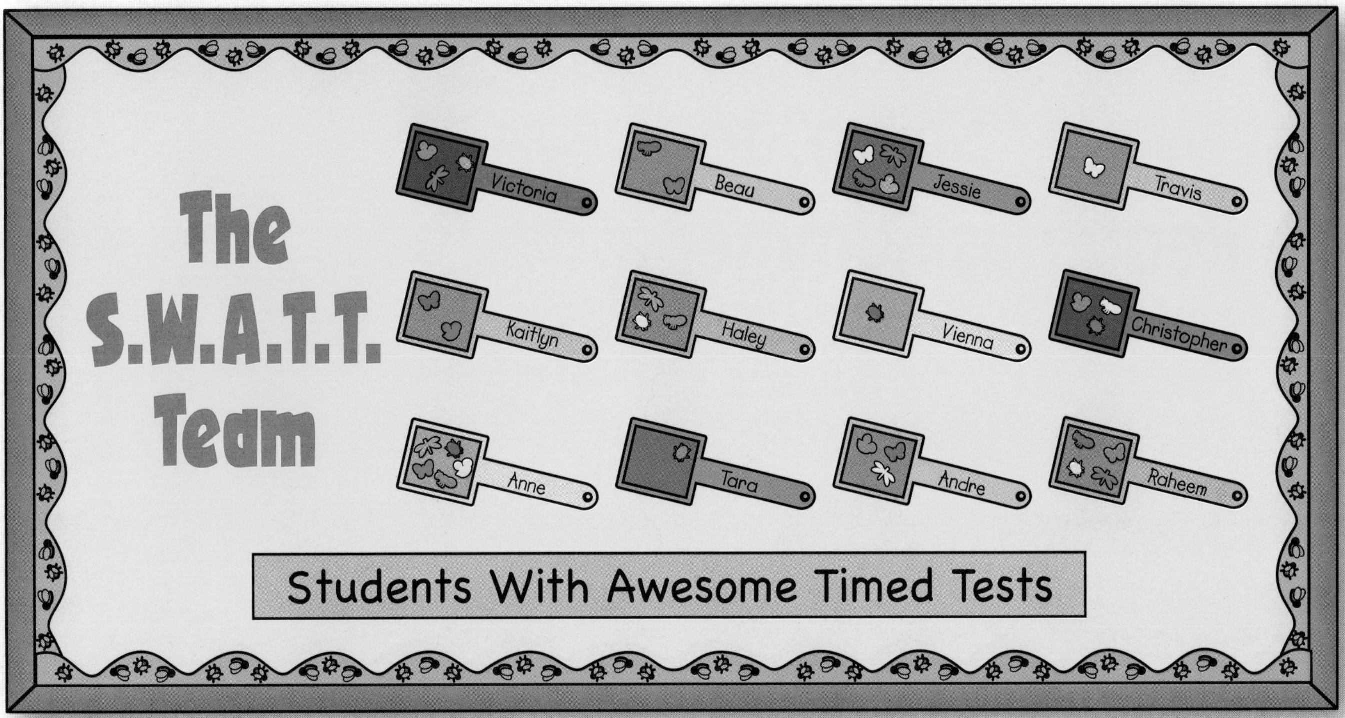
The S.W.A.T.T. Team
Victoria
Beau
Jessie
Travis
Kaitlyn
Haley
Vienna
Christopher
Anne
Tara
Andre
Raheem
Students With Awesome Timed Tests

Motivate students to learn their facts with this incentive board. Instruct each child to personalize a copy of a flyswatter pattern from page 285 and cut it out. Post the flyswatters on a board. Each time a child earns a predetermined score on a timed test, give the student a foam bug sticker to display on his flyswatter.

Jeannie Pavlik, Pittsville Elementary, Pittsville, WI

Don't "Frog-et"
Get a good night's sleep.
Eat breakfast.
Arrive on time.
Wear comfy clothes.
Bring a good book to read.

To prepare students for state testing, post this "un-frog-ettable" display. Cut out several paper frogs and paper ovals (lily pads). Write testing reminders on separate white paper strips and then trim the edges of the strips to make speech bubbles. Post the frogs, lily pads, and speech bubbles on a display titled as shown.

Stephanie Wanek
Brentwood Elementary
Overland Park, KS

Classroom Displays

We're "Shore" to Read This Summer
This summer, I plan to read nonfiction books about sharks. They are cool, and I want to learn more about them.
Name Oliver

Encourage summer reading with this seaside display. Cover a board with blue paper (water) and yellow paper (sand). Enlarge the seagull pattern from the top of page 286 and post it. Next, have each student complete a copy of the shell from page 286, naming a book, series, or genre he would like to read over the summer and explaining why. Then direct the child to color the shell, cut it out, and post it on the sand. Encourage students to visit you in the fall to tell you about their summer readings.

Colleen Dabney, Williamsburg, VA

That's a Wrap!
My favorite memory from second grade was the egg drop. It was fun to figure out how to best keep my real egg from breaking.
Cece

Wrap up one school year while preparing for the next! Cover your classroom door with wrapping paper and title it as shown. Have each child write on a half sheet of paper her favorite memory from the school year. Next, guide the student to use a half-sheet of construction paper, paper scraps, and gift bows to make a gift-shaped cover. Instruct the child to staple the cover atop her writing paper. Post the projects on the door. In the fall, update the title to read "Unwrap a New Year."

Lynette Prinz, Jefferson Elementary, Wyandotte, MI

Roxy Recommends...

Are you good at following a clue?
Do you wonder what a detective might do?
Do you enjoy figuring out what a solution might be?
Then I recommend that you read a mystery!
Lauryn My favorite mystery is
Aubrey I loved
Austin I loved
Ruby I liked
Jasmine I read
Hunter I read
Jackson I read
Autumn I read
Riley I read
Hunter I read
Karsen I read
Tanisha I read
Bryce I read
Hayden I really liked
The Case of the Missing Chicken

Introduce your students to Roxy, a sly fox who knows all about books. To prepare, enlarge and laminate a copy of the fox pattern below. Cut out the pattern, add gear that complements a book or genre you want students to read, and post it on a board titled as shown. Use a wipe-off marker to write a reading recommendation on the speech bubble; then invite each student to write a response on a sticky note and post it on the board.

Lisa Waters
Penn Alexander School
Philadelphia, PA

Roxy the Fox Pattern

Use with "Roxy Recommends…" above.

TEC43052

Monkey Pattern

Use with “Swinging Through the Writing Process” on page 272.

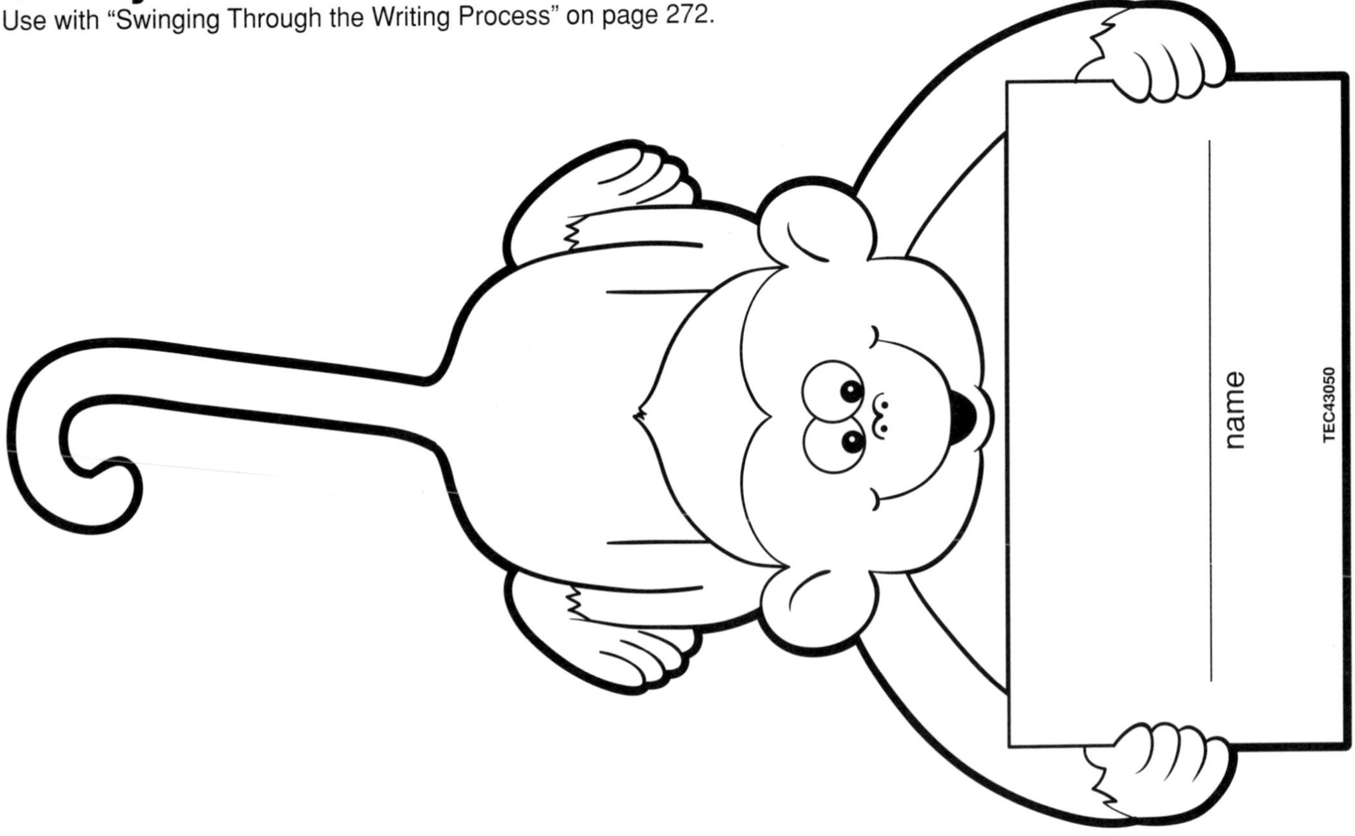
name
TEC43050

Candy Corn Pattern

Use with “Our Favorite Corny Jokes and Riddles” on page 274.

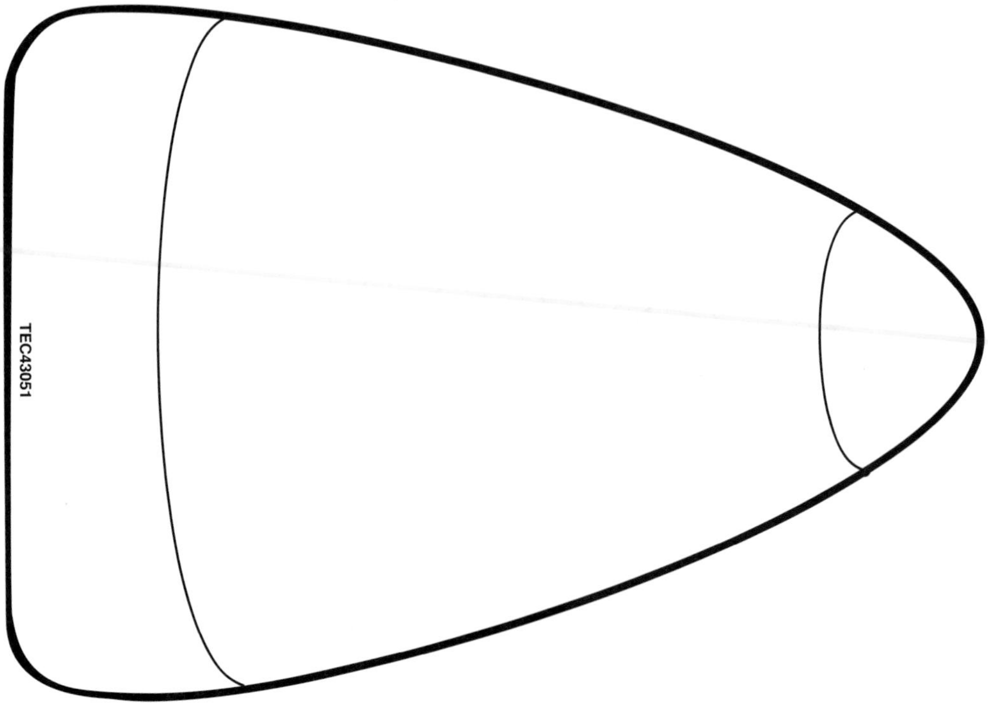
TEC43051

Fish Tank and Fish Patterns

Use with "Teacher's Pet of the Week" on page 273.

TEC43050

TEC43050

Turkey Pattern

Use with "A Thankful Flock" on page 274.

Food
Home
Family
School
Friends
is thankful for...
TEC43051

Bird and Birdhouse Patterns

Use with "Perched on Place Value" on page 275.

TEC43052

TEC43052

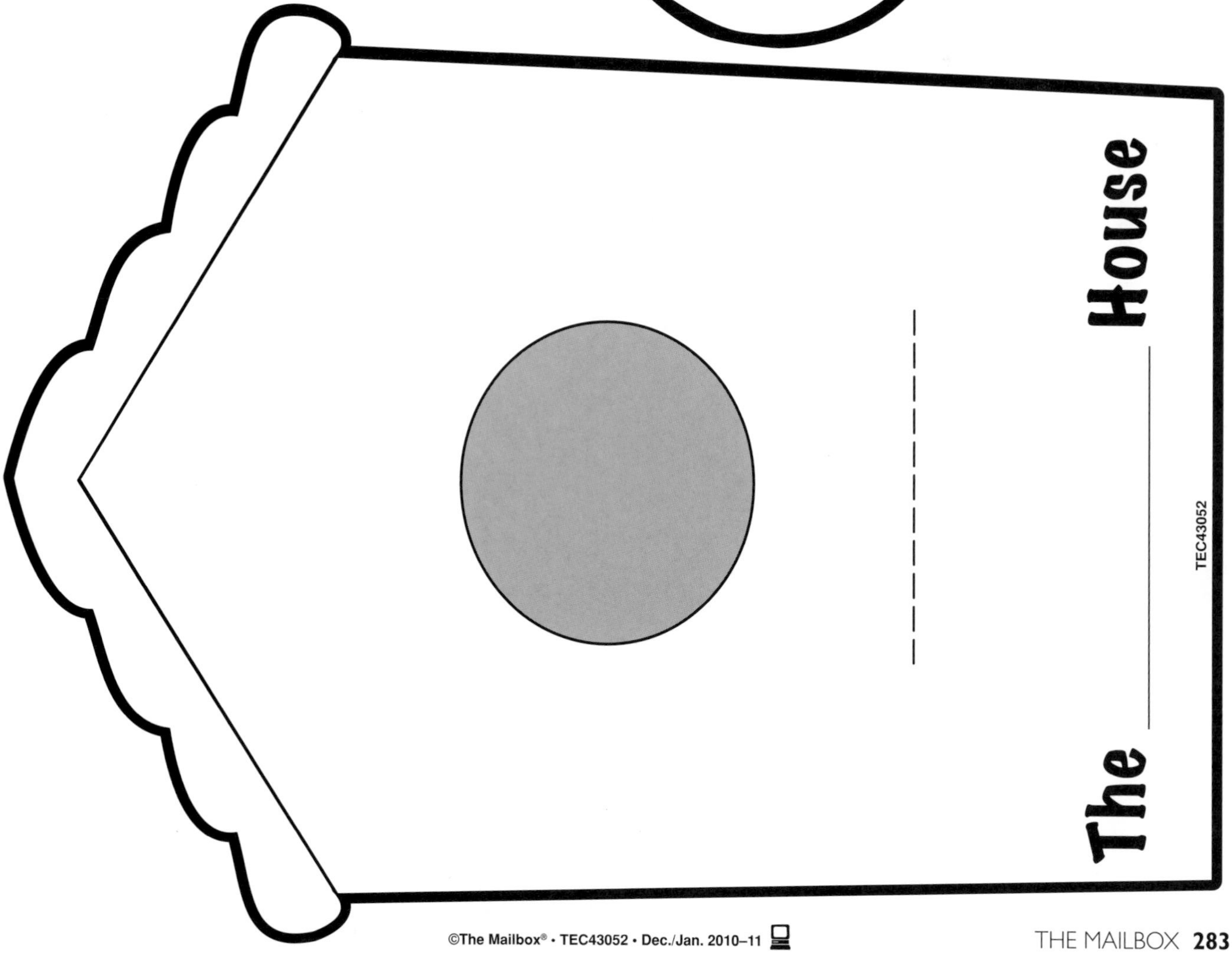
The ______ House
TEC43052

Four-Leaf Clover Pattern

Use with "Luckily for Me…" on page 276.

Luckily for me, ________
Name ________
TEC43053

Flower Pattern

Use with "We're Springing Forward!" on page 276.

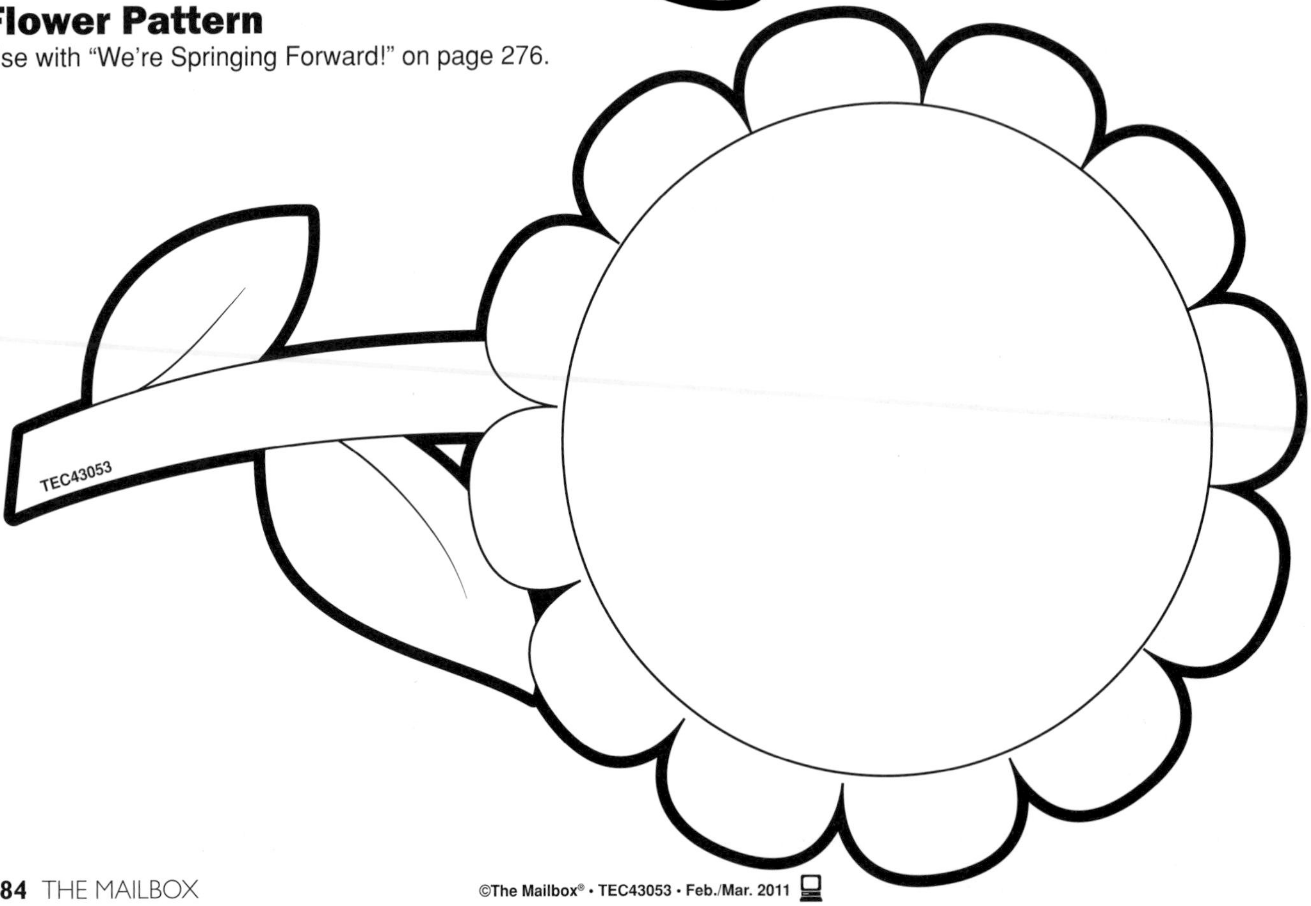
TEC43053

Flyswatter Patterns

Use with "The S.W.A.T.T. Team" on page 277.

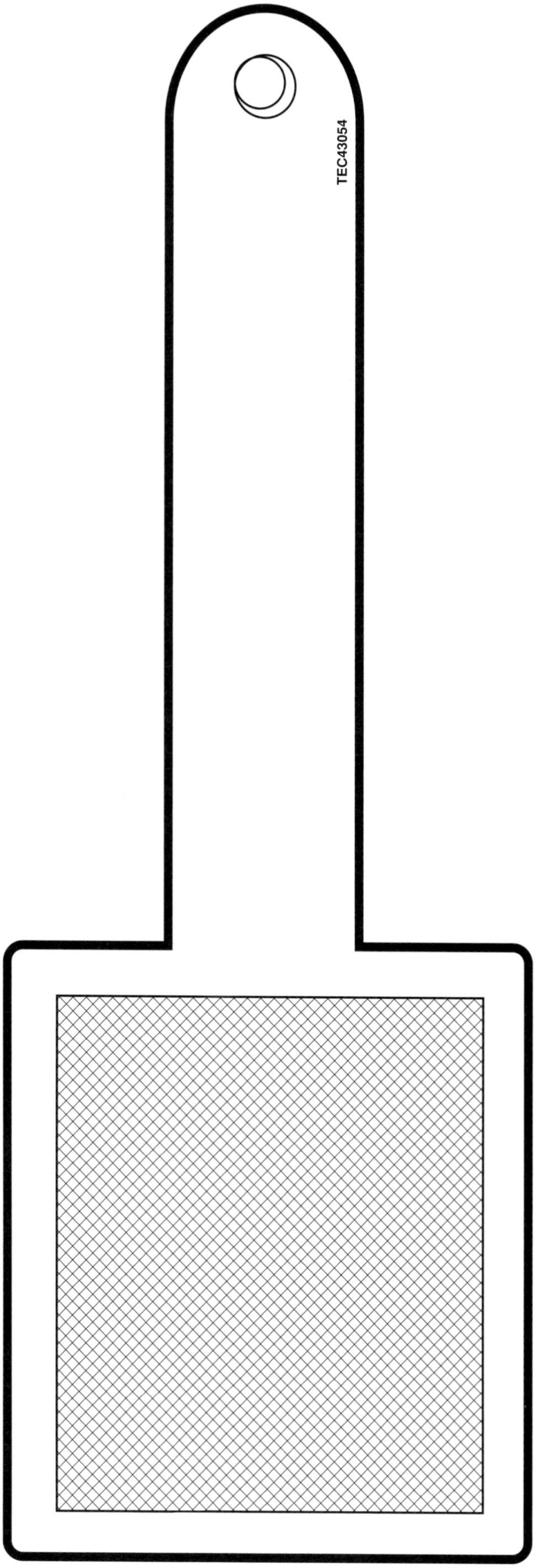
TEC43054

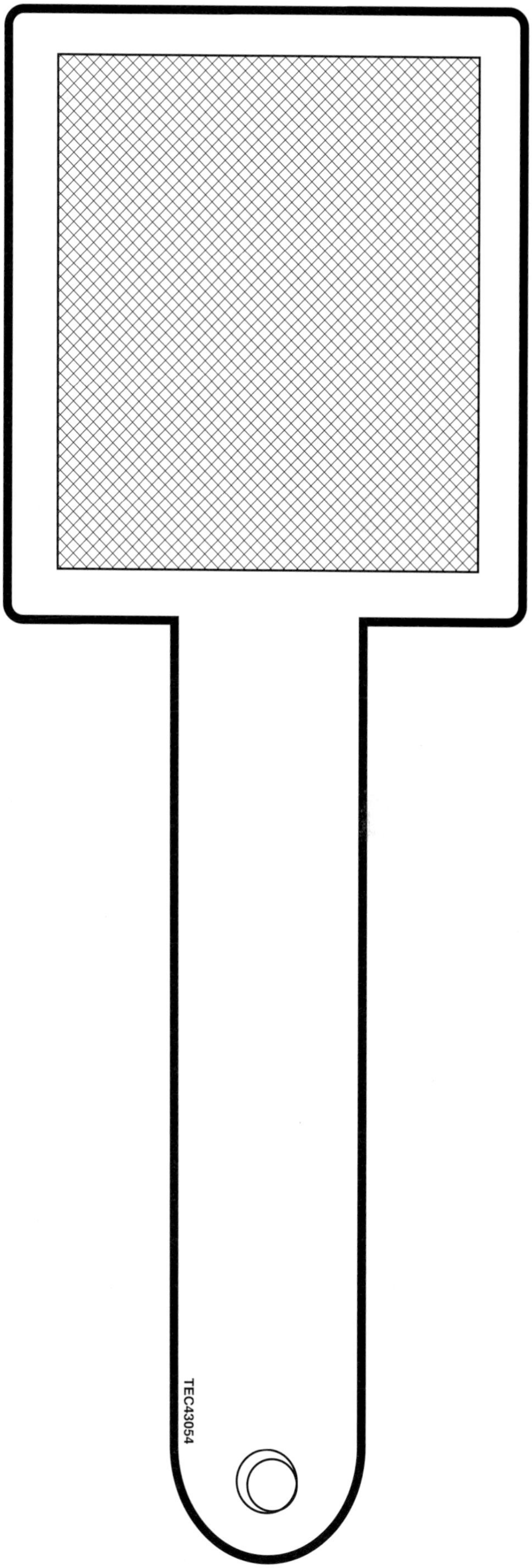
TEC43054

Seagull and Shell Patterns

Use with "We're 'Shore' to Read This Summer" on page 278.

TEC43055

This summer, I plan to read ______________________

____

____

____

____

____

____

Name ________________________________

TEC43055

Management Tips & Timesavers

Management Tips & Timesavers

All-Star Approach

Score points with students when you give your behavior system a sports theme! On the first day of school, introduce yourself as the coach and refer to any support teachers as the assistant coaches. Tell students they are your team players. Then reveal sports-related names for your policies and procedures, rules, consequences, and classroom helpers as shown. Remind students that if everyone works together as a team, they're sure to have an all-star year!

- ★ The Game Plan (procedures)
- ★ The Rules of the Game (classroom rules)
- ★ Penalties (consequences)
- ★ Team Managers (classroom helpers)
- ★ Coach (teacher)
- ★ Assistant Coaches (support teachers)

Carla Basile, Pharr Elementary, Snellville, GA

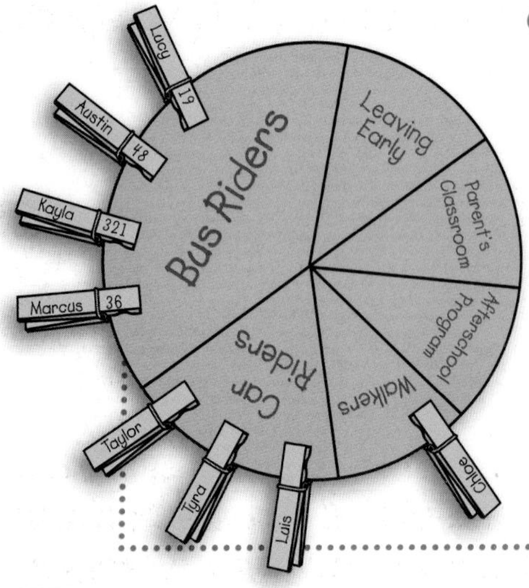
Bus Riders
Leaving Early
Parent's Classroom
Afterschool Program
Walkers
Car Riders
Lacy 19
Austin 48
Kayla 321
Marcus 36
Taylor
Tyra
Luis
Chloe

Dismissal Wheel

Keeping track of who goes where at dismissal time is "wheely" easy with this unique tip! To prepare, divide a large cardboard circle into sections and label each section with a category that names where your students go at dismissal. Also include one section for students leaving early. Next, personalize a class supply of clothespins with students' names. (Also write the bus number by the name of each bus rider.) Post the wheel in a central location and place a basket containing the clothespins nearby. Every morning, direct each child to clip his pin on the appropriate section. Refer to the wheel at the end of the day to guide students to the right locations. After all the children have left for the day, remove the pins and return them to the basket.

Cathy Farr, North Brookfield Elementary, North Brookfield, MA

Bug Box and Firefly Book

This simple system limits tattling and promotes a positive classroom environment. To prepare, label a shoebox and a spiral notebook as shown. Explain to students that the bug box is a place where anyone (including you) can write on a slip of paper a school concern that is bugging her while the firefly book is a special place to write about an example of another student brightening her day. At the end of the week, hold a class meeting and read aloud the bug box problems, being careful to omit any student names. Then have the class discuss ways to solve each problem. End the meeting on a positive note by sharing what's written in the firefly book.

Firefly Book
Bug Box

Megan Stauffer, Ritter Elementary, Allentown, PA

Jazzy Jobs

Looking for a way to spice up your student job titles? Try these! Introduce the titles shown and discuss the job description for each. If desired, have each student apply for his top choice by writing sentences that explain why he thinks he should be chosen for the job.

Meredith Bogush, Center City Public Charter Schools, Washington, DC

Job Titles and Descriptions

Bathroom Bouncer (one male and one female)—monitors the number of people in the bathroom at a time
Board Hygienist—erases, cleans, and readies the board for the next day
Botanist—plant caretaker
Composer—turns the CD player, radio, or MP3 player on and off
Electrician—plugs in the overhead or document projector and turns off the lights
Line-Segment Leader—line leader
Secret Agent—carries notes from place to place

Macey

Special Spot

Manage early finishers by assigning each child her very own quiet spot. At the beginning of the year, write each student's name on a decorative cutout and tape it to the floor or to a wall, cabinet, desk, or piece of furniture close to the floor. Explain to students that these cutouts mark their quiet spots and that, whenever they finish assignments early, they may sit or lie on the floor near their cutouts and read quietly. If desired, invite students to share their assigned locations with a friend for a special reward!

April Leischner, J. D. Lever Elementary, Aiken, SC

Building Behavior

This classroom management system allows students to check their own behavior while practicing calendar skills. At the beginning of each month, tape a blank monthly calendar to each student's desk. When he arrives at school each day, instruct the child to write the day's date, retrieve five linking cubes from a basket, and place them on his desk. Monitor students' behavior throughout the day; if a child's behavior does not meet your expectations, ask him to return a cube. Then, at the end of the day, count each child's cubes and write the number on his calendar. For students who end the day with all five cubes, stamp their calendars. At the end of the week, reward students who earned a stamp every day with a small prize, such as a homework pass.

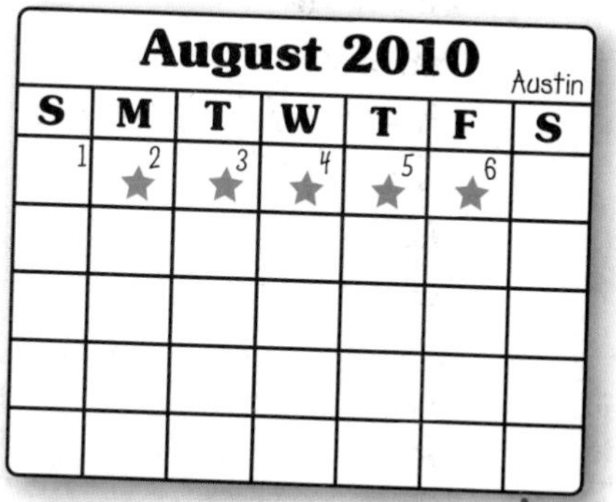
August 2010
Austin
S M T W T F S
1 2 3 4 5 6

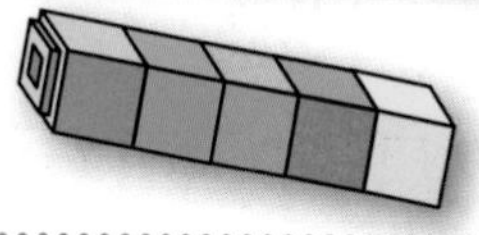

Kindra King, Snow Hill Primary, Snow Hill, NC

Great work!
Please sign and return.
Please complete.
Much better!

Just Print and Stick!

Here's a quick and easy way to comment on students' papers without having to write the comments each time! Use your computer to print labels programmed with common phrases, such as the ones shown. Then, when you need to write a comment on a child's paper or request a parent's signature, just choose the appropriate label and stick it on her paper.

Tara Kicklighter, Bunnell Elementary, Bunnell, FL

Management Tips & Timesavers

It's Mr. Sponge Time!

Looking for a way to quickly communicate with students when you have to attend to a technical glitch or an unexpected visitor? Give Mr. Sponge a try! Add wiggle eyes to an ordinary household sponge, draw a mouth, and attach a magnet to the back. Explain to students that whenever they see Mr. Sponge on the board, they should work quietly on a sponge activity, such as practicing their spelling words or math facts independently.

Melissa Boaz, Frost Elementary, Richmond, TX

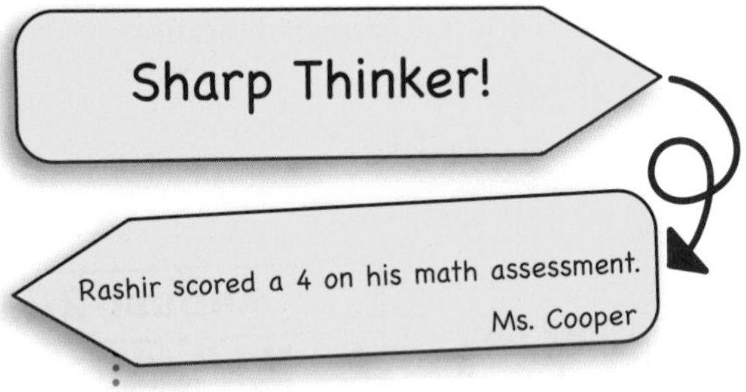
Sharp Thinker!
Rashir scored a 4 on his math assessment.
Ms. Cooper

Cutout Shape	Saying
hand	"High Five!"
apple	"The Apple of My Eye!"
pencil	"Sharp Thinker!"
cookie	"One Smart Cookie!"
star	"Out of This World!"

Way to Go!

Report students' excellent efforts when you send home these creative notes. After a child does something noteworthy, choose a saying from the list and program its matching cutout with the message shown. Then add a brief explanation on the back. It's a great way to communicate with parents and promote positive behavior throughout the year.

Jennifer Cooper, Park Hills Elementary, Hanover, PA

Friendly Reminders

Here's an easy system to help students remember which paperwork needs to go home. Label three cups as shown and, for each cup, program a class supply of craft sticks with students' names or numbers. Give each child his sticks and then place the cups in a location near your desk. When a child needs to take work home to correct it, complete it, or simply have it signed and returned, have him place a craft stick in the matching cup. Then, at the end of the day, refer to the cups to remind students what they need to pack.

Cézanne Flowers, Green Hills Elementary, Millbrae, CA

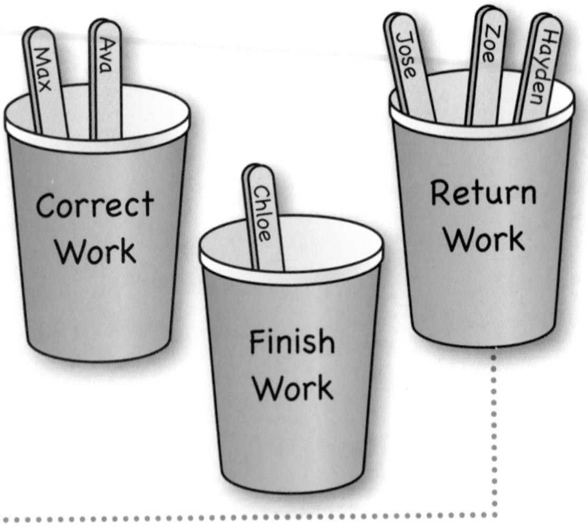
Max
Ava
Correct Work
Chloe
Finish Work
Jose
Zoe
Hayden
Return Work

Wear It Proudly!

Star Speller

Motivate students to do their best by rewarding them with these wearable awards. In advance, gather a set of lanyards with tags and program each one with a different achievement, such as the one shown. When a child deserves recognition, give him a lanyard to wear for the day. If desired, allow him to choose a prize when he returns the lanyard to you at the end of the school day.

Henri Pelham, John Glenn Elementary, San Antonio, TX

And the Answer Is...

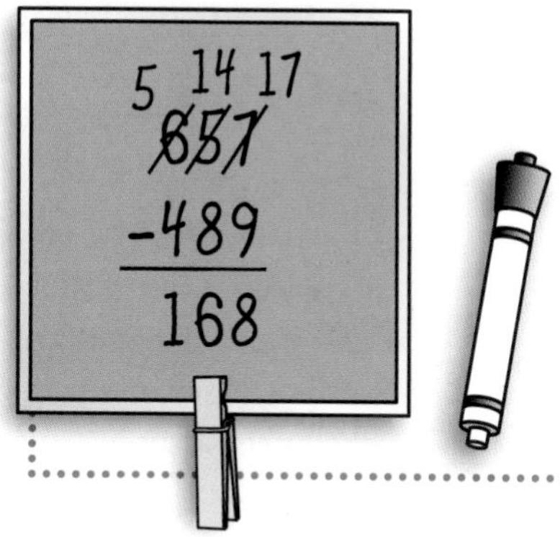
5 14 17
657
-489
168

Encourage classroom participation with these fun answer paddles. Cut and laminate a class supply of 6" x 6" squares of tagboard. Then clip a clothespin to the bottom of each one to create an answer paddle. Give each child one paddle and a wipe-off marker. After you ask a question, have each student write her answer on the paddle and hold it up. With a quick glance, you can see who's on the right track!

Colleen Dabney, Williamsburg, VA

Good Behavior Adds Up!

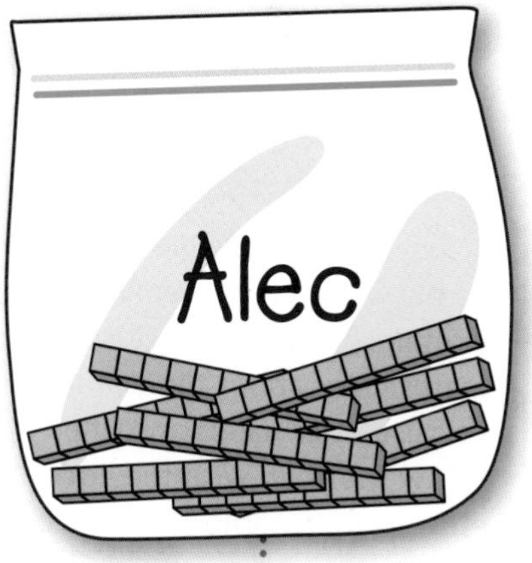
Alec

Promote positive behavior with this math-inspired reward system. Direct each child to place a resealable plastic bag on his desk. Each time a child exhibits good behavior, reward him with a place value ten rod. When he has earned ten rods, direct him to exchange the rods for a hundred flat. After the student has collected a predetermined number of flats, reward him with a small prize. **To adapt this idea for other math concepts,** give students fraction pieces to make a whole, pattern blocks to create a predetermined shape, or reproducible inches to make a foot or yard.

Brittney Lane, Eastern Wayne Elementary, Goldsboro, NC

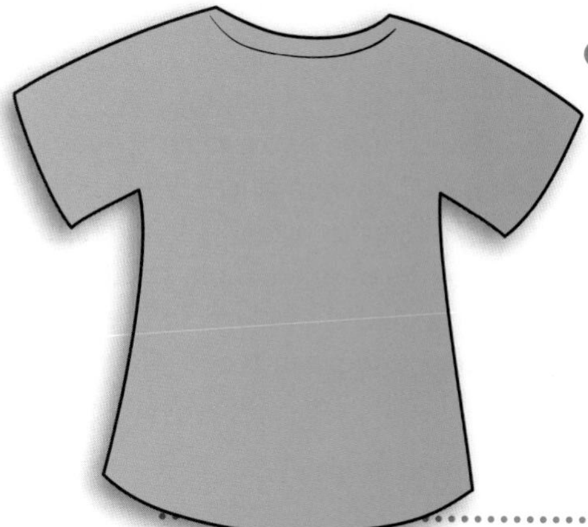

See the Tees

With this colorful tip, keeping students with their assigned work groups has never been easier. Assign each small group a different color and provide them with a set of T-shirts in the matching color. Before students begin work, have them put on their shirts. You can quickly identify students who are not working with the correct group, and addressing a particular group will be a cinch when you refer to them by their group color. Plus students who rejoin the class after pull-out instruction will have no trouble finding their groups.

Susan Soenksen, Carlson Elementary, Rockford, IL

Management Tips & Timesavers

Special Delivery

You're a Winner to Me!
Dear Sean,
I like how you offered to help Nick with his project. You are a good citizen and a great friend. I am proud of you!
Ms. Franzmann

Special Delivery

Send the message that you appreciate positive behaviors and efforts with this simple idea. Use art supplies to decorate a cardboard tube. Then write a motivating message on a copy of a teacher's note from page 296. Roll the note, slip it inside the tube, and place it on the student's desk. After the student has read the message, ask him to return the tube so you can send a message to another student.

Kate Franzmann, Barneveld, WI

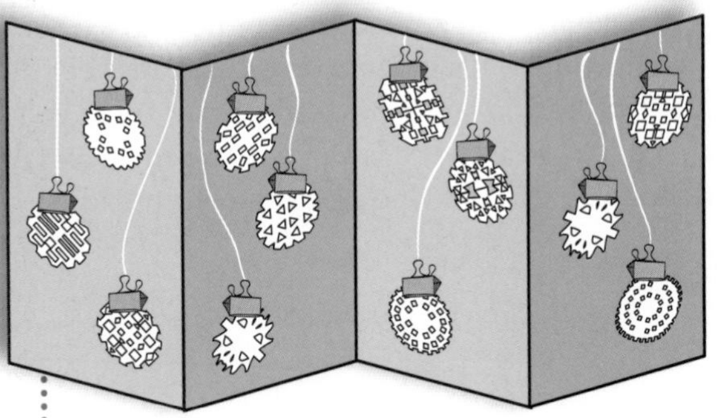

Divide and Conquer

Here's an idea that helps you divide your classroom, disguise a cluttered area, or create an extra bulletin board. Set up a folding screen or a four-panel board like the one shown. To display student work, pin fishing lines from the top and use binder clips to attach papers to the ends of the lines.

Jeannie Pavlik, Pittsville Elementary, Pittsville, WI

Name That Animal

This animal likes to live where it's cold.

Engage students during transitions with an animal guessing game. Write names of different animals on separate paper strips and store them in a container. During transition time, have a student select a strip and give his classmates clues about the animal (without saying its name). Encourage students to raise their hands and offer guesses as to which animal is being described. Allow the child with the correct guess to be the next to give clues. For extra fun, encourage the student giving clues to use sound effects for one of his clues.

penguin

Gerri Primak, Charlotte, NC

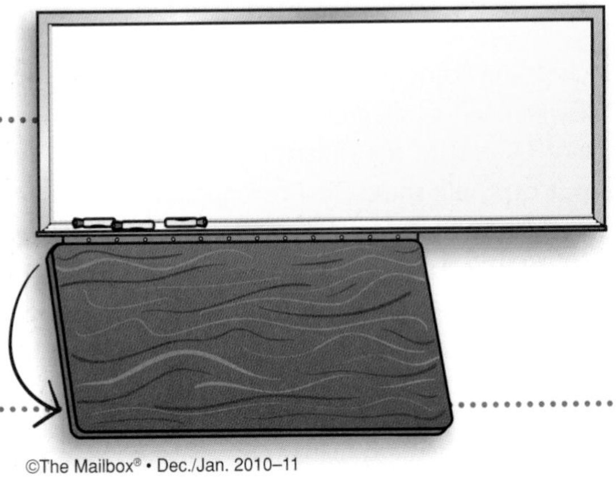

There When You Need It!

This nifty trick allows you to have extra table space when it's needed and open space when it isn't. With your custodian's help, use strong hinges to attach a folding table below your board. When you need extra table space, simply pull it away from the wall and unfold the legs. To create open space again, fold the legs underneath and allow the table to lie against the wall.

Jeannie Pavlik

Do-Good Leprechauns

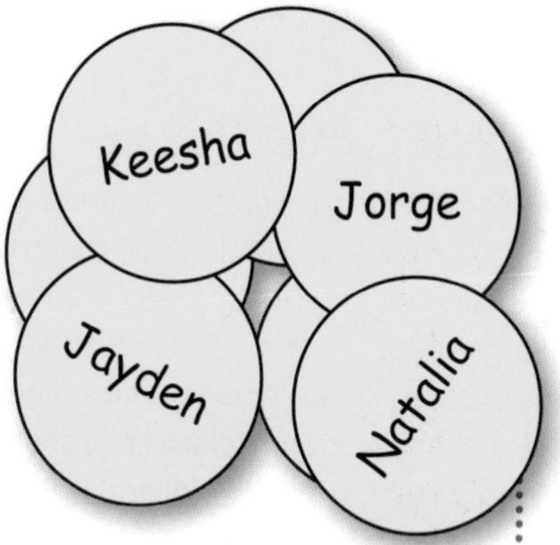
Keesha
Jorge
Jayden
Natalia

Encourage students to do good deeds and make them feel lucky with this fun tip. The week before St. Patrick's Day, prepare a class supply of paper coins, each labeled with a different student's name. Have each child secretly draw a coin. Then explain that, during the next week, each student will perform a good deed for his assigned classmate without revealing his own identity. On St. Patrick's Day, have each child tell the class about the good deed that was done for her and then invite her to guess the name of her secret leprechaun.

Adrienne Averetta, Long Beach, CA

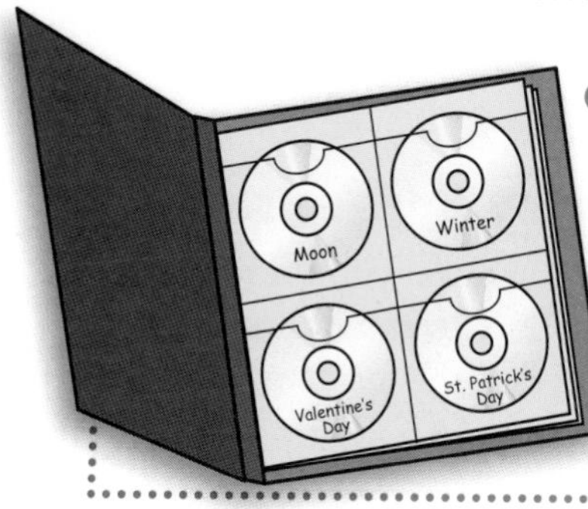
Moon
Winter
Valentine's Day
St. Patrick's Day

Stop the Paper Trail!

This simple system keeps custom-made reproducibles sorted and organized. For each unit, make a computer file containing lesson plans, worksheets, and forms used. Burn the files onto a CD, label the CD with the unit's title, and then file each CD in a CD binder. When it's time to teach the unit again, pop the CD into the computer and you'll have all the papers you need!

Nicholas Sveum, Edgerton Elementary, Edgerton, WI

It's All in the Cards

Looking for a quick and easy way to assign cooperative groups? Try this. Set aside a class supply of playing cards, being sure to include four suits for each number set aside. For example, to prepare for a class of 24 students, set aside all suits of cards two through seven. To use the cards, have each child draw one and direct the student to form a group with the classmates whose numbers match hers. Then, when it's time to assign jobs within a group, use the cards' suits, as shown.

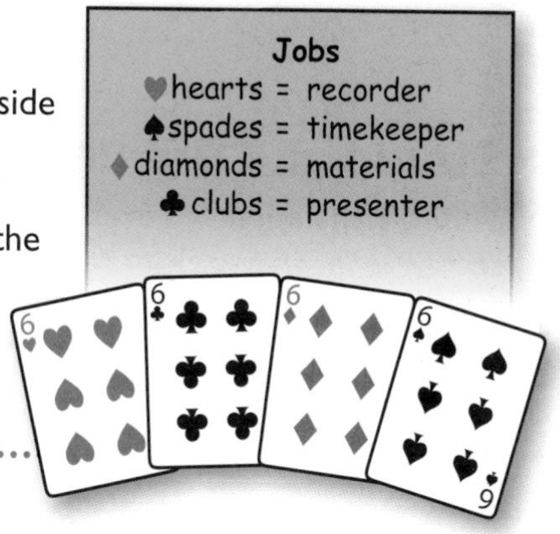
Jobs
♥hearts = recorder
♠spades = timekeeper
♦diamonds = materials
♣clubs = presenter

Leslie Wright, Aviara Oaks Elementary, Carlsbad, CA

Jessica
Top Dog
Luisa

Top Dog

No bones about it, this fun dog-themed reward system inspires students to return their homework! At the end of the week, reward each student who turned in every assignment on time by giving her a bone pattern. Have the child personalize, decorate, and cut out the pattern. Then staple each cutout to a display titled "Homework Top Dogs." At the end of the month, reward students who returned all their homework assignments with a pet tag pattern. Have each student personalize, decorate, and cut out the tag. Then help her hole-punch the tag, thread yarn through the hole, and loosely tie it around her neck to wear proudly.

Sheila Stock, Home Elementary, Stickney, IL

Management Tips & Timesavers

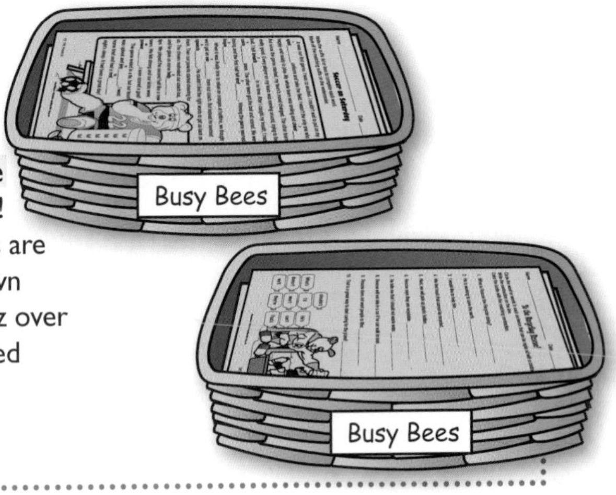
Busy Bees
Busy Bees

Busy Bee Baskets

Looking for a way to keep students working independently while you're leading small groups? Prepare Busy Bee Baskets for students! Each week, choose practice sheets appropriate for the skills students are studying or that you wish to review. Place each set of sheets in its own basket. When students complete their assigned work, have them buzz over to a basket and select an activity. For students who need differentiated practice, prepare individualized Busy Bee Binders instead.

Cindy Ward, Yellow Branch Elementary, Rustburg, VA

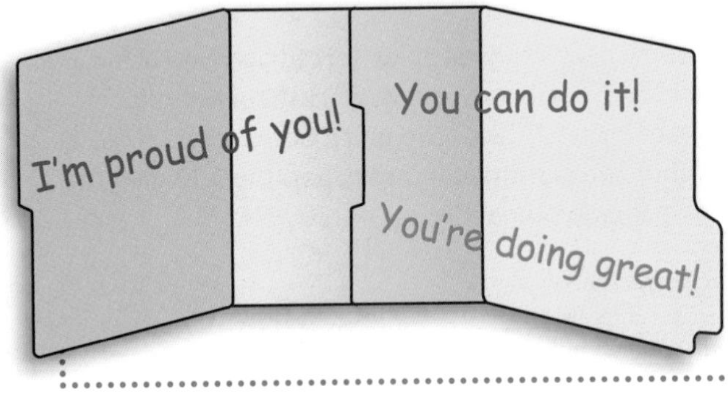
I'm proud of you!
You can do it!
You're doing great!

Inspirational Privacy Screens

Keep students on task during tests with these file folder study carrels. Overlap two folders to the desired size and then tape them together. Program the inside of each study carrel with motivational messages.

Cherie Griepp, Bingham Elementary, Springfield, MO

Stored and Organized

Recycled containers from cleaning wipes make perfect storage containers. Clean the empty containers and fill them with student supplies or center materials. Not only are they easy to store, but the transparent tops also let you see the contents at a glance!

Pam Wolfe, Brookside Elementary, Kingsport, TN

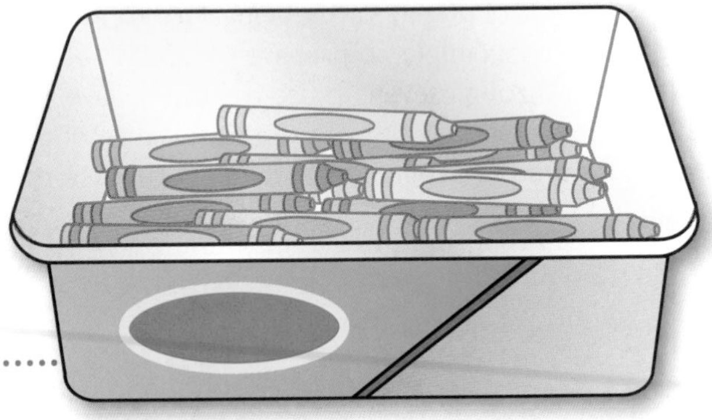

Ms. Cagle's Class

Handy Hall Passes

Sturdy and convenient, students will have no trouble keeping up with these inexpensive hall passes! To make one, drill a hole in one end of a paint stir stick. Then decorate the stick, tie a ribbon through the hole, and hang it within students' reach. Encourage students to hang the pass by its ribbon in the restroom and when returning it to the classroom.

Jamie Cagle, Monroe Avenue Elementary, Hamlet, NC

Management Tips & Timesavers

Practical Paint Dispenser

Keep your empty plastic sports-drink bottles this summer—they make great paint dispensers! Collect bottles that have pop-up tops. Then, using a funnel, pour tempera paint from a large container into a bottle. Screw on the cap and store the bottle. When students need paint, simply pop up the top and squeeze!

Sweet Reminder

Remind students how to move in line with this simple statement. Before you leave a location or whenever you see students sandwiched together in the hall, tell them, "Stack yourselves like pancakes, but leave room in between for syrup." Not only will the silly reminder amuse your students, but it will help them remember to be respectful of their classmates' personal space too.

Colleen Reninger, Worth Elementary, Worth, IL

June

Getting Organized

Use plastic lidded storage totes to sort your monthly teaching materials. Designate one tote for each month of the school year. In each tote, place hanging files; in each file, place materials such as holiday-related activities, bulletin board ideas, stickers, and read-aloud books. Store the totes in a convenient location. Each month, remove the appropriate tote from storage. Not only will you have what you need ready to use, but the handled lid also allows you to take the tote home as needed for planning or restocking supplies.

Jean Hiller, Canton Charter Academy, Canton, MI

You're a Winner to Me!

TEC43052

Super Work!

TEC43052

 Note to the teacher: Use with "Special Delivery" on page 292.

Our Readers Write

Our Readers Write

Bounce Back to School

I set the tone for a fun-filled year by preparing a welcome gift for each student. In advance, I purchase a class supply of bouncy balls at a discount store and attach a welcome note to each one. On the first day of school, I have the special gift waiting on each child's desk.

Elaine Hazel, Southside Primary, Palestine, TX

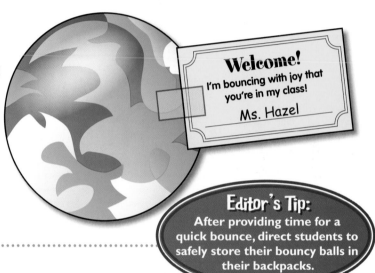

Welcome!
I'm bouncing with joy that you're in my class!
Ms. Hazel

Editor's Tip: After providing time for a quick bounce, direct students to safely store their bouncy balls in their backpacks.

It's a Math Mystery!

With this easy routine, I make my math posters meaningful references instead of just classroom decor. At the beginning of the year, I post all my math posters on one wall. Then I cover each one with a large piece of paper and draw a large question mark on it. As we begin a new math topic, I uncover the corresponding poster, giving it a grand entrance and directing students to its content.

Steph McHugh, Bristol Bay Elementary, Yorkville, IL

?
To solve, use
t you already know!
16 + 10 = 26.
9 is one less than 16 + 10.
Take 1 away from 26.
The answer is
25!

Birthday Desk

Looking for a fun way to celebrate birthdays in your classroom? I decorate an extra desk for birthdays and then set it aside. On a student's birthday, I invite her to sit at the birthday desk. My students love the extra attention and appreciate that I remembered their special days.

Melisa Gutierrez, Dorothy Stinson School, Safford, AZ

HAPPY BIRTHDAY

Emergency Preparations

Here's a dismissal tip I use to monitor the adults who are allowed to pick up my students from school. At the beginning of the school year, I have each parent complete an index card listing the names and phone numbers of all the adults who can pick up his child from school. I also take a picture of each child's parents or guardians and attach it to the back of her card. I keep these cards clipped together and refer to them when needed.

Connie Thomas, Blue River Valley Elementary, Mount Summit, IN

Hayden
Parents
Debbie Short 555-0101
Lyn Short 555-0102
Other Adults
Jean House 555-0103
Tom House 555-0104
Robbie Stockton 555-0105

Tracking Tool

Plastic dusting wands make fun tracking tools for my student readers. I gather a supply of wands and store them in my guided reading area. When it's time to read, I offer a wand to each child and she's ready to track!

Allyson Massey, Robert Wilson Elementary, Corpus Christi, TX

Number Line

I use this quick time filler any time my students are waiting in line. I ask the first student in line to choose a number between one and ten. Then I ask the second child to either add or subtract a number of my choice to the first student's number. I continue the pattern as I go down the line. This is a great way to practice mental math with my students while encouraging them to stay quiet and pay attention.

Jill Santa, St. Elizabeth Elementary, Pittsburgh, PA

Star Effort!

This special frame displays my students' work in an eye-catching and motivating way. I decorate a plastic picture frame as shown and display it where students can see it. Each week, I choose one assignment to showcase and slip it inside the frame. My students love to see their work displayed, and they can't wait to be chosen!

Christina Bainbridge, Central Elementary, White Pigeon, MI

Star Effort!
I love your story! Great Job!

Label That Paper!

To prevent nameless and dateless papers, I teach my students this chant. It works great!

Nancy Farrell, Grassy Creek Elementary, Indianapolis, IN

Name and Date Chant

First name, *(pause)*
Last name, *(pause)*
Then don't stop!
Add the date at the top!

Our Readers Write

The Why Tree

To encourage questioning and researching skills in my classroom, I created "The Why Tree." I make a tree out of bulletin board paper and post it on a wall. Then I make leaf cutouts on white paper and place them near the tree. Any time a student has a question about a subject we are studying, he writes it on a leaf and posts it on the tree. During free time or center time, a student researches the answer to one of the questions. She writes the answer on the corresponding leaf, lightly colors it, and reposts the leaf on the tree.

Christine Smith, St. Lucie West K-8 School, Port St. Lucie, FL

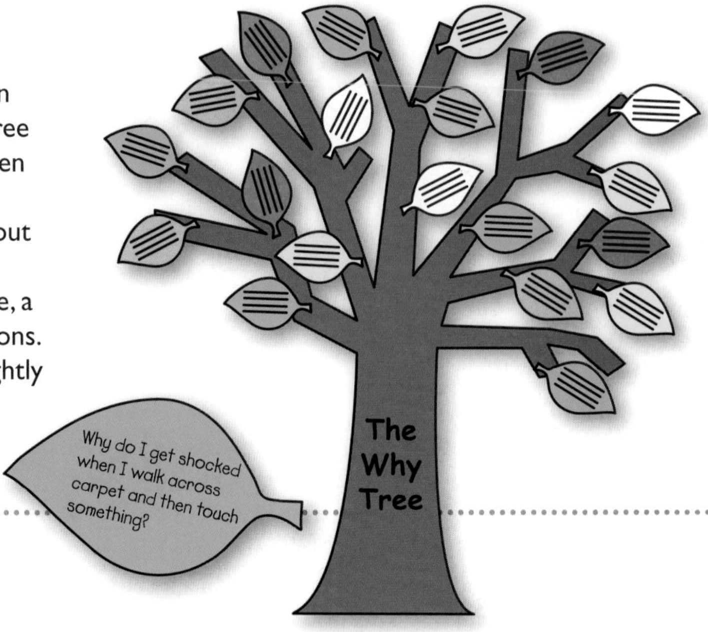
Why do I get shocked when I walk across carpet and then touch something?
The Why Tree

Making It Fit

Since my classroom has limited wall space, I use my cabinet doors and the area below my chalkboard to display my word wall. I laminate poster board and cut it to fit these spaces. Then I secure the pieces in place with strong tape and write different alphabet headings at the top of each one. When I need to add a new word to the word wall, I simply write it with a wipe-off marker. At the end of the year, all I have to do is wipe the pieces clean.

Rachel Lugo, Lynnhaven Elementary, Virginia Beach, VA

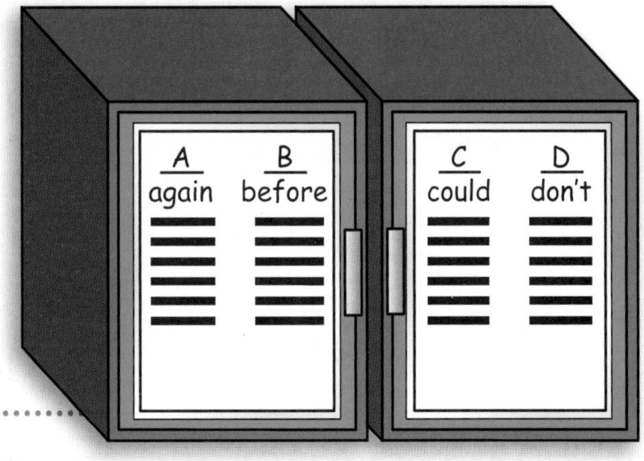
A
again
B
before
C
could
D
don't

Low-Cost Supplies

I'm always looking for ways to save money on classroom materials, so rather than buying candy year after year for students to use in math activities, I use this clever trick. First, I buy a large bag of candy and distribute the pieces at random on separate sheets of paper. Then I photograph each set, print the photos, and laminate them. They're ready to use whenever students need a graphing activity and can be reused with future students.

Andrea Leverton
Alpac Elementary
Pacific, WA

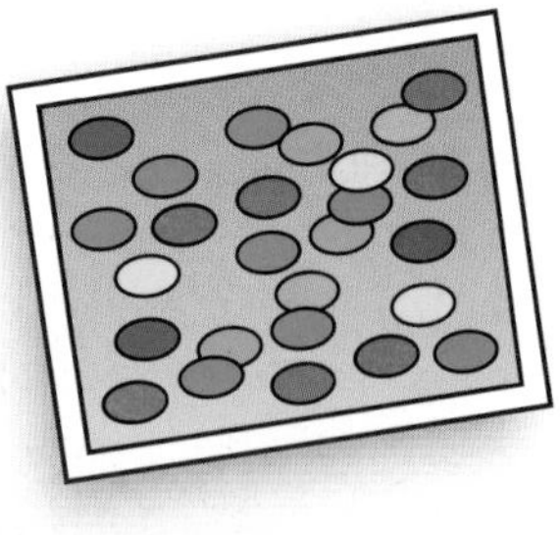

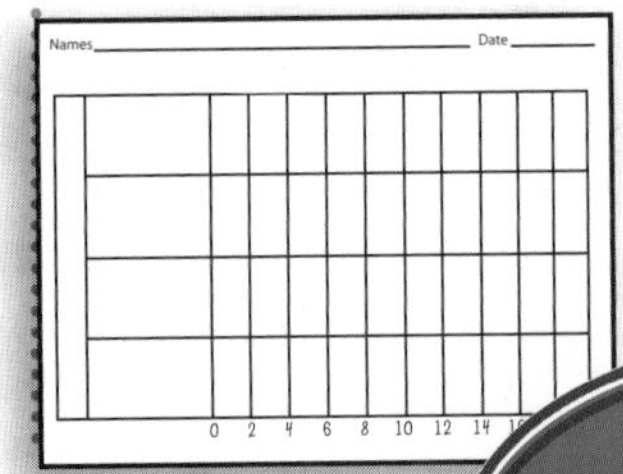
Names
Date
0 2 4 6 8 10 12 14

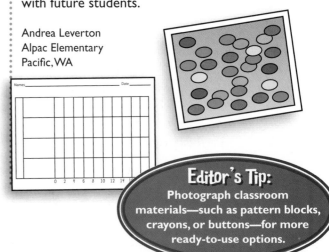

Editor's Tip:
Photograph classroom materials—such as pattern blocks, crayons, or buttons—for more ready-to-use options.

It's Time to Party!

Instead of holding a class party, I branch out across my grade level and throw a block party. Each class brings a designated food or drink to the party. Students in each class also wear matching nametags, and every teacher plans a whole-group game to play. It's a great way to set the stage for collaboration across the grade level and allows students to visit with former classmates!

Randi Austin, Stoutland R-2 Elementary, Stoutland, MO

Pencil Stub City

To help my students let go of their stubby pencils, I create a happy little place for the stubs to retire. I decorate a shoe box and label it "Stub City." Then I explain that Stub City is a fun place where all the stubs like to live. When a student's pencil is shorter than his tallest finger, he writes his initials on the stub, and takes it on a one-way trip to Stub City. Then I give him a new pencil.

Pat Biancardi, Homan Elementary, Schererville, IN

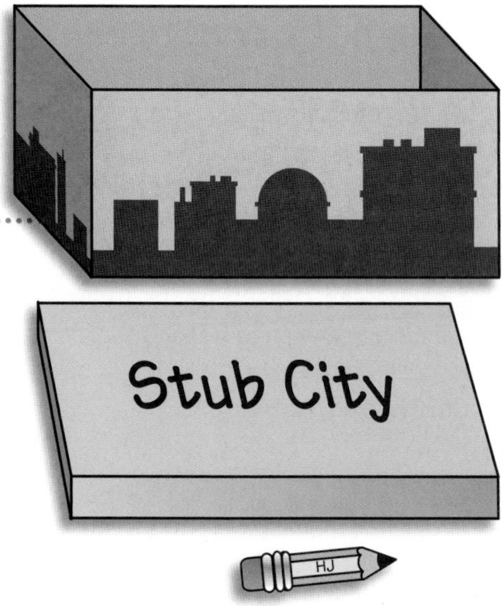
Stub City
HJ

Sequential Order, Please!

To help my students understand the concepts of sequencing and order for reading activities, I assign each of them a number. When we're ready to leave the room, I ask them to line up in sequential order. By using this term daily, my students better understand what it means to sequence the main events of a story. As an added bonus, it also cuts down on cutting in line!

Janice Green, Foster Village Elementary, North Richland Hills, TX

Basket Buddy

I motivate my students to keep our classroom clean by adding a friendly face to our trash can. I look for pictures of fun animals and objects from magazines, posters, clip art, and the Internet. I also cut out a paper speech bubble. Then I laminate the picture and speech bubble, write a catchy reminder, and tape the cutouts to the trash can. As the year progresses, I invite students to prepare a character and reminder to display on the trash can.

Lisa Waters
Penn Alexander School
Philadelphia, PA

"Whoooo" is wise enough to know this is where our trash must go?

No More Sticky Mess

Want to eliminate sticky residues around your classroom? Try these simple tips! I use a small dot of hot glue to hold temporary tags in place. When I remove a tag, I simply pop off the glue dot with a razor blade or a plastic gift card. For things that need a stronger bond, I use packing tape. Since the tape leaves behind residue, I spray on foam shaving cream, let it sit for a while, and then scrape it off with a razor blade or an old plastic gift card.

Amanda Rudolph, Shady Brook Elementary, Kannapolis, NC

Dominic

Our Readers Write

Putting Partners Together

Here's a simple idea for assigning partners. First, I cut postcards and the covers of holiday cards in half. Then I laminate them for durability. I give each child one half and have him find the student with the matching piece. When he finds the student, he's found his partner!

Amanda Heaven, Navajo Elementary, Navajo, NM

Merry
Christmas

100 Words About Me!

To build excitement for the 100th day of school, I have my students make personalized booklets. To start, I make a notebook for each child by folding and stapling three 8½" x 11" sheets of paper. Then I have each student decorate the cover, draw ten lines on each sheet, and number the lines from 1 to 100. Every week, I challenge each child to write ten new words to describe herself. If she runs out of words, I encourage her to check with classmates and family members for ideas. On the 100th day, I have students reread their words to reinforce how wonderful they truly are.

Patricia Herk, Saint Sylvester School, Pittsburgh, PA

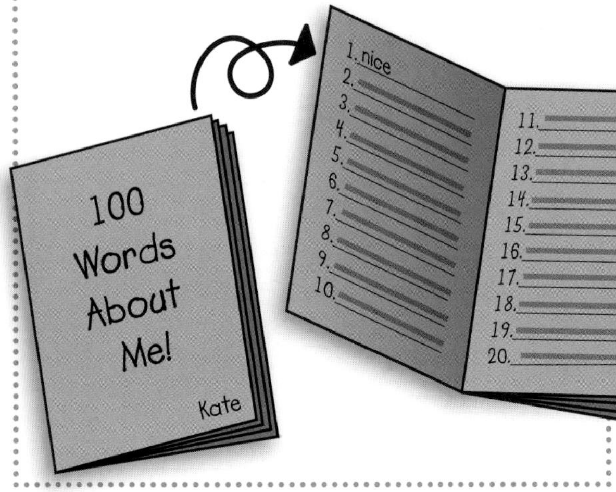
100 Words About Me!
Kate
1. nice
2.
3.
4.
5.
6.
7.
8.
9.
10.
11.
12.
13.
14.
15.
16.
17.
18.
19.
20.

Ideas in a Hurry

To easily locate ideas I want to use from *The Mailbox®* magazine, I set up this simple system. After reviewing an issue, I copy the "Skills in Your Issue" page and highlight the skills I want to use. Then I insert the page inside a plastic sheet protector and place it in a binder. I repeat this for each issue, organizing the pages by issue in the resulting reference notebook. The few minutes I use to prepare these pages save me a lot of time later!

Anne-Marie Christopher, Rossman School, St. Louis, MO

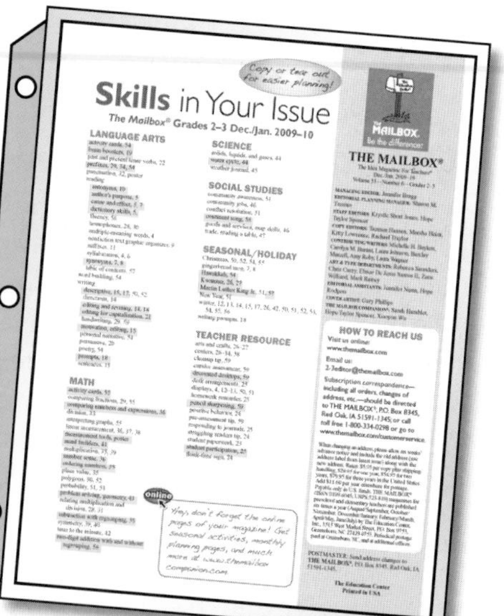
Copy or tear out for easier planning!
Skills in Your Issue
The Mailbox® Grades 2–3 Dec./Jan. 2009–10
LANGUAGE ARTS
SCIENCE
SOCIAL STUDIES
SEASONAL/HOLIDAY
TEACHER RESOURCE
MATH
THE MAILBOX®
HOW TO REACH US

Easily Marked Markers

So I can easily identify my permanent markers, I color the end of each one the same color as its ink. Then I place the markers point-side down in a cup. This way, the ink still flows to the tip so the markers don't dry out. Even better, I don't have to pull each marker out and look at its cap to find the one I need!

Wendy Barnett, Sunnyside Elementary, Dodge City, KS

On Display

Recycled CD cases make great student display shelves. I unhinge the pieces of each case and reattach them backward. Then I label each shelf with a different student's name. The shelves can be easily hung on a board or used on a flat surface.

Jeannie Pavlik, Pittsville Elementary, Pittsville, WI

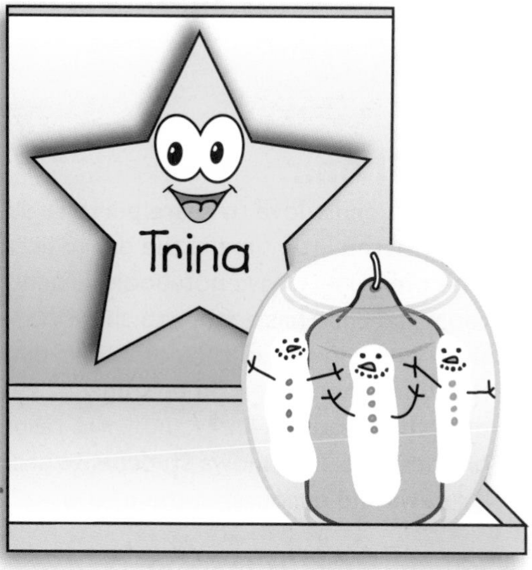
Trina

Travel Log

When students take extended trips with their families, I send along one travel log page for each day they are gone. Each day, the child writes a summary of his activities and draws a picture of his favorite one. When the student returns to school, he shares his entries with the class and adds his pages to our class journal. Then, at the end of the year, I return the entries to the students. What a great way to help my students practice sequencing and summarizing while they're away!

Chrissy Pastor, East High Street Elementary, Elizabethtown, PA

Vocabulary Album

I use an inexpensive 4" x 6" photo album to organize vocabulary flash cards. I insert a list of the week's words in the front and then place each flash card inside a separate sleeve. Then, when we review words or play a game, I know exactly where the cards are and simply flash them from the album.

Lauren Levine, Clementon Elementary, Clementon, NJ

runoff
condensation

Mentors in Training

I encourage my students to master certain skills by training them to become mentors. When a child masters a skill, I write the skill and her name on a sentence strip. Then I post it on the "Mentor Wall" in our room. When another student is having difficulty with a skill, he checks the wall to find a child who can help. Both students benefit from the interaction, and the mentor's confidence and self-esteem grow from helping others.

Mari Gonzalez, Schertz Elementary, Schertz, TX

Our Readers Write

Sweet Encouragement

By establishing a strong home-school connection, my students feel loved and supported during state testing. A few weeks ahead of time, I send home blank notecards and envelopes. I also include a letter asking each child's family to write words of encouragement on the card. I direct them to seal the notecard in the envelope and return it to school. Before students arrive on the first day of testing, I attach a small piece of candy to each envelope and place the envelopes on students' desks. What a great way to start an important day!

Krystle Short Jones, Charlotte, NC

Dear Cam,
What an exciting day to show what you know! You have worked hard this year and have learned a lot. Relax and do your very best. We love you and are so proud of you.
Love,
Mom, Dad, and Reese

Editor's Tip: For students whose families don't return the card, invite the principal or another special staff member to write a message.

Pages of Samples

Looking for examples of persuasive writing to share with your budding writers? I've found that monthly travel magazines do the trick! The magazines are full of articles written to convince readers to visit different places and events. After sharing these with my students, they have a much better idea of what persuasive writing is all about.

Ana Jolly
McGarity Elementary
Hiram, GA

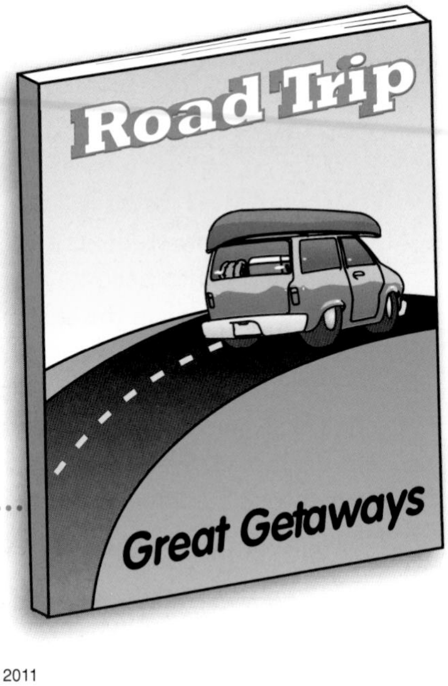
Road Trip
Great Getaways

Tied and Tethered

To keep my students' table groups intact, I use bungee cords. First, I place the desks in my desired arrangement. Then I wrap a bungee cord around each set of touching desk legs. I hook the ends of the cord together and there you have it—the desks become one group and won't come apart or slide on top of each other!

Paige Foltz, Pleasant Elementary, Norwalk, OH

And Then...

My students love to share personal stories. Since there's little time in the day to accommodate everyone, I leave notebooks around my room. If a child has a story to share, he writes a short entry in one of the notebooks during his free time. Then, when other students have free time, they read the entry and write responses or questions. This allows students to share their big news and encourages them to write!

Cori Mack, Chaparral Elementary, Gilbert, AZ

Our Readers Write

The Brainy Bunch

I make a unique signal to indicate think time to my students. First, I use crayons and tagboard to make a brain-shape cutout. Then I glue the cutout to one end of a ruler. Whenever I raise the signal, my students know to think carefully and not raise their hands to respond until the signal comes down.

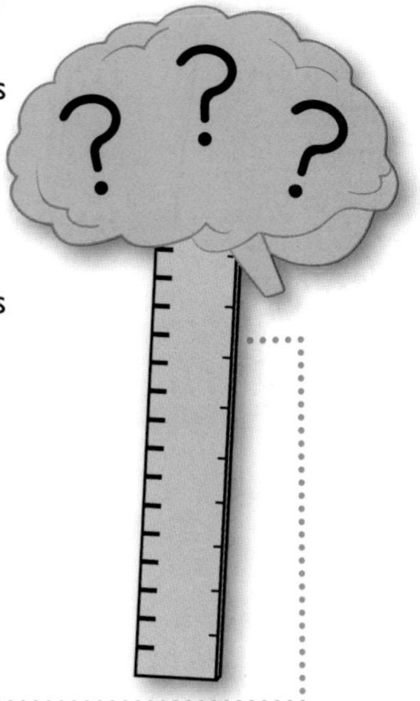

? ? ?

Gina Zimmerman
Edgerton Elementary
Edgerton, KS

Borders at Your Fingertips

In my classroom, an over-the-closet shoe bag serves as a handy storage organizer. When I take down bulletin boards, I tightly roll each border, secure the end with a paper clip, and tuck it into one of the clear pockets. My borders are neat and tidy, and I can easily see my choices.

Amy Loser
Limestone Walters Elementary
Peoria, IL

Storage for Small Treasures

Here's an easy way to store and display fragile classroom materials. I glue seashells, dried flowers, or other small trinkets I want to share with my students inside a clear box frame. Students can easily see the contents, while the boxes keep the materials safe from busy hands. Plus the contents make great discussion starters and writing prompts.

Jane Walsh, Sweetwater Elementary, Lithia Springs, GA

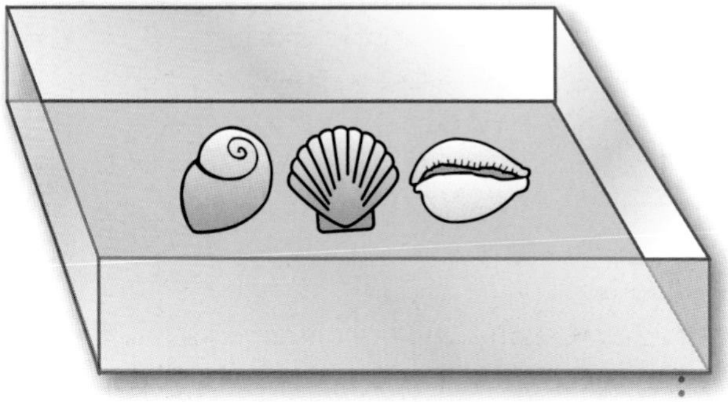

Extra Practice

To make every minute count, I tuck in a word-skills lesson whenever we have a few minutes to spare. I have students refer to a recent reading and challenge them to identify words that match a named skill such as a specific vowel sound, or specific word types such as compound words or contractions. If we have more time, I draw a chart on the board and list each word in the matching column.

Leslie Lessard, Hatfield Elementary, Hatfield, MA

short i sound	long o sound	compound words
milk fish	coat hope loaf	lighthouse strawberry

Our Readers Write

Important Helper

This simple gift is sure to make your student teacher feel special. With our student teacher out of the room, I have my students list words and ideas that explain why she is important to us. Then I ask each student to follow a format similar to that used by Margaret Wise Brown in *The Important Book* to write a book page about our student teacher. I gather the student pages and some pages of photos from the school year and then bind them together to make a book for her to keep. No doubt your student teacher will love the book as much as ours did!

Marie Chen, Village School, Campbell, CA

The important thing about Miss Garcia is that she's fun! She made a game about fractions, told silly jokes about animals, and played kickball with us at recess. But the important thing about Miss Garcia is that she's fun!

Editor's Tip:
Include a copy of *The Important Book* with your student-made book.

Teachers' Night In

Who says documenting and organizing at the end of the school year can't be fun? My coworkers and I turn these tasks into a party! We all stay after school on a designated day, order pizza for dinner, and work on entering grades, updating permanent folders, and completing other tasks that must be done before the school year ends. Teachers who finish their tasks early even help the others! It's a fun way to avoid year-end stress and get our obligations taken care of!

Sandi Norton, Valley Springs Elementary, Harrison, AR

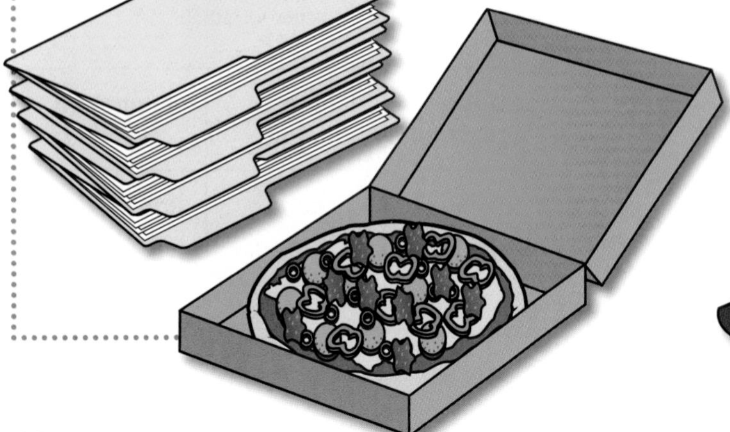

Class Hat Day

I like to combine a student spirit day, Hat Day, with fun learning experiences. First, I get permission for my students to wear baseball caps on a designated day; then I invite my students to participate in Hat Day. On that day, I use the hats in a variety of activities, such as sorting and graphing them by colors, teams, or symbols; hypothesizing and testing which hat can be tossed the farthest; and writing imaginative narratives from a hat's point of view. It's a fun way to top off a great year!

Colleen Dabney, Williamsburg, VA

W

Answer Keys

Page 36

1. fr	2. cr	3. br	4. br	5. gr
6. br	7. gr	8. fr	9. cr	
10. gr	11. fr	12. gr	13. fr	
14. cr	15. br	16. cr		

Order may vary.

br	**cr**	**fr**	**gr**
bread	crisp	frame	grin
broken	crowd	frost	grandpa
bring	cricket	fruit	green
braid	crumb	fresh	ground

Page 37

1. W	7. H
2. T	8. L
3. C	9. E
4. N	10. A
5. D	11. I
6. O	12. F

HE WANTED TO CATCH ALL THE FLIES!

Page 38

1. S: speedy, A: slow
2. S: begin, A: finish
3. S: pal, A: enemy
4. S: small, A: big
5. S: tidy, A: messy
6. S: rich, A: poor
7. S: brawny, A: weak
8. S: stuck, A: loose
9. S: right, A: wrong
10. S: ill, A: healthy
11. S: chase, A: lead
12. S: gentle, A: rough

Bonus: Answers will vary.

Page 39

1. Main idea: The shoe store is very busy today.
   Unneeded detail: It is a pretty, sunny day.

2. Main idea: The shoe store sells all kinds of shoes.
   Unneeded detail: The clerk must ring up lots of orders.

3. Main idea: My whole family is getting new shoes.
   Unneeded detail: My big toe hurts in those shoes.

4. Main idea: My sister needs new shoes.
   Unneeded detail: My brother wants cowboy boots.

Page 40

1. red	5. blue	9. blue
2. red	6. blue	10. red
3. blue	7. red	11. red
4. red	8. red	12. blue

Bonus: Answers will vary.

Page 41

1. Hazel saved money at the food store because she used coupons.
2. Harry saved his money for four months. As a result, Harry had enough money to buy the exercise wheel he always wanted.
3. Hildy lost her paycheck. She put the paycheck in her pocket, which had a hole in it. Poor Hildy!
4. Hal and Hallie pooled their money. Together they were able to buy a tunnel the entire family could use. Fun!
5. Hugh hid his money so no one could find it. He forgot where he put it.
6. Hannah put her babysitting money in the bank. Her money earned interest, which means her money amount grew.
7. Hank got a raise at work because he works hard, gets along with the other workers, and has a great attitude!
8. Henrietta spent her birthday money on candy. Not only did she buy something that didn't last very long, but she also got two cavities from the candy!

Bonus: Answers will vary.

Page 42

1. reptile
2. camouflage
3. hibernate
4. scales
5. pit organ
6. molt
7. Jacobson's organ
8. constrictor
9. fangs
10. venom

keratin

Bonus: Answers will vary but should include that both the glossary and index are found in the back of a book and list words found in the book in alphabetical order. A glossary gives the definition of each word, while an index gives the word's page number.

Page 43

1. squirrel
2. little dog
3. dog trainer
4. big dog
5. dog owner
6. stick

Bonus: Answers will vary but should be written from a child's point of view.

Page 44

1. Fancy Nancy
2. in the morning on the first day of third grade
3. upstairs in Fancy Nancy's bedroom; downstairs by the coatrack
4. Fancy Nancy can't find her lucky hat. After she puts on a headband, she finds her hat hanging on the coatrack.

Page 45

1. ABCB
2. The child is unhappy because it's winter but there hasn't been any snow yet.
3. The weather is more like autumn than winter.
4. to entertain
5. Answers will vary.

Bonus: Rhyming pairs include *luck, stuck; down, brown;* and *sad, glad.* Lists may vary.

Page 54

3, 4, 6. Answers may vary.

1. Possible words from *second grader* include *add, adder, adds, and, can, case, crane, creed, dad, dads, dander, dare, dares, deacon, dead, dear, deer, dog, dogs, god, gods, grade, grades, grease, greed, nag, nags, near, need, no, nod, nods, nor, on, one, race, races, rag, rags, ran, rare, read, reads, rear, red, sad, seen,* and *scene.* Possible words from *third grader* include *air, aid, at, dad, dear, dig, dirt, dither, drag, drat, gear, grade, hard, hat, hate, hear, her, herd, hid, hide, hire, hit, rag, rage, raid, rare, rat, rate, read, rear, red, rid, ride, rig, tag, tiger,* and *trade.*
2. I am a dear friend. The seal is in the water.
   Tom's it. I want to be Steve's friend.
   How is he? What do you see?
5. An apple is on the table. Is an apple on the table?
   Jack will be going with us. Will Jack be going with us?
7. States or state capitals: Maine, Maryland, Massachusetts, Michigan, Minnesota, Mississippi, Missouri, Montana, Madison, Montgomery, Montpelier
   Days or months: Monday, March, May
8. Nouns: flea, meat, meet, sea, see, stair, stare, tide, toe, tow;
   Verbs: flee, meet, see, stare, tide, tied, toe, tow

Page 55
1, 2, 8. Answers may vary.

3. A. Each consecutive word has one additional syllable.
   B. The last letter of the first word is the first letter of the next word (and so on).
   C. All the words are in the *-ame* family, or they all rhyme.
   D. All the words are spelled the same in their singular and plural forms.

4. Order may vary.
   Singular: glass, dress, kiss, lens, boss, bus
   Plural: turkeys, rivers, plates, holidays, meals, houses

5.

ht	heat, hoot	brd	braid, bread, breed
b	bay, bee, boo, buy	trt	trait, treat, trout
mn	main, mean, moon	grn	grain, green, groan

6. Possible synonyms include *alarming, dire, direful, dreadful, fearsome, forbidding, formidable, frightening, frightful, hair-raising, horrendous, horrible, horrifying, intimidating, redoubtable, scary, shocking, terrible,* and *terrifying.*

7.

Past Tense	Present Tense	Future Tense
wrote	am writing	will write
juggled	am juggling	will juggle
ate	am eating	will eat
traveled	am traveling	will travel
rested	am resting	will rest

Page 56
Answers for 3, 4, and 6–9 will vary.
1. What do you get when you cross a tiger with a snowman? Frostbite.
   Why don't mountains get cold in the winter? They wear snowcaps.
2. Answers will vary. Possible answers include *act, an, at, case, cat, cold, colt, cot, dot, lot, lotto, nap, not, nose, pain, pair, piano, pin, pine, rip, sat, saw, so, soap, son, taco, tap, to, toes, told, ton, tones, tot, was,* and *watt.*
5. to look over: browse
   easily broken: brittle
   never used before: brand-new
   to observe a holiday: celebrate
   sweet houses are made of this: gingerbread

Page 57
Answers for 1, 2, and 8 will vary.

3.

	u	s	e
r	o	p	e
c	a	r	s
	b	i	g
	o	n	
h	u	g	

4. Shelly Henry Brittany Lexie
   Gus James Wendy Courtney
   Sentences will vary.
5. A. bicycle B. champion C. telephone
   D. teenager E. airplane F. examination
   G. refrigerator H. gasoline I. automobile
6. The early bird catches the worm.
7. A. the ability to grow plants well
   B. jealous
   C. permission to proceed

Page 58
Answers for 2–4 and 8 will vary.

1.

afraid	daisy	grade
baseball	daylight	hallway
became	escape	May
bricklayer	explain	praise

5. Possible answers include the following:
   bass: a fish or a deep tone
   does: more than one female deer or a form of the verb *do*
   sow: a female hog or to plant a seed
   Each word has an animal as one of its meanings and is a one-syllable word.
   close: near or to shut
   lead: to guide or a chemical element
   tear: to pull apart or a drop of liquid
   Each word has an action verb as one of its meanings and is a one-syllable word.
6. A. ladybug, B. farmhouse, C. nightgown, D. seafood
7. bear, cub; cat, kitten; deer, fawn; goat, kid; owl, owlet; sea lion, pup; sheep, lamb; toad, tadpole; whale, calf

Page 59
1. Possible answers include *after, are, art, at, ate, earth, eat, fare, fat, fate, fear, hare, hat, hate, hater, he, hear, heart, heat, rat, tar, tea, tear,* and *the.*
2. towel, toy, treasure, treats, trip, tugboat; Words could be ordered from fewest letters to most letters or from most letters to fewest letters.
3. hot dog
4. A. big twig B. toad's code C. glad dad D. best nest E. top cop
5. Each word is spelled the same way, whether you start at the first letter or the last (palindrome). Possible words to add to the set include *civic, dad, deed, kayak, level, madam, mom, pop, racecar, redder,* and *tot.*
6. very easy, living without modern conveniences, eats very little; Sentences will vary.
7. Answers will vary.
8. glass or cup, slice, Independence Day

Page 95

1. **.**	4. **.**	7. **!**	10. **!**
2. **?**	5. **.**	8. **!**	11. **?**
3. **!**	6. **?**	9. **?**	12. **.**

Bonus Box: Sentences will vary.

Page 96

1. boxes, yellow	2. dogs, brown	3. houses, brown
4. churches, yellow	5. bones, brown	6. dishes, yellow
7. dresses, yellow	8. collars, brown	9. bowls, brown
10. treats, brown	11. leashes, yellow	12. classes, yellow

Bonus Box: Sentences will vary.

Page 97

1. W	2. E	3. G	
4. U	5. I	6. S	7. F
8. M	9. Y	10. T	11. C
12. N	13. R	14. L	15. A

IT WAS FEELING CRUMMY!

Bonus: Answers will vary.

Page 98
The bones with the following words should be outlined: *brushes, works, thinks, finds, takes, wonders, calls, sets, holds, digs.*

1. thinks	6. takes
2. sets	7. calls
3. digs	8. holds
4. finds	9. wonders
5. brushes	10. works

Bonus: Answers will vary.

Page 99

march 28, 2011

Ahoy, Pirate pete!
What a trip we had looking for treasure! we have made many stops. On sunday we anchored in Pirate's Cove. The map pointed to a hidden spot. We dug and dug. All we found was a forgotten box of valentine's day cards.
On tuesday we hiked to gold hill. The map took us to a hidden cave. There we found some halloween candy from last october. It wasn't gold, but it was yummy!
Yesterday we landed on treasure island. What luck! A big treasure chest was sitting right there by the shore. Captain john's keys were hanging on a palm tree. We peeked inside the treasure chest and took a sample of captain John's loot. To be fair, we left some cards and candy in its place.
how was your week? I hope it's been a "booty-ful" one!

your friend,
parrot Pegleg

Bonus: Letters will vary.

Page 100
1. Digger
2. Cookie
3. Puddles
4. Snuggles
5. Powder
6. Champ
7–12. Sentences will vary.

Bonus: Answers will vary.

Page 102

1. H	2. X
3. Y	4. M
5. W	6. C
7. E	8. Z
9. K	10. Q
11. O	12. F
13. V	14. J
15. H	

THE BATS SLEEP DURING THE DAY.

Page 103

1. its
2. her
3. his
4. their
5. its
6. her
7. his
8. Our
9. their
10. my

Bonus: 1. class 2. Nellie Nugget 3. Rusty Rooster 4. teams 5. team 6. Ms. Hen 7. Rusty Rooster 8. teammates 9. Feathers and Peepster 10. I

Page 126

Each answer should have a crown drawn around it.

A. 6 B. 3 C. 8 D. 4 E. 7
F. 9 G. 4 H. 6 I. 8 J. 2
K. 4 L. 9 M. 5

Page 130

	A. 24	B. 63	C. 25
D. 81	E. 16	F. 21	G. 9
H. 27	I. 42	J. 64	K. 28
L. 35	M. 36	N. 54	
O. 9	P. 10	Q. 18	

Bonus: Students should circle problems A, E, I, J, K, M, N, P, and Q.

Page 131

1, 4, 7. Answers may vary.

2. Order may vary. 14 + 60 = 74, 14 + 25 = 39, 14 + 31 = 45, 14 + 82 = 96, 14 + 13 = 27.
3. short letters ||||| ||||| ||||

   tall letters ||||| ||

   long letters |||||
5. Order may vary. 147, 150; 174, 170; 417, 420; 471, 470; 714, 710; 741, 740.
6. Clocks should show 4:55, 6:10, and 7:25.
8. 1,597; 2,536; 2,548; 4,507; 4,593

Page 132

2, 4, 6. Answers may vary.

1. Possible numbers include 106, 208, 213, 249, 309, 312, 358, 405, 504, 601, 802, 853, 869, 903, 942, and 968.
3. 41¢
5. A. 4,360 B. 5,361 C. 4,261 D. 4,371
7. 256, 260; 265, 270; 526, 530; 562, 560; 625, 630; 652, 650
8. A. 7:25 B. 6:35 C. 6:05 D. 7:40 E. 9:05

Page 133

1. Answers will vary.
2. Yes. If the pattern continues, it will be 30°F on Saturday, which is two degrees below freezing.
3. Shape A has symmetry.
4. Answers will vary. A. B. C. D.

5. A. 100 B. 1,000 C. 10 D. 10,000 E. 1
6. Order may vary. Possible answers include 4 x 9 = 36, 4 x 7 = 28, 7 x 6 = 42, 6 x 4 = 24, 4 x 8 = 32, 8 x 3 = 24, 3 x 5 = 15, 5 x 9 = 45, 9 x 7 = 63, 9 x 3 = 27, 7 x 4 = 28, and 3 x 4 = 12.
7. A. $5.41 B. $3.12 C. $4.63 D. $6.76
8. A. 6,512 + 1,368 = 7,880 B. 1,281 + 5,457 = 6,738
   C. 6,512 – 1,368 = 5,144 D. 5,457 – 1,281 = 4,176

Page 134

Answers for 2 and 7 will vary.

1. Order of numbers will vary.
   A. 152, 156, 251, 256, 651, 652
   B. 215, 216, 251, 256, 261, 265
   C. 126, 156, 216, 256, 516, 526
3. A. $1.25 B. $1.15 C. $1.57 D. $1.60
4. □ = 3, ○ = 5, △ = 2
5. Order will vary. 8 x 3 = 24, 8 x 7 = 56, 8 x 6 = 48, 8 x 2 = 16, 9 x 3 = 27, 9 x 7 = 63, 9 x 6 = 54, 9 x 2 = 18, 5 x 3 = 15, 5 x 7 = 35, 5 x 6 = 30, 5 x 2 = 10, 4 x 3 = 12, 4 x 7 = 28, 4 x 6 = 24, 4 x 2 = 8.
6. A. cube, square pyramid
   B. cone, cylinder
   C. triangular pyramid, triangular prism
   D. rectangular prism, rectangular pyramid
8. A. right B. acute C. obtuse
   D. acute E. obtuse F. acute
   G. obtuse H. right I. acute

Page 135

1.

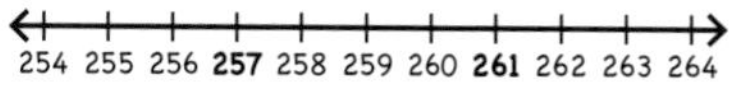
254 255 256 257 258 259 260 261 262 263 264

Number sentences will vary.

2. A. 51¢ B. 47¢ C. 87¢ D. 40¢ E. 36¢
3. Pulling out an *A* is the most likely outcome and pulling out a *B* is the least likely outcome. Answers for an impossible outcome will vary but should be any letter other than *B*, *A*, or *N*.

4–6. Answers will vary.

7. $\frac{3}{5}$; The other fractions are equivalent.
8. Answers will vary. Possible combinations are 16 cups; 8 pints; 12 cups, 1 quart; 12 cups, 2 pints; 8 cups, 2 quarts; 8 cups, 4 pints; 8 cups, 2 pints, 1 quart; 4 cups, 6 pints; 4 cups, 3 quarts; 4 cups, 4 pints, 1 quart; 4 cups, 2 pints, 2 quarts; 6 pints, 1 quart; 4 pints, 2 quarts; 4 quarts; 2 pints, 3 quarts; and 2 cups, 1 pint, 3 quarts.

Page 136

1. 2, 9, 16, 23, 30

2, 3. Answers will vary.

4. 600, 595, 590; minus five. Patterns will vary.
5. star, circle
6. (2 + 4) ÷ 3 = 2; (10 ÷ 2) x 4 = 20
7. 48 ÷ 6 = 8, 9 – 1 = 8, 2 x 4 = 8, 5 + 3 = 8
8. Order may vary. Two half-dollars, two dimes; two half-dollars, two nickels, one dime; two half-dollars, four nickels; one half-dollar, two quarters, two dimes; four quarters, two dimes

Page 137

A. Champ
B. Rocky
C. Rover
D. Princess
E. Bella
F. Pepper
G. Daisy
H. Max
I. Duke
J. Lucky
K. Spot
L. Lady

Bonus: Clues will vary.

Page 138

A. **400**	B. 600
C. 500	D. **300**
E. 400	F. **600**
G. **200**	H. 700
I. 300	J. 200
K. **500**	L. **700**
M. **400**	N. **300**
O. 500	P. **200**
Q. 600	R. 700

Bonus Box: 100, 800; Explanations may vary.

Page 139

A. 9 (pink)
B. 14 (yellow)
C. 10 (orange)
D. 10 (orange)
E. 18 (yellow)
F. 12 (yellow)
G. 8 (yellow)
H. 15 (pink)
I. 10 (orange)
J. 17 (pink)
K. 10 (orange)
L. 16 (yellow)
M. 11 (pink)
N. 10 (orange)
O. 13 (pink)

Bonus Box: 18; Explanations may vary.

Page 140

A. 43 + 51 =	60	70	80	**90**
B. 18 + 27 =	30	40	**50**	60
C. 63 + 29 =	60	70	80	**90**
D. 26 + 22 =	30	40	**50**	60
E. 34 + 33 =	50	**60**	70	80
F. 81 + 12 =	70	80	**90**	100
G. 12 + 11 =	10	**20**	30	40
H. 39 + 24 =	**60**	70	80	90
I. 57 + 14 =	60	**70**	80	90
J. 44 + 37 =	60	70	**80**	90
K. 68 + 31 =	70	80	90	**100**
L. 13 + 28 =	20	30	**40**	50

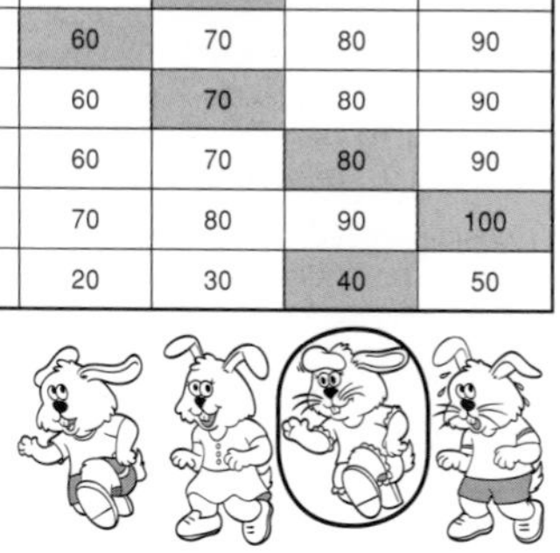

Bonus Box: Answers may vary.

Page 141

A. 56 B. 48 C. 64
D. 10 E. 25 F. 27
G. 24 H. 14 I. 16
J. 42 K. 49 L. 45
M. 81 N. 12 O. 21
P. 9 Q. 35 R. 54
S. 28 T. 40 U. 72
V. 32 W. 18 X. 36

1	30	7	9	60	11	29
88	23	52	10	3	69	8
13	25	40	45	42	16	50
75	4	84	48	17	55	62
24	63	44	18	74	38	36
27	22	5	81	26	2	28
32	72	34	12	20	14	54
19	35	56	21	49	64	6

Page 142

A. $\frac{3}{8}$ B. $\frac{1}{3}$ C. $\frac{3}{6}$ or $\frac{1}{2}$ D. $\frac{6}{7}$ E. $\frac{1}{2}$ F. $\frac{2}{4}$ or $\frac{1}{2}$
G. $\frac{3}{9}$ or $\frac{1}{3}$ H. $\frac{2}{10}$ or $\frac{1}{5}$ I. $\frac{1}{4}$ J. $\frac{3}{4}$
K. $\frac{4}{5}$ L. $\frac{2}{3}$ M. $\frac{8}{12}$ or $\frac{2}{3}$ N. $\frac{1}{2}$

Bonus:
A. $\frac{5}{8}$ B. $\frac{2}{3}$ C. $\frac{3}{6}$ or $\frac{1}{2}$ D. $\frac{1}{7}$ E. $\frac{1}{2}$ F. $\frac{2}{4}$ or $\frac{1}{2}$
G. $\frac{6}{9}$ or $\frac{2}{3}$ H. $\frac{8}{10}$ or $\frac{4}{5}$ I. $\frac{3}{4}$ J. $\frac{1}{4}$
K. $\frac{1}{5}$ L. $\frac{1}{3}$ M. $\frac{4}{12}$ or $\frac{1}{3}$ N. $\frac{1}{2}$

Page 143

A. $\frac{3}{4}$ B. $\frac{3}{8}$
C. $\frac{4}{7}$ D. $\frac{6}{10}$
E. $\frac{1}{3}$ F. $\frac{6}{7}$
G. $\frac{5}{6}$ H. $\frac{2}{5}$
I. $\frac{3}{8}$ J. $\frac{1}{6}$
K. $\frac{4}{5}$ L. $\frac{2}{3}$
M. $\frac{1}{4}$ N. $\frac{3}{10}$

Bonus: Fractions include $\frac{2}{8}$, $\frac{3}{8}$, $\frac{5}{8}$, and $\frac{6}{8}$. Story problems and answers will vary.

Page 144

A. 65, yes D. 67, no
B. 86, yes E. 80, no
C. 57, no F. 75, yes

Page 145

1. September 3, 13
2. fish sticks, taco
3. September 13, hot dog
4. pizza, 14

Bonus Box: Answers may vary.

Page 146

A. 6 B. 5 C. 9 D. 7 E. 6 F. 4

Bonus: 5 inches

Page 148

Order will vary.

Less than one pound: penny, soap, die, macaroni, stamp, chip
More than one pound: hammer, computer, dog, bike, chair, brick

Bonus: Answers will vary.

Page 149

A. 50 points B. 100 extra points C. 200 points
D. 250 points E. 350 extra points F. 450 points
G. 450 points H. 600 points I. 750 points

Bonus: Answers will vary. Possible patterns include the following: Each answer in the top row is double the previous number; the answers in the middle row increase by 100; the answers in the bottom row increase by 150; the answers in the left column increase by 200 and require finding the difference; the answers in the middle column increase by 250 and are solved with multiplication or repeated addition; and the answers in the right column increase by 250 and use addition with regrouping.

Page 150

A. \$2.00 B. \$3.00
C. \$4.00 D. \$6.00
E. \$5.00 F. \$3.00
G. \$4.00 H. \$2.00

Bonus: 2 yards of heart fabric

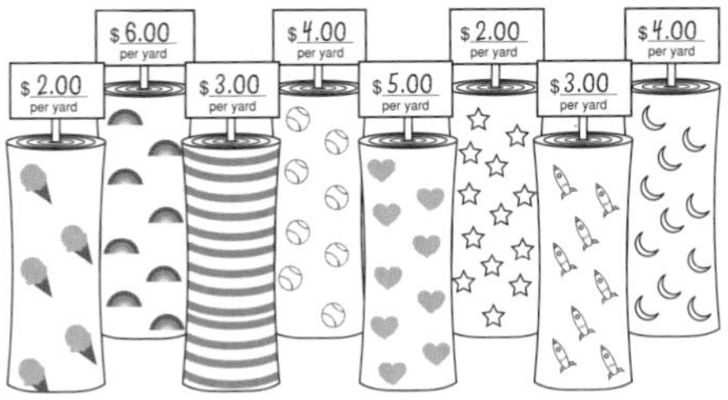

$2.00 per yard
$6.00 per yard
$3.00 per yard
$4.00 per yard
$5.00 per yard
$2.00 per yard
$3.00 per yard
$4.00 per yard

Page 192

Mr. Moustache: 13 circles, 5 triangles, 4 rectangles, 2 trapezoids
Ms. Matchy-Matchy: 16 circles, 8 triangles, 6 rectangles, 2 hexagons

Page 230

"Around the Classroom"
Answers may vary. Possible groupings include one-syllable words and two-syllable words; singular words and plural words; people and things; and number of vowels.

"My Fun Grandpa"
Possible answers include *airplane, barefoot, bathrobe, butterfly, eyebrows, football, grandpa, mailbox, newspaper, outside, rainbow, sidewalk, skateboard,* and *sunglasses.*

Page 231

"Sport Star"

18 − 9 = 9	13 − 6 = 7	16 − 7 = 9	15 − 8 = 7
16 − 8 = 8	17 − 7 = 10	14 − 9 = 5	12 − 6 = 6
14 − 7 = 7	15 − 6 = 9	13 − 8 = 5	17 − 9 = 8

"Pick a Puzzle"
982; 1,002; 1,028; 1,082; 1,209. Numbers added to the list will vary.

"Tools They Love"

Our Favorite Art Supplies
Crayons
Markers
Colored pencils
0 2 4 6 8 10 12

Sentences will vary.

Page 232

"Feasting on Words"

(baked) (cared) cleaned (gobbled) munched (placed)
pulled (scraped) (stored) thanked washed (wiped)

Page 233

"Bobbing for Numbers"
Order may vary.

94, ninety-four
76, seventy-six
110, one hundred ten
61, sixty-one
45, forty-five
83, eighty-three
39, thirty-nine
52, fifty-two
18, eighteen
100, one hundred

"A Football Fan"
Possible estimates: 108 + 872 = 980; 108 + 346 = 460; 108 + 513 = 620; 108 + 251 = 360; 108 + 629 = 740; 108 + 108 = 220; 872 + 108 = 980; 872 + 346 = 1,220; 872 + 513 = 1,380; 872 + 251 = 1,120; 872 + 629 = 1,500; 872 + 872 = 1,740; 346 + 108 = 460; 346 + 872 = 1,220; 346 + 513 = 860; 346 + 251 = 600; 346 + 629 = 980; 346 + 346 = 700; 513 + 108 = 620; 513 + 872 = 1,380; 513 + 346 = 860; 513 + 251 = 760; 513 + 629 = 1,140; 513 + 513 = 1,020; 251 + 108 = 360; 251 + 872 = 1,120; 251 + 346 = 600; 251 + 513 = 760; 251 + 629 = 880; 251 + 251 = 500; 629 + 108 = 740; 629 + 872 = 1,500; 629 + 346 = 980; 629 + 513 = 1,140; 629 + 251 = 880; 629 + 629 = 1,260

Page 234

"A Busy Lady"

Things to Do Before Christmas:
Dec.
ft.
lb.
Rd.
Mr.

Things to Do After Christmas:
Jan.
Sat.
Dr.
Jr.
St.

Page 235
"Gift Boxes Galore"
Students should draw boxes around problems B, D, and E.
A. 67 B. 53 C. 89
D. 80 E. 75

"A Chilly Day"
Possible sets include 3 coffees, $2.75 change; 2 coffees, 1 spiced milk, $2.40 change; 1 coffee, 1 spiced milk, 1 apple cider, $0.35 change; 2 coffees, 1 hot cocoa, no change; 1 coffee, 1 spiced milk, 1 tea with lemon, $0.50 change; 2 spiced milks, 1 apple cider, no change; 3 spiced milks, $1.70 change; 2 spiced milks, 1 tea with lemon, $0.15 change.

Page 237
"Have a Heart"
Order may vary. Possible problems and answers are
90 – 59 = 31, 90 – 47 = 43, 90 – 38 = 52, 90 – 25 = 65, 82 – 59 = 23, 82 – 47 = 35, 82 – 38 = 44, 82 – 25 = 57, 71 – 59 = 12, 71 – 47 = 24, 71 – 38 = 33, 71 – 25 = 46, 63 – 59 = 4, 63 – 47 = 16, 63 – 38 = 25, and 63 – 25 = 38.

Page 238
"Fun in the Sun"
Adverbs that tell how are *gleefully, slowly, swiftly, bravely, loudly, softly, gently, closely, happily, proudly, brightly,* and *cheerfully.*

Sentences will vary.

Page 239
"Leapfrog!"
Count by twos: 2, 4, 6, 8, 10, 12, 14, 16, 18, 20, 22, 24, 26, 28, 30, 32, 34, 36, 38, 40, 42, 44, 46, 48, 50, 52, 54, 56, 58, 60, 62, 64, 66, 68, 70, 72, 74, 76, 78, 80
Count by fours: 4, 8, 12, 16, 20, 24, 28, 32, 36, 40, 44, 48, 52, 56, 60, 64, 68, 72, 76, 80
Count by fives: 5, 10, 15, 20, 25, 30, 35, 40, 45, 50, 55, 60, 65, 70, 75, 80
Count by eights: 8, 16, 24, 32, 40, 48, 56, 64, 72, 80
Count by tens: 10, 20, 30, 40, 50, 60, 70, 80

Page 240
"Star of the Sea"

spreads	walks	
filtering	hunted	
feeding	crawling	
pointed	divides	branched
builds	passed	attaching

Page 241
"Mix 'n' Match Milk Shakes"
Order may vary.
vanilla and chocolate, vanilla and strawberry, vanilla and mint, vanilla and peanut butter, vanilla and bubble gum, chocolate and strawberry, chocolate and mint, chocolate and peanut butter, chocolate and bubble gum, strawberry and mint, strawberry and peanut butter, strawberry and bubble gum, mint and peanut butter, mint and bubble gum, peanut butter and bubble gum; six

"The Flip-Flops"
3, 6: 3 x 6 = 18, 18 ÷ 6 = 3
5, 8: 5 x 8 = 40, 40 ÷ 8 = 5
9, 7: 9 x 7 = 63, 63 ÷ 7 = 9
4, 4: 4 x 4 = 16, 16 ÷ 4 = 4
6, 2: 6 x 2 = 12, 12 ÷ 2 = 6
7, 8: 7 x 8 = 56, 56 ÷ 8 = 7

"Afraid of the Dark"
Problems will vary. Possible answers are 24 ÷ 3 = 8, 24 ÷ 6 = 4, 24 ÷ 8 = 3, 30 ÷ 3 = 10, 30 ÷ 5 = 6, 30 ÷ 6 = 5, 45 ÷ 3 = 15, 45 ÷ 5 = 9, 45 ÷ 9 = 5, 48 ÷ 3 = 16, 48 ÷ 6 = 8, 48 ÷ 8 = 6, 54 ÷ 3 = 18, 54 ÷ 6 = 9, 54 ÷ 9 = 6, 72 ÷ 3 = 24, 72 ÷ 6 = 12, 72 ÷ 8 = 9, and 72 ÷ 9 = 8.

Page 242
1. 12 minutes
2. 20 fifth graders
3. 40 children
4. closed
5. girl

Page 243
"Labor Day Picnic"
A. orange B. yellow C. yellow D. red
E. yellow F. orange G. orange H. yellow
I. red J. yellow K. yellow L. orange

"At a Cookout"
Order may vary.
Two syllables: lawyer, builder, teacher, waiter, singer, plumber
Three syllables: landscaper, conductor, musician, carpenter, reporter, accountant
Four syllables: secretary, librarian

Page 244
Answers and order may vary.
Write two facts about any constitution: A constitution is a statement that tells what a group of people believe in. The group may be a club or it might be a government. The constitution tells how the group will be run and how its leaders will be picked. It tells how rules or laws will be made. Often it is written down.

Write two facts about the U.S. Constitution: The Constitution of the United States was written in 1787. The men who wrote it wanted to set up a strong government for the country. The Constitution they wrote set up the three parts of government (called branches) that we still have today. The Constitution lists the key rights for American citizens. The basic laws of the U.S. are found in this written statement.

Page 246
1. husks
2. tassel
3. stalk
4. prop roots
5. kernels
6. 15 to 20

7–8. Answers may vary.

Page 247
"A Fine-Feathered Friend"
Circled words: thursday, november, october, mr. bradford, wednesday, friday, ms. feathers, december
Words written on feathers: Order may vary. Thursday, November, October, Mr. Bradford, Wednesday, Friday, Ms. Feathers, December

Bonus Box: Sentences will vary.

"My Thanksgiving Plans"
aunt bertie hosts Thanksgiving dinner every year. it is a hard job, because I have a big family. it takes some work to get everyone to her house in new jersey. I have cousins in maryland, florida, new york, and texas. my grandparents live in new mexico and maine. we have to start making travel plans in june just to make it all work out. But it is always worth it. We have tons of fun and eat lots of great food. Then, on the friday after thanksgiving, we always start our christmas shopping. I love Thanksgiving at Aunt Bertie's house!

Bonus Box: Paragraphs will vary.

Page 248
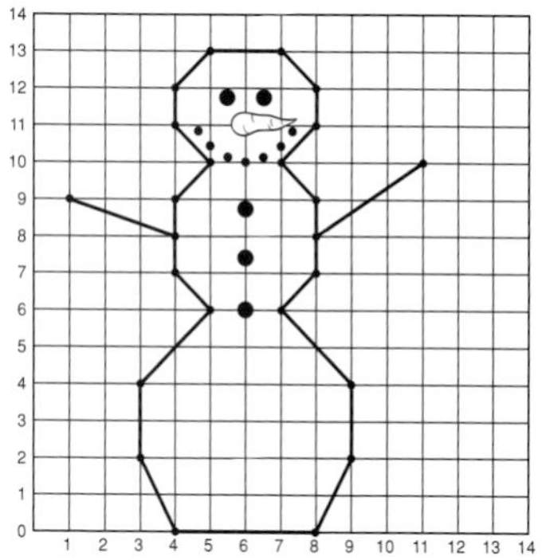

Page 249
"Trim the Tree"
A. 20° B. 33° C. 57°
D. 44° E. 72° F. 24°
Bonus: Drawings will vary.

"Pine Pals"
A. 72°F, warm
B. 58°F, cool
C. 44°F, cold
D. 90°F, hot
E. 14°F, cold
Bonus: Explanations may vary.

Page 250

1. no; He was the middle child of three
2. yes; Martin worked hard in school. He skipped both ninth and twelfth grades. That means he was just 15 when he started college!
3. yes; Dr. King spent the rest of his adult life working for equal rights. He felt that all people should be treated the same way.
4. yes; Dr. King is only one of two Americans whose birthday is marked with a national holiday. Dr. King's efforts made an impact on many. Even after he died, people wanted to continue his work for peace and equal rights.

Page 251

1. equally
2. less
3. more
4. most
5. less
6. more
7. least
8. equally

Bonus: Answers will vary.

Page 252

1. 12
2. the tiger
3. the snake
4. the sheep
5. 2016
6. the rat; The last year on the table is 2019, so the pattern will start again at 2020 with the rat.
7. the rabbit
8. 12, 2023

Bonus: Answers will vary.

Page 253

"Hand in Hand"

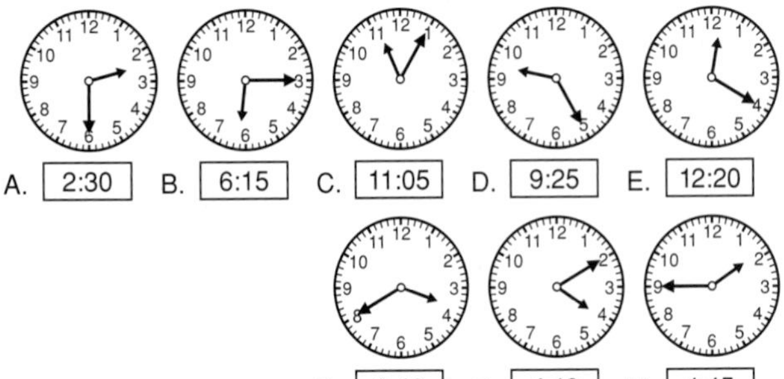

A. 2:30 B. 6:15 C. 11:05 D. 9:25 E. 12:20

F. 3:40 G. 4:10 H. 1:45

Bonus: 

"Be My 'Valen-time'"

A. 6:13 B. 4:51 C. 3:04 D. 11:26
E. 1:42 F. 10:36 G. 5:09 H. 8:21

Bonus: A. 6:15 B. 4:53 C. 3:06 D. 11:28 E. 1:44 F. 10:38 G. 5:11 H. 8:23

Page 254

A. 5 I. 1
B. 12 J. 6
C. 3 K. 21
D. 24 L. 2
E. 96 M. 27
F. 7 N. 15
G. 48 O. 9
H. 72 P. 8

Bonus: 2 yards; Explanations will vary.

Page 255

"'Eggs-tra' Special Delivery"

A. 12 ÷ 4 = 3	
B. 9 ÷ 3 = 3	
C. 6 ÷ 3 = 2	
D. 8 ÷ 2 = 4	
E. 12 ÷ 2 = 6	
F. 10 ÷ 2 = 5	
G. 4 ÷ 2 = 2	
H. 12 ÷ 3 = 4	

Bonus: ,
15 ÷ 3 = 5

"An Easter Artist"

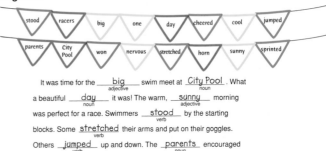

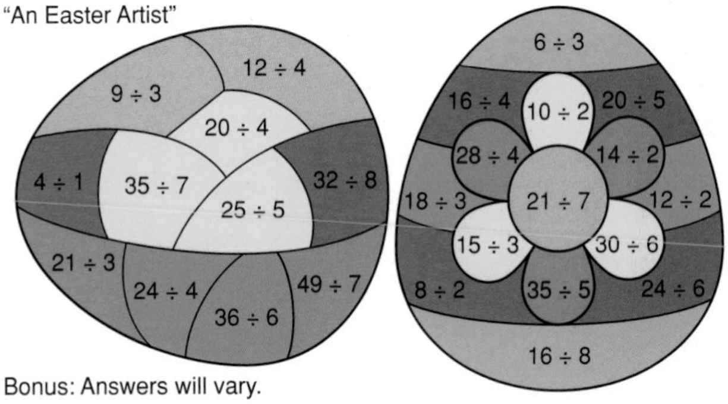
9 ÷ 3
12 ÷ 4
20 ÷ 4
4 ÷ 1
35 ÷ 7
25 ÷ 5
32 ÷ 8
21 ÷ 3
24 ÷ 4
36 ÷ 6
49 ÷ 7
6 ÷ 3
16 ÷ 4
10 ÷ 2
20 ÷ 5
28 ÷ 4
14 ÷ 2
18 ÷ 3
21 ÷ 7
12 ÷ 2
15 ÷ 3
30 ÷ 6
8 ÷ 2
35 ÷ 5
24 ÷ 6
16 ÷ 8

Bonus: Answers will vary.

Page 256

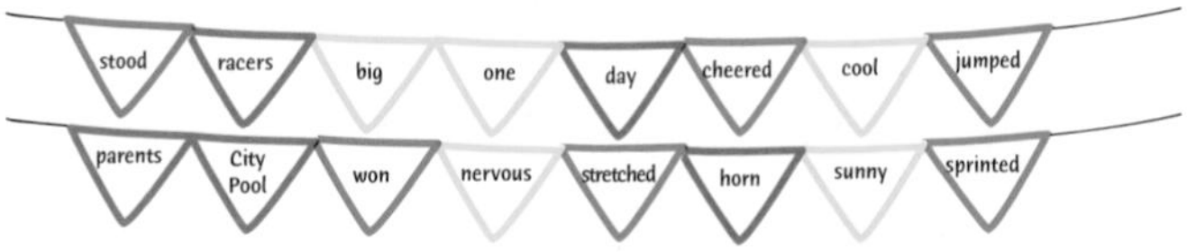
stood
racers
big
one
day
cheered
cool
jumped
parents
City Pool
won
nervous
stretched
horn
sunny
sprinted

It was time for the big (adjective) swim meet at City Pool (noun). What a beautiful day (noun) it was! The warm, sunny (adjective) morning was perfect for a race. Swimmers stood (verb) by the starting blocks. Some stretched (verb) their arms and put on their goggles. Others jumped (verb) up and down. The parents (noun) encouraged their nervous (adjective) children with kind words.

Soon, the horn (noun) blew. The racers (noun) dived off the blocks. They sprinted (verb) through the cool (adjective) water. Everyone who watched from the pool deck cheered (verb). Before long, one (adjective) swimmer touched the wall. He won (verb) the race!

Page 257

A. Sonny B. Sunday
C. 163 shells D. 174 shells E. 132 shells F. 22 shells
G. 5 shells H. Sandy I. 51 shells J. Friday

Bonus: Answers will vary but should include finding the largest number in the column for Saturday and then moving left across its row to find the name.

Page 258

"One Cool Cat"

1. Katie loves to run jump and hop outside.
2. She cools off with treats that are sweet cold and tasty.
3. Ice pops ice cream and fruit are her favorite snacks.
4. Katie likes orange lime or cherry ice pops.
5. She tops her ice cream with sprinkles whipped cream and a cherry.
6. Katie knows it's better to snack on watermelon grapes and pineapple.

Bonus: Sentences will vary.

"The Ice Cream Man!"

1. Carlos shouts "I hear Mr. Frosty!"
2. Kyle exclaims "There he is!"
3. Mr. Frosty asks "What would you like?"
4. "I'd like a cherry ice" Carlos answers.
5. Kyle asks "May I have a mint cone?"
6. "Here you go" Mr. Frosty says.
7. "Thank you" the boys reply.
8. Mr. Frosty smiles and says "Stay cool!"

Bonus: Sentences will vary.

INDEX

ISBN 978-161276140-4
9 781612 761404